LIBERAL SOCIALISM APPLIED

The Applied Welfare Economics
of a Liberal Socialist Economy

by

Burnham Putnam Beckwith, Ph.D.

Published by B. P. Beckwith
656 Lytton Ave. (C430), Palo Alto, CA. 94301
Price:—$12.00, postpaid

HB
171
B35
1974
v. 2

© 1978 by Burnham P. Beckwith
Manufactured in the United States of America

PREFACE

This book is really the second volume of Liberal Socialism (1974), the second, radically revised and expanded edition of The Economic Theory of a Socialist Economy, published by Stanford University Press in 1949. The first edition was twice reprinted in English, was published in Spanish by Aguilar, and was listed in Books for College Libraries: A Selected List of 53,400 Titles, edited by M.J. Voight (American Library Association, 1967).

The first volume of this second edition was retitled Liberal Socialism, the Pure Welfare Economics of a Liberal Socialist Economy, in order to describe its contents more accurately, and was published by Exposition Press in 1974. Although it covered only two thirds of the subject matter of the first edition, it was not named Volume One because we did not then expect to be able to publish a second volume on applied theory. If the two volumes of this second edition are ever republished in like format, this volume should be retitled Liberal Socialism, Volume Two, the Applied Economics of a Liberal Socialist Economy.

The first volume of Liberal Socialism is primarily concerned with general theories like those of price determination, output determination, and income determination, theories applicable to many or all economic activities. This second volume covers the application of these general theories to individual industries and government agencies. It also states many new principles applicable only to individual industries and groups of like industries.

The one-volume first edition of this treatise contains in Part Seven, Applied Theory (pp. 327-432), six chapters on individual industries — Agriculture, Transportation, Marketing, Foreign Trade, Public Utilities, and Housing. Liberal Socialism Applied includes revised and expanded versions of all these chapters, plus eight new chapters on other major industries and on ideal city planning. The greatly expanded treatment of city planning is perhaps the most important new feature of this work. We have explained for the first time the marked effects of city planning on ideal price and output determination for firms located in planned cities.

In Liberal Socialism (1974) we devoted an entire chapter to banking, and another to education since all industries rely upon their operation. Every industry should make all payments through banks, and should employ workers trained in public schools. We found it convenient to treat applied as well as pure theory in these chapters. Hence, this volume contains no chapters on banking or education.

Moreover, some capitalist industries require little if any discussion in this volume because they would largely or entirely cease to exist in a socialist economy. Among such industries are those made up of investment bankers, trust companies, title insurance firms, corporate and tax lawyers, security and commodity brokers, real estate brokers, advertising agencies, and debt collectors.

The application of most of the general economic principles stated in <u>Liberal Socialism</u> is usually fairly obvious, and needs little further explanation here. Therefore, we shall not repeat and apply in every chapter basic principles such as the rule that each price should balance supply and demand, or the rule that planning of future prices is uneconomic. We shall discuss the application of such general principles only when we believe they should not be applied, or when the need for their application seems to require special emphasis or explanation.

So far as we are aware, no other western socialist economist has ever tried to systematically apply modern, non-Marxist socialist welfare economics to the practical problems of most individual industries in a fully socialist economy. East European Marxist economists have published many books on the economic problems of individual socialist industries, but their analysis is usually naive and unsound because they have rejected marginal analysis, the most useful tool of modern economic analysis. A few sophisticated western economists have discussed incidentally the application of one or two general welfare principles to the operation of one or more socialist industries, but nothing like <u>Liberal Socialism Applied</u> has ever been published.

The title of this volume includes the term <u>applied</u>, which may suggest to some readers that it deals chiefly with immediately practical and/or politically feasible solutions to current economic problem. In fact, like <u>Liberal Socialism</u>, it deals almost entirely with <u>ideal solutions</u> in a fully socialist advanced economy. This does not mean that we disapprove of political compromise. Such compromise is essential to social peace and progress. But, in order to compromise intelligently, progressive political leaders must know what is ideal. They cannot determine their goals or the value of a compromise, unless they know what is ideal. Thus, our consistent emphasis upon optimum or ideal solutions to economic problems does not imply any rejection or depreciation of political compromise.

In this connection, it is noteworthy that it is easier to prescribe in advance what is ideal than what is politically feasible. Political forces change much faster and much more often than the best theories of ideal economic policy. For instance, orthodox economists have taught for two centuries that free trade is ideal in advanced countries, but during this long period the political feasibility of free trade has differed from decade to decade, and from country to country in each decade.

Full achievement of the economic system and policies advocated in this book will result in a radical reorganization and redirection of nearly all the industries and agencies discussed. But we believe that such changes can and should be achieved by gradual reform, not by a sudden violent or peaceful revolution. And we also urge that most individual reforms be tested in individual metropolitan areas or regions before being adopted nationally. We need far more deliberate social experimentation, and far less ideological dogmatism.

One of the great defects of competitive capitalism is that it cannot assure central management and rationalization of each industry. A capitalist firm may be rationally organized and managed, but the industry of which it is a part cannot be so organized and managed. The major function of this book is to explain how entire industries can and should be reorganized, rationalized, and managed in a fully socialist economy. Such reorganization and coordination is quite different from the kind of economic planning, namely price-output planning, discussed and rejected in _Liberal Socialism_.

In our book, _The Next 500 Years, a Scientific Prediction of Future Social Trends_ (1967), we discussed 12 methods of predicting such trends, including extrapolation of past trends, study of current trends in public and expert opinion, and improvement of the social sciences. Nearly all of the prescriptive social theories stated in _Liberal Socialism Applied_ could easily be restated as firm predictions of future social trends or events and supported by one or more of the 12 methods of social prediction stated and applied in _The Next 500 Years_. If this were done, _Liberal Socialism Applied_ would become an elaboration of those chapters in _The Next 500 Years_ which deal with the subjects discussed in both books, primarily Chapters V to XII. We are in fact confident that most of the social policies advocated in _Liberal Socialism Applied_ will acutally be adopted in most advanced countries within the next 500 years.

This volume contains no bibliography for three reasons: (1) <u>Liberal Socialism</u> contains a long annotated bibliography which can serve in part for this volume also, (2) we have not had time to review much of the extensive capitalist literature on the rationalization of the industries discussed in this book, and (3) little of this literature deals with problems of ideal socialist rationalization.

In closing, we hope the reader will bear in mind that no one can be an expert on all the industries covered in this volume, and that this book is merely a pioneer survey of a vast and largely unexplored territory. We hope that it will stimulate other authors to write more polished and sophisticated works on the same subject. The entire world is moving gradually but inevitably towards liberal socialism. Therefore, the economic theory of liberal socialism will become ever more important and useful.

TABLE OF CONTENTS

Preface

I. AGRICULTURE 1
   A. The Reorganization of Agriculture   2
   B. Price and Output Determination   10
   C. Other Operating Policies   16
   D. Research and Development   21

II. MINERAL PRODUCTION 23
   A. Organization   23
   B. Oil Production and Distribution   24
   C. Coal Mining and Distribution   26
   D. Conservation   28
   E. Price Determination   39
   F. Ideal Inventories   41
   G. Mining and Oil Towns   42

III. NEW-CITY PLANNING 43
   A. The Need for Planned New Cities   43
   B. National City-Planning Policies   48
   C. Possible Forms of Ideal Cities   54
   D. Principles of New-City Planning   57

IV. CITY-UNIT PLANNING 80
   A. City-Center Planning   80
   B. Town Planning   84
   C. Village Planning   94
   D. Community Planning   99
   E. Neighborhood Planning   101
   F. The Reconstruction of Old Cities   102

V. INTERCITY TRANSPORTATION 106
   A. Organization   106
   B. Operating Policies   110
   C. Price Policies   117
   D. Investment in Transport Facilities   127
   E. Taxation   128

VI. MANUFACTURING 131
   A. Organization   131
   B. Product Simplification   135
   C. Product Improvement   136
   D. Price-Output Control   138
   E. Incentives for Managers   146
   F. Job Satisfaction   147

VII.	MARKETING	158
	A. Marketing by Producers	158
	B. Wholesale Marketing	160
	C. Retail Marketing	165
VIII.	FOREIGN TRADE	178
	A. The Advantages of Foreign Trade	178
	B. Methods of Increasing Foreign Trade	181
	C. The Disadvantages of Foreign Trade	183
	D. Methods of Restricting Foreign Trade	184
	E. The Conduct of Foreign Trade	186
	F. Foreign Finance	191
IX.	PUBLIC UTILITIES	192
	A. Utility Construction in New Cities	193
	B. Consolidation of Utilities	193
	C. The Development of Central Heating	196
	D. Water Utilities	197
	E. Controlling Investment in Public Utilities	199
	F. The Pricing of Utility Services	200
X.	INSURANCE	207
	A. The Functions of Insurance	208
	B. Organization	211
	C. General Operating Policies	212
	D. Kinds of Socialist Insurance	218
XI.	HEALTH CARE	229
	A. Organization and Personnel	229
	B. Health Care Policies	235
	C. Medical Education and Research	246
	D. Financing Health Care	249
XII.	PUBLISHING	254
	A. Organization	254
	B. Newspapers	257
	C. Periodicals	262
	D. Books	267
	E. Output and Price Control	275
	F. The Microprint Revolution	276
	G. Libraries and Bookstores	277
XIII.	BROADCASTING	281
	A. Organization	281
	B. Program Creation and Selection	285
	C. Output Control	291
	D. Financing Free Broadcasts	293
	E. Program Announcement and Rating	294

XIV.	LAW ENFORCEMENT	297
	A. Organization of Law Enforcement	298
	B. Reform of the Criminal Law	301
	C. The Organization of Police	302
	D. Reform of Police Methods	306
	E. Court Trials	312
	F. Criminal Penalties	321
	G. Scientific Research	325
	INDEX	326
	ABOUT THE AUTHOR	331

CHAPTER I

AGRICULTURE

Until a few decades ago agriculture was by far the largest industry in every advanced country. Its chief product, food, is still the most essential of all economic goods, and the many raw materials it produces support most other industries. In one sense, all production begins with the production of raw foods and other raw materials. Hence, we begin our statement of applied socialist welfare economics with a chapter on agriculture.

Although agriculture once gave employment to almost 90% of the population in all countries, this percentage has been falling steadily in advanced countries for some 200 years. In the U.S., farm population fell from 30% to 5% of total population between 1920 and 1970, and will probably continue to fall for many years.

Agriculture long presented a difficult problem to socialist theorists and leaders. The individualistic organization of agriculture was a serious obstacle to the political success of the socialist movement because peasants or farmers were until recently the largest social class, because most of them owned land or hoped to become landowners, and because they lived in the country, remote from urban centers of civilization and socialist influence. The recent rapid decline in farm population, however, has made conversion of peasants and farmers to socialism far less important, and progress in transportation and communication has made it much easier for socialist propagandists to reach them.

Agriculture is the last large industry to remain in the stage of economic individualism, the stage in economic evolution which ordinarily follows fuedalism, and precedes capitalism. Since socialism is the natural and inevitable outgrowth of capitalism, it is much easier to introduce socialist methods of organization and production in an industry which has attained the stage of capitalism, than in an industry which has not yet reached that stage of development. Socialism must transform agriculture directly from an individualistic into a socialistic industry. It is this necessity for the omission of one stage of economic evolution which makes agriculture a difficult problem for socialist welfare economists.

The fact agriculture is still in the stage of individualism in most capitalist countries does not prove that capitalist and socialist forms of organization are unsuited to agriculture; it merely proves that evolution does not proceed at the same pace in all industries. Different branches of industry have passed from individualism to capitalism at different times, and the fact that, at any given time, certain branches of industry were still individualistic while others had already attained the stage of capitalism, did not, as later development has demonstrated, prove that the backward industries were unsuited to capitalist forms of organization and production.

Since agriculture in advanced capitalist countries is still highly individualistic, it suffers much less from the evils of oligopoly — sales effort, oligopolistic pricing, etc. — than do most other industries. But, for the same reason, the socialization of agriculture would require much greater changes in the life style and economic activities of those engaged in agriculture than it would require of other workers. It follows that the socialization of agriculture is now both far less urgent and far less politically feasible than the socialization of most other industries, and should therefore be postponed until nearly all other industries have been socialized. It should also be carried out more slowly.

However, the ownership of farm land could be quickly and easily socialized without affecting the individualistic operation of family farms. And large corporate farms should be socialized long before family farms are eliminated.

A. The Reorganization of Agriculture

The socialization of agriculture would permit and make economic a radical reorganization of agriculture, especially in those countries where most farmers still live on isolated individual farms. The chief elements of this reorganization, in addition to socialization of ownership, should be: (1) complete centralization of control, (2) the creation of giant state farms, (3) the concentration of farm workers in farm towns, (4) an increased division of labor on each farm, and (5) increased specialization by most farms.

Centralization of Control — In a mature liberal socialist economy, nearly all agriculture — including forestry, animal husbandry, and most primary agricultural raw material processing — should be managed by a single national agency, the Division of Agriculture. The chief unit of this division should be the Farm Trust, which should supervise all farms and farm towns.

The division should also include a Lumber Trust which supervises all forests and lumber mills, but we shall not discuss its operation in this chapter.

The chief unit of the Farm Trust should be a Farm Management Branch. In the U.S., such a branch should be divided into about a dozen regional units, each of which supervises, through area offices, the 100 to 200 giant farms and farm towns in its region. Most of these farms would be mixed farms, so organization of farm operations along crop lines would be impractical. But national and regional staffs of crop experts should be available to advise all area supervisors and giant farm managers.

All farm managers, area supervisors, and regional supervisors should be appointed and supervised by their immediate supervisors. And all investment funds should be distributed through this bureaucratic network.

National, regional, and area supervisors should loan needed funds to farm managers, supervise their operations, provide them with specialized professional advice, and assist them in other ways. But they should not tell any farm manager what crops to plant or what prices to charge. In other words, there should be no national or regional price or output control or planning. Each local farm manager should decide what crops to plant, what factors to use, and how to combine them. Prices should be fixed by independent price experts.

The Farm Trust should have a Marketing Branch which markets all raw and processed farm products not consumed on the farm or in the farm town where they are produced. This branch should operate all wheat elevators, warehouses, and other facilities where such products are stored. It should sell only to processors, manufacturers, and wholesalers.

The Farm Trust should also include a Price Branch which determines the prices of all goods handled by the Marketing Branch. The Price Branch should be separated from and independent of the Marketing Division and the Farm Operations Branch to assure that prices will be fixed so as to clear markets, not so as to earn higher profits for one or both of these other divisions.

The Scale of Production — The industrial revolution and the rise of capitalism have had less effect upon the scale of production in agriculture than in any other major industry. The increase in the scale of production in manufacturing, transportation, and commerce has resulted in the steady socialization of production in these fields. In capitalist agriculture, however, the most common unit of production is still the individual family farm. Hence the transition to socialism will occasion a more radical increase in the scale of production in this field than in any other large industry.

Under socialism the size of the average farm ought to be vastly increased for a number of reasons. Large-scale farming permits in agriculture that division of labor which has so greatly increased the productivity of factory labor. It permits more extensive use of the ablest and best-trained farm managers and agronomists, who ought to be placed in control of large farms so as to give the maximum scope to their talents. It reduces the cost of fences and the unused ground they occupy. It makes economic the use of more expensive and more specialized labor-saving machinery. It permits tractors and other machines to move long distances within fields without frequently stopping and turning around. Finally, it will greatly aid the collection of isolated farm families into farm towns.

If large-scale farms are so much more efficient than family farms, why have they not displaced the latter in advanced competitive capitalist countries? There are numerous reasons. Few individual farmers have the capital required to organize and operate giant farms. For this purpose the corporate form of organization is ideal, but some American states have prohibited farming by corporations. Where they are permitted, corporate farms suffer from serious discrimination in taxation. They must pay corporation income taxes up to half of their net income, and then their stockholders must pay personal income taxes higher than those paid by owners of family farms. And corporate farms may be required to pay social security taxes and other levies from which family farms are exempt.

For several decades the U.S. government has restricted the total national output of one or more farm crops, often by assigning individual acreage quotas to individual farms, based on past output. Such quota systems limit the growth of giant farms.

To help family farms survive, the U.S. federal government has created a national system of free advice by county agricultural agents and has subsidized agricultural R and D. Large corporations can afford to establish and finance their own R and D, but family farmers cannot. The federal government also heavily subsidizes mail service and electrical service in rural areas. Moreover, federal, state, and local governments have used taxes collected in urban areas to subsidize rural schools and the construction and maintenance of rural roads and highways. The creation of giant farms and the concentration of farm workers in farm towns would make such subsidies unnecessary.

The federal government has invested billions of dollars in land reclamation and irrigation projects, and has striven to restrict the benefits of these projects to family farms.

These are only a few of the many ways in which the U.S. discriminates against giant farms in favor of family farms for non-economic, ideological reasons. Yet in spite of this discrimination, giant farms pay higher wages, produce superior products, earn higher profits, and are expanding their share of total farm output.

Only careful calculation and continued experimentation can determine how large a specific kind of farm should be. The optimum farm size will be different for each kind of farm. The principal factor limiting optimum size will be the cost in money and time of transporting workers to and from the places they work. As explained later, all farm workers should live in farm towns, which would greatly increase such costs.

If farm workers are driven to the from their field work in trucks or busses, it should be economic for most farm towns to farm nearly all land within a radius of 10 to 20 miles. The smaller the number of workers per acre, especially on the most remote acres, the larger a farm can be without creating excessive transport costs. And most giant socialist farms should be located and/or laid out so that the crops on the most remote acres require the least labor per acre.

The ideal size of a socialist farm would depend more upon the ideal size of its farm town than upon the ideal scale of farm operation. The members of farm families should spend almost ten times as many hours per week in the farm town as in the farm fields or barns. Hence, it would be far more important for them to live in a town of some minimum size than to work on a farm of ideal size. In other words, the benefits of town life are so great that they can more than offset considerable waste of time in traveling to and from fields distant from a farm town.

<u>Farm Towns</u>— Isolated individual farmhouses should be abandoned under socialism. Nearly all farm workers and executives should live in farm towns of 6 to 20 thousand population.

Notable economic benefits would result from the concentration of farm population in towns. In the first place, most farm children would attend better schools. Education, like all other economic activities, can be done more efficiently and cheaply on a large scale than on a small scale. That is why, for the same expenditure, urban schools are everywhere able to give a superior education. The little red schoolhouse, with one teacher and 6 to 12 grades, is inefficient. Consolidated country schools require pupils to travel long distance to and from school. Concentration of farm population in towns would provide better schools much closer to their students. Moreover, educational and cultural advantages for farm adults would also be increased. Adults would be much nearer a lecture hall, a radio station, and an adult evening school.

A similar increase in opportunities for amusement, recreation, and social life would result from concentration of farm population. Theaters, clubhouses, swimming pools, tennis courts, golf courses, etc., would be more readily accessible to all farm workers. Cable TV could be installed in all homes.

Concentration of farm population in towns would markedly reduce the cost of all public utility services. Water, gas, electricity, sewer, and telephone connections cannot be provided as economically for isolated farmhouses as for town dwellings.

The cost of country roads and highways would be greatly reduced by the elimination of isolated farmhouses and the small fields which go with them. If the size of fields were increased ten to a hundredfold, country roads would be much farther apart than at present, and the total mileage necessary to serve a given area would be greatly reduced.

Concentration of farm dwellings in towns would make house construction and maintenance more economical since both construction and maintenance work could then be done on a larger scale and with an increased division of labor. And the time that plumbers, carpenters, and other building-trade workers now spend in going to and from isolated farmhouses would be saved.

Other advantages of housing farm workers in towns are the increased facility for shopping and the increased economy in distributing goods. When living in isolated farmhouses, farmers and their wives must travel for many miles to reach the village store. This wastes time and money. In a socialist farm town, every family would be within a five- or ten-minute walk, not ride, of a larger and more efficient retail store.

Likewise, living in towns would enable farm workers to buy bakery bread and pasteurized creamery milk, to send their soiled clothes to a modern laundry or dry-cleaning plant, and in many other ways would permit them to benefit from the increased division of labor made possible by urban life.

Concentration of farm population in towns would facilitate management of the large farms which, for other reasons, ought to be typical of socialist agriculture. A thousand farm workers can be controlled as a unit far more effectively if they live in the same town than if they are scattered among isolated farmhouses. It would be easier to use time cards, to group men in gangs according to daily needs, to inspect machinery and equipment after use, to secure daily cost and production reports, and so forth, if all workers set out from and returned to the same central point each day.

One further advantage of village life is significant. If farmers lived in towns and worked on large farms, they would be able to work in groups much more of the time. Social labor is more interesting and less wearisome than isolated individual labor. Conversation and companionship make the time pass more quickly and may stimulate competition in speed or efficiency.

Nearly all primary food-processing plants, those which first process fresh, perishable farm products — dairies, canneries, wineries, frozen food plants, etc. — should be located in farm towns so as to minimize the time between harvesting and processing perishable food. Also, some plants processing non-perishable foods and raw materials — grain elevators, flour mills, lumber mills, cotton gins, cotton spinning mills, etc. — should be located in farm towns in order to minimize total transportation costs. Farm raw materials are heavier and more bulky than the processed products make from them. Moreover, some processing plants could be operated so as to compensate for seasonal fluctuations in the employment of farm workers. For instance, some workers who harvest crops in the summer and fall could work in lumber mills or cotton mills in the winter. It is far easier to provide work for idle farm workers who live in town than to provide it for those who live on isolated farms.

A socialist farm town should be large enough to house and service all farm workers, all employees of local processing industries, and all workers in town stores, offices, and other non-farm activities. Farms and farm-product processing plants are export industries, i.e., their products are shipped to other towns and cities. To serve 100 export-plant workers, about 100 workers in local non-export activities are needed. And for each worker in a socialist society there may be one non-worker. Therefore, a socialist farm town of 20,000 population might provide only 5,000 workers in export plants. If half of this labor force is employed in farm-product processing plants, only 2,500 workers would be left for farm work. By 2050 A.D., most American farms of 500,000 to 1,000,000 acres should require less than 2,500 farm workers.

The Division of Labor — The division of labor in individualistic agriculture is very incomplete. The manager of a typical large family farm raises more than one kind of plant and/or animal, does his own accounting, markets all of his products, buys his own seeds, supplies and equipment, and so forth. He cannot be an expert in all of these widely differing occupations, and is often quite incompetent in one or more of them.

The creation of giant state farms would permit a vastly increased division of labor on American farms. Economic calculation and cost accounting could be done by professionally trained economists and accountants. Farm machinery, supplies, and seeds could be purchased by experts who specialize in one kind of machine, supply item, or seed. Farm machinery could be repaired in the local farm town by skilled mechanics, each of whom specializes in one kind of machine and has tools and equipment designed for use on that kind of machine. All farm products could be marketed by a national monopoly which employs experts who specialize in individual farm products.

Moreover, the division of labor among field hands could also be greatly increased. Some workers could specialize in repairing fences and buildings, and others in repairing irrigation and drainage ditches and pipes. Some could specialize in the cultivation of one crop, and others in the cultivation of another crop. These are only a few illustrations of the many ways in which the division of labor could and should be increased on giant socialist state farms.

Specialization — Specialization among private American farms has been growing for over 100 years and will continue to grow. In 1900 the typical family farm produced grain, fruit, garden vegetables, chickens, eggs, pork, beef and dairy products. Today it specializes in a single product or pair of complementary products, like corn and hogs.

Giant socialist farms should specialize far more intensively than the family farms they replace. Of course, the mere merger of many private farms into a single socialist farm would increase the number of farm products per farm, but such a merger should drastically reduce both the variety of products produced on the land of most old farms and the total number of products in each area. The former kind of specializations should be achieved by concentrating some kinds of production — raising trees, caring for dairy cows, fattening cattle and hogs, etc. — in certain areas of the new giant farm, i.e., by greatly increasing the scale of such production. The latter kind of specialization should be achieved by closing down certain farm activities not well suited to the land, climate, and facilities of the new giant farm.

Diversified farming has certain advantages under capitalism that would not continue under socialism. It reduces the risk from crop failures. This is a serious risk for owners of small private farms, but no crop failure could bankrupt a giant socialist farm, which would be fully insured against all risks.

Diversified farming also makes the family farm more self-sufficient and reduces the need to drive to town and buy food in town stores. But all workers on a giant socialist farm should live in a farm town, so there would be no gain from reducing their purchases in town stores.

Thirdly, diversified farming spreads the demand for farm labor over a greater part of the year and reduces seasonal idleness or unemployment. This is more beneficial on small private farms than on giant socialist farms because the latter can operate local manufacturing and food-processing plants during months when the demand for field workers is low. Moreover, a giant socialist farm could shift its field hands from one part of the farm to another one producing a different crop, even if it were far less diversified than a typical family farm, because it would produce more different crops.

Specialization increases the scale of production of each crop on each specialized farm, and therefore yields all the advantages of large-scale production — a greater division of labor among men and machines, the use of larger machines and more specialized equipment, quantity discounts on purchases, and so forth. It often permits a more productive use of land which is best suited to a single use. It also reduces the average distance farm products must be transported to reach the nearest primary processing plant.

Moreover, the progress of agricultural technology has made and will continue to make specialization ever more economic. It is costly to spray a few fruit trees on each farm or field, or to care for a few sick animals on each farm or on each unit of a giant farm. Fruit trees and animals can be cared for much better and more economically when they are concentrated in very large orchards or herds. And the number of farm pesticides, growth stimulants, fertilizers, animal medicines, and other technological farm aids will continue to grow as a result of future scientific progress. The most economic use of most such aids requires concentration of production and specialization of tools, equipment, and workers.

Of course, specialization should never be carried so far that it prevents desirable crop rotation, but a giant socialist farm which practices crop rotation may specialize in one rotation schedule and produce great quantities of the crops in this schedule.

Collective vs. State Farm — In a socialist state all farms should be state farms whose employees work for wages, not collective or cooperative farms. Since the latter are still very common in most socialist countries, they deserve some critical attention here.

On a cooperative farm, workers share in the losses due to bad weather and low prices as well as in the unusual profits due to good weather and high prices, and this results in wide and harmful fluctuations in their earnings. Such earnings should vary with personal effort, not with the weather and/or selling prices.

Moreover, collective farmers elect their managers, and this often results in the election of popular but incompetent leaders. And even competent elected managers find if difficult to enforce discipline on those who elect them. Also, locally elected managers may feel free to ignore the advice and orders of officials of the national department of agriculture. To enforce their orders and policies, these officials must be able to hire and fire local farm managers.

Furthermore, it is more difficult politically to determine and collect ideal real estate rentals from collective farms than from state farms. Collective farmers feel more like land owners than do wage workers on state farms, and as semi-owners they feel that they should not be required to pay farm rentals. In fact, Soviet collective farmers do not pay such rentals. As a result, those collective farmers who are lucky enough to farm rich land near markets, and/or to have more farm real estate per worker, earn much more than equally hard-working collective farmers who farm poor remote land and/or have less real estate per worker.

The organization of individual family farms into large collective farms may be a politically useful half-way measure in the gradual transition from an individualistic to a socialistic system of agriculture, but any transitional collective farms should eventually be reorganized as state farms.

B. Price and Output Determination

In socialist agriculture, as in competitive capitalist agriculture, price determination and output determination should influence each other strongly and directly — that is why we treat them both in this section — but they should be separately determined by separate and independent executives.

<u>Pricing Farm Products</u> — The original wholesale prices of socialist farm products should be fixed by local price experts in the Price Branch of the Farm Trust. Subsequent wholesale and retail prices should be fixed by wholesalers and retailers in the Marketing Trust.

The most basic and general of all socialist welfare pricing rules is that prices should balance supply and demand. Therefore, pricing experts should fix the price of each farm product at each point of original sale so that it balances supply (including any desired inventory reduction) and demand (including any desired inventory build-up).

The ideal method of pricing storable farm products differs from the ideal method of pricing perishable farm products. The prices of storable farm products should remain stable for weeks at a time, and, while price is stable, demand and supply should be balanced by inventory changes. This vital welfare pricing rule has been completely ignored in capitalist countries. For instance, in the U.S. the prices of wheat and cotton actually change many times each day, like the prices of stocks and bonds. As a result, the managers of plants which use wheat and cotton as raw materials are usually unable to react wisely to any market price before it has been changed, and their production schedules cannot be based upon current raw material costs. In a socialist America the prices of wheat and cotton should rarely change more than six times a year.

If storable farm products are imported from or exported to foreign countries where prices fluctuate more frequently, domestic inventories should serve as cushions or insulators which prevent foreign price changes from immediately affecting domestic prices, except when foreign prices change by more than some minimum amount (5%?) and/or the new price persists for some minimum period (one month?). During any such minimum period a socialist state should first react to foreign price changes by changing its imports or exports. Only if these changes in imports or exports and other events do not restore foreign prices to their previous levels should the socialist state change its own domestic prices for the goods in question. Domestic prices should not respond quickly to small changes in foreign prices, but they should never remain continuously above foreign prices (plus or minus shipping costs). The Foreign Trade Trust should import or export farm products whenever this is profitable, and such imports and exports should in time affect domestic prices.

The domestic prices of a storable farm product in different marketing areas should never differ by more than the cost of transport from one area to another. Whenever they differ by more than this amount, enough of the product should be shipped from low-price areas to high-price areas to reduce price differences to the cost of transport. Such inventory shifts would occur if the Marketing Branch tried to obtain the maximum total revenue from its sales without discriminating among buyers, as it should.

The prices of perishable farm products should of course be fixed so as to balance supply and demand. They should change far more often than those of storable products because it is much more costly to store them and because they deteriorate when stored. The wholesale prices of the most perishable products should often change several times a week, but they should probably not change several times a day, as they do in capitalist produce markets. A socialist monopoly could predict daily supplies and sales in each area much more accurately than any competitive capitalist firm can do this now.

Farm Rental Determination — In Liberal Socialism we distinguished between land rent (an inevitable intramarginal surplus) and land rental (an optional payment for the use of land). We drew a similar distinction between quasi-rent and a rental payment for the use of capital goods or improvements. We explained that it is usually impractical to determine separately an ideal land rental and an ideal quasi-rental when capital has been invested in farm land and buildings. Therefore, we proposed that lessees of socialist real estate should pay a single rental determined so as to measure the sum of land rent and quasi-rent on old improvements. In addition, socialist farm managers should pay interest on funds borrowed to make improvements.

If each giant socialist farm included nearly all farm land closer to its farm town than to any other farm town, there would be little if any competition for the use of most pieces of farm land. Thus, most farm land rentals could not be properly determined by competitive bidding. They would have to be determined administratively.

If farm managers are told to maximize their intramarginal profits, and if they are evaluated, paid, and promoted on the basis of the profits they earn, as they should be, they will often use any influence they have on the determination of farm rentals to achieve unduly low rentals, in order to overstate their intramarginal profits. Therefore, farm rentals should be fixed by an impartial outside agency, the National Bureau of Real Estate. This agency should receive copies of all farm financial reports which could help it to fix ideal farm rentals.

Farm rentals should be fixed so that average profits and wage rates on different similar farms are almost equal. Farm workers who farm rich land should earn no more than like workers who farm poor land. Rentals should fall only on intramarginal surpluses.

If they affect any marginal cost, they will make money marginal costs less accurate measures of real marginal costs, and therefore less useful in economic calculation. One good way to help prevent possible rental increases from affecting marginal costs and marginal output decisions is to fix rentals for a period of years. Then a later decision to increase output during this period would not increase current rental charges. For this reason, basic farm rentals probably should not be revised more often than once every five years. They should be based upon assumptions of average weather and average management.

Each giant socialist farm should pay a single total real estate rental for all property in its farm town and all its farm land. The rentals for each housing unit in the town should be separately determined and should vary more often. They should be fixed by each farm manager so as to balance supply and demand for each type of housing. Other local real estate rentals should be based upon agricultural land rent and land improvement costs because there could be little competitive bidding for specialized facilities in a monopolistic socialist farm town.

Cost Accounting — Cost accounting is an essential means of profit maximization, and should be far more widely and intensively used by farmers in capitalist countries, but socialist farm managers should strive to maximize welfare, not profits, and should therefore rely primarily on economic welfare calculation, i.e., on total and marginal cost-benefit analysis. Nevertheless, cost accounting would still be essential as a basis for such felicific calculus.

Every giant socialist farm should have an accounting unit which should prepare accurate cost reports, operating statements, balance sheets, etc., at periodic intervals. National control over individual farms would be based largely upon these periodic accounting reports which must be designed to facilitate such control. All farms should use a uniform system of cost accounting in order to make possible comparison of reports from different farms.

While cost accounting is essential, it should be used solely to help reduce costs per unit of output, evaluate farm managers, and control outputs. It should never be used to fix prices or wage rates. Both farm prices and farm wage rates should be set so as to balance supply and demand, not so as to help make prices equal costs, or vice versa.

A giant socialist farm should rely on the single local branch of the Banking Trust for most of its financial accounting. All payments by and to the farm would pass through this branch bank, which should classify them and report them to the farm accounting office. This office should not duplicate or verify these financial accounts, which should be checked only by bank auditors. It should confine its efforts to cost accounting, economic calculation, and the preparation of periodic accounting statements. It would not have to keep records of accounts due or payable because all transactions should be cash transactions. Every purchase or sale should result in an immediate bank debit and credit.

Socialist farm accountants should never try to determine average costs of production for individual farm products. They should concentrate on determining marginal costs (defined as necessary current variable cost), marginal profits, and marginal losses for each farm product, and the chief marginal cost components. They should also calculate total annual profits and losses per farm, but not per individual farm product.

Output Control — In determining the outputs of individual farm products and total farm output, socialist farm managers should operate under certain rules and constraints. The most important of these rules and constraints are that: (1) farm rentals should be predetermined by an outside agency, normally for a period of several years, (2) managers should not allow their land to deteriorate, and should maintain their fixed improvements, (3) the prices of farm products should be determined by an outside independent agency, so as to balance supply and demand for each product, (4) all farm wage rates should be fixed so as to balance supply and demand, and the application of this rule should be enforced by an outside agency, and (5) the farm town should rarely if ever be expanded or rebuilt to house additional workers, and farm-house housing should rarely remain vacant for long. These constraints have been (1-3) or will be discussed more fully elsewhere in this chapter.

A socialist farm manager can change his output of any farm product in two ways: (1) by using more or less lumpy or fixed factors, with the needed variable factors, and (2) by using more or less of one or more variable factors only. Most changes in output achieved by the first method are relatively large, and most achieved by the second method are relatively small.

Acting within the specified constraints, each manager should control the output of each and all of his products in such a way as to maximize the sum of consumers' surplus and net intramarginal profits over a period of years. On each piece of land he should plant the crop which he believes will make the largest contribution to this sum, and he should increase or decrease the application of each variable factor on this land whenever he expects the change in factor use will increase this sum. In other words, the use of variable factors on each piece of land should be increased until marginal cost equals marginal product, i.e., price, in a typical or average crop year.

Each individual lumpy output decision of a socialist farm manager should be based on total, not marginal, cost-benefit analysis. This rule is most important in the case of a decision to start producing a new crop, which may require the construction of new buildings, the purchase of new equipment, and vocational training of some workers, but it is also applicable when a lumpy increase in the output of an old crop is being considered. Any such increase requires a lumpy investment in labor, seed, fertilizer, land use, and other factors which will not yield a return for several months or years.

In the vast majority of cases, the effects of a proposed lumpy output change upon consumers' surplus can be ignored because it is too small to be significant. Nearly all farm products are produced in such large amounts that the shift of a single field from one crop to another can have no significant effect upon consumers' surplus. However, when a new crop is first produced, or an old crop is introduced into a new area, or the total output of an old crop in its old market area is increased by more than some minimum proportion (10 to 20%?), the effect on consumers' surplus may be large enough to deserve measurement and consideration. In all other cases, farm managers should consider the effect of proposed output changes on intramarginal profit only.

It may seem that socialist farm and/or farm-town managers should try to control the outputs of individual products in such a way as to minimize seasonal fluctuations in their demand for labor, and that this policy would conflict with a policy of maximizing intramarginal profits. But if wage rates fluctuate seasonally in an ideal way, low wage rates would assure optimum employment and output in periods of minimum demand for labor, and high wage rates would reduce the demand for labor ideally in periods of maximum demand for labor.

Sound wage-rate variations would also persuade workers to provide much less work in off-peak periods. These demand and supply changes should result in marked seasonal variations in the average weekly hours of labor, from perhaps 20 to 50 hours per week during each year, on many farms.

A giant socialist farm and farm town should almost always operate at ideal capacity with full employment. It should rarely reduce its workforce in order to reduce its output. Such a reduction would result in housing vacancies and unused production facilities and equipment. A socialist farm should occasionally shift some fields from one crop to another in order to maximize rent and quasi-rent surpluses, but it should hardly ever reduce its total output and workforce in order to end marginal losses or increase its intra-marginal surplus.

Labor-saving inventions in socialist agriculture should normally result in increased output and/or lower rental income from farm towns, but not in work-force reductions and vacant housing in existing farm towns. Such inventions should, however, reduce the rate of investment in farm towns until the investment in old farm towns is again yielding more than a satisfactory rental income.

When a decline in farm prices reduces the income of a socialist farm, the net burden should fall on rental income from farm property, not on the real wages of farm workers. Neither real wages nor the number of jobs should be reduced until repeated annual losses have eliminated all rental income and proven that a future restoration of such income is unlikely. In a growing socialist economy, such continuing farm losses should be very rare.

C. Other Operating Policies

Wage Rates — The wage rates of farm-town and farm workers should be determined so as to balance the supply of and demand for workers in each craft or profession during each shift. Every local worker should be able to demand and secure any local job for which he is qualified. Wage-rate changes should be the chief means used to induce workers to take or leave farm jobs.

Nearly all such wage rates should vary cyclically during the day, week, month, and year so as to attract the ideal number of workers to each shift, to each day's work (there should be no holidays), and to work during peak and off-peak weeks and months.

No farm manager should be allowed to reduce his average wage rates in order to increase his reported profits. An outside agency should constantly supervise each farm's wage-rate determination to prevent such monopsonistic exploitation. And every farm manager should be graded, rewarded, and promoted partly on the basis of his average wage rate as well as upon the basis of his unit costs and his profit and loss statements. Proper application of wage policies, with sound rental determination, should result in average real wage rates being almost equal on all farms in equally popular climate zones. Wage rates should, of course, be higher in harsh climates than in mild climates.

The executives of a socialist Farm Trust should try to induce every worker to make an optimum productive effort by rewarding individual workers and teams of workers according to their output. Farm work is especially suitable for the use of individual and group piece rates and/or bonuses, because most farm workers control their own efforts most of the time. Their output is not controlled by the speed of an assembly line.

Individual piece rates should be used whenever the individual controls his output and this output can be measured at a reasonable cost. Team or group rates should be used whenever output is measurable and is controlled collectively by a team of workers.

When the output per worker is determined by the speed of an assembly line or machine, wage payments should vary with the number of errors caught by inspectors and supervisors, and also with absence and tardiness rates.

Farm managers and executives should be given special efficiency bonuses whenever they achieve a reduction in relevant production costs per unit of output. Relevant cost reductions are those due to managerial decision, and exclude savings due to factor-cost changes, good weather, and other non-managerial causes.

All workers and executives should be continuously encouraged to suggest cost-saving improvements in farm tools, machines, equipment, and methods of cultivation. Those who make useful suggestions should usually receive bonuses which vary with the capital value of the total expected savings. Those whose suggestions are not accepted should be told why their suggestions have not been used, and should be encouraged to try again.

Several non-monetary rewards should be offered to superior workers and executives. For instance, they should receive special mention and praise in the farm-town newspaper and/or on some local radio or TV program, should be fiven special cups or medals, and should have first choice of vacation periods and facilities.

Other Personnel Policies — In a mature socialist society most farm workers would be born and raised in farm towns and would work on the farm around their native town. But farm managers should be required to hire all qualified applicants for each class of farm work, regardless of where they come from, within a month or two after receiving an application, provided local housing is available. And housing would be available if wage rates and housing rentals are properly fixed.

If too many persons apply for any kind of farm work on any farm, the wage rates for such work and/or the hours of labor should be altered until demand equals supply, but no qualified individual applicant should ever be denied desired employment.

If an unqualified, i.e., untrained, adult applies for farm work which requires little training, he should be taken on as an apprentice and trained on the job at his expense. However, most non-professional farm workers should be trained in vocational secondary schools at public expense before they seek their first job. Only those who change their occupation after leaving school should be required to pay for their retraining as farm workers.

In most branches of agriculture the need for labor varies seasonally, being highest during harvest months. In the U.S. the demand for seasonal labor is met by employing migrant seasonal farm workers, most of whom are married and have children who travel with them. In a socialist society the demand for seasonal labor should be filled largely by high school and college students, especially those who live in farm towns. School calendars should be planned to enable students to take seasonal farm jobs with minimum interference with their studies.

Seasonal needs for farm labor should also be met in part by shifting workers from farm-town jobs to farm jobs. For instance, many local teachers, librarians, barbers, repair men, office clerks, and store clerks should become temporary farm workers during periods of peak demand for farm labor. This would improve their health by giving them more outdoor exercise and would broaden their life experience. It would also reduce the demand for migrant workers, whose way of life is harmful, especially to children.

Finally, the hours of labor per day and week for year-round farm workers should vary throughout the year so as to minimize the need for seasonal labor. Such workers should take all their vacations, 4 to 6 weeks a year, during those seasons when the demand for farm labor is lowest, and their hours of labor should also be sharply reduced during these seasons. On the other hand, during the season of peak demand, all farm workers should work up to 50 hours a week.

If migrant farm workers with families are used, they should be organized in stable communities which move together in comfortable house trailers with trailer schools and other normal community facilities.

No farm worker should ever be required to retire because of age or a partial disability. The hours of labor for aged or partially disabled workers should be less than for most other workers, and special jobs suitable for these workers should be created, but no one capable of useful labor should be denied work or forced to retire. Moreover, the managers of a socialist farm should make continuous efforts to persuade all local residents not in school or in a hospital to seek full or part-time work.

To facilitate greater female participation in the local labor force, every farm town should provide free public care and/or education for all children whenever both parents are working. And ample part-time jobs for mothers with young children should be provided.

Farm Machinery — Every increase in the size of a farm makes it economic to use larger and/or more specialized farm machines and equipment. The average size of a tractor or a seeder is much bigger on large capitalist farms than on small family farms. A giant farm usually has larger fields as well as more acreage devoted to each crop, and can utilize large farm machines more fully.

Since socialist farms should be far larger than the average capitalist farm, they should use much larger farm machines. This would reduce cultivation costs substantially. One tractor driver can operate a large tractor pulling a six-row seeder almost as easily as he can operate a small tractor pulling a two-row seeder.

The farm machines now in use on American farms have been designed for use on existing private farms. Few of them would be suitable for use on giant socialist farms. Therefore, the Research and Development Branch of the Farm Trust should develop new types and models of farm machines much larger and more labor-saving than any now in use.

The managers of giant socialist state farms should be able to obtain needed capital funds more easily and at lower rates than private farmers because such loans would be more secure and because socialist farms could borrow from the national government. Most loans to private farmers are relatively risky because the farm is small and/or under-financed. The owner-operator may get sick or die at any time, and a single crop failure may bankrupt him, even if he remains healthy and competent.

With much more adequate supplies of capital funds, giant socialist farms could markedly increase their investment in farm machinery and equipment per farm worker. Thus they would benefit both from the use of larger and more efficient farm machines and equipment and from a much more adequate and economical supply of capital funds to invest in such capital goods.

Some expensive farm machines which are needed for only a few days on each farm — combines, cotton-pickers, etc. — should be provided and operated by migrant communities of specialized farm workers who live in mobile homes and move from farm to farm. Since the same crop must be planted, harrowed, or harvested at different times in different areas such migrant teams and machines can perform the same service at different times in different areas. Normally, they should move from south to north during the spring and from north to south during the fall.

Conservation — All socialist farms should be required to prevent or offset depletion and destruction of the land they use. So far as possible, they should replace all lost minerals, and should prevent the structure and composition of the soil from deteriorating. They should use all economic methods to prevent erosion, and should offset the effects of unprevented erosion by positive measures to improve the soil. It is uneconomic to feed one generation by depleting the soil to be passed on to the next generation. Soil depletion resembles living on capital, and is equally uneconomic, for the same reasons.

Instead of depleting the soil to be left to the next generation, a socialist society should try to increase this estate. It should level, lime, enrich, irrigate, drain and otherwise improve millions of acres of land each year. It should bring fresh water from Alaska and Canada to irrigate millions of acres of arid soil on the Great Plains and in the American Southwest. It should crush billions of tons of rocks each year in order to turn rocky wastes into fertile fields and to rebuild eroded fields. It should plant millions of acres of trees each year to assure ample future supplies of lumber, to protect land from wind and water erosion, and to rebuild exhausted soils.

If farm soil is not fully conserved, the money costs of farm products do not measure the full real costs of production because they ignore depletion. And depletion may occur and be significant even when land increases in value due to technological progress or growth in demand.

Every farm town should have a sewage system which collects all solid human waste, purifies it, and prepares it for use as liquid or solid fertilizer on nearby land. This system should also be used to collect, purify, and transport some animal waste, at least that from barns and feeding lots. Transport and use of both human and animal wastes in liquid form will probably often be more economical than transport and application in solid form, especially on irrigated fields. In any case, no farm-town sewage of any kind should ever be placed in or allowed to flow into rivers of lakes.

Socialist farms located near large cities should receive purified organic sewage in liquid form by pipeline from the nearest city and should apply it to their fields in liquid form, usually mixed with irrigation water.

To prevent farm managers from inflating their profits or reducing their costs by mining their soil, a socialist Farm Trust should employ soil testers who visit each farm each year and test the soil on a good sample of all fields. The reports of such soil tests should be used both to evaluate the work of all farm managers and to help determine the measures needed to prevent soil depletion.

Of course, each farm manager should do his own soil testing to help determine his operating methods. The soil testers employed by the Farm Trust should perform a function like that of outside auditors who check bank accounts.

D. Research and Development

The Farm Trust should include a Research Branch which carries out applied research and development on all methods, tools, machines, equipment, seeds, plants, animals, and other means of agricultural production. Probably over 10% of the total net income of this trust should be spent on such applied R and D, but the funds should come from a national investment agency, not from an addition to the prices of products. All spending on R and D should be treated as an investment, not as a price-determining cost of production.

When private firms invest in R and D, they are usually able to appropriate only a minor part of the social gains from their investment. Hence, investment in R and D is always grossly inadequate in capitalist countries. Fortunately, capitalist governments have been increasing public investment in R and D, especially in agricultural R and D. As a result, the output of farm products per acre, and, more important, per worker, has grown rapidly in advanced countries in recent decades. The opportunities for further progress in seed selection, plant breeding, animal breeding, and other fields seem almost unlimited. The average social yield from investments in agricultural R and D is still probably over 50% a year. For instance, the social gains from the development of hybrid corn have been larger than all the funds previously spent on agricultural R and D in the U.S.

Expenditures on agricultural R and D should be increased until the social return from such investment falls to the level of the average return from other investments, measured by the uniform national rate of interest. The social return includes additional land rent and consumers' and workers' surpluses, as well as the benefits measured by total relevant quasi-rent.

In a liberal socialist country the improved
methods of seed selection and cultivation developed
each year by R and D would be applied far more quickly
and extensively than in an individualistic capitalist
economy. All socialist farms should be managed by professionally trained agronomists responsible to like
superiors, who would apply improved methods as soon as
they have been created and properly tested. Individual
managers of family farms often refuse to adopt such
methods for many years. It follows that money spent
for agricultural R and D would be more productive
under socialism, and this would help to justify higher
investment in R and D.

CHAPTER II

MINERAL PRODUCTION

In 1970 raw material production accounted for 1.7% of U.S. GNP. Since then the sudden drastic increase in the world price of petroleum and its effect on gas and coal prices may have doubled this percentage. Moreover, in this chapter we discuss the refining, transportation, and sale of coal, ore, gas, and oil, as well as their production.

The relative costs of raw materials are likely to increase gradually and indefinitely because the costs of finding and extracting most minerals will probably rise faster than GNP as the richest deposits are exhausted and ever lower-grade deposits must be exploited. Moreover, the industrialization of backward countries will increase the demand for minerals much faster than it will increase the demand for most other products. However, the relative costs of transporting and processing raw minerals should decline steadily as a result of technological progress.

A. Organization

The production, refining, and distribution of petroleum and natural gas differ so much from the production, processing, and distribution of other mineral products that they should be carried on by a separate national organization, the Oil and Gas Trust. This trust should also manage the intercity pipelines which distribute oil, gas, and other goods. And it should drill and operate the deep wells which extract steam, sulphur, and other chemicals in liquid form from underground.

The mining and initial processing of all other mineral products except water should be managed by a single national Mining Trust. Both trusts should be supervised by a Division of Minerals.

Vertical integration of the oil industry, from producing well to gasoline service station, is desirable because it permits a smooth flow of oil and refined products from the oil field to the consumer. The storage and transport facilities used by this industry are peculiar to it, and unsuitable for use by other industries.

1. Prospecting

In a capitalist society, prospecting for mineral resources is carried out in an uncoordinated way by thousands of independent individuals and firms, each of which looks for one or a few minerals only, and conceals most of the results of its search. As a result, there is an incredible duplication of effort, and no assurance that any area has been properly prospected. Moreover, most prospectors are badly trained and/or cannot afford to use the best available equipment and methods. And scientific research and development on prospecting methods and equipment is far below the optimum level.

The American oil industry spends over a billion dollars a year in its search for new oil and gas fields, but nearly all the results of such prospecting are kept secret. So valuable is this secret data that large American oil firms spend many millions of dollars each year trying to prevent the leakage or theft of such data and/or trying to secure such data from their competitors, often by dishonest methods.

In a socialist society all prospecting for new mineral resources should be carried on by a single national geological survey unit responsible jointly to the heads of the Oil and Gas Trust and the Mining Trust. When any individual prospector or survey team covers an area, it should look for all kinds of mineral resources (including water), not just gold, oil, or any other mineral.

Moreover, the entire nation should be covered systematically by professionally trained geologists equipped with the best equipment, and all survey results should be preserved in a single office and made available to all interested trusts and departments. This system would radically reduce the cost of discovering mineral resources and/or would greatly increase the known reserves of all minerals.

B. Oil Production and Distribution

Competitive exploitation of an oil or gas field is very wasteful. Each producer tries to extract as much oil or gas as possible before the field is exhausted. Far too many costly wells are drilled, and little effort is made to conserve underground pressure. It does not pay to inject the optimum volume of water or gas into a field in order to extract more oil if some or most of the benefit accrues to competitors. In a socialist economy every oil and gas pool should be exploited by a monopoly which drills no more wells than are socially justified, and which uses all economically sound methods to maintain or raise underground pressure and otherwise maximize total oil or gas recovery.

When oil extraction produces natural gas which cannot be sold, it should not be burned or flared, a common practice under capitalism. Instead, it should be pumped back into the geological layer from which the oil is drawn, in order to maintain underground pressure and preserve the gas for future use.

The oil produced in a single capitalist oil field may flow to several different refineries for processing, some nearby and some remote. All the oil produced in a typical socialist oil field should be processed in a single refinery, the one nearest the oil field, if it is big enough. And all the products of each refinery should be sold to the nearest customers. No refinery should sell in the marketing area of another refinery.

In capitalist countries there is a vast amount of cross-shipment of petroleum and petroleum products because of competition between private oil firms. Petroleum products produced in California are shipped to Texas, and some of those produced in Pennsylvania and Texas are shipped to California. Gasoline tank trucks pass each other carrying like gasoline in opposite directions on most American highways every day, often every hour of the day. In a socialist economy all such cross-shipment of oil and oil products should be ended.

The number of petroleum refineries in the U.S., now well over 400, should be reduced below 100. No metropolitan area or group of nearby planned new cities should be served by more than one refinery. The average distance between refineries should be over 200 miles.

Every increase in the size of a refinery reduces in-plant production costs per unit of output. The chief sound reason for having more than one giant refinery in the U.S. is to reduce transport costs to and from refineries. However, petroleum and most of its products can be transported (by pipeline and tanker) more cheaply than other fuels and raw materials. Hence, transport costs are less of an objection to large-scale processing plants in this industry than in most others.

If oil and/or oil products must be imported by sea by an oil-producing country, all such imports should arrive at those ports most distant from the oil fields of the recipient nation. For instance, such U.S. imports should be received in New England harbors and should supply all of New England's demand before any like imported oil and/or oil products are received in New York City or Philadelphia. And all imported oil should be refined in the regions where the refined products are consumed. No oil or oil products imported into the U.S. should be landed in Texas, Louisiana, Mississippi, or other oil-exporting regions, a common practice under capitalism because of competition. The same rules apply also to the importation of liquified natural gas.

In America today over 100 different brands of gasoline, lubricating oil, and other petroleum products are sold, and most producers claim falsely that their products are the best for some uses. In a socialist economy the variety of each refinery product should be drastically reduced, probably by over 90%. Careful testing should be carried on continuously to determine which variety of each product is best suited for each use, and only that single variety should be produced and sold for that use. The decision as to which variety of gasoline a private car owner should buy and use should be made by the nearest refinery, not by the customer. Gas stations should usually sell only one variety, and if they sell more than one, they should decide which one each customer buys. Few if any drivers are competent to choose wisely between different kinds of gasoline and lubricating oil.

The simplification of refinery products would sharply reduce the cost per gallon of refining, transporting, storing, and retailing such goods. It would permit a marked increase in the scale of most refinery operations and would drastically reduce the variety and number of tank trucks, storage tanks, and retail gas pumps needed.

The number of gas stations in the U.S. should be reduced by over 80%. All stations should be at least one mile apart.

C. Coal Mining and Distribution

Coal mining is by far the largest mining industry in most advanced countries, and it will become relatively much more important as coal replaces oil and gas in many uses.

In 1970 there were still over 6500 coal mines in the U.S. Most of these were much too small to be efficient. Many were unsafe and survived only by paying below-average wages. A socialist Mining Trust should close down the great majority of these mines, enlarge some of them, and concentrate coal production in less than 600 large, safe, efficient, mechanized mines. This would sharply increase the output per miner, and would drastically reduce the number of mine accidents and illnesses caused by mine conditions.

Because of competition and business fluctuations (which would end under socialism) capitalist coal mines are unwilling to build up optimum inventories of coal in off-peak periods. When demand falls off seasonally, they reduce their output and discharge workers until demand picks up again. The unemployed workers bear most of the social costs of such profit-maximizing policies. A socialist coal monopoly could predict demand much more accurately than any single competitive firm, and it should bear the full social costs of seasonal unemployment. It should largely eliminate seasonal fluctuations in coal-mining employment and coal output by building up optimum stocks of coal in the warmer months of the year.

Of course, some small seasonal fluctuations in coal production might be economic, to reduce storage costs and coal deterioration. But they should not result in any seasonal unemployment. They should be offset by seasonal vacations and by seasonal variations in the hours of labor.

In 1970 about 60% of all coal consumed in the U.S. was burned to generate electricity. It is cheaper to transmit electricity long distances than to ship coal. Therefore, most large power plants should be located adjacent to the coal mines which provide their coal. Only those power plants needed to provide heat for urban central heating systems should be located in or near cities. This policy would help to reduce air pollution in urban areas, as well as reducing the cost of electricity.

For similar reasons, plants which convert coal into synthetic gas and chemicals should also be located near coal mines rather than near urban areas. Synthetic gas can be moved by pipeline more cheaply than the coal used to produce it can be moved by rail. Moreover, most gas and chemical plants pollute the air, and therefore should not be located in or near urban areas.

In capitalist countries coal-mine operators have rarely if ever been required to pay for all the external diseconomies they cause — water pollution, air pollution, industrial accidents and illness, etc. In a socialist economy the Mining Trust should pay special taxes and insurance rates which fully measure such costs.

Open-strip mines already account for 20% of U.S. coal output and this share is certain to increase greatly. They are especially destructive of land. Many critics have argued that they should be required to restore stripped land to its original condition, even if the restoration costs are far greater than the value of the restored land. This policy would be uneconomic. Investment in land restoration, like all other investment, should yield a net social benefit, which means that it should be economic after allowing for interest costs and consumers' surpluses.

While full restoration of land damaged by mining is often uneconomic, any resulting depreciation in land value should be converted into a marginal money cost of mining, like depletion.

Underground mining is still one of the most dangerous and disagreeable occupations, and capitalist insurance benefits and wage rates do not fully measure the relevant real costs. In a socialist economy insurance benefits should fully cover the high costs to miners of mining accidents and industrial illness. And, if all miners were free to choose their occupation, underground miners' wages would have to be raised substantially above wage rates in more pleasant occupations. Both reforms would speed up the shift from underground coal mining to strip mining because the latter is less dangerous and less unpleasant.

Most miners who continue to work underground should do so for only half a shift, three or four hours a day. For the rest of their shift they should be given aboveground work. Such daily job changes would be desirable for many workers in other industries, but the need for them in underground mining is especially great.

D. Conservation

We use the term conservation here to include all effective practices adopted primarily in order to reduce the consumption of scarce irreplaceable minerals. In a broad sense, all sound economic practices conserve some of the factors in production, usually including one or more minerals. But the term conservation is commonly applied only to practices adopted primarily to conserve the stock of irreplaceable resources.

Conservation practices may be divided into two major classes: (1) those which are profitable, and (2) those which are not profitable.

It is hardly necessary to argue here that profitable conservation practices should be adopted under socialism. The difficult question is whether unprofitable conservation practices should be adopted. In Liberal Socialism (pp. 117-18) we argued against the adoption of unprofitable measures. However, we now doubt this conclusion. Therefore, we shall state and criticize the major arguments for and against this conclusion, and leave the reader free to reach his own conclusion.

1. The Case Against Unprofitable Conservation

As the supply of any mineral declines and/or its relative cost increases, all old conservation measures will be applied more vigorously, at a higher cost, and new conservation measures will become profitable and be adopted. These measures include the increased use of old substitute raw materials, the discovery and invention of new substitute raw materials, the increased production of old substitute end products, improvement in methods of discovering the relevant natural reserves, improvement in refining methods, increased recycling of the mineral, and simple delay in the exploitation of known resources.

For instance, the use of most irreplaceable natural resources could be very sharply reduced by rehousing the American population in new planned cities designed to reduce most living costs, especially the costs of urban travel to and from work, stores, clinics, and other urban facilities. We shall offer a theory of such ideal socialist new-city planning in Chapters III and IV. Many other economic policies which would incidentally conserve mineral resources are suggested in other chapters of this book.

The exploitation of known reserves often yields a profit which is less than 5% of the value of the mineral extracted. In such cases it is profitable to leave the mineral in the ground whenever its real price is rising more than 0.55% a year. If the profit is less than 1%, as in the case of many copper and silver mines, it is profitable to leave the mineral in the ground as long as its real price is rising more than 0.011% a year. We are assuming here that the real interest rate is 10% or less, and that there are no property taxes on mineral resources. Thus, any steady rise in the relative price of a mineral should result in substantial delay in its exploitation, without the adoption of any unprofitable conservation practices.

There is good reason to believe that technological progress will continue at as high a rate in the future as in the recent past, a period during which many synthetic substitutes for minerals have been developed, many new sources of energy have been discovered or invented, and many other methods of profitable conservation have been developed.

Some critics of conservation have argued that future technological progress may sharply decrease the value of most irreplaceable mineral resources, and that therefore conservation of these resources will be both unprofitable and uneconomic. They cite the case of Chilean nitrate deposits, whose value fell after engineers learned how to extract nitrogen from the air. It is true that whenever such technological progress seems very probable before existing low-cost resources have been exhausted, conservation is much less needed.

Moreover, it is likely that the growth rate of world population will decline drastically during the next 50 years, and that in advanced countries, the chief mineral consumers, population will cease growing in a few decades. These population trends will tend to reduce the growth rate of mineral consumption.

A final argument against unprofitable conservation is that it is unreasonable, and therefore politically impractical in democratic states, to ask the present generation to sacrifice for future generations who are likely to be richer, healthier, and happier than the present generation.

2. The Case for Unprofitable Conservation

The current market demand for and price of an irreplaceable mineral measures only the current marginal benefit from consumption and discounted benefits from future consumption. The market discount of the benefit from future consumption increases rapidly as we look further into the future. Consequently, the needs of our posterity 100 or 200 years from now are virtually ignored. But most men want to promote the welfare of their posterity, even for centuries. And this want will become more intense as men become more prosperous and better educated. One of the best ways to satisfy this growing want is to adopt collective conservation and carry it well beyond the limit of profitable conservation. How far beyond will depend upon the intensity of this collective want, which will grow as the years pass. But it is possible that the voters of an advanced democratic socialist state will approve of a substantial amount of unprofitable collective conservation.

Some futurists have predicted that the current rapid depletion of world mineral resources will continue or accelerate, and that this will soon result in the start of a long, perhaps drastic decline in our standard of living. Such predictions strengthen the case for unprofitable collective conservation. No individual can partially protect his posterity against the risk of economic decline by practicing either profitable or unprofitable conservation. But a majority of the voters of a large country can do so collectively by practicing sufficient unprofitable conservation.

As insurance, unprofitable conservation may be economic even though the losses insured against never occur. The mere elimination of risk may amply justify it. A wise house owner does not consider his fire insurance unjustified merely because his insured house does not burn down. He knows in advance that the risk of a fire is small. Thus conservation of mineral resources may be beneficial insurance even if the risk of national disaster due to future lack of such resources is very small. Even an imaginary risk may justify conservation because insurance reassures the insured.

Conservation of irreplaceable mineral resources resembles saving and investment. Abstaining from the extraction and use of such minerals is like abstaining from the consumption of consumers' goods. Leaving mineral reserves in the ground corresponds to depositing gold reserves in underground vaults, but is more productive. The mineral reserves are far more likely to increase in value indefinitely, and the storage costs are lower, indeed usually nil. They are highly-leveraged investments, and increase in relative value each year 10 to 100 times faster than refined minerals.

Collective action can increase the total volume of both saving and conservation. Each individual is willing to save or conserve much more to achieve a national goal when he knows that everyone else is participating appropriately, which is possible only with compulsory collective saving and conservation. Hence, he will vote for a much larger per capita volume of compulsory collective saving or unprofitable conservation than he would otherwise practice voluntarily and individually.

We turn now to the second plausible reason for unprofitable conservation, defense needs. In a world of independent armed states with conflicting national interests and policies, each nation must be prepared to resist attack. To do so, it must have assured access to adequate supplies of those minerals essential to military preparedness and action, in other words, to nearly all widely used minerals. And the most certain and secure mineral supplies are those obtainable from domestic natural resources. To preserve such domestic supplies may require conservation programs which would be unprofitable in the absence of conservation taxes and subsidies. Like all defense spending, unprofitable conservation of minerals needed for future defense activities is necessarily collective, compulsory, and unprofitable.

Critics of this defense argument may, however, reply that large, continued spending on defense will itself help to force up mineral prices enough to make profitable all the conservation needed for defense purposes.

While we are in doubt as to whether any unprofitable expansion of mineral conservation is economic, we have no doubts concerning the ideal method of expanding such conservation.

3. Taxes and Subsidies

The best method of pushing conservation beyond the profit-maximization limit is to impose taxes on the domestic extraction of the scarcest irreplaceable minerals. Such taxation would affect all domestic users and consumers of these minerals equally. It would decentralize decisions concerning specific conservation practices. Each user would be free to use substitute minerals or fuels, to start or expand a recycling program, to redesign his products so as to prolong its life and facilitate repairs, to raise his selling prices, and so forth. And each final consumer would be free to react to these changes and alter his consumption as he pleases.

Moreover, the imposition of an ideal extraction tax would enable each local plant manager to determine precisely how far he should carry each conservation measure. He would need only to carry each measure as far as it is profitable. The tax would raise the cost of the taxed minerals to each user and make new and/or increased conservation measures profitable, but the local user could still use the same principles of output control and factor combination, the same methods of marginal and total analysis. No central planning of local conservation practices would be required.

Centralized national determination of individual conservation rules for local plant managers is a part of, or at least closely resembles, the kind of centralized national economic planning discussed and rejected in our Liberal Socialism. Nearly all of the arguments against such planning stated there (pp. 206-11) apply also against centralized determination of local conservation measures. Only the local plant manager is able to collect and respond promptly to all the changing local data which should influence his decisions on local conservation proposals. And we defined liberal socialism as the kind of socialism which decentralizes such economic decision-making.

While capitalist governments rarely impose mineral extraction taxes, many private owners of mineral reserves allow other firms to exploit these reserves and require payment of a mineral royalty per unit of output. Such royalty payments raise marginal costs and have the same conservation effects as extraction taxes.

If extraction taxes are imposed on two or more minerals, they should vary, often widely, from mineral to mineral. The shorter the expected life of any domestive mineral resource (including expected future discoveries), the higher the tax should be. The more essential the mineral, the higher the tax should be.

Extraction taxes on domestic mineral output would stimulate the importation and use of foreign minerals, which would both conserve domestic resources and lessen the rise in domestic mineral prices. The larger the foreign supplies of a domestically scarce mineral, the greater are the potential domestic benefits from any domestic extraction tax.

The same reasons which may justify the imposition of extraction or excise taxes on domestic extraction of irreplaceable minerals may seem to justify the granting of subsidies to importers of such minerals. Both policies would conserve domestic mineral resources for consumption by our posterity and by our military forces. Both would increase imports and reduce domestic extraction of these minerals. On the other hand, import subsidies would raise domestic mineral consumption and speed up exhaustion of world mineral resources. And subsidies require higher taxes on all taxpayers, regardless of their consumption of scarce minerals. Therefore, extraction taxes on domestic mineral producers are preferable to subsidies on imported minerals, and render the latter unnecessary.

Instead of using extraction taxes and import subsidies to encourage conservation of irreplaceable mineral resources, many capitalist states have imposed property taxes and import tariffs, both of which hasten the depletion of domestic mineral resources. For instance, most local governments in the U.S. impose substantial property taxes on proven mineral resources (which make conservation much more costly), and the American federal government has imposed import tariffs on several raw minerals and on many metallic products. In a socialist economy there should be no property taxes on mineral resources (or on any other property), and no import tariffs on irreplaceable minerals or goods made from them.

It has often been claimed that tariffs on mineral imports are needed to maintain a domestic output level high enough to meet military needs in times of war. But the resulting expansion of domestic output merely hastens the arrival of the day when domestic producers will be forced to reduce their output. The best way for any nation to prepare for possible wartime military needs for scarce minerals is to build up reserve stocks, preferably by importation, and conserve its limited domestic mineral resources.

4. More R and D on Conservation

Men have learned how to extract nitrogen from the air and certain minerals from sea water at costs low enough to make these processes economic. The development of such processes turns irreplaceable minerals produced under increasing costs into readily replaceable minerals produced under decreasing costs. It ends the need for special conservation measures for these minerals.

It is almost certain that men will learn how to extract economically other minerals from the air and sea water or to economically recover mineral nodules from the ocean floor. The benefits of converting scarce irreplaceable minerals into abundant, replaceable minerals are so great, and so incompletely measured by money profits, that investment in the relevant R and D should be increased well above the limit justified by prospective money profits. Most of the benefits of R and D accrue to the public. The large resulting consumers' and workers' surpluses should be carefully estimated and fully considered in the total cost-benefit analysis used to control such investment.

For the same reason, investment in R and D to discover or create substitutes for mineral fuels and raw materials should also be carried well beyond the limits justified by money profits alone. Since many useful substitutes have already been found, it is certain that more will be discovered or created.

In extractive industries producing mineral raw materials the benefits of R and D projects which increase supplies or reduce demand are especially large because such projects usually prevent or reduce an otherwise inevitable increase in marginal costs. Any subsequent rise in such costs increases the value of the savings made possible by all previous relevant R and D projects. Thus it is much more likely that R and D projects in mineral-producing and using industries will prove economic than that similar projects in other industries will do so.

For all of these reasons, investment in R and D projects which may reduce the costs of mineral products should be increased by 100 to 500% in a socialist economy. At least 10% of the revenue from the sale of primary mineral materials should be invested in such R and D.

5. User-Plant Conservation Practices

Whether or not mineral extraction taxes are imposed in order to promote mineral conservation, many old conservation practices by local manufacturing plants and other users will become more profitable as mineral prices rise faster than the price level. Moreover, this relative mineral price rise will make some new conservation practices economic. A brief discussion of such new or expanded conservation practices is appropriate here.

In order to decide whether or not to adopt a specific new conservation measure, local plant executives must engage in total cost-benefit analysis. Each such measure involves lumpy intramarginal disbenefits (costs and/or benefit losses) and lumpy intramarginal benefits, usually continuing over several years. The benefits lost and the benefits secured both include some consumers' surplus and some producers' surplus, which are lumpy intramarginal quantities. To evaluate a proposed local conservation measure, the welfare economist must estimate, add up, and compare the total lumpy disbenefits and the total lumpy benefits. Marginal analysis is not applicable to such measures.

In a liberal socialist economy, additional local plant conservation stimulated by rising real mineral prices should include: (a) increased use of substitutes for scarce minerals, (b) more recycling and reuse of mineral products, (c) more standardization and simplification of such products, (d) more repairs and longer use of these products and (e) more attention to mineral conservation in the design of new buildings and appliances.

More Substitutes — Every rise in relative mineral prices will induce local managers of mineral-using plants to increase their use of old mineral substitutes and look for new ones. Managers will also reduce the output of those end products most affected by higher mineral prices and increase their output of substitute finished products less affected by higher mineral prices.

For instance, they will produce fewer gold and silver watch cases, and more stainless steel cases; less silver tableware, and more stainless steel tableware; less metallic furniture and more wooden furniture; less metallic pipe and more plastic pipe, and fewer metallic cans and more glass bottles and plastic containers.

Moreover, most factories and power plants which burn oil or natural gas will change to coal or to some other substitute fuel if oil and natural gas prices continue to rise relatively. And many more residential buildings will be heated by steam or hot water from coal-burning power plants instead of by their own oil or gas-burning furnaces.

One of the best ways to conserve irreplaceable mineral fuels and raw materials is to develop satisfactory new substitutes for minerals. For instance, continued research on the use of nuclear fuels, solar power, geothermal power, tidal currents, and other alternative sources of energy may drastically reduce the demand for oil and coal, and therefore greatly prolong the life of existing supplies of these mineral fuels. And further research on plastic substitutes for metallic raw materials should reduce the use of metal per unit of output of most durable goods.

Large amounts of mineral fuel should be conserved by burning urban combustible trash in local power and heating plants. All urban trash should be collected by a single agency in each city and classified into combustible and non-combustible components. The combustible components should be processed to convert them into a suitable power-plant fuel and burned in the nearest power plant.

The non-combustible components should be further classified so that each metallic element can be shipped to the nearest metal-processing plant and recycled. These practices will reduce the net costs of trash disposal as well as conserve irreplaceable mineral resources.

More Recycling — Any rise in the real prices of minerals will make it profitable to collect and recycle much larger quantities of used and discarded mineral products — especially goods consisting partly or wholly or aluminum, copper, nickel, lead, and precious metals. This will reduce the demand for all newly mined minerals.

To further stimulate recycling, all retail stores should require deposits on glass and metallic containers high enough to assure collection and reuse or recycling of 90% of such containers. Most glass containers should be washed and reused, and most metallic containers should be recycled. It is much easier and cheaper to recycle glass containers than to recycle metal containers. Glass does not corrode and is easier to wash and clean. Hence, more glass containers should be used.

All dirty oil drained from automobiles should be saved, collected, re-refined, and reused. The grouping together of all gas stations under a single socialist Oil Trust would greatly ease the adoption and application of such a conservation policy. Privately owned gas stations find it more profitable to sell costly new oil than cheap re-refined oil.

Standardization — We have emphasized elsewhere that standardization and simplification would sharply reduce both manufacturing and marketing costs. Here we wish to note that it would also result in significant conservation of irreplaceable minerals by reducing factory, wholesale, and retail inventories of all metallic parts and products, by reducing the costs of repairing metallic goods, by facilitating reuse of containers and of parts of junked machines, and by ending style cycles designed to speed up obsolescence and stimulate conspicuous consumption.

In capitalist countries most metallic products are deliberately designed for a short life, and new, usually unimproved, models are produced each year in order to induce consumers to junk their old metallic products as soon as possible. Moreover, so many different sytles and models of each good are produced each year that consumers and repairmen find it difficult or impossible to obtain repair parts, and rarely learn how to install them properly and/or quickly before new models require different parts.

The variety of different colors, shapes, and sizes of containers should be reduced by 99%. This would not only reduce sharply the cost of producing, distributing, and stocking them, but would also facilitate both collection and reuse of them and the melting and recycling of the material in them. Nearly all glass containers should be colorless to reduce sorting problems.

If glass containers were properly designed and standardized, most used glass containers could be shipped to the nearest glass-container user for reuse. It would no longer be necessary to ship them back to the original user.

The easier and cheaper it becomes to use glass containers, the less demand there will be for metal containers. And the supply of raw materials used for making glass is far less limited than the supplies of minerals used to make metal containers.

More Repairs — Each rise in real mineral prices will increase the relative prices of all goods made partly or wholly of minerals, and this will induce consumers to use such goods for a longer time before discarding them. In order to prolong their use, they will spend more on repairing old goods, but they will also prolong their use of non-repaired goods merely because replacement would cost more.

Any measure which reduces the costs of repairing old machines and the metal parts of other goods will induce consumers to have more old machines and parts repaired instead of replaced. The adoption of socialism would assure the introduction of many such measures. Only a few deserve mention here.

Under capitalism the prices of repair parts are usually far higher than the original cost of production, often four or five times as high, because producers want to encourage the junking of old products, because they desire monopoly profits, and because the incredible number of models of each durable good greatly increases the costs of producing and storing new spare parts for old models. Socialist simplification and standardization of durable goods and components would sharply reduce the cost of producing and storing new spare parts for old models.

Since capitalist repairmen compete with each other in each city area, the average distance traveled by repairmen to reach their customers is more than twice as long as it would be under monopoly. And monopoly would permit far more specialization among repairmen, which would allow them to use more specialized tools and equipment and to become much more proficient in the repair work they specialize in. This would make the repair and continued use of old durable goods more common.

In a model socialist town (described in Chapter IV) all automobile repair should be performed in a single garage by mechanics who specialize in one repair service on one kind of car. And the variety of cars in use should be reduced by over 90%. Furthermore, all cars should be designed for a life of over 20 years, and for easy installation of standardized repair parts. Moreover, nearly all metallic parts of junked cars should be removed, reconditioned when necessary, and used to repair other cars. And all new cars should be designed to permit the use of such old parts.

Redesigning Buildings and Appliances — For reasons given earlier, fuel prices will continue to rise faster than the price level for centuries. Mineral extraction taxes would speed up this trend. Therefore it will become more and more desirable to design new buildings so that they require less fuel and less fuel-consuming utility services.

In a capitalist society most buildings are constructed for sale or rent to consumers who are unaware of fuel use and costs and/or who will not or can not pay for optimum investment in fuel-conservation equipment and construction. Moreover, builders know that most buyers and renters are uninformed or improvident and do not insist on optimum fuel-conservation features. And builders also find it easy to misrepresent, hide, or obscure the facts about fuel-conservation features.

If a private speculative builder invests all that he should to conserve fuel in the structures he erects, he loses sales to less scrupulous competitors. Also, he knows that he will not have to pay the uneconomically high fuel costs due to his underinvestment in fuel-conservation features. There is an inevitable conflict of interest between private builders and building occupants which results in marked under-investment in building fuel-conservation features under capitalism. The adoption of liberal socialism will end this conflict by uniting the interests of builders and building users. This will result in much more careful consideration and disclosure of fuel and utility service costs, and in greater efforts to reduce them.

The consumption of fuel to heat and cool buildings and to heat water can be substantially reduced by increased investment in insulation, by substituting central heating and cooling for small individual furnaces and air-cooling systems, by proper location and orientation of buildings, by planting shade trees, by installing solar heating equipment, and by housing people in apartments and row houses or duplexes rather than in separate houses. The fuel-conservation merits of all of these measures will increase as real fuel costs rise.

There is a conflict of interest between private manufacturers and users of domestic gas and electrical appliances and light bulbs similar to that between builders and buyers of buildings. Manufacturers know that they can increase sales and profits by skimping on spending to reduce energy consumption, and that most consumers are partially unaware of the resulting increases in operating costs. In a socialist society all domestic appliances and light bulbs should be redesigned to reduce energy consumption. Every dollar of additional cost which saves enough energy to amortize and pay interest on this added cost is economic.

E. Price Determination

Every mine and oil field should charge prices which balance supply and demand at the source. Each consumer not located at the source of the minerals it buys should pay the same uniform equilibrium source price, plus the costs of delivery. Then the mine or oil field should increase its output until its marginal outlay (including any extraction tax) equals the equilibrium price. If joint products are produced, the sum of the joint prices should equal the joint marginal outlay.

Since all industries which extract minerals from the earth have increasing costs, it is financially profitable for them to charge prices which equal marginal outlays. Nearly all non-extractive industries have decreasing costs. For them, socially ideal prices are unprofitable. Therefore, under capitalism the prices of raw minerals are much closer to marginal costs than the prices of manufactured goods, and would be much less affected by application of sound socialist price-output determination.

In a socialist economy there would be no need for commodity exchanges to help determine mineral prices or to bring buyers and sellers together. All prices should be locally determined, and all buyers of minerals should buy from the national marketing office of the mineral-producing trusts. These trusts should always ship their products from the cheapest source, usually that nearest the buyer, charging local prices plus delivery charges.

The prices of coal and any other mineral product with a seasonally fluctuating demand should vary seasonally so as to optimize output and inventory fluctuations. Consumers who buy during peak-demand periods should pay off-peak prices, plus relevant storage costs. These seasonal price fluctuations should be regular, i.e., uniform from year to year, and announced in advance, so that consumers can plan their consumption so as to minimize their total costs.

While all mineral prices should be locally determined, they should be fixed by pricing experts responsible to national trust headquarters, not to local managers or executives, who would be tempted to use price changes to conceal errors in output control or factor combination.

In America today the prices of some mineral products change several times every day of the year. In a socialist America non-seasonal price changes should probably occur less than once in three months. It would be far easier to predict demand and supply because there would be no business fluctuations and no competition. And buyers require some time to react properly to price changes. On the other hand, no mineral prices should remain unchanged for years as some do in the USSR.

In capitalist countries producers of mineral products often sign long-term contracts which provide for specified monthly or annual deliveries at specified prices. No such contracts should be permitted under liberal socialism. Consumers of mineral products should frequently inform producers as to their future needs at various possible prices, i.e., should submit estimated future demand schedules, but the prices charged should always be current equilibrium prices, not prices set by old contracts. The use of contract prices above or below current prices is uneconomic because it prevents ideal output control, the balancing of current real marginal cost against current real marginal benefit as measured by current equilibrium price.

For the same reason, mineral prices should never be fixed in advance by economic plans (see LS, pp. 74, 206-11).

F. Ideal Inventories

Inventories of raw and processed mineral products should always be large enough to assure stable operations of the plants which use these products. When a plant curtails its output because of a lack of fuel or raw materials, the social loss is very substantial.

It is far more important for socialist trusts to maintain adequate stocks of essential fuels and raw materials like oil and copper than to maintain adequate stocks of finished goods. If a consumer is temporarily unable to obtain a given finished good, he can usually delay his purchase or buy a close substitute, with relatively little real cost to him, but, if a plant is unable to obtain needed fuel or raw materials, it must ordinarily close down and throw many people out of work. Hence, inventories of raw and processed mineral products should normally be more than adequate to meet normal expected demand.

The national mineral trusts, not the consuming trusts, should determine and maintain optimum reserve inventories of mineral fuels and materials. Under capitalism each firm must build up raw material and coal inventories sufficient to protect itself against unforeseen emergencies because it cannot rely on aid from its competitors or from independent suppliers. The creation of socialist monopolies in each industry would permit concentration of emergency inventories, and common or mutual use of them.

A single central agency can achieve ideal regional or national reserve inventories of any mineral much more easily than can local plant managers. It can maintain a reserve stock available to all buyers, which would sharply reduce the duplication of reserve stocks in the hands of users. Moreover, large storage tanks and warehouses are cheaper to build and protect per unit of capacity than are smaller tanks and warehouses.

When a nation is dependent on imports of essential mineral products, it should maintain relatively large reserve inventories of these products. The more likely is the interruption of any import trade, the larger the extra inventory should be.

Whenever a plant must reduce its operations due to lack of any mineral or other raw material, supply, or fuel, the trust responsible for maintaining adequate reserve inventories and filling orders promptly should compensate the shutdown plant for all resulting losses, including the wages paid to its idle workers.

This practice would help the central government to evaluate the work of mineral trust executives.

G. Mining and Oil Towns

Most miners, oil field workers, refinery workers and other associated workers should live in small towns, built chiefly for them, near mines and oil fields. They should not live scattered over the countryside or in distant towns and cities. They should be able to walk or cycle to work in twenty minutes or less.

Most mine and oil towns should include one or more primary processing plants, a mine- or well-equipment warehouse and repair shop, and all the retail stores, offices and repair shops needed to serve the local population. Thus a mine or oil field and associated plants employing one thousand workers would require a town large enough to house and service 3 to 4 thousand persons.

The case for housing miners and oil field workers in towns rather than in rural areas is essentially the same as that stated in the previous chapter for housing farm workers in farm towns.

CHAPTER III

NEW-CITY PLANNING

Two hundred years ago, over 80% of the world's people were engaged in agriculture. Today the great majority of the population in all advanced countries live in non-agricultural towns and cities, and this majority will continue to grow until over 90% live in urban areas.
The size, shape, and structure of towns and cities greatly influence the economic activities of all their residents. For instance, they determine the number of jobs, the kinds of jobs, the type and efficiency of urban transportation, the variety and costs of public utility services, opportunities for recreation and amusement, the average distance between home and job, the location of schools, the quality and amount of housing, the amount and kinds of street traffic, and many other conditions of urban life.
As explained later in this chapter, many planned new socialist cities should be built, and all old cities should be wrecked and replaced by entirely new planned cities. In other words, all the industries discussed in later chapters should eventually operate under conditions largely determined by socialist city planners. That is why we are stating a theory of ideal socialist new-city planning before explaining how individual socialist urban industries should be managed.
A planned socialist city should consist of a city center or nucleus and surrounding, largely self-sufficient towns. In this chapter we shall state and discuss the city-planning principles which should determine the structure of the city as a whole and/or those which apply to all parts of a planned city. In the following chapter we shall propose principals which should apply primarily to certain individual units of a planned city — towns, villages, communities, etc.

A. The Need for Planned New Cities

A Criticism of Unplanned Cities — Nearly all existing cities are the misshapen products of a long period of erratic, unplanned growth. Each new street, building, factory, or subdivision has been designed and built with little if any consideration of the effect of this project upon the city as a whole. Consequently, new construction usually makes old areas of the city less pleasant and useful by increasing congestion, limiting views, creating unpleasant noise, making access to the country more difficult, etc. Moreover, the cost per dwelling unit of building one more house or apartment building in an old city is much higher than the cost when thousands of units are built simultaneously in the construction of a new planned city. To expand the housing capacity of an old city by building additions to it is as inefficient as expanding the capacity of an old auto by adding an extension to it. When new cities and new cars are properly planned and built, every component of each city or car is perfectly proportioned to the whole. Any enlargement of an old component or addition of a new one is costly and inharmonious.

The continued growth of a city requires periodic enlargement of all public utility systems and all other public facilities — city hall, jail, courthouse, post office, airport, etc. — which serve the entire city. Most public utility lines run under paved city streets which must be dug up to enlarge the old water mains, gas mains, and sewer pipes. It costs much more to install new, larger public utility lines beneath busy old streets than to install them in the unpaved streets of cities under construction. It also increases traffic congestion.

Population growth in an old city increases the volume of traffic on main streets until it is necessary to widen or supplement them. But widening old streets or building new freeways may cost several million dollars a mile, and may displace many old residents. Moreover, the noise and air pollution caused by the additional and/or faster traffic disturbs all tenants and residents who work or live near the widened streets or new freeways.

The expansion of a growing business district often requires the demolition of adjacent houses and apartment buildings long before they have become worthless. In a well-planned new city such wasteful demolition of useful buildings would be far less common because the city would not need to expand after it has been built.

Growth is responsible for many of the defects and wastes of unplanned capitalist cities, but there are other serious defects. Most areas of old capitalist cities are depressingly ugly. San Francisco is often called one of the most beautiful cities in the world, but in fact only its location is beautiful. The central business district consists of a collection of widely differing, incongruous, non-symmetrical structures. A graceful skyscraper may have a runty, dirty two-story structure on one side and a mammoth glass box jammed against the other side.

In most American cities, junk-yards, parking lots, garages, gas works and other necessary but ugly facilities are exposed to public view. Indeed, they are often found in the most conspicuous locations, for instance on main streets and freeways. A large blighted area of slum and semislum housing surrounds the center of each large American city. And the newest houses and apartments often have weed-filled vacant lots or abandoned buildings next to them. Their residents may have no view but a bare street or the side or back of a nearby building.

Modern capitalist cities are also inefficient and uneconomic. In large cities most workers spend one to two hours a day traveling to and from their workplaces. Wives and children likewise waste many hours a month in traveling excessive distances to schools and shops. And such travel — on noisy, dangerous streets — causes general nervous tension, thousands of accidents, and city-wide smog.

In an unplanned capitalist city, places to live and places to work are built by different men, and therefore are rarely located so as to minimize travel to and from work, shops, schools, etc. The cost of travel to and from work is an external or unpaid cost to employers. And individual workers acting alone can do little to reduce this cost. Certainly they cannot decentralize a city. An individual firm may locate a new plant in a suburb, if the zoning laws permit this, but it can rarely build a new suburb planned to minimize travel time, street traffic, traffic accidents, smog, etc. And when it can do so, it usually does not do so because the executives prefer to keep their offices near downtown banks, brokers, wholesalers, labor markets, and other facilities.

<u>Why Cities Grow Too Large</u> — Large unplanned cities tend to grow indefinitely. Greater New York City now includes some 18 million persons and is still growing. Futurists predict it will become part of a single giant megalopolis extending from Boston to Washington, D.C. And the same process of unlimited agglomeration of urban population is apparent in most other metropolitan areas.

Why do large cities tend to grow far larger than any city planner considers optimum? Such excessive growth is due to economic individualism and to lack of proper social control. Both the capitalist entrepreneur and the communist trust usually find it profitable or expedient to build a new factory in or near an old large city in order to draw upon its supply of labor, to be close to a large market, to enable executives to enjoy the cultural advantages of metropolitan life, to utilize existing housing and public utility services, and so forth.

The construction of a new factory in an old metropolitan area saves the cost of constructing housing and other facilities. It causes large external costs — air pollution, congestion, street widening, longer travel distances, etc. — but these external costs are not borne by the owners of the new factory. Consequently locating a new factory in an existing large city usually benefits the plant owner, in spite of the fact that it injures the city and the nation.

In order to locate a new factory or office in a new town, or in a small old town, a capitalist or socialist trust must build streets, housing, schools, utilities, and all other facilities for urban life. Few capitalist firms have sufficient capital to build new towns, and those which have prefer to use their capital in other, more profitable ways. Even in communist countries, state trusts are reluctant to build new towns because this requires specialized knowledge and greatly increases the capital outlay per unit of output. Moscow, like New York, has continued to grow far beyond its ideal size because communist trusts consider their own economic interests, not those of the city or the country as a whole. Only firm national control can limit the growth of cities in communist or capitalist countries.

Growth of population in a capitalist city normally increases real estate values throughout most of the old city and the surrounding rural areas. Moreover, it increases the sales and profits of most local businessmen. Therefore, the great majority of propertyowners and businessmen favor continued urban growth. And they usually control the city government. Most workers suffer from the increased congestion, noise, pollution, transport costs, etc., but they are unable or unwilling to vote against urban expansion. They are told that expansion will reduce local unemployment, but not that it will attract many new job-seekers who will compete with them for local housing and jobs.

The Advantage of City Planning — We have been describing the serious defects of unplanned cities and indefinite urban growth in order to suggest the great need for comprehensive planning and rapid construction of entire new cities. We shall now state the advantages of such city planning and building more directly.

Comprehensive planning of new cities enables planners to coordinate every feature of a city with every other feature. Factories and other places of employment can be planned so that they will provide work nearer home for all who live in the new city. And enough housing can be built to provide for the planned population.

Planners can locate all buildings in a new socialist city so that there is adequate space between them and so that their occupants can enjoy the optimum amount of fresh air, sunshine, privacy, and quiet. There are no private property boundaries to limit the size or location of individual structures. And glaring conflicts in architectural styles and building sizes can be avoided. City planners alone can create architectural order and harmony throughout a city.

All the streets, transport facilities, and other public utilities of a planned new city can be designed to fit the needs of a known population and industry, which should not expand after the city has been built. Moreover, all the utility cables and pipes can be installed before the streets are paved, and all the streets can be paved before any buildings are erected.

Planners of new cities can also design thousands of adjacent buildings so that they consist of the same prefabricated parts, panels, rooms, or complete apartments. This sharply reduces construction costs. The simultaneous construction of all buildings on each street or in each area also helps to reduce construction costs, for it permits a greater division of labor among workers, and sharply reduces their travel time between buildings.

Those who plan an entire new city can also locate housing, places of employment, schools, shopping centers, etc., in such a way as to reduce drastically the amount of time required by resident workers to travel to and from their jobs, by housewives to travel to and from stores, by children to travel to and from school, and by delivery and repair men to travel to and from the homes they serve. In sum, new-city planners can radically reduce the amount of urban traffic and the resulting smog, noise, vibration, and accidents without limiting private-car use. They can also design cities so as to permit drastic limitation of private-car use with minimum inconvenience to urban residents.

In planning the location and size of each building, city planners can consider and allow for its effect upon all nearby buildings and their occupants. For city planners, most costs and benefits which are external to the private builder, and therefore are ignored, become internal costs and benefits which are considered. A private builder in an old city does not care whether he destroys the view from another building, but a new-city planner does care because he will be judged by the total benefit or value of the new city, not by that of a single new building. Planning internalizes many external economies and diseconomies.

Reasons for Concentrating on New-City Planning — The problem of planning the reconstruction of existing cities is now, and will long remain, more urgent and difficult than the problem of planning new cities. Nevertheless, in this and the following chapter we shall largely restrict our discussion to the theory of new-city planning, for a number of reasons.

First, it is impossible to plan the reconstruction of an old city unless one has a clear idea of what an ideal new city should be like.

Secondly, urban reconstruction problems differ from city to city, and also depend upon how fast reconstruction must be carried out. We do not have space here to consider all such unique individual problems.

Thirdly, we believe that many new cities should be built in all countries because the population is increasing and/or because many old cities are far too large.

Fourth, the concentration of construction work on the building of new cities would facilitate the eventual reconstruction of excessively large old cities by radically reducing their population before reconstruction begins.

Fifth, new cities can be built much more rapidly and cheaply than old cities can or should be completely reconstructed. There is usually little or no cost of demolition.

Sixth, the first entirely new planned socialist cities will serve as invaluable demonstrations of the benefits of complete city planning if they are well planned. And, if they are poorly planned, their defects will become obvious and will help city planners to improve their theories and practices before any old city is torn down.

Finally, it is much easier to state a general theory of ideal socialist new-city planning than to state a theory of ideal urban reconstruction applicable to a wide variety of old cities in many different geographical areas.

While we propose to concentrate here on the general theory of ideal socialist new-city planning, we shall offer a few concluding remarks in Chapter IV on the application of this theory to the complete reconstruction of old cities.

B. National City-Planning Policies

There are certain national housing and construction policies which should be agreed upon in advance because they are prerequisites for a sound socialist program of new-city planning and construction. They include the following principles:

1. In an advanced socialist country over 90% of the population should live in cities.

2. All population increments and much of the old urban population should be housed in new planned cities.

3. New cities should be located in superior climatic areas.

4. The production and regional distribution of water, gas, petroleum products, and electricity should be planned by national, not city, planners.

5. The national government should establish national antipollution policies which guide all new-city planners.

6. New-city planning should be subject to national conservation laws and policies.

7. The national government should create and finance a national city-planning and construction agency endowed with full power to plan and build new cities efficiently.

Universal Urbanization — The technological revolution in agriculture is so far along and so rapid that it will soon be possible for 2% of the population in advanced countries to feed the other 98% using city-made machines and chemicals. Thus it will shortly be possible for almost everyone to live in cities. Is this desirable?

For generations young people reared on farms and in small towns have flocked to the city to secure better jobs and to enjoy the many advantages of city life. The city offers more and cheaper public utility services, more commercial amusement and recreation, superior educational and cultural facilities, a richer social life, and better medical care, as well as higher wages and a wider variety of employment.

It costs much less per person to provide adequate public utility services — gas, water, electricity, sewage, telephone, cable TV, public transit, etc. — for city dwellers than for country dwellers because the former live much closer together. For the same reason, urban schools and cultural facilities can be larger and can provide superior and more varied services. A small town cannot afford a zoo, a botanical garden, an aquarium, a planetarium, a museum, a stadium, a legitimate theater, an opera house, a university, and other cultural and entertainment facilities found in large cities.

Moreover, as a result of the industrial revolution factory workers are far more productive than self-employed artisans and domestic workers. And the larger the factory, office, store, or warehouse, the greater is the productivity of labor. Small towns cannot provide enough labor to man factories, offices, department stores, etc., which are large enough to achieve most of the economies of large-scale production.

In a socialist country nearly all farm workers should live in farm towns in order to gain some of the advantages of urban life, but no small town can provide the major cultural, educational, recreational, and amusement services available in large cities.

It is true, of course, that life in capitalist cities, especially in very large ones, has serious disadvantages — congestion, noise, smell, numerous eyesores, etc. However, all of these evils could be eliminated or greatly reduced by the adoption of socialism, including socialist city planning.

For these reasons the socialist government of an advanced country should plan to house and employ almost its entire population in cities large enough to provide nearly all the advantages of metropolitan life. Only farm workers, miners, forest workers, and such should live in small towns.

The Scale of New-City Construction — All old cities of over 600,000 population are too large (see Sec. D, below). Their populations should be steadily reduced rather than increased. Moreover, all old towns and cities are so badly planned that they should eventually be demolished and replaced by new planned towns or cities (see Ch. IV, Sec. F, below). And the population of each new planned city should decline continuously, probably by over 1% a year after the first few years because its people will want more and more housing and/or garden space as their real incomes rise. It follows that a socialist government should plan to build enough new planned cities each year to house both the entire national increase in population and a part of the population of all old cities.

In the U.S. about two million new housing units were built in 1970. If these were all built in new planned garden cities of the type advanced here, they would provide enough new housing for 10 to 15 new cities.

Locating New Cities — The location of existing American cities was largely determined by history, by transportation lines, by local natural resources, and by other factors which should have far less effect upon the location of planned new cities. Nearly all old cities began as very small towns which had to rely on existing transport routes and services. By contrast, a planned new city would be large enough to justify the construction of adequate transport facilities connecting it with the existing national rail and highway networks. Moreover, transportation has become so cheap and efficient that there is now far less need to locate new cities so as to minimize transport costs. And real transport costs per ton-mile will continue to decline indefinitely.

New York, Philadelphia, and other large east-coast American cities are much too large, partly because too many immigrants from Europe landed on the east coast and stayed in the ports where they landed, or in nearby cities. Profit-making capitalists then built factories in or near these cities in order to be near large supplies of cheap labor. No one ever stopped to consider whether large cities ought to be built on the east coast. Moreover, the United States did not annex the west coast until 1847, and transportation to this coast did not become cheap and easy until the 1880's. A socialist government, however, could and should build new cities where they should now be located, not where historical accidents or profit-seeking firms would locate them.

Nearly all new socialist cities in large advanced countries should be located where the climate and/or recreational opportunities are superior, not where raw materials are cheap and/or markets are nearby. Every rise in real wages makes commodity production and distribution costs less important, and climate and recreation more important. Fortunately, the best climate areas are usually on seacoasts, lakefronts, and river banks, where both natural recreational opportunities and transport possibilities are superior.

Nearly all new U.S. cities should be built in the Far West, the Southwest, and Florida, the areas which have the finest all-year climates in North America. Most of the people now living in the Midwest and Northeast should be moved to the Far West and Southwest, especially to the coastal states. Americans have long been moving to these areas, but a socialist government could greatly expand this migration merely by guaranteeing good jobs and housing in planned new cities to all in-migrants.

Other factors being equal, location of a new city beside a large body of water is preferable to location away from water. Temperatures are more equable near large lakes and oceans, and most people enjoy walking beside, boating on, swimming in, and/or viewing large bodies of water. Moreover, ample water for urban use is more easily available. And location near the ocean or a navigable river may reduce transport costs.

However, no new city should be located on both sides of a river, lake, or bay because this would increase the risk of flood damage, require the construction of costly bridges, and make it more difficult to get from one part of the city to the other. Rivers should run through the outer greenbelts around new cities, not through the cities themselves.

Since most planned socialist cities should be located in those areas which have the most pleasant climate, and since such areas make up only a small part of each country, new cities should often be placed quite close together. For instance, both the European and the California Rivieras should eventually be completely urbanized from one end to the other, except for needed greenbelts, parks, and recreation areas. Greenbelts between adjacent cities should, of course, be much wider than greenbelts around isolated cities.

National Utility Planning — The production and national distribution of water, gas, petroleum products, and electricity should be planned by national, not city, planners. No planned city should contain a plant producing artificial gas, desalted water, or electricity, except as a by-product.

Only a large regional or national agency can create, conserve, and supply pure fresh water economically and can produce and supply gas and electricity at minimum cost. Moreover, dams and gas storage tanks should be located outside of urban areas, for safety reasons. However, if a new city is to be heated by low-pressure steam from an electrical generating plant, the plant should be in or near the planned city.

Since fresh water can now be transported economically for hundreds of miles and can be obtained by desalting sea water, new-city planners should never have to worry about water supplies. A national Public Utility Trust should be responsible for providing adequate water for all new cities.

All electrical generating plants should be connected to a national network of power lines designed so as to minimize the need for surplus capacity and permit optimum use of all power plants, especially low-cost power plants. Only a national agency can design and properly manage such a national super-power system. New-city planners should merely inform this agency of the probable power consumption of each new planned city as far in advance as possible.

National Pollution Control — The planning and control of local air and water pollution is a national problem. The harm caused by such pollution is not confined to the city responsible for it. Indeed, most of this harm may fall on the residents of other areas. Therefore, the planners and governments of individual cities never have sufficient incentives to reduce air and water pollution to the optimum level, the level at which the marginal social costs and benefits of pollution are equal. For this reason, the central government of a socialist state should establish ideal antipollution taxes and regulations which all new-city planners would have to consider when planning the transport, heating, sewage, and other pollution-causing facilities of a new city.

<u>Conservation Policies</u> — All new-city planning and construction agencies should be subject to and be guided by national conservation laws and policies, some of which would apply directly to the use of fuels and building materials in new cities. For instance, the national government might prohibit or limit the use of copper pipe, electric stoves, incandescent lighting, home washing machines, and/or redwood lumber. And it might specify the amount of insulation and the degree to which buildings must be fireproof.

However, the national government should not prepare or enforce a detailed building code since socialist city planners would know much more about local building costs and needs than the central government, and would have no reason to deceive and cheat new-city tenants. To conserve irreplaceable minerals, the central government should rely chiefly on extraction taxes rather than on laws to enforce specific desired conservation practices.

<u>Need for a New-City Planning Agency</u> — A socialist government should create a national agency large enough and powerful enough to plan and build all required new cities without undue delays in planning or construction. This agency should be able to use any land it needs without going through long and/or costly legal procedures.

For reasons to be discussed later, a socialist new-city planning and construction agency should build entire cities all at once, not gradually over a long period. Therefore, such agencies would require enormous capital funds, would employ very large work forces, and would need the authority to build very large facilities for export firms. They must be allowed to determine the size and intracity location of all new industrial and commercial plants. They should be required to consult with the state agencies which will operate such facilities, but the final decision concerning plant size and local location should be left to the new-city planning agency. It is much more important that new cities be beautiful, salubrious, and efficient than that their export plants achieve the minimum possible production costs.

C. Possible Forms of Ideal Cities

Most proposed new cities may be classified by their overall form or shape into three major classes: (1) round or nearly round, (2) linear or nearly linear, and (3) megastructure cities. These terms are not very satisfactory, but we know of no more suitable ones. Class (1) includes all multistructure cities which are not obviously linear.

Round Cities — The chief advantage of a round city over a linear city is that, with any given density of population, it can be designed so as to minimize the average distance between residential units and the city center, the nearest town center, the local shopping center, and local schools. The radius of a circle limiting a round city is much shorter than half the length of the axis running through a linear city of equal population and density. Minimizing these travel distances may not eliminate travel time, because mass transport along a linear city axis may be more frequent but it does make it possible for more people to walk or cycle to and from work, shops, and schools, and therefore permits a much greater reduction in motor-vehicle traffic on city streets.

Moreover, a round city can be designed so as to provide many more streets and paths leading to city, town, and village centers, which helps to minimize traffic of all kinds on each through street. And it is much easier to plan these streets and paths so that they pass through parks or can be beautified with trees and shrubs.

Linear Cities — A linear city is one built along a major axis or corridor which includes one or more main transportation lines — highway, subway, railroad, etc. Its chief advantage is that it can grow at either end with a minimum of disturbance to and reconstruction of old areas of the city, and without making it more difficult for old residents to reach the nearby greenbelt or countryside.

Since a linear city is long and narrow, every residence is close both to the nearest greenbelt or countryside and to all main-line transport systems. However, such transport lines are usually noisy, and residents of a linear city suffer from such noise much more than residents of a round city.

Most linear-city plans locate industrial and other major export plants on one side of the main transport axis, and residential areas on the other side. Employees of export firms must therefore cross this noisy and dangerous highway and rail line on their way to and from work. Of course, overpasses and underpasses can be provided, but it is usually difficult to persuade all workers to use such often inconvenient facilities.

In a linear city the average distance between residences and the city center is much greater than in a round city. To reach the city center most residents must use fast, noisy, main-line transport. In a planned round city they can usually cycle or ride a slow, quiet electric bus. Moreover, delivery trucks operating from a linear city center have to travel much farther to serve all residents. Finally, every extension in the length of a linear city requires a costly expansion and reconstruction of the old city center serving the new residents.

In a linear city it is also more difficult to provide town and village community centers — shops, schools, clinics, etc. — which are in the center of the communities they serve. Of course, a linear city could be wide enough to permit the construction of nearly round villages like those in a round city, but this would make it more difficult for residents to use the main traffic corridor leading to the relatively distant city center.

Megastructure Cities — The third class of planned new cities includes those which are entirely housed in a single immense building, a megastructure, and those which consist of a city center and separate towns, each of which is housed in a megastructure or in a very small number of such buildings.

Megastructure towns and cities may take many forms and their advantages and disadvantages depend in part on their form. But all share certain common advantages. Heating and cooling costs per cubic foot of space are substantially lower in large buildings than in detached or semidetached houses because the external exposure per unit of space is less. Moreover, megastructures can provide protected internal passageways between all parts of the town or city, which is a great advantage in very hot or very cold climates. And housing thousands of families in a single building sharply reduces the cost per family of providing local streets and utilities — water, gas, telephone, cable TV, etc. It also minimizes the average distance residents must travel to visit each other, to go shopping, to go to and from work, to attend school, etc. And it enables the average resident to reach the surrounding greenbelt and/or countryside more quickly. However, for this reason the nearby areas of the greenbelt would be much more congested than those about a round city or alongside a linear city.

A tall one-building town or city has additional advantages. It enables many residents to have sweeping views from their windows, which are especially attractive when the city is beside the sea or a lake, or near a scenic mountain range. Furthermore, elevator passenger transport is more rapid and convenient than outdoor road transport and replaces much of it. It may also be more economical since it eliminates the need for many streets and motor vehicles. In a tall one-building city all residents could travel to school, work, shops, clinics, etc., without using any external streets. Some electric cars might be needed for horizontal intrastructure movement, but not nearly as many as would be needed in a garden city because the distances would be very much shorter.

The chief, and we believe fatal, disadvantage of a tall one-building town or city is that construction costs per cubic foot of rentable space rise steadily for every additional story above the third or fourth floor because the addition of each floor requires a stronger steel frame for all lower floors, more space on each lower floor for elevators and stairways, larger water pipes and air-conditioning ducts through each lower floor, etc. Tall buildings are profitable in large unplanned capitalist cities only because land values in certain areas are very high, far higher than they should ever be in a well-planned new city.

Another serious disadvantage of all one-building towns or cities is that they would house families so close together that they would often disturb each other. Children playing, adults talking loudly, radio and TV receivers blaring, young people dancing in adjacent corridors or apartments would frequently disturb neighbors. Soundproofing would reduce this evil, at a substantial cost, but probably could not reduce it enough at a reasonable cost.

Furthermore, residents of tall buildings must travel further to reach outdoor gardens and playgrounds, and this is especially inconvenient for children and mothers. Also, fire and earthquake risks are greater for occupants of tall buildings than for residents of equally well-built low buildings, and power failures cause more inconvenience. It is very tiring to climb more than five stories by foot when elevators cease to operate.

<u>Mixed-Form Cities</u> — It is possible of course to design a new city which would contain some round garden towns, some linear towns, and one or more megastructure towns. Many mixed-form city plans are conceivable.

Perhaps the most promising mixed form is that which would house the city nucleus in one or two tall megastructures surrounded by a greenbelt and garden-city towns. Another promising mixed form is similar except that each town center also would consist of a single megastructure surrounded by garden villages. The use of megastructures to house city and town centers would help to make cities and towns more compact, thus reducing average travel time to jobs and shopping centers.

A low, extensive, one-building city could contain many internal garden courts or could be built in the shape of a linear city. It might be planned so as to gain many of the advantages of a round city or so as to gain many of those of a linear city. Moreover, the average tenant in such a city could reach outside gardens much more quickly and easily than the average tenant of a tall one-building city. And, if the buildings were only four stories high or less, no elevators would be required, and tenants would benefit from the exercise of climbing stairs.

The theory of how to plan a one-building city or town differs radically from the theory of how to build a multibuilding round or linear city. There is less difference between the planning theory of a round new city and that of a linear city, but each theory deserves separate treatment. This discussion is devoted to the theory of how to plan a multibuilding, round, garden city. Many of the basic principles stated here could be applied, in whole or in part, to the planning of linear and/or megastructure cities but we shall rarely note or explain such application.

We have chosen to concentrate upon the theory of round garden-city planning because we believe properly planned new round cities would be much superior to any linear or megastructure cities in temperate areas. Most other students of new-city planning seem to share this conclusion.

D. Principles of Overall New-City Planning

This section is devoted to a statement and justification of the basic general principles which should be applied in the overall planning of a new round socialist garden city. It includes only the most general principles, those which apply to the city as a whole. Principles which apply solely to the planning of certain parts of a new city, for instance, to the city center, will be discussed in the next chapter.

<u>Complete</u> <u>Planning</u> <u>before</u> <u>Construction</u> — The most important general principle of socialist city planning is that each new city should be completely planned, except as to minor architectural details, before construction is begun. Complete city planning includes determining the location, size, and use of each

building, as well as planning all streets, parks, and public utility systems. Only such comprehensive advance planning can assure that every part of a planned city is properly coordinated with every other part. Such coordination cannot be achieved by piecemeal planning, or without planning.

This is a basic principle because most of the principles of planning discussed below could only be applied by planners able to plan entire cities. For instance, planners could not plan cities so as to minimize internal travel time and costs unless they could determine the location of all housing and places of employment, as well as all streets and freeways. And they could not determine the ideal layout and size of public utility lines unless they knew in advance the kind, size, and use of each building on each street.

Ideal New-City Size — Each new city should be large enough to provide those cultural, educational, recreational, medical, and retail services and facilities which are now available only in large cities and which cannot be economically provided in small cities and towns. Such facilities include zoos, stadiums, theatres, universities, specialized hospitals, large libraries, art museums, and other facilities rarely found in small cities.

It is true, of course, that the larger the city the more of such facilities can be economically provided. But, beyond a certain optimum point, the advantages of increased size are more than offset by the disadvantages, most motably the additional distance which the average resident must travel in order to use these facilities. Hence, if a planned city is large enough to provide one of each of these facilities, it is probably large enough.

The chief inherent disadvantage of any increase in city size is that it lengthens the average distance which residents must travel to reach the city center and the countryside. It also increases traffic, accidents, and noise on main streets leading to and through the city center. But, by planned decentralization of major export plants and shopping areas, socialist new-city planners could radically reduce these disadvantages of large cities. They could plan decentralized cities of half a million population which would suffer less from these disadvantages than do capitalist cities one tenth that size. Therefore, it would not be necessary to limit new-city population below the half-million level.

Few if any American cities of less than one million now provide all of the cultural and social opportunities of a great city. However, the American standard of living will continue to rise steadily, and this will slowly reduce the size of the minimum city population needed to support such facilities. By 2020 A.D., an American city of 500,000 population should be able to support all the distinctively metropolitan facilities and services which now require a population of 1,000,000 to support them.

In sum, a planned city should be large enough to provide nearly all the cultural and recreational facilities and services now found only in large cities. Growth beyond the minimum size necessary to permit economical provision of these urban advantages would be undesirable since it would increase unduly the mean distance between the average residence and these facilities, and between the average residence and the countryside. For all these reasons, the population of a new socialist city designed for initial occupation in the U.S. in the year 2020 should probably be over 400,000 and less than 600,000 persons.

No Growth — Each new city should be planned without any provision for future growth in area or population. No space should be reserved for such growth, and no facilities should be planned so as to have surplus capacity or unused space available to care for additional people. Rather, city planners should always expect the population of a new city to decline slowly but steadily after it has been fully occupied.

No new city should be permitted to grow in population or area because such growth would require periodic reconstruction of all old buildings and facilities serving the entire city — main streets, public utility plants, main utility lines, the city hall, the central hospital, etc. Moreover, any population growth in an ideal planned city would eventually make it too large and congested. It is always much more economical to provide for additional population by building new cities rather than by enlarging and reconstructing old ones.

It follows that the plan for a new city should provide for immediate use of all land in the city. There should be no vacant lots or areas left to accumulate weeds and debris until this land is needed to care for additional population. Even if some land is reserved for future building to meet growing needs, it should be used meanwhile as well-maintained park or play areas. There should never be any unused land in a planned socialist city.

Instead of growing, the population of a planned new garden city should deline slowly but continuously after it has been built and fully populated. Personal real income will continue to rise steadily in all advanced countries. When men earn more money, they normally want more spacious and/or more luxurious living quarters, more garden and park space, more and better recreational and cultural facilities, etc. In the past, these new needs were met by building additional, better housing and facilities, usually in new suburbs. But an ideal planned city should be surrounded by a permanent greenbelt. And public parks and greenbelts should be expanded rather than built upon as average real income rises.

If the population of a planned garden city declines continuously, it will be possible not only to allow each resident more housing and garden or park space, but also to supply him with more public utility, commercial, and other public services of each kind without replacing any original public facilities.

It may be objected that our rejection of urban growth in both new and old cities would make it impossible for men to move freely from one city to another and choose their place of residence. However, proper control of local rent charges and wage levels would assure that any person could migrate to and settle in any city with a declining population. If too many people want to settle in any town or city, rentals should be raised and wages lowered until demand equals supply for every kind of local job and housing unit.

Rapid Construction — Each new city should be planned for immediate construction, and should be built all at once, as a single construction project. It should not be built piecemeal, one section or community at a time. No part of a new planned city could function properly without all the other parts. Moreover, every delay in the completion of any part of a planned new city increases unnecessarily the interest cost incurred before all new facilities can be completely occupied and/or utilized. For instance, if the nucleus of a planned new city is designed to serve ten satellite towns, delay in building any of the latter results in incomplete utilization of the costly buildings in the nucleus, and therefore raises per-person costs for all residents. On the other hand, constructing one or more of the surrounding towns before the nucleus is built, a more common practice, seriously inconveniences the occupants of these communities because they must do without the many services which an urban nucleus provides.

Furthermore, when some new buildings in a neighborhood are built and occupied before adjacent buildings are completed, the noise, dust, vibration, and street congestion due to continued construction annoy all occupants of nearby buildings. Hence, nearly all buildings in each town should be completed before any new residents move in.

Finally, it is much cheaper to build a large number of nearby streets and buildings at the same time than to build them at different times. Indeed, every increase in the scale of construction lowers unit costs.

When all the houses in a new city are built at the same time by the same contractor, he can buy his raw materials in larger quantities at lower prices, can prefabricate more parts of each house, can achieve a much greater division of labor among his workers, can use more costly and/or specialized equipment and tools, can use the same architectural plans over and over again, can borrow money more cheaply, and can spread his overhead costs over a much larger number of units.

New planned capitalist cities are built gradually over a period of 20 to 50 years because private city builders cannot induce workers and employers to move into their new cities fast enough to fill them up quickly. Moreover, they usually lack the capital funds required to build an entire new city all at once. They normally depend upon the sale of lots and buildings in the initial part of a new city to finance construction in other later parts. As a result, costs per housing unit are much higher than they would be if the entire city were built all at once. A socialist state, which should own all industry, would find it far easier to finance and build rapidly an entire new city, and to provide work immediately for the entire new-city population. Moreover, it could easily fix rents and wages in the new city so as to induce enough people to move into it to achieve full occupancy in a very short period. The fact that a socialist government could build large new planned cities all at once and immediately fill them with people employed locally is a major and virtually ignored argument for socialism.

To build an entire new planned city as a single rapid-construction project would require a very large force of workers. They should be housed in mobile housing and served by mobile communal facilities. The entire construction staff, all their mobile facilities, and the staff for these facilities should be a stable permanent community which moves from one new-city construction site to another. In other words, none of these workers should have permanent homes in old cities from which they travel long distances to and from buildings sites. However, their communities should be as stable, and their mobile homes and communal facilities should be as commodious and pleasant as those they would enjoy if they had fixed permanent homes.

Minimizing Reconstruction Costs — The fifth basic general principle of socialist city planning is that each new city should be planned so as to facilitate and minimize the cost of the predictable continuous reconstruction which will be made necessary by a steady rise in average real income and a steady decline in the population.

The chief predictable reconstruction costs will be those of enabling residents to enjoy ever more spacious and/or luxurious housing, gardens, parks, stores, and other urban facilities. When real income per person rises, consumers spend part of their additional income to buy or rent larger and more spacious homes and grounds and to shop in more luxurious stores. Scientific research could easily determine the extent of such effects.

There will be few if any domestic servants in a mature socialist state. And most wives will work outside the home, and have two children only. Hence, there must be some optimum limit beyond which the average demand for housing space per family will not increase. And the intensity of demand for such space will decline steadily as this limit is approached. This limit will probably be less than 600 square feet per person. Thus, if a planned socialist city provides 400 square feet per person to begin with, the maximum average housing-space expansion over a period of centuries should be less than 50%.

In a capitalist city most housing is allowed to deteriorate gradually over long periods, and is occupied by lower and lower social classes as the decades pass. In a planned socialist city, most housing should be periodically improved and occupied by persons with higher and higher incomes (usually the same persons) as the years pass. While some housing might be allowed to deteriorate just before it is replaced, no neighborhood should be allowed to do so.

The least expensive and spacious building in a well-planned city should be the first to be removed, reconstructed, or wrecked and replaced. Hence, the city planners should design the smallest houses for use during the shortest periods, and the most luxurious and spacious for use during the longest periods. The cheapest housing in a new city should be mobile homes, which should initially house at least 10% of all families. This would help to minimize reconstruction costs for many years since these mobile homes could be easily moved away, rebuilt, and used elsewhere as population falls and as room for new more spacious homes is needed.

The least luxurious nonmobile housing should be temporary housing designed to be used only for 20 to 30 years. The cheapest permanent housing in a new city should be designed for periodic interior reconstruction and renovation. The most luxurious permanent housing should be constructed of the most permanent materials and designed for little if any future reconstruction. New and more luxurious housing for the tenants of the last class of housing should be built in space freed by removing mobile homes or wrecking temporary housing.

Another way to plan for and achieve at minimum cost a steady enlargement of housing units in a city with a stable or slowly declining population is to plan apartment buildings so that adjacent apartments can eventually be combined into larger units. Such combination would often be doubly desirable since it would reduce the total number of housing units as well as increase the supply of more spacious units.

After the first fifty years, the chief method used to expand housing space per person in an ideal planned city should be vertical expansion. One- or two-story buildings should be expanded into or replaced by higher structures.

New housing should always be superior to any existing housing in quality and spaciousness, and should replace the cheapest existing housing. Thus reconstruction should slowly convert the least desirable residential areas into superior ones. This policy would minimize the number of reconstruction projects required to achieve any desired improvement in total housing. It would also minimize the economic waste due to the wrecking of existing usable houses.

As real incomes rise, the demand for commercial and office space will rise much faster than the demand for housing space, and the rate of increase will decrease little if any as income rises indefinitely. Lack of domestic servants will limit the expansion of housing space, but not the growth of retail sales and personal services per family. Therefore, socialist city planners should plan for a 100% increase in store and nonexport office space per resident every 50 years or so. The best way to do this would be to plan for low-rise buildings which can gradually add one story after another, at minimum cost, indefinitely.

<u>Greenbelts</u> — Every major unit of a new city, except the town centers, should be encircled by a permanent greenbelt. The larger the unit, the wider the greenbelt should be. The greenbelt around the city center and each town should average over a mile in width, and that around the entire city should average over two miles in width, but a neighborhood might need a greenbelt only two or three hundred feet wide.

Greenbelts should be reserved for freeways and for recreational use — golf courses, archery ranges, riding paths, walks, etc. No industrial plants or commercial facilities — except some used for recreation — should be located in greenbelts.

Greenbelts should cover over half of the area of a planned new socialist city, but they would not be very costly because the land they occupy would be purchased at prices based on local agricultural rentals. The creation of new parks and greenbelts in or around old capitalist cities costs over ten times as much because the value of this land has risen greatly due to the chance of future urban use.

Moreover, the creation of extensive greenbelts would permit and justify a greater population density achieved by the reduction of space devoted to private yards and gardens in the residential areas of planned new cities. When greenbelts are nearby, people need private gardens less. And the cost per acre of maintaining public parks and greenbelts is much less than that of maintaining private gardens.

A greenbelt should include no farm land except small orchards for public picking. Its chief function should be to provide city dwellers with ample areas for recreation — sport, walking, picnicing, nature studies, etc. Most of the area in greenbelts should be open forest. The trees would provide a scenic view from all dwellings near the greenbelt and from all tall buildings in the city. They would also muffle the noise from freeways, railroads, and airports.

Decentralization of New Cities — All new cities should be highly decentralized in order to: (1) minimize the average distance people must travel to and from work, schools, shops, clinics, and recreational areas, (2) reduce the density of population, (3) promote agreeable social relationships among the residents of each division of the city, and (4) reduce differences in urban land values.

Planned decentralization of business activities should permit every worker to live within a mile or two of his place of work, so that he can easily walk or cycle to and from work on most days of the year, and should permit him to walk to and from a nearby shopping center on good days. It should also minimize both the number of trips which the average person must make to the center of the city, and the distance from the average home to recreational areas, especially the greenbelts.

These goals should be achieved by decentralization of economic activities in each city, not by increasing the density of population in residential areas. Rather, one of the gains from planned decentralization should be a decrease in the density of population. Decentralization of business activities makes possible a decrease in the density of urban population because it greatly reduces the need to travel to and from the city center, and to and from other suburbs. And a decrease in population density is socially desirable because it permits the creation of more parks, playgrounds, and greenbelt areas, and increases domestic quiet and privacy. It also enables planners to locate and design housing units so that most occupants can enjoy more sunshine, a better view, and a private garden.

Planned urban decentralization would promote agreeable social relationships and activities. It would help people get acquainted by enabling fellow workers to reside in the same community, shop in the same local stores, and send their children to the same schools. It would also make it much easier for people with common interests in certain sports or cultural activities to live together in neighborhoods planned to meet their special needs.

Low Land Rentals — A new city should be designed so that the land used does not yield a total land rental much greater than it would yield as agricultural land. Of course, land rental is only a part, often a minor part, of an urban property rental, which includes quasi-rent on all capital improvements. Nevertheless, the application of this planning rule would sharply reduce nearly all urban rental charges, especially those for commercial, industrial, and office buildings.

Land rent is a pure intramarginal surplus, an unearned income which can be seized by the state without affecting marginal costs of production and market prices. In a socialist society, where land is socially owned, it accrues to the state. But in a planned socialist city it would nevertheless be better to minimize it by controlling suitably the supply of each kind of urban land.

Under capitalism the creation of a new town or city increases the value of the land over 100%. That is the chief reason for the growing efforts of capitalist firms to create entire new communities. When their salesmen sell lots or tracts in these new communities, they explain that the land in question has risen steadily in market value since the community was established and predict that it will continue to do so indefinitely and rapidly. And their predictions have often come true.

In old capitalist cities some choice lots in the best business areas are worth over a million dollars. In a planned socialist city they should be worth little if any more than the land would sell for as farm land.

There are several planning principles which socialist city planners could and should apply in order to minimize land values in a new city. First, they should provide enough land for each commercial and industrial use to prevent any increase in the value of such land. Secondly, they should decentralize all commercial and industrial activities in order to reduce radically the demand for land in the center of the new city. Thirdly, they should plan all residential areas so that no class of housing is scarce enough to yield a land rental above the agricultural level. Finally, they should prevent any increase in the demand for land and space due to population growth by housing all population increments in new cities, not in old.

Each socialist retail store should be a local monopoly, and therefore could easily charge prices high enough to yield a high land rental. But such prices would be economic only if lower prices resulted in store overcrowding and higher selling margins. Socialist city planners could easily prevent the need for such high land rentals by planning in each shopping area retail stores large enough to prevent store crowding when retail prices are low enough to yield only the desired low land rental.

Decentralization of employment and shopping areas would greatly reduce the land rentals earned by downtown stores and offices. It would also greatly increase the number of homes conveniently close to shopping centers, and thus reduce the relative advantage of living in homes close to shopping centers. Furthermore, socialist planners could and should notably increase the number of parks and recreational facilities and locate them so that residents of houses less conveniently located for shopping would be more conveniently located for recreation. Many other methods could be used to make different residential areas almost equally attractive and desired.

When the land area chosen for a planned city is irregular, hilly, or beside water, it may be impossible to lay out residential lots so that all are equally desirable. For instance, tenants may be willing to pay more for houses with a view, and the views from different houses may vary widely. In such cases, land rentals per site should vary, but the total land rentals from all sites should not exceed the total comparable agricultural land rental.

Universal Monopoly — Socialist new-city planners should design all retail and other local productive facilities for use only by local monopolies. They should not provide facilities for two or more competing firms in any shopping center, industrial area, or office building.

The economic argument for monopoly — valid in both planned and unplanned cities — is too long to repeat here. It was stated in detail in our <u>Liberal</u> <u>Socialism</u>. Here we shall note only the additional argument for monopoly in planned new cities.

It is much easier to plan a new city in which all agencies are monopolies than to plan one in which there are two or more competing units in most shopping centers and industrial areas. City planners can never be sure that competing agencies will volunteer to rent and operate all commercial and industrial facilities in a planned new town, or that, if enough volunteer, they will have adequate capital and will provide adequate services and jobs. Moreover, even if competitors do all of these things initially, some of them are sure to over- or underestimate local costs and demand later on. It is much more difficult for a competitor to predict his sales and demand than it is for a monopolist to do so. Hence, competitive firms go bankrupt much more often, which would require repeated reallocation and/or reconstruction of commercial and industrial plants.

Competition among export firms can, and often has, resulted in the failure of individual firms which provide a larger share of the total employment of an entire town. The residents of a planned socialist new town should not be subject to such risks. Moreover, it is uneconomic to invest immense sums in planning and building a new city whose houses and plants may experience a high vacancy rate because of the competitive failure of one or more of its major export firms.

<u>Building Height</u> — The tenth principle of socialist new-city planning is that no residential building and few office buildings should be more than four stories high. The precise limit will depend upon current technology and local conditions.

We have explained why a planned new city should be highly decentralized and why there should be no competition between units in the same industry. In unplanned centralized cities where competing units bid against each other for limited space in business districts, land rentals rise far above agricultural rentals, often a hundred times as high. This makes it profitable to build tall buildings in order to reduce land rental per square foot of building space. Properly planned decentralization of a new city would largely eliminate the concentration of street traffic, retail buying, and business activities which now make some locations far more valuable than others. If urban land rentals in new cities are thus minimized, the major economic argument for erecting tall buildings, the lower land rental per square foot of floor space, will be greatly weakened.

Increasing the height of a one-story apartment or office building from one or two, three, or perhaps even four floors reduces the building costs as well as the land rental per square foot of rentable space because it does not increase proportionately the cost of the foundation, the plumbing system, the electrical system, the heating and hot-water plant, etc. It also allows the ceiling beams of one floor to serve as the floor beams of the floor above. And heating and cooling costs vary inversely with building size. On the other hand, building above one story wastes space on stairways and, perhaps, on elevator shafts. The taller an elevator building, the greater the waste of space on elevator shafts, and every building of more than four floors needs an elevator as well as a stairway. Moreover, the cost of steel beams and concrete pillars per square foot of space rises steadily as additional floors are added.

Furthermore, the risk of heavy loss of life from fire and earthquake is much greater in high buildings than in well-constructed low buildings, and this risk alone may be sufficient to rule out high buildings in planned new cities, especially in those near known earthquake faults or active volcanoes.

The chief economic advantage of building tall apartment houses is that this reduces land rental per dwelling unit, but the cost of saving land in this way is very high. P.A. Stone estimated in 1963 that the cost of land saved by building 12-story instead of two-story dwellings in England was over $150,000 an acre. It would be much higher now because construction costs have more than doubled since 1963.

The above analysis of land costs, construction costs, heating costs, and insurance costs implies that no buildings of more than four stories should be erected in a planned new socialist city. But there are other considerations which would justify some exceptions to this rule.

First, the well-planned location of a few tall buildings in each city or town center may make the city or town more attractive to the eye. A city consisting entirely of low buildings is likely to be much less impressive and inspiring than one with some handsome tall buildings.

Secondly, some tenants enjoy the view from a tall building, especially one with a view over water, mountains, or the countryside, and are quite willing to pay higher rents in order to be able to enjoy such views.

Finally, and most important, the construction of tall buildings in a planned new city reduces the area of the city, which shortens nearly all travel times — from house to work, to shops, to schools, to the city center, etc. — and this in turn permits more people to walk or cycle to their local destinations. This advantage is most marked in the case of tall office buildings, for they do not house children and do not need so much garden and play space around them, and they attract many more daily visitors from a distance than do tall apartment buildings.

These considerations suggest that there should be one or more tall buildings in each city center, and one in each town center in a planned new city. Perhaps there should also be one or two tall apartment buildings in each town. But the case for tall apartment buildings is much weaker.

Since construction costs per cubic foot of rentable space rise with every increase in building height, few if any tall buildings in a planned socialist city should have more than 12 stories.

Number of Workplaces — Socialist new-city planners should provide enough jobs or workplaces to provide work for all residents who want to work. No new-city resident should have to seek work outside his city unless he is trained for very specialized work offered only in other cities, and then he should usually go to live where such work is available.

The mere creation and peopling of a new city creates a very large number of local service jobs — jobs for workers who serve the local population — in stores, clinics, repair shops, banks, etc. Such local jobs should provide work for around half of the local labor force. Their creation does not require much special planning by city planners, who must, in any case, provide the right number of stores, clinics, shops, etc. What does require special planning is the provision of the proper number of workplaces in major export offices or plants.

In planning jobs and workplaces for all prospective residents of a planned new city with a predetermined population, socialist city planners should first estimate the number of jobs in each local, nonexport trade and profession — retail stores, repair shops, local government, medical clinics, schools, etc. These estimates should be easy to make because they can be based largely on statistics concerning the number of such jobs in existing cities. After these estimates have been made and added up, the total should be deducted from the total planned workforce in the new city to determine the number of export jobs and workplaces needed. This total in turn should be divided among the constituent planned towns according to their planned population to determine the size of the export plant needed for each town.

Import-Export Balance — Socialist new-city planners should provide for export plants and offices which will export enough goods and services to pay for all the goods and services which will be imported annually after the new city is fully populated and its workforce is fully employed. In brief, city planners must plan for an import-export balance.

Import requirements for a socialist city are determined largely by the size of the workforce, which varies with population and the average real wage. We have already explained how the population of a planned new city should be determined. Real wages should equal the national average. Thus the chief remaining controllable factors are the size and kind of export plants and offices.

In new-city planning it is necessary to classify all plants and offices into two groups, export producers and nonexport producers. The first group includes all local business and government agencies which provide tangible goods or services largely or entirely for consumption or use outside the city in question. The latter group includes those which provide goods and services largely or entirely for residents of and organizations in the new city.

A city, like a nation, must export in order to import. And, since individual cities are far less self-sufficient than individual nations, they must export a far larger share of their output. Most American cities now export bewteen one third and two thirds of their total output (measured as value added), which means that between one third and two thirds of the labor force in a planned new American city should be employed in producing export goods.

The problem of balancing the exports and imports of a nation has been discussed in thousands of books and articles. The problem of balancing the imports and exports of a single city has received very little attention, but is much more important.

When imports exceed exports in a capitalist city, the residents gradually lose capital funds or must borrow to maintain them. If such a loss continues long enough, local employers discharge workers and unemployed workers leave the city to work elsewhere. A single city cannot devalue its currency in order to preserve employment. It must shrink in size as a result of any continuing "unfavorable" balance of trade. A nation usually benefits from such an "unfavorable" balance — which enables it to increase consumption — and does not lose population thereby, but a city can only waste away. Therefore, it is much more important for a city to achieve adequate exports than for a nation to do so. As the practice of new-city planning grows, more and more attention will be given to the problem of urban import-export balancing. Eventually, more books and articles will be devoted to this problem than to that of balancing national imports and exports. Of course, in both cases it is the overall balance of payments, not commodity movements alone, which must be balanced.

In planning a new city so that its exports will equal its imports, city planners should concentrate their efforts on determining the kind and size of major export plants, those which export 80 to 100% of their output. In a socialist country nearly all factories would be major export plants. In many planned towns there should be only one such plant, a large factory which ships over 80% of its output to other cities and countries.

The national or regional offices of national trusts and government departments are major urban export plants because they largely serve branches and divisions in other cities.

All R and D plants or offices are major export plants because they serve the nation as a whole, not local residents only. Colleges and universities which draw most of their students from outside the city are also major export plants.

In a socialist economy every major export plant would be a local branch of a national government agency and the planners of a new city would have to arrange with one or more such agencies for the establishment of local branches in their new city. This task should be far easier in a socialist than in a capitalist state. The number of such national agencies would be far smaller, and each would be required by the government to expand enough to give work to all jobseekers and to cooperate fully with new-city planners. Profit-making would be subordinated to job creation, and the national government would save and invest each year enough to provide for the creation of new cities, including the construction of adequate export plants and offices in each new city.

Motorcar Use — A new socialist city should be designed so as to minimize motorcar traffic. The use of private cars in U.S. cities should be reduced by 95%. Nearly all urban passenger movement should be by foot, by cycle, or by mass transit. Taxis should be allowed in residential areas only for occasional use by cripples, invalids, and persons carrying baggage. If a socialist city of properly decentralized, little mass transport will be required in residential areas, and that little should be provided by electric trolley buses which never move faster than ten miles per hour. This speed should also be strictly enforced against all commercial vehicles on residential and commercial streets.

Private cars should be garaged or parked on the outer edges of towns or villages, with access only to a greenbelt freeway. All parts of the city should be connected by pedestrian and cycle paths which do not cross any main streets or freeways at ground level.

Fast, frequent, electric-powered bus service should be provided on freeways between town centers, between these centers and the city center, and between all centers and the extracity union passenger terminal. Freeways which enter towns should be used only for entrance and exit, and only by commercial vehicles.

Virtual elimination of private car use in residential communities would radically reduce the number of automobile accidents and the amount of smog and unpleasant noise. It would permit and justify a great reduction in the cost and area of city streets and parking lots. It would promote the wholesome exercises of walking and cycling. It would sharply reduce crime by making it more difficult for criminals to get away from the scene of a crime, and by largely ending car thefts. It would save most families over $2,000 a year (1975) in car ownership costs.

Finally, and perhaps most important of all, the virtual elimination of private-car use in built-up urban areas would radically reduce the consumption of scarce irreplaceable natural resources. The growing cost and scarcity of such resources is likely to become a major brake on future economic progress in all countries. In advanced countries the manufacture of private passenger cars now consumes enormous quantities of irreplaceable metals — steel, lead, nickel, copper, etc. — and the operation of such cars consumes vast quantities of petroleum products. Therefore, an 80% cut in the production and use of such vehicles would sharply reduce the national consumption of many irreplaceable natural resources.

Central Heating and Hot Water — In a planned socialist city all buildings should receive their heat and hot water from central heating plants, probably from electrical power plants. Central heat and hot water could come from a single city power plant located in the city center, or from a town power plant located in the town center. The last alternative seems the most reasonable, partly because much heat is lost when it is transported several miles.

The average American family spends far more for heat and hot water than it spends for electricity, so it is more important to reduce the cost of heat and hot water than to reduce the cost of electricity. A giant regional power plant could reduce slightly the cost of electricity, but it could not supply heat and hot water nearly as cheaply as a town or city power plant. Such local power plants should be just large enough to supply local needs for heat and hot water. If plants of this size do not produce enough electricity to meet local needs, additional electricity should come from large regional power plants.

Centralized outside production of heat and hot water for urban buildings is much cheaper than decentralized production within each building because a large central plant costs much less to build and operate than many thousands of individual furnaces and heaters. Moreover, the metals used to build individual furnaces and heaters and the fuels they burn come from irreplaceable natural resources which ought to be carefully conserved. And the elimination of domestic furnaces and heaters would prevent many destructive explosions and fires, and many deaths due to asphyxiation. It would also save housing space. Finally, the elimination of domestic furnaces would make retail purchase, storage, and handling of coal and oil unnecessary.

It is much easier and cheaper to provide centralized heat and hot water for an entire new planned city built complete at one time by a single agency than to provide such heating in an old capitalist city where heating is controlled by thousands of independent property owners, most of whom already have an independent heating system. Central heating is most economical only when it serves every building in an area, when it is installed simultaneously in all buildings as original equipment, and when there are no vacant lots between buildings.

<u>The Elimination of Gas Utilities</u> — New socialist towns and cities should have no gas utility. Central heat and hot-water systems should replace gas furnaces and stoves as means of heating buildings, and electric cooking stoves should replace gas cooking stoves in these towns and cities.

Many new American homes are already equipped with electric stoves and hot-water heaters, in spite of the fact that natural gas is available at low rates. As gas fields are depleted, gas rates will rise steadily, much faster than the costs of coal and nuclear power. Growing demand for natural gas as a chemical raw material will help to raise gas prices.

In old cities with large gas utility systems little can be saved by reducing the domestic use of gas. But when an entire new city is built, large savings in capital investment can be achieved by not building a local gas plant and/or a city-wide gas distribution system. Moreover, central supply of heat and hot water would end the need for gas furnaces and hot-water heaters in each building. The resulting total capital savings would outweigh any likely resulting increase in current operating costs due to increased use of other utility services.

Electric cooking stoves and hot-water heaters have several advantages over their gas competitors. They are safer because they cause fewer fires, explosions, and cases of asphyxiation. They are cleaner because they produce less soot and fumes. As a result, they do not require the installation of vents or chimneys in each room where they are used.

Competition between electric and gas utilities in capitalist cities permits individual residents to choose between the use of electricity and gas for heating and cooking, but here as elsewhere competition requires unnecessary duplication of facilities and services, and therefore increases costs. No individual consumer can achieve the economies of monopoly by choosing electricity rather than gas. Only new-city planners can eliminate one utility entirely and thus reduce wasteful competition. And such planning is far easier under socialism than under capitalism.

Sewage Disposal — In a planned garden city every dwelling should have an indoor toilet designed to minimize water consumption, and every dwelling should be connected with a sewer main. All sewer mains should carry sewage to a disposal plant which treats sewage so as to make it free from germs and odor and suitable for use as a dry or liquid fertilizer. Most or all of it should be carried in liquid form by canal or pipeline to nearby farms where it should be used for irrigation and fertilization. This use of human and food waste would drastically reduce water pollution and the demand for synthetic fertilizers. It would minimize the cost of reducing water pollution.

Every kitchen sink should be equipped with a garbage pulverizer, and nearly all waste food, bones, and vegetable trimmings should be disposed of through this pulverizer. Then, if all food containers were washed before being put in a garbage container, these containers would not attract flies, cockroaches, rodents, and other animals and would not produce offensive odors. Moreover, the use of garbage pulverizers would radically reduce the cost of garbage collection.

Cable TV — In a planned new socialist city every dwelling unit and many offices and stores should be equipped with cable-TV lines. In most homes there should be cable-TV connections in every room except the bathroom.

Transmission of TV broadcasts by cable rather than by air greatly increases the number of programs which can be provided at the same time. It also improves the reception of most programs.

TV cables could be installed underground with other utility lines at a very early stage in the construction of a planned city. This would minimize installation costs, which are relatively much higher in an old city. Moreover, by providing cable-TV service for every house on every street, new-city planners could minimize the cost per family of cable-TV service.

Within a few decades it will become technically feasible for cable-TV lines to carry many channels. It is already economic and desirable to double the number of TV programs available to urban viewers. And every future increase in average real family income will increase the demand for additional TV programs. Hence, in a planned new socialist city cable-TV lines should carry at least twenty channels, and perhaps many more.

Every residence in such a city should be equipped with both a telephone and a cable-TV outlet. Hence, the telephone line should be included in the TV cable in order to reduce the cost of manufacturing and installing both lines.

Locating Railroads and Highways — No railroad line or intercity highway should enter or pass through a planned new city. Railroad freight and passenger stations should be placed in the outer greenbelt, outside the circumferential freeway running through this greenbelt. Most rail passengers should move to and from the railroad station by taxi or by some means of mass transit. All freight should be moved to and from off-rail points by electric trucks, few of which pass through residential areas.

By keeping railroads outside the city, planners would save the cost of building expensive highway over- or under-passes, would reduce noise and vibration within the city, would diminish downtown street congestion, would avoid creating some urban eyesores, would permit trains to move faster, and would save scarce urban space for other uses. The costs of transhipping more freight to and from trucks are the chief disadvantages, but these costs could be greatly reduced by containerization of all freight.

Like railroad trains, truck and auto traffic on main intercity freeways cause unpleasant noise, vibration, and air pollution. Therefore, all such freeways should pass around rather than through planned cities. And towns within new cities should be planned so that little if any intracity highway traffic goes through them. All main intracity roads should run through the greenbelts separating towns from each other, and should be sunken and banked to reduce noise spread. All traffic on these freeways should move at speeds under 40 miles per hour, mostly to and from local points only.

The intercity truck terminal should be located next to the rail terminal so that freight can be easily transferred from trucks to railroad cars. The main intercity bus terminal should be located at the airport so that passengers can move easily and quickly from buses to planes. And no planned city should have more than one intercity truck or rail terminal.

Airport Location — The airport for a new city should be located far enough outside the city so that plane noises disturb few if any city residents. Only one airport would be needed for a planned new city, and it should be located so that no plane has to fly over the city in order to land or take off, except in very unusual circumstances. Moreover, all private and commercial planes should be penalized for noise pollution whenever they do fly over a planned new city. Such cities should be so small, so located, and so compact that it would nearly always be possible for planes to fly around them, except when several are located close together.

While a new-city airport should be located outside the outer-ring freeway, it should be as close to railroad station as possible in order to facilitate the movement of freight and passengers from one means of transport to another.

Whenever new cities are located less than perhaps 20 miles apart, they should be served by the same airport. A single airport could serve up to four different nearby planned cities. The costs of airport operation fall, and the quality of service rises, with every increase in the scale of operations.

Warehouse Location — All wholesale warehouses should be located outside the city, adjacent to the land freight terminals, and close to the airport. This would facilitate rail and truck deliveries to wholesale warehouses, would reduce truck traffic and the demand for space in the city center, and would not unduly increase the average distance from warehouses to retail outlets.

Lumber yards also should be located next to railroad freight terminals for the same reasons, and because they are ugly, noisy, and require considerable space. Similar reasoning applies to both wholesale and retail dealers in other building materials, farm machinery, used cars, new cars, and junk. The purchase of an automobile or a tractor is so important and so unusual that buyers would not mind traveling a few extra miles to reach a dealer who stocked all new and used models available in their city. And the proper display and demonstration of such varied and bulky merchandise requires a great deal of space.

Most of the workers employed in the railroad station and nearby facilities should be housed in the nearest villages of the closest town of a planned new garden city.

<u>Urban Beautification</u> — The 20th basic principle of socialist new-city planning is that city planners should try to make each new city as beautiful as possible within given budgetary limits. It is always possible to make any city more beautiful by spending more money on landscaping and architecture, but such spending must be limited because men have many other unsatisfied wants. However, as average personal real income continues to rise, men will want to spend an ever larger share of their income on making their homes and cities more attractive, and city planners should plan for future as well as present needs. They should initially overinvest in urban beautification in each new city, and should plan so as to facilitate future beautification projects. For this reason alone, each new socialist city should be more attractive than any old city.

Private architects employed by private persons usually try to make single buildings attractive. City planners should do the same, but should also locate buildings so that the pattern they form is itself pleasing, and so that each beautiful building can be easily observed and enjoyed by passersby and by occupants of nearby buildings. City planners should design streets, squares, and complexes of buildings which please the viewer because they reveal harmony, order, and agreeable contrasts. Every feature of a planned new-city — streets, paths, street lamps, telephone poles, police stations, etc. — should be designed so as to harmonize with other nearby structures and spaces and make the neighborhood more attractive.

Men are willing to spend collectively more money per person for urban beautification projects than they are willing to spend individually. Most of the benefits of individual beautification projects accrue to neighbors and passersby. Thus a man who is unwilling to paint his house or maintain his garden may become willing to do so when all his fellow citizens agree to do the same. City planners can satisfy such collective wants, and they can also coerce antisocial and/or uncultured minorities.

<u>Pollution Control</u> — City planners should plan new cities so as to reduce air and water pollution to the optimum degree, whenever the public can and will pay

the costs. Air pollution is used here to include unpleasant noises and odors, as well as smoke and smog.

City planners should locate those few export plants which continue to produce significant air pollution so that their smoke and/or odor rarely blows over residential areas. They should also see that each power plant, factory, or other potential source of air and/ or water pollution is designed so that such pollution is minimized to the optimum degree.

The richer the country, the more it can and will want to spend to minimize air and water pollution. New cities will endure for generations during which real wage rates will rise steadily. Hence, city planners should design cities so that they will long satisfy rising future demands for clean air and so that additional, future antipollution steps will be as feasible and inexpensive as possible.

The placing of all freeways in greenbelts, the prohibition of private car traffic in residential and commercial areas, the decentralization of commerce and industry, the location of housing near places of employment, the creation of a retail delivery monopoly, and the application of other city-planning principles already stated would reduce air pollution very sharply.

Public Recreational Facilities — Nearly all expensive urban recreational and athletic facilities should be planned for public, not private use. For instance, no houses should be built with private swimming pools, tennis courts, badminton courts, or putting greens. It is uneconomic to build such costly and space-consuming facilities for use by one family only. They should be used by many families. Since family incomes will be far less unequal under socialism, the demand for such private luxuries will be far less than under capitalism.

For the same reasons, few if any houses in a new socialist city should have large private grounds and/ or gardens. Public parks and gardens should largely replace private grounds and gardens. This would greatly increase the use of and benefit from such areas, and would also reduce the cost per acre of maintaining them. Full-time professional gardeners who care for all parks in a city can use equipment too costly for individual home owners to buy and can reduce gardening costs in other ways.

Furniture — In a new socialist town or city, all housing units should be largely or entirely furnished by the builder. This policy would sharply reduce the cost of furniture, would reduce the capital requirements of tenants, and would save most of the cost to the tenant of moving his furniture from one dwelling to another.

The retail marketing of furniture now costs about as much as the manufacture of furniture. A socialist construction trust could buy furniture by the carload at wholesale prices and have it delivered at the construction site. This would save nearly all the costs of retailing. Moreover, the trust could employ professional interior decorators who would choose furniture more wisely than most tenants.

When furniture is moved from one dwelling to another, it rarely fits in well in the new dwelling. It is usually too large or too small, or the wrong color or style. And such movement is very costly. It often costs more to move old furniture than the furniture is worth, but the furniture is moved anyway, partly to save the time and expense involved in looking for suitable new or used furniture. Moreover, movement frequently damages furniture and/or the doors and halls through which it is moved. And furniture in movement is unavailable for use, which may compel new tenants to live in hotels for a time.

<u>Street</u> <u>and</u> <u>Area</u> <u>Names</u> — All city and town streets should be numbered, lettered, and/or named (Allen for A Street) so as to help people find them most easily. This idea is well over a hundred years old, but most American streets are not so named. As a result, delivery men, mailmen, police, firemen, and visitors waste hundreds of millions of hours and much gasoline each year looking for unfamiliar addresses. And aid for those in distress often arrives too late because it is hard to find the address. Finally, the cost of addressing envelopes to persons who live on streets and/or in towns with long names is much higher than it need be.

Every geographical unit of a city or town should also be named so as to help people find it quickly. For instance, the towns around a city center might be named North Town, Northeast Town, East Town, and so forth, or, better yet, simply NT, NET, ET, and so forth.

All buildings should, of course, be numbered in such a way as to help visitors find them quickly. This is already done in most American cities, but not yet in Japan.

Postal area numbers or zip codes should include both city symbols and city unit symbols. All cities should have numbers indicating their location. Thus the zip code for NE Town in city A4 would begin with A4NE.

CHAPTER IV

CITY-UNIT PLANNING

In this second chapter on city planning, we discuss the planning of five different kinds of units of a planned new socialist city — city centers, towns, villages, communities, and neighborhoods — in that order. We also comment on the replacement of old unplanned cities by new planned socialist cities.

A. City-Center Planning

As explained earlier, a planned new socialist city should be highly decentralized. It should consist of a city center surrounded by a wide greenbelt and, beyond the greenbelt, by largely independent and self-sufficient towns. We shall now explain first how such city centers should be planned.

This discussion of city-center planning falls into two parts: (1) what facilities should be included in the city center, and (2) how the city center should be laid out.

1. City-Center Facilities

City centers should include all facilities used by the residents of all surrounding towns. They should also house nearly all of the workers who man these facilities and the retail and service facilities needed to care for city-center residents.

The following list of specific facilities which should be included in each city center should clarify the above general rules, but it is meant to be illustrative and suggestive, not definitive.

Medical Complex — The city center should contain specialized health offices and hospital facilities used by the residents of all towns in the city. These facilities should supplement rather than duplicate the services and facilities provided in town hospitals. They should include the more costly and rarely used equipment and provide the most specialized and/or most rarely needed health services.

Central City Library — The city center should contain a library serving the entire city and the city university. This library should contain several million books and periodical files not found in local town libraries.

University — Each city center should contain a non-residential university which offers most liberal arts courses and trains many professional and paraprofessional workers for local employment. This university should not duplicate career training offered in any town junior college or in any regional or national residential university.

City-center universities should draw students from throughout the city. They should primarily train local students for local jobs, and therefore should not include professional schools whose students come from other cities and whose graduates go to other cities. Such professional schools should be provided only by residential universities, which should be located in town centers because they are major export plants. Thus a planned new socialist garden city could include a university town like Cambridge or Palo Alto, but no residential university should be located in a city center.

Museums, Zoos, and Botanical Gardens — The city center and its greenbelt should contain all local museums, an aquarium, a zoo, and a botanical garden because such places are visited by persons from all parts of a city, and placing them in the city center would make them most easily accessible.

Theaters — The city center should contain all theaters and concert halls which draw patrons from all towns in the city. The towns would be too small to support any local theaters except cinemas.

Broadcasting Studios and Towers — These facilities should be located in the city center to enable visitors from all over the city to reach the studios most easily and to improve average broadcast reception.

Major Facilities for Athletic Events — The city center should contain a stadium, a baseball field, and any other sport facilities used chiefly for events which draw fans from all over the city.

Administrative Offices — Any national trust or department which operates local units — stores, clinics, offices, power plants, etc. — in each town within a new city might need a local administrative office to supervise local operations. Such administrative offices should be located in the city center in order to minimize the travel time between such offices and the units they supervise.

Government Offices — The city hall, the courts, the jail, the district attorney, and other government offices which draw visitors from throughout the city or send employees throughout the city should be located in the city center to minimize average travel time.

However, offices which do all or nearly all their business by mail and phone should not be located there. They should be export industries in town centers.

Department Store — The city center should contain one big department store which is largely or entirely restricted to the sale of the kind of expensive merchandise consumers buy infrequently, so-called shopping goods.

Newspaper Office and Printing Plant — The editorial office and printing plant of the city newspaper should be located in the city center because reporters and newspaper distributors would travel to and from all parts of the city and because more news stories would break in the city center than in any other part of the city.

Hotel — The city center should contain one or more hotels or motels for use by visitors who wish to visit offices or residents of the city center or who wish to visit or sightsee throughout the city.

Restaurants — The city center should contain several bars and restaurants for use by residents of and visitors to the center.

Parking Lots — The city center should have four or more large parking lots on its margin, but nine out of ten visitors should walk, cycle, or ride the buses to and from the city center, so these parking lots should occupy less than 2% of the area of the city center (as compared with 50% in some large U.S. cities).

Amusement Area — Each city center should contain an amusement area, a combination of Coney Island and Disneyland, which provides a wide variety of commercial amusements not available elsewhere in the city and draws patronage from throughout the city.

Residential Village — Nearly all persons employed in the city center should live in one or more residential villages in this center so that they can walk or cycle to work in less than fifteen minutes. Such city-center villages should contain much the same kind of housing, schools, shops, offices, etc., as residential villages in nearby towns. The planning of such villages is discussed later.

There should be no central post office, no wholesale warehouses, no rail or intercity bus terminal, no highway-truck terminal, and no corporate headquarters in a new-city city center. The post office, warehouses, and terminals should be adjacent to or near the airport, outside the outer circumferential freeway. Each national or regional trust or department headquarters should be treated as an export plant and located in some town center.

There should be no gas stations or garage within the city center, except perhaps one gas station at each parking lot on the fringe of the city center.

2. City-Center Layout

The city center of a planned new round city should be round or oval in shape. It should be located in the center of the city, and surrounded by a greenbelt. The city center should be between one and two miles in width, and the greenbelt between one half and one mile in width. A freeway should encircle the city center, in or near the center of this greenbelt, and should connect with the parking lots and bus depots on the fringe of the city center, but no freeway should run through the city center.

No private cars and taxis should be allowed to circulate within the city center, except to enter and leave the marginal parking areas. Hence, there need be very few streets within the center.

City center streets should be but one or two lanes wide. They should be used only by slow electric trucks and buses. No parking should be allowed on city streets. Trucks should load and unload in basements or in special off-street areas. All streets should be tree-lined, and all sidewalks should be separated from both buildings and street pavements by a green parking at least six feet wide. Free transportation by slowly moving buses (10 miles an hour) should be provided throughout the center. To reduce traffic on intracity freeways and to minimize the area used for parking in the city center, the city should provide fast cheap bus service between each town center and the nearest city-center parking lot.

In regions of cold winters, all buildings in new-city city centers should be connected by heated underground pedestrian tunnels so that visitors can walk about the city center without feeling the winter climate. On very hot summer days these tunnels and the buildings they connect should be airconditioned.

The area of each new city center should be minimized in order to enable most visitors to walk from their bus depot or parking lot to their destinations and in order to reduce the average distance from town centers to the city center. Hence, each city center should probably contain two or more eight- to twelve-story buildings, at least one tall office building and one tall retail store. The university also might be housed in a single tall building. The construction of such tall buildings would not only reduce the area of the city center but would also make it easier for tenants to visit each other, and for the public to visit two or more offices, classrooms, or store departments.

Every building in the city center outside the residential areas should be free-standing and surrounded by a garden or lawn at least 20 feet wide. Moreover, it should be designed so that all sides are pleasing. The taller the building, the wider the surrounding area should be.

All educational and cultural facilities in the city center — university, theaters, library, museums, etc. — should be grouped together. Likewise, all government offices and facilities involved in crime prevention, detection, and treatment should be near each other. Newspaper and broadcasting facilities should be very close together, probably in the same building, and adjacent to the educational-cultural complex. There should be only one, large department store, and it should probably be grouped with the single hotel and one or more restaurants and bars in another complex. Most major athletic facilities should be near the university so they can be used by students as well as by professional athletes.

The residential village which houses and serves most families whose adult members are employed in the city center should be located in the center of the city center so that workers can live as close as possible to the places where they are employed and so that visitors to the city center will rarely travel through any part of this village to reach the facilities they have come to patronize. And the shopping center of this residential village should be placed in the center of the village in order to enable residents to reach it as easily as possible.

The size of the department stores and most other facilities in the city center would depend upon their hours of operation, which in turn should depend primarily upon how many shifts they are operated. In a later discussion of export firms we shall explain why these units should operate two or more four- to six-hour shifts per day. Most stores and offices in the city center should operate the same number and length of shifts in order to serve export workers on all shifts equally well. This would reduce radically, by at least one half, the size of the buildings needed to house the city-center department store and most other city-center facilities.

B. Town Planning

A planned socialist city of 400 to 600 thousand population should include six to ten district towns surrounding the city center but separated from it and from each other by greenbelts at least a half mile wide. Each town should be compact and largely self-sufficient. It should provide nearly all jobs, housing, schools, retail stores, recreational facilities, clinics, etc., needed by its residents.

Such a town could be housed in a single giant building or in a complex of a few very large buildings. We shall discuss later the advantages and disadvantages of such megastructure towns. However, for reasons already partly stated in Chapter III, this discussion is largely restricted to the planning theory of round garden cities.

Each garden town should be divided into a town center and eight to twelve distinct residential villages around the town center. The villages could not be self-sufficient because many of their residents would be employed outside the village, usually in the town center. Therefore, there should be no greenbelt around the town center, but there should be some green space between villages, both to provide more accessible open space and to make villages more distinct.

Export Plants — The central feature of the great majority of towns in planned socialist cities should be a single major export plant located in the town center and employing 40 to 60% of the town's workforce. Indeed, the chief economic function of any such town would be to operate its major export plant and house, feed, supply, and in other ways serve the workers employed in this plant. We use the term export plant to denote any urban plant or office whose output is largely consumed outside the town in which it is located, i.e., is exported.

All export plants should be located in town centers or just outside the city. Inoffensive export plants, those which do not disturb their neighbors, should be located in town centers in order to place them as close as possible to the homes of their employees. Offensive plants — steel mills, oil refineries, some chemical plants, etc. — produce so much noise, vibration, smoke, fumes, odor, fire risk, etc., that they should be built outside the town which houses their workers. Such plants, a small minority of all export plants, should be placed beyond the outer greenbelt, just across from the town which houses their workers. Even in these cases, the average distance workers travel to work should rarely if ever exceed two miles.

For reasons given later, no export plant located in a town center should employ much more than 18,000 workers. This would limit opportunities for reducing unit costs by hiring more workers and increasing the scale of operations. However, each export plant would still be free to increase its scale of production by further specialization, for instance, by producing only one model of its product, or one part of one model, instead of producing two or more models and all their parts.

The typical new town should have only one export plant because this policy would increase its scale of production and therefore lower its unit costs. This policy would make the future of the town dependent upon the sales of a single plant. Under capitalism such dependency is dangerous and uneconomic because an export plant may have ruthless competitors who can drive it out of business. Under socialism, however, there should be no competition, no style cycles, no advertising, no forced obsolescence, no business depressions, and so forth. Each industry should be a monopoly and socialist monopolies would rarely find it economic to close down an export plant. They could easily plan their plant construction programs so as to avoid any serious overcapacity.

We explained earlier why each new planned city should be decentralized by dividing it into largely self-sufficient towns. This rule implies that each town should be planned so that it will export to other towns, cities, and areas enough goods to pay for all imported goods. The final plan for any new town should therefore include a table showing the total expected town imports and exports. If preliminary estimates show an estimated surplus or deficit of exports, the plan should be corrected.

<u>Town Size and Population</u> — Every town in a planned city should be small enough so that nearly all its residents can walk to schools, to shops, and to work within the town in less than twenty minutes. Since adults walk about three to four miles an hour and since persons employed in a town center could live in those areas nearest the town center, where the population should be most dense, the suggested 20-minute walk limit would allow a town to cover up to 12 square miles.

If a new town is small enough so that most workers can walk to work or open country in twenty minutes, and can cycle to work or open country in seven minutes, intratown use of private cars can be virtually ended, and the urban areas used for streets, car parking, service stations, private and public garages, etc., can be radically reduced. No families will require two cars, and most will do without a private auto. Finally, walking and cycling provide much-needed exercise. Taken altogether, these and other advantages far outweigh the benefit from any reduction in internal plant production costs permitted by employing more workers and increasing the export-plant scale of operations above our suggested limit.

The larger the town, the larger will be its potential workforce, and therefore the larger and more efficient its major export plant. However, it is more desirable to enable all town residents to live near greenbelts, shops, and jobs than to minimize the internal costs of export plants.

If we assume average densities of 4 to 6 thousand persons a square mile (7 to 10 per acre) within the town limits (excluding only the greenbelt around the town), we can conclude that an ideal town (12 square miles in area) could house 50 to 75 thousand residents. Of these, over half would work, about half of them in the export plant, which could therefore have 12 to 18 thousand employees. This would nearly always permit a large enough scale of operations to achieve over 90% of the maximum internal cost reduction achievable from an optimum increase in the scale of production. Moreover, those few plants outside any town could draw workers from two adjacent towns to achieve a larger scale of production.

Since the ideal size of a town depends largely on the need to minimize automobile traffic, on the need to minimize export-plant production costs, and on other internal town needs, it does not vary with the size of the city. To increase the planned population of a planned new city, planners should increase the size of the city center and the number, not the size, of the towns in the new city.

Town Centers — Town centers should function for towns much as city centers function for cities. They should contain — in addition to export plants — only those facilities and offices which serve residents throughout the town. They should not contain facilities which serve chiefly the area of a single village or neighborhood within the town.

To be more specific, a town center should contain, in addition to any export plant:

1. A large department store
2. A supermarket grocery store
3. One or more moving picture theaters
4. A bus station
5. A real estate rental and maintenance office
6. Repair shops for clothing, furniture, and appliances
7. A clinic and hospital
8. A large high school and junior college
9. A public library
10. A town hall

11. A hotel
   12. One or more restaurants
   13. A police and fire station
   14. One or more churches

   This list is meant to be suggestive rather than complete and authoritative.
   Town centers should not contain any gas stations, garages, wholesale warehouses, railroad stations or yards, museums, zoos, opera houses, jails, amusement areas, stadiums, etc. And the schools, hospitals, stores, and offices they do contain should not duplicate the services of similar units in the city center.
   Most town centers should contain two or more tall buildings (eight to twelve stories) in order to reduce the area of the town center and make its services more easily accessible to town residents. Usually, the major export plant should occupy one tall building, and a combination store and office building another.
   The town-center high school and junior college should be designed so that its classrooms, auditorium, library, and athletic facilities can be used by nonstudents when not being used by students. For instance, the auditorium should be planned so that it can be used for church services, plays, moving picture shows, and musical events. And the swimming pool should be designed for public use in the evening, on weekends, and during vacation periods.
   The streets and plazas of town centers should be far more attractive than those in capitalist business districts. The elimination of private motor vehicles and fast, noisy mass-transit vehicles would do much to achieve this result. Town-center streets and squares should be lined with trees and flowering plants, ornamented with fountains and murals, and furnished with benches and bicycle racks.
   On the other hand, town centers should contain no large parks and should not be surrounded by a greenbelt because both features would increase the distance which town residents must travel to reach some or all parts of the town center. This effect is much more serious in the case of greenbelts around town centers than in the case of greenbelts around city center because the average resident of an ideal city would travel to his town center several times as often as he would travel to his city center.
   <u>Multi-shift Operations</u> — The size of the buildings housing most town-center activities, and therefore the area of the town center, would depend upon the number of hours or shifts these facilities are used. For one-shift operation, most buildings would have to be

almost twice as large as for two-shift operation, and
almost three times as large as for three-shift operation. To plan a new city properly one must first
decide how many hours and shifts each facility is to
operate. The application of this rule to town-center
planning is especially important because town centers
should include most major export plants, which should
employ about half of all workers and which would be
most suitable for multi-shift operation because most
of them would be highly mechanized and would produce
storable goods.

The advantages and disadvantages of multi-shift
operation were discussed in <u>Liberal Socialism</u> (pp.
140-41). Here we shall only note that, other factors
being equal, every rise in the amount of fixed costs
per dollar of wage cost and every decline in the hours
of labor increases the advantages of multi-shift operation. When fixed cost exceeds variable cost for one-shift operation — a common situation — the addition
of a second shift permits at least a 50% increase in
wage rates for both shifts. And the share of fixed
costs in total costs has long been rising and will
continue to rise indefinitely.

To simplify this discussion, let us arbitrarily
assume here that the export plant in a given new town
should operate for two six-hour shifts. If this plant
operates two shifts, all other facilities in the town
center should also operate at least two shifts in
order to serve workers on both shifts.

<u>Town Streets</u> — A self-sufficient, decentralized
town in a planned new socialist city should have only
three or four outlets to the freeways which run
through the surrounding greenbelts. One of these
should be a two-lane freeway carrying bus traffic
from the town center directly to the city center. This
traffic would not be heavy enough to justify construction of a subway or an elevated line, but would be
heavy enough to justify the departure of a bus every
five minutes or oftener.

There should also be a two-lane freeway running
across town as part of a freeway ring around the city
connecting adjacent towns with each other. This would
be used primarily by buses and trucks carrying people
and goods to and from town centers.

In residential areas these freeways should be
depressed and hidden by shrubbery in order to minimize
noise pollution. Within the town center both freeways
should probably run underground.

Except for these freeways, nearly all intratown
streets should carry only local traffic. Most such
traffic would be slow-moving and light in weight.
There would be little need for parking space on or

off these streets because nearly all private-car use within towns should be prohibited. Only a few handicapped persons should be permitted to use small electric cars, which would require very little parking space.

Few if any heavy trucks should be permitted to use these narrow intratown streets, so their paving could be much thinner, narrower, and much less costly than that on the residential streets of unplanned capitalist cities. The creation of monopolies to handle local delivery service, local building maintenance, local gardening, local repair services, etc., would greatly reduce the local street mileage of the light trucks performing these services, which would help to reduce the need for wide streets and thick paving.

Mass Transit — If a planned new city is properly decentralized, i.e., divided into self-sufficient towns and well-integrated villages, most residents will be able to walk or cycle to and from jobs, shops, and schools, so there will be relatively little need for mass transit, even if the use of private cars is largely prohibited. Therefore, socialist new-city planners should not plan for a subway system, or even a streetcar system. Instead, they should plan for a system of small, slow electric buses to carry passengers within each town, and for a system of larger, faster electric buses to carry passengers between town centers and city centers. Both systems should charge fares in order to encourage walking and cycling. In old existing cities mass transit should be free in order to reduce private auto use, but in a planned new town such auto use should simply be prohibited.

The demand for mass transit will of course be much heavier when the weather is bad, and it is expensive to provide large buses which are used only a small part of the year. Bus capacity should be sufficient to provide seats for all during peak-hour use in good weather. This would permit each bus to carry twice as many peak-hour passengers when the weather is bad. Also, trailers could be attached to buses during peak hours in bad weather.

Private-Car Terminals — As explained in Chapter III, few if any privately owned or rented automobiles should be allowed to move about within a well-planned socialist unit town or city center. Therefore, all intercity travelers who arrive or depart by private car and who lack a local private garage or parking space should arrive at and depart from an intercity private car terminal. No unit town or city center should have more than one such terminal, which should be located on the edge of the surrounding greenbelt.

This terminal should contain a car and bicycle rental office, a garage, a hotel or motel, a tourist information office, a restaurant, and other tourist facilities. Those who arrive by car at such a terminal could turn in their rental car and rent a bicycle or small electric car to enter the town or city center. They could also enter by bus, but not by their intercity car.

Housing Types — Socialist city planners should try to provide enough of each class of housing so that the rental income from that class will just cover the full cost of providing that housing. Individual rentals should be determined by supply and demand, but the supply of each class of housing should be planned so as to result in a total rental income which just covers total construction, interest, land rent, maintenance, and all other relevant outlays over the life of the housing. Estimates of the demand for each class of housing in a proposed new city should, of course, be largely based on actual demand in existing cities, especially in similar planned cities.

When planning the housing in a new town, planners should prepare a table showing the number of families who will live there classified by size and income. They should then plan the new housing so that every family will be able to find a dwelling of desired type and size at the rental they can afford to pay. No worker employed in a new socialist town should have to live elsewhere in order to have a dwelling of suitable size and cost. Since socialist city planners could determine the type of industry to be located in each new town and since all firms and agencies in the new town would be branches of national monopolies, it would be relatively easy for these planners to secure data on all prospective payrolls in the new town.

The great majority of people in England and America now want to live in detached one-family houses with a private yard. And in other advanced countries the preference for such housing has long been growing. As real incomes continue to rise, more and more families will be able to afford such housing. However, the housing preference of prospective residents of planned new socialist cities would be quite different.

The residents of detached houses on spacious lots in the suburbs of capitalist cities use private cars to go to and from work and shops. The drastic curtailment of private-car use desirable for other reasons — smog and noise reduction, accident prevention, mineral conservation, etc. — would make life in communities of detached houses much less attractive. Even if mass transport were provided, it would be much less frequent and/or costly in such communities because distances would be longer and patronage smaller. Every increase in the density of population reduces mass transport costs, and permits more frequent service.

Furthermore, a socialist government would abolish laws which now favor private ownership of detached houses, such as that which permits U.S. homeowners to deduct property taxes and mortgage interest from their income subject to income tax, and would stop the continuous inflation which now enriches homeowners at the expense of mortgage owners. Most American property taxes and zoning laws now discriminate heavily against multi-family housing.

Also important is the fact that family incomes in socialist cities will be far less unequal than they now are in advanced capitalist states. As a result, the cost range of new housing will be much narrower. No residents will be able to afford costly mansions and grounds, and the poorest families will be able to afford comfortable new apartments or row houses. No family will be able to afford a full-time servant, so no dwellings containing servant quarters should be built. And a very liberal provision of public parks and greenbelts should further reduce the demand for private gardens and yards.

Moreover, average family size in new socialist cities will probably be smaller than it is today. In particular, the proportion of families with three or more children will be much smaller. And facilities for child care outside the home will be far more extensive.

The proportion of urban married women who work outside their homes has been growing for at least 50 years and will continue to grow for many years. This trend also will reduce the relative demand for detached houses because such houses require more time to be spent on housekeeping and gardening. A garden apartment complex with adequate child-care and food services is the ideal home for a family of two working adults and one to three children.

Finally, the cost of power and fuel for air-conditioning and heating will probably rise faster than other housing costs during the next century or two. And such costs are much lower in multi-family buildings than in detached homes because common walls and floors conserve both coolness and heat.

For these reasons it is likely that the demand for multi-family housing, especially row houses and apartments, will be far larger in new socialist cities than in the suburbs of old U.S. cities.

One-Building Towns — An entire town could easily be housed in a single immense building. The six-story pentagon in Washington, D.C., now provides office space, restaurants, stores, bus terminals, etc., for 30,000 workers. A taller or larger building could house all of a town of 60,000 people.

Housing an entire town in a giant building, or a cluster of them, would yield certain advantages. It would make it possible for everyone to ride or walk to school, work, or stores without going outdoors. This would be most advantageous on days when the weather is bad, and therefore in areas where the climate is very cold or hot, or both by turn.

Moreover, such housing would minimize the average distance between homes and jobs, schools, and stores, which would save much of the time now devoted to travel between them. It would also sharply reduce the need for private cars, mass transport, and paved streets. And it would lower heating and cooling costs because it would cut the area of exterior wall and roof per unit of floor space. It would facilitate automatic delivery of mail and retail purchases to individual homes. It would make it easier for neighbors to get acquainted and visit each other because they would use common facilities — halls, patios, swimming pools, etc. — and because they would live closer together.

On the other hand, housing an entire town in a single building, or in a small cluster of them, has serious disadvantages. It would make it much more difficult to have a private garden or patio, and to walk or play outdoors in uncongested public parks, gardens, and woods. It would sharply increase residential housing costs because a giant multi-floor building must be much more substantially constructed — with heavier walls, floors, and foundation — and must provide many wide interior halls and elevators. And tenants would be more frequently and seriously bothered by noise and vibration from adjacent apartments and halls. Most apartment rooms would have windows on only one side, and the average window view would be inferior. Such factors might arouse feelings of mild claustrophobia and/or institutionalization in many tenants.

The only way to determine whether people prefer to live and work in megastructures or in garden communities is to build both and then study their inhabitants. But we believe that the great majority of people living in agreeable climates will prefer garden communities, and therefore we have largely confined our discussion to such communities.

C. Village Planning

As explained earlier, an ideal new city should be highly decentralized in order to minimize street traffic, congestion, noise, pollution, and time wasted in traveling to and from work and shops. The most important application of this general principle should be the creation of relatively self-sufficient towns, but each town should also be decentralized to a lesser extent in order to place schools and local village shops near all residents.

Each town should therefore include 8 to 12 semi-self-sufficient residential villages, in addition to the town center. Each village should have 4 to 6 thousand residents. Villages should be separated from each other, but not from the town center, by narrow greenbelts containing paths leading both to the wide circumferential town greenbelt and to the town center.

Size and Population — The chief economic activity in most villages and neighborhoods of a planned town should be education. Therefore the structure of a town should depend upon the structure of the educational system. Most villages should have just enough population to support a single intermediate school (ages 10 to 14?) of a near-ideal size. This size would depend in part upon the maximum distance pupils should walk or cycle to get to school. No school buses should be used to carry normal children to and from school, except perhaps in regions with a severe winter climate. Busing is costly and deprives children of needed exercise.

Children will soon start going to school at ages 3 and 4 and such young children ought not to have to travel far to reach school. Therefore, elementary pupils (ages 3-9?) should attend schools located in community rather than village centers.

The physical size of a planned new village would depend upon population density as well as upon the number of people it houses. Density of population in a residential area depends largely upon the type of housing. We have suggested that while the great majority of Americans now prefer detached houses, this preference will become much weaker in a new socialist garden city. However, it is possible to house all the residents of a 6,000-person village in detached houses on 50 x 80 foot lots without using more than one half of a square mile.

If a village occupies less than one square mile of ground, no child would have to walk more than half a mile to reach an intermediate school in the center of the village. The average distance would be about one third of a mile. Children age 10 to 14 could easily walk or cycle this distance to school, especially since street traffic in a socialist planned city would be less than 10% of its 1975 level in U.S. cities, and would move much more slowly.

In a village of 6,000 persons there should be almost 100 children of each age. It may seem that a school with 100 children of each age from 10-14 is likely to be too large, because class sizes should be reduced to less than 20. However, the larger the school, the lower the building and maintenance costs per pupil and/or the greater the variety of course and facilities which can be provided. Moreover, each intermediate school should offer several channels and/or methods of instruction for each age group of pupils.

Of course, the educational structure and the ideal size for each kind of school should be largely determined by educators and school officials, not by city planners, but only new-city planners and builders can provide schools of the ideal size and class in the ideal locations. Moreover, it would be costly to alter the size, use, and location of finished school buildings.

Since the ideal size and population of a planned village should depend almost entirely upon educational and other local internal factors, they should not depend upon the size of the city or town of which they are a part. To increase the planned area and population of a planned town, city planners should enlarge the town center and the number, but not the size, of the villages to be included in the new town.

<u>Village Centers</u> — Each village should have a village center which should contain the facilities needed to provide all educational, medical, recreational, retail, financial, and other services used only or largely by local village residents and by residents of all areas of the village. It should contain no major export plant, and no facility which serves primarily residents of other towns or of other villages in the same town, or residents of only one area in the village.

In addition to an intermediate school, a typical village center should include a supermarket, a junior department store, a church, a clubhouse, a movie theater, a clinic, a branch library, and other facilities used frequently and/or almost exclusively by village residents. These facilities should be planned so as to supplement rather than duplicate those provided in the town center. For instance, the medico-dental services offered in the village clinic should be those most frequently required, while those offered in the town clinic should be those less frequently required.

The provision of such facilities in village centers would reduce the distance shoppers must travel to and from retail and service facilities. It would also enable the workers employed in these village centers to live closer to their jobs. Hence, many more shoppers would walk to shopping centers, and many more workers would walk to and from their places of employment.

Streets and Transport — Each village in a planned socialist city should be planned so as to minimize the area devoted to residential streets. Such streets should be less than 16 feet wide. In most new American subdivisions streets occupy 10 to 20% of the land, and private driveways, garages, and parking spaces take up another 10 to 20%. In a well-planned new village where intratown private car use is prohibited these motor-vehicle facilities should require less than 5% of the land area.

In a planned village, streets and schools should be located so that nearly all young children can go to and from school without crossing or walking on any street, and so that older children need cross only one or two streets. Almost every house or apartment building should have a greenbelt or park in the rear, and these areas should contain paths which lead most children to school and most parents to stores and work without crossing more than one street.

One of the reasons why socialist new-city planners should make wide use of residential superblocks and cluster housing is that both arrangements reduce the number of street intersections and/or the amount of street space required to serve a given residential population. Housing people in row houses or apartment buildings has the same result. The construction of garden apartment buildings in superblocks combines and multiplies these effects.

Village Layout — Within each village the density of population should be highest in the neighborhoods nearest the town center, and lowest in those nearest the outer greenbelt. The best location for the densest housing and the largest apartment buildings, if any are needed, would be between the village center and the town center because this location would help most to reduce street traffic and the daily travel time of village pupils, workers, and shoppers.

Housing for large families — all dwellings with three or more bedrooms — should be placed relatively close to schools. Housing for small families should be relatively remote from schools. Such planning would reduce the average distance children must travel to and from school, and would enable children to make more frequent use of school playgrounds, which should, of course, be open and supervised throughout the day and part of the night every day of the year.

City planners should plan each village so that there is more public than private open space in each village. Public parks and gardens cost less per acre to maintain because they are larger, less divided by fences, and can be cared for by professional gardeners using more specialized equipment. Moreover, they can be used and enjoyed by more persons. And, since they are larger, they can provide space for tennis courts, swimming pools, walks, and other facilities which cannot be installed in the typical private yard because they are usually too expensive and/or too extensive.

One-Building Villages — Housing an entire village in a single large building or groups of such buildings is much more feasible than so housing an entire town. It would not do as much to shorten the average distance from home to job or school but it would reduce by 80 to 90% the size of the structure, and thus radically reduce the disadvantages of living in such large buildings.

Moreover, if one village in a town were so housed, it would provide a wider diversity of housing. Hence, it seems likely that at least one village in most new towns should be largely housed in a single giant building or in a small cluster of large buildings. Such villages would be most suitable for childless couples and single persons.

The design of a one-building village belongs more to architecture than to city planning. And the theory of how to design a one-building village or town differs radically from the theory of how to design a new garden village or town. Furthermore, we believe that the great majority of people will prefer to live in garden communities and villages. Hence, we have little to say here about the design of one-building communities.

Single-Shift Villages — The major export plant and other facilities in the center of each town would employ 40 to 60% of all workers in the town, and most of these facilities should operate two or more shifts a day, seven days a week, throughout the year. So far as possible, the workers on each shift should live together in the same villages. This would permit operation of most village-center facilities — school, store, clinic, clubhouses, etc. — on those shifts which best meet the needs of the village population. It would also promote social life. Neighbors would sleep, work, shop, and relax at the same time, and night-shift workers would feel far less alienated and discriminated against. When a village must house members of two different shifts, these shifts should be segregated in neighborhoods within the village, for similar reasons.

When workers on different shifts live in the same building, they often disturb each other. When night-shift workers leave for work or arrive home and carry on household activities, they awaken sleeping day-shift workers, and vice versa. Even when they do not live in the same building, their street and playground use disturbs sleeping members of other shifts.

Moreover, if night-shift workers live together in the same village, their children can follow the same time schedule as their parents. They can sleep and eat when their parents and neighbors do so, and they can attend school when their parents are working. We assume here that night-shift schedules would be only five or six hours long and would permit night-shift workers to sleep about half of each night, so that such workers and their families could be awake and enjoy most daylight hours. Socialism will sharply reduce the hours of labor, and multi-shift operation itself permits a substantial reduction in the hours of labor, especially on night shifts.

City planners must determine in advance the number of hours and shifts each village economic unit is to operate in order to plan its size, its utility connections, its lighting, and so forth. In villages housing members of two or more shifts, most stores, schools, and office could operate two or more shifts, and therefore could be much smaller than in one-shift villages. However, this advantage is probably much less than the benefits of life in a one-shift village.

If workers are not segregated by work shifts, they should be segregated in separate villages by age and/or according to whether or not they have children living at home. This would enable adults and children of similar ages to live closer to each other, which would favor more frequent and pleasant socializing among adults and children.

Childless Villages — One village in each new town should be designed to meet the special needs of young single adults and young childless couples, nearly all of whom should work on night shifts. It should have no schools and playgrounds for children but instead should have many more recreational facilities which have been designed to meet the needs of young childless adults. All housing should be designed for use by single persons and couples. Such segregation of these adults would not only enable them to enjoy homes and recreational facilities more suited to their needs but would also promote closer social relationships among them.

Another village in each town should be designed to meet the special needs of older adults (age 45 to 100?) who are either childless or living apart from their children. It too should contain no schools or playgrounds for children, but it should have a school for adult classes. All of its housing and other facilities should be designed to meet the particular needs of older adults.

D. Community Planning

Most of the arguments for decentralizing a city or town can also be used to justify decentralizing a village. We shall call the semi-self-sufficient units of a village "communities." Each community should contain all public facilities which are used chiefly by local community residents. It should be separated by a narrow greenbelt from other communities.

Area and Population — A village in a planned socialist city should be divided into 4 to 6 distinct and slightly separated communities, each covering 80 to 120 acres and housing 1000 to 2000 people. The chief basis for prescribing this population range is that it would justify a separate elementary school for children aged three to nine. Such schools should be small enough so that young children need not travel far or cross a street in order to reach them. Another basis for this prescription is that the recommended area and population could constitute a single superblock.

Community Centers — There should be a community center in the center of each community. It should contain all public facilities used frequently and almost exclusively by local community residents. These would normally include a community church, a clubhouse, a recreational center, a coffee shop, a small convenience-goods store, a barber shop, a beauty parlor, a laundromat, an elementary school, and a playground for young children. If it houses only adults without young children, no facilities for children would be needed, but many more facilities for adults should be provided.

The recreational facilities provided in community centers should vary from center to center. One center might provide more and/or better tennis courts and another might provide more and/or better badminton courts. Each center should be designed to appeal to a slightly different group of residents. This would give all town residents a wider variety of choice among residential areas, and would also assure fuller local use of recreational facilities. Furthermore, residents who enjoy the same sports and games are more likely to play together, to be congenial, and to become friends.

Community center facilities should supplement rather than duplicate those of village centers. For instance, community centers might provide poolhalls and outdoor badminton courts, while village centers might provide bowling alleys and tennis courts.

The creation of such community centers is desirable for two reasons. It would place some of the most frequently used recreational, educational, retail, and service facilities closer to consumers, within very easy walking distance, and it would promote social relations among the local residents using these facilities.

Community Layout — Many, perhaps most, communities should consist of a single superblock with dwellings around the sides and a large park and community center filling the interior of the block. The entire superblock should be separated from adjacent communities by a greenbelt 200 to 300 feet wide, with a narrow street running through the middle of it. There should be no streets within such a block except a one-lane delivery alley leading to, but not through and beyond, the community center.

We explained earlier that in a very cold or very hot climate, it might be desirable to construct an entire town or village under one roof as a single megastructure. The case for building entire communities in such climates under one roof would be even stronger. And, if a community is inhabited only by adults, the case for building it under one roof, as a large apartment building, would be strong in any climate. Since each town in our ideal city would contain 30 to 50 communities, at least one community in every town should be planned and built as a single structure.

The housing in each village and community should be planned and designed so as to enable families to live as close as possible to the places where adults work and children attend school. If a town has a single high school and junior college located in the town center, as suggested earlier, most of the housing located in communities adjacent to the town center should be designed to fit the needs of families with students attending these schools and/or with one or two adults employed in the town center.

Similarly, in each town the communities most remote from the town center should be planned and largely reserved for families none of whose members work or attend school in the town center, i.e., for familiies whose members work or attend school in their own village or community center.

Within each community the housing closest to the village center, and therefore to the village school, should be planned and designed to meet the special needs of families one or more of whose adults work in the village center and/or of families one or more of whose children attend the village school.

We have proposed that the residents of a planned new socialist city should be segregated according to their place of employment, their work shift, the age of their children, and other factors, but they should not be segregated according to their incomes, as they are in most capitalist towns and cities. The chief reason for this last rule is that income and cultural differences should be far less in a socialist than in a capitalist society. Moreover, inherited cultural and educational differences would be much smaller under socialism. As a result, other differences — in place of employment, in age, in age of children, etc. — would become more important than differences in income as bases for social integration and segregation. It follows that each community in a planned socialist town should provide housing for all income levels, and there should be no communities including only or mostly high-rent or low-rent dwellings.

E. Neighborhood Planning

Every community should be divided into 4 to 6 neighborhood groups of 60 to 100 housing units. These basic housing groups might consist of a cluster of detached houses or duplexes, a group of small apartment buildings, a single apartment building, or a wing or sector of a very large apartment building. The occupants of most such housing groups should share relatively exclusive use of a day nursery, a playground, a badminton court, a swimming pool, one or more laundromats, and/or other facilities suitable for such restricted use.

Recreational facilities should vary from neighborhood to neighborhood. A cluster of detached houses or apartments should be built around or near such facilities and separated by park land from nearby housing groups. A neighborhood would not need a commercial center, but it might well have a manager who performs the functions of an apartment house manager. If most of the tenants have infants, there might also be a night nursery and a resident child nurse. If most of the residents are very old, there should be a resident nurse to care for them.

Day nurseries and kindergartens should usually be placed in neighborhood centers because this would minimize the distance children below age three must walk or be taken to and from the nursery or the kindergarten.

All domestic washing machines, clothes dryers, and dry cleaners should be installed in public neighborhood laundromats, not in private homes. This policy would radically reduce the number and total cost of such machines, would conserve housing space for other uses, and would help to reduce the national consumption of irreplaceable natural raw materials like copper and iron ore. It would also increase personal contacts between neighbors, and thus promote social life in each neighborhood. There should probably be one small public laundry room for every 10 to 20 families.

We have discussed housing specialization among communities. A community would consist of several neighborhoods, each of which could be further specialized in housing and public facilities. For instance, in a community designed and reserved for families with young children one neighborhood should be largely reserved for parents with very young children only, and another should be reserved for parents with children aged six to ten. Similarly, in a community designed for older adults who have no children at home, one neighborhood might be reserved for persons under 70 and another for those over 70. The dwellings and facilities in each neighborhood should be designed to meet the special needs and preferences of its selected residents.

If the stores, schools, and offices in any community center operate two or more shifts a day, the workers on each shift should be housed in neighborhoods reserved for members of the same shift, and any neighborhood facilities should be planned for use by this shift and operated during hours which best meet their needs.

F. The Reconstruction of Old Cities

We turn now from the theory of how to plan the construction of an ideal new socialist city to that of how to plan the reconstruction of an old city.

It is impossible to construct an ideal new planned city by reconstructing an old city piecemeal. The street plan of an ideal new garden city should be entirely different from that of any old unplanned city, and the location of buildings and public utility lines in a new city should be largely determined by the new street plan. Moreover, every reconstructed or new city built on the site of an old city should be divided and surrounded by greenbelts, whose creation would require demolition of all buildings, streets, and facilities in extensive areas. Hence, every old city should be leveled to the ground and nearly all its underground facilities should be dug up or abandoned before a new planned garden city is built on the site of any old city. But such demolition and new construction should be done district by district, not on a citywide scale.

Demolition of old cities and clearing of their sites for new construction is expensive. Why should we not merely abandon them gradually and rehouse their populations in entirely new planned cities built on fresh, unspoilt sites? Abandonment is uneconomic because most old cities occupy sites which have natural or manmade advantages. They are located on harbors or rivers, have adequate supplies of fresh water, are served by railroads and freeways, and so forth. Moreover, an abandoned old city would mar the landscape for many generations. And housing all of their population on new sites would cut into the amount of land available for agriculture. Finally, a great many residents of old cities are sentimentally attached to the place of their birth or long residence, and are willing to pay extra to continue to live there.

An enormous amount of capital funds has been invested in existing cities. And the populations of these cities must continue to live in them until they can be housed in new planned garden cities. A full-scale socialist new-city building program would probably rehouse annually only a very small proportion of the existing U.S. urban population. And all existing old cities are grossly overcrowded. Finally, most of the equipment and building components used to construct new cities must be produced in old cities. Hence the demolition of old cities should not begin until the new-city construction program has rehoused 30 to 50% of the old-city population, i.e., until 10 to 20 years after a massive new-city construction program has begun.

In other words, the best and simplest way to minimize the social cost of demolishing old cities in order to permit their replacement is to wait a decade or two while old buildings age and no new buildings are built. Then when they must be wrecked, the old buildings will be worth much less, and no new buildings will have to be wrecked.

While existing cities are aging in this way, their population should be gradually reduced by inducing more and more of their residents to move to new planned cities. The mere stopping of new construction in old cities would help to produce this desired result since it would reduce the number of jobs in construction projects, and would make old cities look more and more old-fashioned.

The new-city planning and building program in a socialist state should be expanded rapidly until it gives employment to 80 to 90% of the urban construction labor force. In the U.S. this should permit construction of enough new cities to house and employ 3 to 4% of the population each year. With a 1% annual increase in total urban population this would permit a 2 to 3% annual reduction in the population of old cities. There should be hardly any construction of new buildings and facilities in old cities. Rather, many old buildings should be vacated and wrecked as the population of old cities declines. The land area freed thereby should all be converted into public parks and playgrounds.

It may be suggested that the residents of old cities, who make up a great majority of the electorate, would strongly oppose a new-city construction program which would virtually end new construction in old cities. Under capitalism such a restriction of new construction would seriously injure the residents of old cities, especially property-owners, but this need not be so under socialism. For instance, there would be no property-owners. And a socialist government should see to it that residents of stagnating old cities share fully in national economic progress.

The gradual, city-wide demolition of the oldest, ugliest, and poorest buildings in old cities and their replacement by public gardens, parks, and playgrounds would help to improve living conditions in old cities. And all remaining buildings in old cities could be repainted inside and outside more often as real wages rise. A socialist government could and should see that real wage rates in old cities continue to rise as fast as wage rates rise in new cities. And, of course, there should be no unemployment in any old city due to cessation of new construction or to any other cause. If these measures do not suffice to reconcile the residents of old cities to the temporary cessation of new construction in their cities, other measures of compensation should be adopted. In a democratic state it is essential to secure the political support of residents of old cities for any new-city construction programs.

After a third to half of the urban population has been rehoused and re-employed in new planned garden cities, a socialist government should begin to replace old cities. This would require near-complete demolition of old cities. To minimize the inconvenience to the residents of old cities and to prolong the use of the expensive buildings and facilities in old cities, socialist city builders should demolish and replace old cities district by district. Each district so cleared should be just large enough to provide a site for an entire new town (one to two square miles), and this town should be completed and occupied before another district is demolished.

The first district to be cleared for replacement building in an old city should be that having the lowest total assessed value, i.e., the cheapest and/or most rundown buildings and facilities. And each adjacent district chosen later for demolition should have the lowest assessed valuation when chosen. The district with the newest and most valuable buildings and improvements should be the last to be cleared for new-town construction. Since the complete replacement of old cities would probably require at least 30 years, the most valuable buildings and districts of old cities could continue in use for 30 to 40 years after new-city construction has begun.

A complete land-use plan for each replacement city should be prepared before any construction begins. This is true even though, as previously noted, a replacement city should be built town by town, not all at once. To plan and build a single town properly, one must know precisely how it is to be related to all other parts of the city of which it will be a part.

Nearly all the major and minor principles of new-city planning stated earlier in this book should be applied to the planning of replacement towns and cities. The only ones which do not apply are those concerning site selection and rapid simultaneous construction of all parts of a new city.

There are, of course, many things which could be done to improve the conditions of life in old cities waiting to be demolished and replaced. For instance, the provision of free mass transportation throughout the city by bus would greatly reduce congestion, street accidents, noise, and air pollution. But discussion of such temporary measures of urban improvement does not fall within the scope of this chapter. Obviously, few if any costly fixed investments should be made in a declining city scheduled for complete demolition within a few decades.

The U.S. already has many metropolitan areas with over one million population. In most cases it will be desirable to build two or more replacement cities, with wide greenbelts between them, in these areas. For instance, in 1970 the Los Angeles metropolitan area had a population of about seven million, and occupied about 2000 square miles. A new or replacement garden city (including greenbelts) should have only 400 to 600 thousand residents and should occupy only 80 to 120 square miles. Therefore, when the Los Angeles metropolitan area is cleared of old structures it should provide sites for 16 to 24 new ideal planned garden cities with a total population of up to ten million.

CHAPTER V

INTERCITY TRANSPORTATION

As used here, the term transportation includes all commercial movement of commodities and passengers outside the limits of a single plant by any mode of transport. Thus, it includes the services of post offices, express companies, pipe lines, etc., in addition to all other types of railway, highway, air, and water transportation. It does not include private use of private cars.

There is no need for a complete exposition of the economic theory of socialist transportation in this chapter. Much of this theory can be taken over intact from capitalist transportation theory. Nor is there any need to discuss the technical problems peculiar to each of the major forms of transport, for these are not economic problems.

The general principles of price determination, of factor allocation, of management, etc., already set forth in Liberal Socialism apply to transportation unless qualified in this chapter. Only a few of these applications are noted here.

It is noteworthy that the reorganization of industry proposed in Liberal Socialism would have drastic effects upon the demand for transport. For instance, the adoption of universal monopoly would eliminate millions of small stores, farms, and plants and thereby greatly increase the average size and value of individual freight shipments. Moreover, it would eliminate all cross shipment of like freight due to competitive selling in each marketing area. And the adoption of sound socialist freight rates would bring about a relocation of industry which would sharply reduce ton-mile haulage per ton of output. On the other hand, the great increase in output per worker and in the volume of employment made possible by socialism would greatly increase the tonnage of products to be hauled.

A. Organization

The American transport system is more atomized, decentralized, and competitive than any other such system in an advanced country. For instance, the railroad system is completely unified in Great Britain, France, and Germany but in 1975 there were still over

700 railroad companies in the U.S., of whom 73 were Class I line-haul operating firms. Yet the railroad industry is a pure natural monopoly, and competition has greatly increased railroad construction and operating costs.

While the wastes due to competition and atomization are less severe in other American transport industries, they are very great. For instance, competition among airlines has resulted in a seat vacancy rate of almost 50%, and has prevented or sharply limited both the use of the largest, most economical existing airplanes and the development and use of far larger and more economical planes.

Consolidation — In a socialist America all intercity railroads should be consolidated into a single national rail system. This would make it possible to: (1) eliminate all unnecessary and costly duplication of physical facilities and transport services; (2) standardize all railroad locomotives, cars, and equipment; (3) establish union passenger and freight terminals in all cities; (4) operate more through trains; (5) sell round-trip passenger tickets good on all trains; (6) end division of responsibility for accidents and freight damage; (7) end the costly record keeping required to divide through-freight revenues among different railroads; (8) end uneconomic, roundabout routing of trains; (9) increase the division of labor among workers; and (10) achieve other economies made possible by an increase in the scale of railroad operation.

Most American cities are now connected by two or more rail lines. For instance, there are six direct rail routes between St. Louis and Chicago and seven between Omaha and Chicago. These lines often parallel each other for long distances. Between Miles City, Montana, and Spokane, Washington, two main lines run side by side for 760 miles.

Where existing single-track lines parallel each other, a socialist Transportation Trust should use each line for one-way traffic only. Where double-track lines parallel each other, the trust should use one line each way for fast trains and one line each way for slow traffic, as long as all main lines are maintained. In many cases one of the existing lines should be abandoned because its continued maintenance and use is not justified by current or prospective future traffic. In these cases the best parts of two or more rail routes should be integrated in one or more new routes more direct and economical and less polluting and highway-congesting than any of the previous routes. After the best new route has become operational, all through freight traffic should be moved over it. This would yield all the benefits of an increase in the scale of operations. For instance, it would permit the scheduling of many more through trains, which need not waste time detaching or picking up cars at stations along the way.

The consolidation of all American rail lines into a single national system would permit for the first time the creation of through rail lines from the Atlantic coast to the Pacific coast. At present all through freight must be transferred from one rail line to another at Chicago, St. Louis, New Orleans, or some other gateway city. The interchange at these gateways is so slow and so costly that many shippers prefer to truck their freight hundreds of miles for direct loading onto western or eastern railroads rather than have them pass through two or more freight yards and a belt rail line in one of these gateway cities. A socialist railroad trust should lay through lines around these cities and operate through freight trains over these lines under a single railroad management.

Although the merger and reorganization of independent and competing rail systems is more urgent and would yield greater savings than such treatment of any other intercity transport industry, each of these other industries also should be integrated and reorganized as a single system. All the docks in each harbor, all the passenger and freight-handling facilities in each airport, all the truck terminals in each city should be merged and reorganized so as to eliminate wasteful duplication of facilities and services, increase the scale of each operation, standardize equipment, and achieve other economies of centralized, monopolistic operation.

But it would not suffice to form a single monopoly operating each mode of commercial transport. Most passengers and freight shipments move by two or more transport modes on each trip. Therefore, all commercial intercity transport agencies should be units of a single national Transportation Trust. This trust should control all means of intercity transport except pipelines, which should be operated by the trusts whose products move through them.

In the U.S. over half of all highway trucks and passenger buses are owned and operated by non-transport firms. Since they are not operated by common carriers, they usually carry freight in one direction only and return empty. In a socialist economy nearly all such trucks should be owned and operated by the national Transportation Trust. This would permit greater use of each truck, would cheapen repair and maintenance, would facilitate standardization of trucks, and would yield other benefits. Only a few highly specialized trucks, for instance, should be owned and operated by the trust which produce these products.

Similar reasoning applies to the ownership and operation of other non-specialized means of transportation. Thus no non-transport agency should own and operate executive passenger planes.

<u>Coordination</u> — Centralization of control over all forms of transport except pipe lines would permit the achievement of important additional reforms not permitted by the consolidation of individual transport industries. It would permit or facilitate many kinds of coordination between these industries, including the creation of union multi-mode terminals, the use of the same standardized containers by all transport agencies, unified control over the movement of through passengers and freight by two or more transport modes, the creation of union all-mode ticket offices and freight agencies, the standardization of some equipment and supplies throughout all transport industries, an economic choice of the mode of transport for each freight shipment, making one agency responsible for damage or delay to each freight shipment from shipper to consignee, the coordination of passenger schedules for different modes of transport, the publication of passenger schedules giving information on operation by different modes of transport, and centralized purchasing for all transport industries.

<u>Regulation</u> — Under capitalism the organizational structure, operating policies, and rates of all private transport firms are closely and expensively regulated by local, regional, and/or national government agencies. In America, city councils, state legislatures, and Congress have enacted thousands of laws on transportation structure, policies, and rates, and have created numerous administrative agencies to enforce these laws. Such external regulation is essential because private transport firms are monopolies which try to maximize private profit, not social welfare. Under socialism all such detailed regulation of transport industries should be ended. The government should determine the general policies applicable to all industries, such as marginal-cost pricing, but should not approve or disapprove individual decisions. If certain executives fail to carry out general national economic policies, they should be replaced by men who will carry them out. Some central supervision would be necessary to determine how well top executives carry out national policies, but this supervision should be entrusted to a single national transport agency. It should be based largely upon the review of regular statistical reports on transport services,

employment, wage rates, accidents, and so forth. Lawyers and courts should have no part in such supervision. And the total man-hours devoted to such supervision should be at least 95% less than that now devoted to government regulation of private American transport firms.

Operating Units — The main operating units of the coming American Transportation Trust should include: (1) a Railroad Branch, which operates all intercity rail lines and related repair and maintenance shops, (2) an Airline Branch which operates all airlines and aircraft repair and maintenance shops, (3) a Highway Transport Branch which operates all intercity truck and bus lines and their repair and maintenance shops, (4) a Water Transport Branch which operates all intercity boats, barges, and waterways and related repair and maintenance facilities, (5) an Urban Transport Branch which operates all intracity means of public transport and the related repair and maintenance facilities, and (6) a Union Terminal Branch which operates and maintains the intermodal terminals used by the above listed branches.

B. Operating Policies

The creation of a national transportation monopoly and the resulting centralization of control over all forms of transport would permit and should result in drastic changes in the operating policies of each form of transport. Transport technologies and the social conditions affecting transportation are still changing rapidly, but it is possible to predict some of these changes.

Unification of managerial control over all forms of commercial transport would provide for the first time the basis necessary for the most efficient coordination of all methods and agencies of transportation. When different modes of transport are controlled by independent competing firms, each firm places its own interest above those of the industry as a whole, and often seeks to injure its rivals and the public in order to benefit itself. Moreover, independent managers find it impossible to determine what is in the public interest because they do not know what other managers will do. Only unification of management permits ideal coordination of and cooperation between transport agencies.

If highway and rail freight transport are controlled by the same top management, it will be much easier to experiment with various forms of truck-train coordination, and much easier to adopt those forms of coordination which experiments prove to be economic.

110

Traffic Re-allocation among Modes of Transport —
The American railroad network was built by competing
firms without any national plan or other method of
coordinating individual construction projects. This
resulted in a vast amount of unnecessary duplication
of facilities and services. After this rail network
was constructed, paved highways were built to connect
nearly all communities served by railroads, and trucks
and buses began to compete with railroads in an uncoordinated, wasteful way. Although the movement of
freight by rail for over 200 miles is usually cheaper
than such movement by highway, railroad rates were
normally far above relevant costs, especially for
high-value freight, which permitted trucking firms to
charge lower long-haul rates on a great many commodities and take over a large share of the more valuable freight previously shipped by rail. In the late
1960s, intercity trucks carried about one quarter of
U.S. intercity freight ton-miles but received about
three quarters of the money spent on intercity freight
transport. In other words, truck rates averaged three
times as high as average rail rates.

In America, highway transport rates have often
failed to measure all relevant marginal real costs
while rail freight rates have usually been far higher
than relevant marginal real costs. Strong unions
raised rail wage rates above average wage rates long
before they raised highway truckers' wage rates, and
many independent truckers still work excessive hours
for below-average wage rates. Also, railroads have
built, maintained, and paid taxes on their own rail
lines while truckers have used roads built by public
agencies, and have paid gas taxes which often do not
measure fully the relevant costs. Moreover, public
regulatory agencies began to regulate rail rates long
before they began to regulate truck rates, and have
kept rail rates much further above marginal money
costs than they have truck rates. Finally, additional
truck traffic on a highway injures all other traffic.
It makes highway use less pleasant for all persons in
other cars, slows down traffic, and increases the
number and costs of highway accidents, but these
external real costs do not affect the money costs of
truck transport.

Moving long-distance freight by rail is much
cheaper than moving it by road because a single locomotive can pull over 100 times as great a weight as a
single truck. Both the fuel and the labor costs of
moving freight by rail are therefore much lower. Rail
line-haul costs in the U.S. are estimated to be about
20% of truck line-haul costs. Moreover, railroad locomotives can burn coal or use electricity generated in
nuclear or coal-burning power plants, while intercity

trucks will probably continue to require gasoline or other more costly fuels. And highway trucks suffer more accidents and kill many more people than do freight trains.

The chief advantage of truck transport is that trucks can take freight from off-rail shippers and deliver it to off-rail consignees without transshipment, which is now costly and time-consuming. But the universal use of standardized containers will radically reduce truck-train transshipment costs, which will reduce the mileage range within which shipment by road is economic.

The construction of a rail line, like that of a highway, requires a very heavy investment in fixed facilities. Once constructed, either should be fully used before it is expanded or duplicated. In most countries, railroads were built, indeed overbuilt by competing firms, before modern freeways were built, and should have been fully used before any long-distance freight was shifted to highway transport. But uneconomic rail rate determination and unfair competition by truckers resulted in a great shift of freight from rail to highway transport. A socialist transport trust should reverse most of this shift and should see that in the future nearly all long-distance (over 200 miles?) freight moves by rail. Only careful studies under the new economic conditions created by socialism can determine precisely what share of freight should move by rail, but it will certainly be far higher than the share now moved by rail in the U.S. The resulting savings in intercity freight costs should be very large, probably over half of total previous trucking costs.

In America, private road and rail transport firms have coordinated some of their activities by moving loaded trucks on railroad flat cars. Such coordination should be replaced by the use of standardized containers on road and rail lines. Both systems of freight transport require close coordination of road and rail systems, and would therefore be far easier to adopt when road and rail transport are operated by a single top management.

<u>Containerization</u> — The use of large standardized freight containers has been growing for several decades. Their use greatly reduces pilferage, breakage, damage, and the costs of transferring freight from one carrier to another. However, it has been very difficult to persuade thousands of independent private transport firms to standardize their containers. Integration of all such firms into a single socialist transport system would make it far easier to standardize containers and container-handling equipment. And integration of

shippers in each industry into national monopolies would make it much easier to persuade all shippers to use containers. Moreover, the elimination of competition and small-scale production in each industry would greatly increase the size of the average freight shipment, which would make the use of large containers economic more often. Hence, a socialist Transportation Trust should plan for and achieve a far more extensive use of large standardized containers than has been or can be achieved under competitive capitalism.

The same standardized containers should be used on nearly all forms of transport, so that any container can move by several different means of transport on a single trip. All docks, airports, rail terminals, and truck terminals should have standardized container-handling equipment suitable for transferring standardized containers from one kind of carrier to another.

Terminal Unification — Most large American cities have two or more of each kind of transport terminal. A socialist transport trust should eliminate all such duplication of terminal facilities in old cities. All new and reconstructed cities should be free of such duplication from the start.

A well-planned socialist city should have only one non-marine intercity passenger terminal, which should serve all intercity buses, passenger trains, and passenger planes, as well as local passenger buses. And it should have only one non-marine intercity freight terminal, which should handle all intercity rail, road, pipe, and air freight lines. In some cases, a marine terminal should be part of the union terminal.

Since terminal costs now account for about half of all intercity transport costs, integration of all non-marine freight terminals in each socialist city should result in large savings, probably over 20% of total intercity transport costs. For instance, it would make economic much more automation of freight yards, and would increase substantially the length of the average freight train.

One other much-needed form of coordination between different modes of transport is the creation of union ticket, information, and baggage offices which serve all intercity travelers. It should never be necessary to phone or visit more than one local office to obtain full information on all alternative methods of intercity travel. And most printed schedules should include data on all these methods.

In a socialist union passenger terminal the ticket clerk who sells airline tickets should also sell railroad and bus tickets. Indeed, most passenger tickets should include travel by two or more modes of transport. A passenger should never have to buy two separate tickets to complete his trip. And all baggage should be handled by a single agency throughout any trip.

Pick-up and Delivery Service — A socialist transport trust should pick up all freight at the shipper's warehouse and deliver it to the consignee's warehouse. Pick-up and delivery should usually be by truck; intercity transport, by plane, rail car, truck, or ship.

In America today these services are commonly provided by three or more separate private firms, and the consignee rarely knows who is responsible for damage to his shipment. Moreover, the business transactions with these three or more transport agencies are costly, for each prices his service and collects his charges separately. Consolidation of pick-up, transport, and delivery services would improve coordination of them, reduce operating costs, and improve the service rendered to shippers. It would free most shippers and consignees from the burden of having to operate their own, often small and inefficient, trucking service. It would concentrate freight pick-up and delivery trucks in the hands of a single large and efficient agency in each city.

Rerouting Freight Traffic — Much freight now moving by rail should be shifted from high-cost rail lines to low-cost lines. Since competing American railroads are now required to charge the same rates for the same services, high-cost lines often obtain freight that ought to move by a low-cost line. Thus freight moving from New York to California may move by way of New Orleans or Seattle instead of by a much more direct low-cost route. Indeed, freight rates over indirect high-cost routes have often been set below rates over direct, low-cost routes in order to give more business to high-cost lines.

Indirect, high-cost freight shipment is also common on air, water, and highway lines. A socialist transport monopoly should end this practice on all means of transport.

Abandonment of Rail Lines and Stations — We have explained how parallel main railroad lines should be merged, integrated, or abandoned. Many, perhaps most, U.S. branch lines should also be abandoned. Since they usually carry a very small volume of traffic and are paralleled by paved highways, it will be easy to shift their freight and passengers to trucks and buses. The highways must be maintained in any case, but the entire cost of rail-line maintenance falls on rail service.

The American Interstate Commerce Commission (ICC) has repeatedly denied railroad petitions requesting permission to abandon tens of thousands of miles of unprofitable branch lines. It has often decided that unprofitable railroad services should be subsidized out of the profits earned on profitable services. This is an unsound economic policy. It benefits certain shippers at the expense of other shippers and their customers. Under socialism all subsidies should be financed by the national treasury, not by raising some prices above the optimum level, and thereby discriminating against certain consumers.

In order to speed up freight trains and reduce their operating costs, a socialist rail system should cease picking up and dropping freight cars at most small towns on its main routes. Freight to and from these towns should be trucked, usually in containers, to the nearest town large enough to justify operation of a freight depot. The universal use of standardized containers would radically reduce the cost of transferring freight from trucks to freight cars, and thus decrease the need for small railroad freight stations, yards, and sidings. Only careful research can determine how much freight a town must provide or receive to justify having a freight depot, but it seems likely that most freight depots on American mail rail lines should be abandoned.

<u>Unit Trains</u> — The merger of all American railroads into a single integrated network and the great increase in the average size of railroad shippers and consignees due to socialist monopoly would make it economic to increase radically the volume of goods moved by unit trains. Such trains have much lower operating costs because they do not stop at any intermediate freight stations and do not require any switching or other terminal services for individual freight cars. The entire train moves from one terminal to another, often from one shipper to one consignee, without any switching stops enroute.

Until a few years ago the use of unit freight trains on American railroads was prohibited for fear that it would enable large firms to reduce their freight costs and drive smaller competitors out of business. Moreover, even today no American railroad has a transcontinental rail line.

When both containerization and transcontinental unit trains have been adopted by American railroads, it may become economic to ship much freight from East Asia to Europe and the eastern American states by means of American unit trains rather than by means of ships passing through the Panama Canal.

Larger Vehicles and Planes —Within broad limits, as yet unapproached, every increase in the size of a vehicle reduces transport costs per passenger or ton-mile. A large vehicle can be constructed at a lower cost per capacity-unit than a small vehicle. It can also be moved at a lower cost per ton-mile. And loading and unloading costs per ton of freight are lower. Finally, airport air and ground space is already dangerously congested at many airports, and every increase in average plane size reduces the number of planes which must use these airports.

By ending competition among both carriers and shippers, a socialist government would greatly increase the size of the average freight shipment and the number of passengers per departure. Therefore, it should greatly increase the size of rail cars, airplanes, ships, intercity trucks, and intercity buses.

All passenger planes flying from Los Angeles to New York, London, or Tokyo should carry over 500 passengers and/or over 100 tons of freight by 2000 A.D., and ever larger loads thereafter. This increase in size would sharply cut air-transport costs. And flying passenger planes full instead of half full would reduce costs by another 40%.

Intercity freight trucks should also be much larger than they are ever likely to be in a competitive capitalist economy. Such trucks would move only on modern intercity freeways. They would depart from and arrive at terminals located outside cities, and would rarely if ever move over city streets. Therefore, their size would not be limited by the need to turn corners on city streets, park on city streets, etc.

To permit an optimum increase in the size of railroad freight cars and engines, all American rail tracks should be widened. Only careful scientific research of a sort never yet done can determine how wide railways should be, but the width should probably be even wider than those of Russian railways. The carrying capacity of the average freight car should be at least doubled, and perhaps trebled or quadrupled. This would permit the use of much larger containers.

In recent years the increase in the volume of petroleum moved by ships has permitted a ten-fold increase in the maximum size of oil tankers. The elimination of competition between shippers of other products should permit an equal increase in the size of other ocean freighters.

A great increase in the average size of transport vehicles and the elimination of competition between carriers would permit and should result in a drastic reduction in the number of ships, trains, trucks, buses, and/or planes arriving at and departing from each terminal. Passengers and freight could be concentrated in larger vehicles which would depart and arrive less often. This would reduce congestion on all rail lines and highways and in all terminals, which would reduce accident rates and terminal costs.

Reducing Empty-Car Mileage — On American railroads empty-car mileage is about 25% of total car mileage. Railroad cars are owned by individual roads which charge rent for their use by other lines. As a result, each railroad normally tries to return empty foreign cars to the home line as soon as possible.

Of course, when there is a temporary scarcity of cars, a railroad tries to hold on to foreign cars and use them to haul freight on its own lines. This discourages other roads from buying new cars.

A socialist railroad monopoly should never move empty cars unless they are needed at the point to which they are moved. There should be no rental charges which influence empty-car movement. The railroad system should buy and maintain enough cars to permit an optimum reduction in empty-car mileage. Moreover, it should fix freight rates so as to optimize empty-car mileage. And no local division of the rail trust should be allowed to retain empty cars needed more urgently elsewhere.

Over 30% of all highway truck mileage in the U.S. is empty-truck mileage. The highway-trucking industry is so atomized and competitive that it is especially difficult for trucking firms to secure return freight. And ICC regulations prevent many trucks from carrying return freight. A socialist transport trust should therefore find it easy to reduce drastically intercity empty-truck mileage.

C. Price Policies

The general theory of price determination developed in Liberal Socialism should, of course, govern the determination of socialist transport fares and rates, but the application of this theory to transportation would result in far greater changes in pricing methods than would its application to any other major industry. The price theory now applied by most capitalist transport firms is grossly uneconomic.

There is a very extensive literature on capitalist transport pricing practices, but nearly all of this literature is purely descriptive or apologetic. For instance, a great deal of it treats of the way judges have interpreted laws concerning rate regulation. And most prescriptive capitalist rate theory prescribes how judges and transport executives should interpret such laws. But the idea that lawyers and judges, rather than economists, should formulate and/or interpret transport pricing policies is unscientific and irrational. It amounts to a rejection of political economy. In a socialist economy all pricing policies should be formulated and interpreted by economists. If any economist performs such functions badly, he should be replaced by another economist, but should never be replaced or overruled by a judge or other non-economist.

It is often claimed that the different transport services provided by a single rail route, train, truck, freight car, or other carrier are joint products and that therefore the special price theory applicable to joint products should be applied to most or all transport services. However, we have defined joint products as those which must be produced together — like cotton fibre and cotton seed — not as those which may be produced together (LS, pp. 196, 283), and therefore believe that no transport services should be classified as joint products.

No Price Discrimination — Socialist freight rates should not discriminate among shippers or commodities. They should both balance supply and demand and measure marginal costs per unit of service — ton miles or some other composite physical unit. They should not be based upon the value of the product. If shippers of different products buy identical transport services, or services with the same marginal costs, they should be charged the same rate, regardless of the nature and value of the goods shipped. If they buy services with different costs, they ought to pay different rates, and the rate differentials should usually be based upon differences in marginal costs.

To allow for differences in bulk, the transport trust should include the weight of the carrier — railroad car, truck, or plane — in the total weight on which freight rates are based. Rates based on the weight of the cargo only cannot measure and vary with marginal costs. Classification of freight by bulk or value is a crude, costly, and unsatisfactory method of allowing for differences in bulk per ton. Counting in the weight of the carrier is a simple and accurate method of determining freight charges, one which allows for the bulk as well as the weight of shipments.

When a transport firm uses cars of different weight to carry the same weight and bulk of freight, the rate charged should be based on the weight of the heaviest car because marginal freight movement requires their use.

In both the U.S. and the USSR, freight rates are based largely on ability to pay, and they differ widely and unequally from relevant marginal costs. For instance, the rate per ton-mile of a valuable manufactured good may be ten or even twenty times as high as the rate on a raw material like coal or gravel. As a result, factories are located much closer to the markets for their finished products than to the sources of their raw materials, and this raises total transport volume and costs far above the optimum level.

Certain bourgeois economists have attempted to justify rates based upon ability to pay by asserting that it is impossible to determine accurately the costs of rendering individual transport services. But the fact that a task cannot be performed perfectly is not a conclusive reason why it should not be performed at all. Even if this reason were conclusive against rates based on cost, it would not prove that rates based on ability to pay are desirable. Rather, it would suggest that all rates should be equal. However, it is possible to estimate nearly all specific transport costs with sufficient accuracy to justify rates based on costs.

A more important argument in favor of rates based upon ability to pay, and one which is persuasive under capitalism, runs as follows. About two thirds of the total costs of operating a railroad are fixed costs which do not increase when the volume of traffic increases. Interest, rent, and salary overhead will be the chief fixed costs under socialism. Taxes are an important fixed cost under capitalism. The fact that two thirds of railroad costs are fixed costs means that it may be profitable to the private owners of a railroad and to society as a whole to increase the volume of railroad freight whenever idle capacity exists, even if the additional freight does not pay the estimated (imaginary) average cost of railroad service. So long as the additional freight covers the variable costs and contributes something to the fixed costs, it is worth carrying if the low rate quoted on the additional freight does not apply to the previous volume of business. Such a situation is common. Since railroads carry many different types of commodities over many routes, a new low rate can apply to one kind of commodity and one route only, which makes it possible to grant special low rates to some shippers only. Thus, special low rates which serve to move additional freight benefit everyone concerned under capitalism.

The situation is quite different under socialism. It is still economic to move more freight whenever idle capacity exists and this additional freight can pay the marginal cost of moving it. However, and this is the vital point, it is no longer necessary for any carrier to be self-supporting, and all rates can and should equal marginal costs. Any deficit a carrier incurs by charging ideal freight rates can and should be met by the government. The resulting ideal freight rates will yield consumers' and producers' surpluses much more than adequate to cover ideal deficits and any resulting tax increase. And they will result in a more economic location of all new factories and cities.

Another argument in favor of ending freight rate discrimination and charging uniform rates for all freight is that this would save hundreds of millions of dollars now spent each year by carriers in order to fix, publish, and collect discriminatory rates, and by shippers to determine which of thousands of different rates applies to each of their shipments. The classification books now published by American railroads are as large as a New York City phone directory, and only an expert can understand and use them.

The basic principle that prices should equal marginal costs also rules out discrimination between one-way and round-trip passengers. The marginal costs of carrying one-way passengers are the same as those for carrying round-trip passengers. Hence, all should pay the same passenger fares.

Capitalist firms can afford to charge lower rates for round trips because their rates for one-way trips are well above marginal costs. And they can get additional business by charging less per passenger mile for round trips. A socialist transport trust should charge ideal rates for one-way trips, so any reduction for round trips would be uneconomic.

There is another form of railroad rate discrimination prevalent under capitalism that should have no place in a socialist economy. Railroads have often cut through rates between competitive points below the average for local rates. The excuse offered for this type of rate discrimination is that the railroad must compete for the through business. It is better to obtain some of the through traffic at any rate which will yield a surplus over marginal costs and will contribute something to fixed costs, it is argued, than to permit all the through traffic to go by other lines or by ship, with the result that local freight will have to meet all fixed charges of the railroad.

It is perfectly true that if excess railway capacity exists, rates should be cut until the capacity is entirely utilized, provided rates still cover variable costs. But, if it is necessary to cut through rates for this purpose, local rates should be cut in proportion. The same reasoning applies here as in the case of different rates on different kinds of merchandize.

This does not mean that ton-mile charges should be the same for long and short hauls. Railroad rates should be composed of two parts, one to cover terminal costs, the other to cover line-haul costs. The former does not vary with the length of the haul, but the latter does. Hence, total charges per mile for long hauls should always be less than those for shorter individual hauls.

Some Soviet freight rates per ton-mile increase with distance. The purpose is to induce trusts to locate nearer their markets and/or sources of supply. This is an uneconomic pricing policy because marginal transport costs fall continuously as the distance increases, and transport rates should measure marginal costs, except when higher rates are needed to prevent congestion.

Soviet railroads also charge lower rates for hauling freight over more costly roundabout routes in order to avoid congestion on direct low-cost routes. This policy too is uneconomic. The proper way is to raise rates on congested routes, not to lower them on alternative routes. The resulting profits on the low-cost routes would then stimulate expansion of capacity on these routes.

Soviet railroads have granted large discounts on freight rates for coal hauled to Moscow from the nearest coal basin in order to discourage the import of coal from more distant basins. This pricing policy is uneconomic. If coal prices at near and distant fields, and transport rates from them, are properly determined, and if buyers try to economize, no special rate discounts for coal shipped from nearby fields is justifiable. If rail lines from distant coal fields are congested, transport rates should be raised for all freight over these lines, not for coal only.

More Frequent Rate Changes — In both capitalist and communist countries, transport rates often remain fixed for many months or years at a time. Capitalist rates have been changed more often in recent years, but chiefly because of inflation, not to balance the supply of and demand for individual transport services. They are fixed so as to yield a total income which covers total costs, not so as to achieve optimum use of transport facilities. As a result, transport volume is usually well below, often far below, the optimum level. For instance, most American commercial passenger planes have been flying half empty for years. But some planes fly full and others nearly empty.

The demand for transport service of any kind over any route varies unpredictably from week to week and month to month. Therefore, if transport rates should balance supply and demand, they too should fluctuate from month to month irregularly, as well as seasonally and predictably.

When storable goods are unsold because their prices are too high, they can be stored until sales increase or their prices are cut. Hence, a price reduction is not urgent. But when potential services are unsold, they cannot be stored and are lost. Hence, it is essential that the prices of services should always be low enough to assure capacity output and consumption. When sales are insufficient, service prices above marginal costs should be cut immediately, if not earlier. And, due to lack of inventories, they should be raised immediately when demand exceeds capacity. In sum, the prices of services, including transport services, should fluctuate more than the prices of storable goods and should respond much more quickly to changes in demand. For these reasons, service prices should be fixed by service producers, who would be the first to notice small changes in demand.

The prices of many listed securities and commodities now change every minute or hour on capitalist security and commodity exchanges. If all shippers could instantly learn of and react to transport rate changes, and if such rate changes were costless, transport rates should change every hour of every day. But rate changes create real costs, and require time to produce desired results. Careful research will be needed to determine how often each rate should change, but it is likely that few rates should change irregularly more often than once a month. However, few if any rates should remain fixed for more than three months.

Two-Class Fares and Rates — No passenger airplane, bus, ship, or train should depart on a long intercity trip with empty saleable seats. The best way to fill all seats is to sell two classes of tickets, one which guarantees a seat on the desired carrier and one which allows the purchaser to occupy a seat which would otherwise be empty. The price of the first class of tickets should be high enough to assure a seat on the desired carrier and to fill, on the average, perhaps 80% of all seats. The ideal percentage can only be determined by scientific research. The fluctuating standby fares should be low enough to fill all seats not occupied by class-one ticket holders, and to keep waiting lines at optimum levels. The total income from both classes of passengers should at least cover the average total marginal costs of each flight.

It may seem that the same two-price system should be used to assure full use of all space on freight carriers. However, the departure of freight carriers can usually be delayed until they are full without serious inconvenience to shippers. And the waiting time of a ton of passengers is worth far more than an equal waiting time of a ton of ordinary freight. Hence, it would probably be uneconomic to establish a two-class system of freight rates.

Separate Line-Haul and Terminal Freight Rates — The marginal costs of transport can be divided into two chief elements which vary independently of each other, namely line-haul costs and terminal costs. Line-haul costs are the costs of hauling trains between terminals. Terminal costs include all cost incurred in terminals. Few people realize that terminal costs amount to about half of transport costs.

Since terminal costs do not vary with the distance a shipment is moved, but do vary significanlty from terminal to terminal and according to the type of terminal service, while line-haul costs vary mainly with the gross weight of the train, the route, and the distance, these two components of total marginal costs should be separately calculated for each shipment or class of shipments. Probably all freight rates should be determined and published only as separate line-haul rates, terminal rates, and special charges, which the shipper must put together in order to determine in advance the total charge for any contemplated shipment. But if total charges are published for each possible shipment or class of shipments by each route, they should be based upon separate calculation of line-haul and terminal charges.

If cost accounting and the printing and use of thick rate books cost nothing, separate line-haul and terminal costs should be estimated for each possible line-haul or terminal use. Since cost accounting and thick rate books are very costly, however, the determination and use of freight rates should be simplified to the optimum degree, a point very difficult to determine, by grouping all types of terminal service at all terminals into a limited number of terminal rate classes and by grouping all possible line-hauls into a limited number of line-haul rate classes. It would then be possible to print all basic terminal and line-haul rates on a few pages. However, it would also be necessary to publish classification books classifying all termimals and all possible line-hauls into the classes shown in the short rate table.

In order to save the very substantial costs of using such classification books, it might seem desirable to establish uniform terminal charges for all terminals and uniform line-haul charges for all hauls of equal length. But this would make it impossible to encourage the use of partly idle terminals and routes, or to discourage the use of congested and/or high-cost terminals and routes. It would make all estimates of the marginal costs of freight transport less accurate.

In the case of letters, small packages, and, perhaps, all less-than-carload freight, the convenience to shippers and rate clerks of a simple rate system justifies simple uniform rate systems which ignore differences in marginal costs, but this is not true of carload shipments, which often cost several hundred dollars to move. And under socialism the proportion of freight shipped in carload losts would be much greater than it is today.

Rate Differences to Balance Traffic — Whenever the demand for transport is stronger in one direction than in another, and this necessitates an empty return haul, line-haul rates should be changed in such a way as to achieve an optimum degree of balance between freight movements in the two directions. In order to obtain freight for empty cars being returned to their point of origin, rates should be successively lowered until these empty cars are filled or until the rates reach the level of the marginal costs of such additional freight movement. In the case of empty cars which must be moved anyway, these costs are extremely low.

The total charges for shipping any given commodity in both directions should always be sufficient to at least cover all marginal costs involved. The allocation of these costs to the freight shipped in each direction should be determined by relative demand. The freight moving in the prevailing direction should pay all costs over and above the contribution of the freight moving in the opposite direction. This latter freight, moreover, should contribute nothing over and above the additional costs due solely to its shipment, until the freight movement in both directions is equal. Then the rates on return shipments should be raised to the highest possible point compatible with such balanced freight movement.

Rate Variations to Minimize Traffic Fluctuations — The demand for freight and passenger service is seasonal. In order to cut to the optimum degree seasonal fluctuations in the volume of traffic, the Transportation Trust should regularly vary its line-haul and terminal rates from season to season. During periods of slack demand, each rate should be set at a figure which just covers the low marginal costs prevailing at such times, and during the rest of the time rates should be high enough to cover the higher marginal costs then prevailing or to limit demand to the volume of service scheduled. Moreover, new transport facilities to meet peak demands should not be built until peak-traffic income is high enough to cover both the total fixed and variable costs of the extra capacity that this peak traffic uses.

In spite of the fact that seasonal fluctuations in car loadings are now largely due to the seasonal nature of agriculture, it is possible to eliminate the greater part of these fluctuations by a sound pricing policy. Wheat is harvested in one or two months of the year, but there is no reason why it should move to market immediately after being harvested. The same is true of most farm products, and of coal and lumber. Since freight rates make up a large share of the delivered cost of these commodities, slight variations in freight rates would control the time of their shipment. Of course, fluctuations in the shipment of highly perishable seasonal products cannot be eliminated, but these goods should pay all costs chargeable to them. If refrigerator cars are required to move fruit during only one month of the year, this fruit should on the average be charged the full cost of maintaining these idle cars throughout the rest of the year, and all other fresh produce shipped in refrigerator cars during the peak month should pay the same high rate.

Seasonal fluctuations in the use of specialized equipment such as coal cars and refrigerator cars are much greater than seasonal fluctuations in the total volume of railroad traffic. The rates on the idle specialized equipment should be reduced to bare variable cost during off seasons, and raised high enough to cover the entire year's fixed cost during seasonal peaks, provided, of course, that this will not reduce peak loads below capacity. No price above marginal costs should ever be fixed high enough to reduce production below capacity.

<u>Other Differences in Freight Rates</u> — While freight rates should be uniform for all commodities, except in so far as there are real differences in the marginal costs of moving them, there should be a high degree of diversity in freight rates. Transport costs differ widely from one railroad line to another and from one means of transport to another. These costs should be reflected directly in freight and passenger rates.

Under capitalism railroad rates are made uniform for different roads in spite of the fact that costs differ widely. The ICC aims at a rate schedule which will give the proper average profit on railroad capital as a whole. Under socialism, every single freight haul should pay its way, so far as it is economic to install the cost-accounting system necessary to bring this about. Whenever freight is moved which does not pay its own marginal costs, society is harmed because the real costs of the freight movement exceed the benefit created thereby. On the other hand, if unused capacity exists, every rate above marginal cost checks

125

the shipment of goods which would move at a lower rate, and thus prevents the creation of net social benefits.

All rate structures designed to yield only a proper average profit possess serious defects. They prevent the movement of some freight which ought to be moved, and they make possible the movement of some freight which ought not to be moved. The ideal rate system or structure is one in which every rate just equals the marginal costs involved.

Some compromise with this ideal must be made, of course. Up to a certain point, additional cost accounting is worthwhile because it makes possible the determination of more accurate specific costs and, hence, more economic rates. Beyond this point, the real costs of additional cost accounting outweigh the benefits of additional accuracy in costs and rates. Thus, while rates should agree roughly with costs, and differ as costs differ from one form of transportation to another, from one railroad to another, and from one mile of track to another, great accuracy should not be sought.

Differences in freight rates based upon the size of shipments are justified, so long as they merely reflect actual differences in marginal costs. Small consignments involve three distinct sources of additional expense: separate collection and delivery; separate handling; invoicing, and accounting at the freight depot; and less economical loading of freight cars.

Differences in rates based on type of car used, speed of service, insurance costs, etc., are also proper. All differences in freight rates which are based upon measurable differences in variable costs are justified, provided that the cost of measuring and using these cost variations is not larger than the gain from better pricing.

Rail-Car Rental Charges — It has long been customary for American railroads to impose daily car rental charges, called demurrage charges, on shippers and consignees who retain freight cars beyond a fixed period, such as three days. Under socialism car-rental charges should be retained and developed as a more important element in the railroad rate system, but their amount and use should be quite different.

When any particular type of car is in short supply, a car-rental charge just sufficient to balance supply and demand (including necessary minimum reserves of empty cars) should be imposed on all car-lot shippers for each day the car is in their use. On the other hand, when cars of the type in question are in excess supply at a given terminal, no car-rental charges should be imposed on any shipper, regardless of how long he keeps his cars. When cars are in excess supply, no costs are caused by the retention of cars by shippers, and some benefit to the latter is likely.

Proper car-rental charges would enable shippers and consignees to balance the cost of keeping cars in their possession one or more extra days against the often considerable advantages to them of longer use of railroad cars. Chief among these advantages are reductions of overtime wages and savings in storage costs.

<u>Free</u> Urban Passenger <u>Transport</u> — In <u>Liberal Socialism</u> we explained why first-class mail should be handled free of charge and why local urban mass passenger service also should become a free good (pp. 328-29). It is unnecessary to repeat these explanations here, but we wish to qualify and supplement that treatment of urban passenger transport.

When we argued that all urban mass passenger transport should be free, we were thinking of unplanned capitalist cities in which all residents are allowed to operate private cars on city streets. As explained in Chapters III and IV of this volume, a socialist government should gradually replace all such cities with new planned garden cities so designed that most residents will walk or cycle to work, shops, and schools. In such new cities it would be feasible and desirable to prohibit the use of private cars on nearly all city streets. If this were done, free mass transit would not be needed to persuade residents to reduce their use of private cars on city streets.

Nevertheless, some of the other arguments for free provision of mass transit would still be valid. Free provision would save the costs of hiring conductors to collect fares, or would free vehicle operators of this time-consuming chore. It would also assure increased use of costly transport facilities during off-peak hours, when marginal costs are low or negligible.

On the other hand, free provision would induce many residents to ride when they ought to get much-needed exercise by walking or cycling. And it would increase taxes. We conclude, therefore, that in a planned socialist city local mass transit should not be free during hours of peak use, but should perhaps be free during other hours.

D. Investment in Transport Facilities

As explained in <u>Liberal Socialism</u>, investment in new capital goods or facilities always causes a lumpy, not a marginal, change in factor supply. Hence, every proposed investment should be evaluated by means of total, not marginal, cost-benefit analysis.

Many investments in transport involve very large sums of capital and create very large new transport facilities — airports, railroad lines, railroad terminals, etc. The use of such new facilities can result in large new consumers' surpluses, which should always be considered in total analysis. Such additional surpluses may fully offset a very large financial loss, an ideal deficit, resulting from the relevant investment. Private transport firms cannot bear such losses, and therefore often underinvest in transport facilities A socialist Transportation Trust should be heavily subsidized, so that it can achieve both optimum investment in facilities and optimum use of them after they have been built.

Investment in each form of transport, each route, each item of equipment, and in any other aid to transportation should be increased whenever it is expected that the additional investment will yield a net total benefit over the life of the additional capital goods. The term <u>net total benefit</u> does not mean an increment in total profit, but a net surplus of total revenue and consumers' surplus from the additional services over the total costs of the additional factors used to provide these services.

Every transport industry has decreasing costs. The larger the volume of traffic by any means on any route, the lower the marginal cost when capital facilities have been designed to serve the enlarged volume. Marginal costs rise temporarily when the volume of traffic approaches or exceeds the capacity of given facilities, but every rational expansion of facilities lowers marginal costs. It follows that, whenever investment is optimum, charging non-discriminatory rates equal to marginal costs would result in large deficits, which we have called ideal deficits because they would result from ideal investment and ideal price determination (<u>LS</u>, pp. 239-41).

In a socialist economy ideal deficits should occur in all non-extractive industries, but they should be especially high in railroad and pipe line transportation because fixed costs are relatively very high in these industries, because facility increments are often very large, and because the marginal-cost curves of these industries decline more steeply than such curves in most other non-extractive industries.

For instance, when a single-track railroad is converted into a double-track road, the new railroad can handle over three times as much traffic at faster speeds, but road maintenance costs increase much less than 100%. And fuel costs per ton-mile decrease because locomotives do not have to stop and start as often. Moreover, every increase in the volume of traffic permits the use of more powerful locomotives and longer trains, more unit trains, and more efficient container-handling equipment. Many other such economies could be mentioned.

Ideal deficits in transport industries can easily be avoided, without raising prices above marginal costs, by restricting investment until prices equal to marginal cost become profitable. It is ideal investment which should produce ideal deficits. It should also permit creation of the large consumers' surpluses needed to justify such deficits.

E. Taxation

Transportation costs, prices, and profits have long been seriously affected by taxes, most of which are uneconomic. Under socialism, such taxation should be radically reformed.

There are three basic principles which should govern the taxation of all forms of transport under socialism. First, no general revenue tax (one levied primarily to raise revenue) should fall upon any mode of transport. All property taxes, excise taxes, income taxes, and other business taxes levied solely or primarily to raise revenue should be abolished. This prohibition applies to virtually all taxes now paid by American transport lines.

The second basic principle is that all unpaid real costs (external diseconomies) should be measured by taxes which turn real costs into money costs. This rule applies, of course, to all socialist industries, but its application to transportation is especially important because most methods of transport cause relatively large unpaid costs — air pollution, water pollution, noise, vibration, ugliness, accidents, interference with TV reception, and so forth.

Gasoline taxes can be used to serve several distinct functions — financing insurance, allocating highway costs, reducing congestion, etc. — but a part of every gas tax should measure unpaid marginal road-transport costs — including air pollution, noise, and vibration. Since trucks cause much more of these costs than do private passenger cars, gasoline sold for use in trucks should bear a relatively high sales-tax increment designed to measure unpaid costs.

Airplanes cause air pollution, unpleasant noise, and vibration, and interfere with TV and radio reception. One easy way to allocate unpaid air-pollution costs to planes responsible for them would be to impose a tax on all aviation gasoline. All airplanes should be classified according to the amount of air pollution they produce and the most polluting planes should pay the highest gas taxes. This would provide financial incentives for the design, production, and use of cleaner planes.

Airplanes pollute the air throughout each trip but their noise and TV interference are annoying chiefly when they fly low over urban areas, usually near terminal airports. Gas taxes are a poor means of allocating these real costs. Special additions to terminal charges would be preferable. They should be based upon the amount of noise each plane creates when landing and taking off.

Transportation always involves the risk of losses due to accidents, and many of these losses are unpaid costs. Insurance is economic not only because it converts large unexpected losses into small regular costs but also because it turns many unpaid external costs into paid internal costs. All socialist transport agencies should carry enough accident insurance to convert all costs of transport accidents into paid costs of operation. For most road transport, gas taxes are the best means of financing such insurance.

The third principle which should govern transport taxation is that special price taxes should be used to allocate the user-cost part of street and highway maintenance to those responsible for them. By user costs we mean costs due to highway use. Most road maintenance costs are due to weathering, not to the passage of vehicles.

Price taxes, like prices, should normally measure only real costs at the margin. The best tax to measure highway-use costs is a gas tax, or, more precisely, a special addition to the gas tax, but tire taxes may also be desirable.

The fourth and final principle is that no other unequal tax should be levied on any transport facility or service. Any other tax which falls unequally on different transport facilities or services would discriminate against certain transport services and create money costs which do not measure real costs.

In America today gasoline taxes are used to cover non-user highway maintenance costs and to finance the construction of new highways. In a socialist economy all investment, including that in new highways, should be financed by nationwide saving. No industry should be required or permitted to finance its own investment, and no special sales taxes should be used for this purpose (see LS, p. 127).

CHAPTER VI

MANUFACTURING

Manufacturing is the transformation of raw materials and/or components into more nearly finished portable products. It includes both handicraft production and large-scale mechanized factory production. In advanced countries factories have already largely replaced handicraft shops. In a mature socialist economy nearly all handicraft production will be done as a hobby. In this chapter, therefore, we discuss only manufacturing in large mechanized plants.
Manufacturing produces about 30% of the U.S. national income, and this share has remained stable since 1950. This suggests that most of the talk about a new "post-industrial age" is misleading.

A. Organization

Most plants which process mineral ores, petroleum, and natural gas should probably be located at or near the main supply source and managed by the relevant branches of the mineral-producing trusts. Most plants which process raw agricultural products in farm towns should probably be controlled by the Division of Agriculture. All other manufacturing plants should be operated by: (1) a Division of Metals — including a Steel Trust, an Aluminum Trust, a Non-Ferrous Metals Trust, (2) a Division of Machinery — including a Machine Trust and an Airplane Trust, and (3) a Division of Light Industry — including a Textile Trust, a Clothing Trust, a House Furnishings Trust, a Printing Trust, and a Paper Trust (see LS, p. 114). This organization plan is, of course, very tentative.

Basic Principles of Organization — In Chapter V of Liberal Socialism we stated four basic principles of socialist economic organization which should be applied in every socialist industry, including all manufacturing industries. These principles are: (1) universal monopoly, (2) centralization of ultimate control, (3) decentralization of subordinate decision making, and (4) functional organization. Since these rules were discussed in detail in Liberal Socialism, and, since they apply equally to all industries, we shall merely summarize their application to manufacturing here.

All socialist manufacturing plants should be monopolies. Each plant should supply all consumers within its marketing area. There should be no cross shipment of like goods. Monopolistic organization would end all the wastes of competition and imperfect competition discussed in great detail in our book, <u>The Case for Liberal Socialism</u>, and would permit the achievement of an optimum scale of production in each factory.

Within each plant and each trust, control over all personnel and policies should be completely centralized. All general policies should be formulated at the top, and all executives should be appointed by their immediate superiors. But all executives should delegate to junior executives the decisions which the latter are best qualified and situated to make. For instance, all output and price decisions should be left to local plant managers and price fixers. There should be no centralized price-output planning or current operating control.

The principle of functional management implies that each manufacturing trust should be primarily organized into functional, not regional, units.

<u>Plant Location</u> — The choice of where to locate a new factory may be divided into two parts, the problem of which region or city the plant should be located in and the problem of where the plant should be placed within the city chosen for its location. The first location problem should be solved by the trust which will operate the plant; the second, by the trust which plans and builds new cities. Let us consider first the problem of regional location.

Every new factory should be located so as to yield the maximum total return (quasi-rent) from the investment in it. Correct regional location helps to achieve this goal chiefly by minimizing the sum total of all freight-in and freight-out costs. Freight-in costs are those included in the delivered costs of raw materials, components, fuels, and supplies. Freight-out costs are those paid for the shipment of factory products to buyers.

When raw materials are widely or universally available — air, salt water, sand, clay, wood, etc. — factories should be located as near as possible to the consumers of their products. When raw materials are concentrated in one or a few areas and are heavy or bulky, factories should be located near the source of their chief raw material.

These and other factors which should influence regional location of new factories have been thoroughly and competently discussed by capitalist economists. Their sound conclusions would be equally valid under socialism if socialist freight rates were ideal. The major new factors would be these new ideal freight rates and monopoly, so we discuss them only.

In America, freight rates are now based primarily on ability to pay, not on cost. Under socialism they should be based on marginal cost, which is usually far below any estimate of average cost. The application of this new socialist principle would sharply lower average freight rates and would radically change the rate structure. Most freight rates for factory products are now two to ten times as high as the freight rates on the materials and fuel used to produce these products. Moreover, raw materials are much more heavy and/or bulky than the finished goods made from them. And fuel is entirely consumed in production. Therefore, under socialism nearly all factories using fuel and heavy raw materials obtained from distant sources should be replaced by new factories located much nearer the domestic sources of such fuel and materials, and/or the ports where they are imported. For instance, most U.S. cotton textile plants should be relocated in or near cotton-growing areas, and should be scattered throughout these areas so as to minimize the total cost of shipping cotton to textile mills.

Of course, factory location should also be affected by climate. As average real income continues to rise, most workers will become increasingly willing to accept wage cuts in order to live in areas with a superior climate. The resulting wage differentials will justify the location of many more new factories in areas which enjoy a superior climate but are not as close to sources of fuel and raw materials as areas with less desirable climates.

Under capitalism most new factories are located in or near large old cities in order to be near adequate supplies of skilled labor and good markets. That is one of the chief reasons why many capitalist cities have grown far beyond the ideal size and still continue to grow. As explained in our chapters on new-city planning, nearly all new socialist factories should be located in new cities. This means that the housing and all the other urban facilities needed by the workers in a new factory should be built at the same time the new factory is built, and all of these should make up a new town in a new city.

Capitalist firms try to locate new factories in areas where wage rates are relatively low and unemployment is high. In a socialist economy there should be no unemployment anywhere, and wage rates in a new factory town might have to be initially higher than wage rates in old factory towns in order to attract sufficient workers.

Let us turn now to the problem of intra-city plant location. As explained above, each new plant should be built as an essential major component of a planned now town in a planned new city. The size of each new plant and its specific location within a new town should be determined largely by those who plan and build the new town, not by the executives of the national trust which will operate the new plant. Most new factories should be located in the center of a planned new town and should be just large enough to employ all workers not employed elsewhere in the town.

Plant Size — As explained in Chapter IV, hardly any factory should be so large that it requires a labor force larger than that which could be supplied by a town of ideal size. In other words, the upper limit on plant size should be determined by city planners, not by manufacturing executives. These planners should of course cooperate closely with the top regional executives of each trust for whom they build a new factory, but city planners should have the final work on both intra-city plant location and plant size.

Since nearly all well-planned new towns should be of about the same size and since most manufacturing plants should be located in the center of such towns and employ only local town residents, the great majority of factories should employ about the same number of people. In our chapter on new-city planning, we suggested a town population of 50 to 75 thousand initially, which implies a factory work force of 12 to 18 thousand. This limit would now permit a great increase in the scale of production of nearly all privately owned factories. In 1967, over 99% of U.S. factories had fewer than 1,000 employees, and employed 67% of all factory workers.

A monopolistic organization of socialist manufacturing industries and an ideal simplification of products (discussed below) would permit and should result in a great increase in the size of the average factory and/or a great increase in specialization among factories. Ideal socialist city planning would limit the maximum size of individual factories, but not the degree of their specialization. The latter should be limited primarily by transportation costs which have little effect upon compact, valuable products like watches, electric razors, and electronic components. In a socialist economy, therefore, the entire national output of most models of such goods should be manufactured in a single factory. And nearly all socialist factories should specialize far more intensively than do their capitalist counterparts today.

A factory located in the center of a well-planned new town should never be expanded to permit an increase in its work force. Its output could be expanded by installing improved equipment, by using better materials or more components produced elsewhere, by redesigning products or work processes, by improving employees, and by other means which require no more labor, but output should never be expanded by any measure which would require more workers. Rather, every local plant manager should plan for a gradual but continuous decline in his labor force. As explained earlier, the population, and therefore the work force, of every planned new city and town should decline slowly and indefinitely in order to permit a steady rise in living and housing standards without increasing city or town size.

B. Product Simplification

For reasons explained in <u>Liberal Socialism</u> (pp. 229-30), the diversification of manufactured products under capitalism has proceeded far beyond the optimum level. The transition from capitalism to socialism should therefore radically reduce the variety of manufacturing goods produced in advanced countries. For instance, the number of different styles and models of automobiles produced in the United States should probably be reduced by at least 90%. Moreover, the number of style changes in each decade should be equally reduced.

Such simplification measures would yield many economic benefits. They would make it much easier for garages to obtain and stock repair parts, and for mechanics to learn how to repair automobiles. They would justify the development of new, and the wider use of most old, labor-saving tools and machines in auto repair shops. They would permit a drastic reduction in the inventories of repair parts and automobiles. They would allow a great increase in the scale of production of all automobile components and repair parts, which would markedly reduce manufacturing costs. They would sharply reduce the costs of marketing new and used cars. They would reduce the difficulties consumers have in choosing among different car models, and would permit a wiser choice. Hence, they would probably reduce the costs of manufacturing, repairing, and selling new cars and spare parts by over 25%.

We have taken all these illustrations from the automobile manufacturing, marketing, and repair industries because autos are now the most important manufactured good, but simplification of other goods should make possible notable economies in their manufacture, marketing, and repair.

The radical simplification of products, the monopolistic reorganization of industry, the increase in average factory size, and the much more complete specialization among factories recommended above would make economic a far more complete mechanization and automation of most manufacturing plants. This should result in both a more extensive use of old methods of mechanization and automation and the development and use of new methods of mechanization and automation. Research on these problems would suddenly become far more productive after a socialist reorganization of manufacturing industries, and therefore much larger sums should be invested in such research.

C. Product Improvement

Most manufactured goods now produced in capitalist countries should be radically redesigned if they are to continue in production under socialism. They should be redesigned so as to make them both more durable and much easier to repair. For instance, autos should be designed so that on the average they will last over 20 years instead of only 10 years. Most auto repairs should be made by replacing parts, not by repairing them in the repair shop. If autos were properly designed, it would become almost as easy to replace any part as it now is to replace a wheel. And most parts can be repaired much better and/or more cheaply after they have been detached from a car and sent to a shop specializing in repairing, reconditioning, and/or rebuilding the parts in question.

Under capitalism it is often profitable knowingly to produce goods which wear out or break down before they should because this increases sales. If one oligopolist makes his product more durable and/or easier to repair, and initially profits thereby, the other oligopolists soon follow suit, which ends his advantage and increases costs for all producers more than it increases industry sales. Under private oligopoly, such product improvements are as unprofitable as price cuts.

For similar reasons, capitalist oligopolists often produce home appliances which use far more fuel, water, or electricity than they should. Their salesmen stress low original costs, and fail to advise potential customers of excessively high operating costs. In a socialist economy each home appliance should be designed to minimize total combined operating, depreciation, energy and other costs over the life of the appliance, and consumers should be fully informed concerning such total costs. No appliance catalog or price tag should list original cost only.

If automobiles and their repair parts were radically simplified, standardized, and made far more durable, it would become economic to collect and reuse most of the undamaged parts in all wrecked cars. New cars should be designed so as to facilitate this final disassembly and recycling. Damaged metal parts should be repaired or recycled as scrap metal. Fortunately, the same design features which would simplify removal of parts for repair would also simplify final disassembly and recycling of wrecked-car parts.

Standardization, simplification, monopoly, and elimination of style cycles will also make it economic to design all factory equipment and machines for a longer life. Competition and style cycles now shorten the life of most factories and most equipment and machines in them. Socialist engineers should therefore redesign nearly all factory equipment and machines to make them more durable and more easily repairable. And, when finally wrecked, such machines should provide many usable repair parts.

All manufactured goods should be designed so as to reduce optimally both pollution and the number of accidents resulting from their use. It might be desirable to create a special independent agency to review all manufactured products and determine whether they are optimally safe and non-polluting, but, in any case, all inventors and product designers should be taught how to minimize pollution and accidents by suitable design changes.

Capitalist manufacturers rarely test new materials, parts, and finished goods as carefully as would be socially desirable before these goods are put into mass production. They are well aware that most consumers are poor judges of durability, and that it may be years before consumers learn of defects in the goods they buy. Often one competitor is eager to bring out a new product or model before a competitor does so. And style cycles require so many model changes that there is little time to test mew models which, in any case, will only be produced for a few months.

Simplification of factory products would greatly increase the total output of each model of a good, and this output increase alone would make it economic to spend far more on testing each new model before it is approved for production. Moreover, any socialist trust should give more attention to consumer needs than do profit-seeking private firms. For both reasons, each new factory product should be tested for durability, washability, cleanability, repairability, safety, and pollution effects far more thoroughly than such products are now tested in capitalist countries. And the resulting data should be provided to all potential customers in catalogs, in sales brochures, and on labels or tags attached to each product.

D. Price-Output Control

In a liberal socialist economy every change in the output of a manufactured good should be the result of a previous price change and/or a substitute for a new price change. And each price change should be a result of a previous output change and/or a substitute for a new output change. Hence, we treat output control and price control together in this section. We begin with output control.

Socialist output theory is far more important than socialist price theory. The chief goal of socialist economic policy should be to achieve optimum outputs, not optimum prices. Many economic goods should be provided free of charge. And, even for price goods, price determination should be merely a means of achieving ideal outputs. Hence, output theory, not price theory, is the heart of socialist economic theory. By contrast, orthodox capitalist microeconomics is largely a theory of price determination.

Nearly all of the theory stated here is short-run output theory. It deals only with how to control outputs in existing factories. The problem of when to build new factories or rebuild old ones belongs to the theory of investment. We shall largely ignore the application of general investment theory to factories because it presents no new or special problems except those discussed in our chapters on city planning.

Under capitalism the current output of each factory is strongly influenced by current demand. Such demand should have far less influence on the output of a socialist factory in a planned town. It is nevertheless worth noting here that such demand would fluctuate less than it now fluctuates in advanced capitalist economies.

Each socialist factory should be a monopoly. The mere creation of a monopoly tends to stabilize demand because the total demand for any good changes less than any part of it, especially the demand for the output of one of several competing plants.

Moreover, a socialist manufacturing monopoly should drastically reduce the number of styles and models of nearly all factory products, which would concentrate demand in much larger totals and therefore make them more stable. And socialist equalization of personal incomes would also tend to concentrate demand on a smaller variety of manufactured goods, which would tend to stabilize the demand for each good. Finally, a socialist government would achieve and maintain full employment, which would radically reduce the continuous fluctuations in the total demand for each class of factory product. It would largely end the so-called business cycle.

The stabilization of demand produced by these socialist reforms would make it much easier for socialist factory managers to stabilize the outputs of their plants.

Stable Output at Capacity — The most basic and general principle of socialist factory output control is that nearly all plants should operate at near-capacity levels from the time they are built until they are rebuilt or replaced. Obviously, factories which process perishable seasonal farm and sea products could not operate continuously at capacity, but nearly all other factories should do so, especially those located in new planned socialist factory towns. And within a few decades after the achievement of full socialism, all factories should be so located.

The chief reason why factories so located should operate at near-capacity levels throughout their existence is that each should be originally designed to assure full employment for all would-be workers in the planned town in which it is built. By assuring full employment, it would also assure full occupancy and use of all town housing, commercial buildings, and other local facilities. The investment in the factory itself and in other town facilities, i.e., in the planned town, would be so large, and the marginal costs of factory operation at any below-capacity level would be so small, that near-capacity operation would almost always be economic.

The Shape of the Marginal-Cost Curve — As explained in *Liberal Socialism*, the output of each price good should be increased or decreased until price equals marginal cost, narrowly defined. In a typical factory the marginal-cost curve is flat and low, compared with any so-called average-cost curve, until output rises almost to or beyond capacity. Then, marginal costs rise sharply and indefinitely. Prices equal to marginal costs at output levels substantially below capacity are very unprofitable. Therefore, investment in plant expansion should be limited sufficiently to justify operation of most existing factories at levels near or above capacity, where prices equal to marginal cost can yield an income which in time largely justifies the last increment in investment. This argument for continuous operation at near-capacity level applies to factories in old or unplanned cities, as well as to those in new planned factory towns.

In many large capitalist factories non-marginal costs already amount to much more than half of total costs. And the inevitable progress of technology and economic reform will make non-marginal costs relatively more and more important. For instance, the elimination of business fluctuations, the creation of socialist monopolies, and socialist simplification of manufactured goods will make far more mechanization and higher interest costs economic, even without any further mechanical progress, because each of these reforms will increase the scale of production and/or reduce fluctuations in output. Moreover, managers of socialist factories should begin to treat as fixed or non-marginal expenses certain costs and expenses which capitalists often treat as marginal costs, for instance, advertising, research and development, and selling costs.

A socialist factory and factory town should not be built unless the entire investment (in housing, stores, etc., as well as in factories) is expected to yield a total net benefit equal to the expected total interest cost. The executives who approve such investments will inevitably fail to predict future prices, rentals, and interest rates perfectly. They will often overinvest enough to reduce prices and rentals below the levels which would yield the desired return, but would rarely if ever overinvest enough to reduce the prices of factory products to below-capacity marginal costs. The products of nearly all socialist factories should normally sell for prices which are two to ten times as high as such marginal costs.

When investment in any branch of manufacturing is insufficient, prices will rise and factories will earn excessive profits (quasi rents). The proper eventual response to such investment profits would be to build new factories in new factory towns, not to hire more workers and increase outputs in old factory towns, which would have no vacant housing and unused urban facilities. Moreover, it is usually uneconomic to increase the output of old factories above capacity levels.

There should be no idle standby manufacturing plants in a socialist economy because there should be no standby workers and standby towns to house such workers. If it is economic to prepare for unexpected increases in future demand, this should be done by building up inventories, not by maintaining standby factories or capacity. Of course, such demand increases would be far less likely under socialism than they now are under capitalism.

When new labor-saving machines and/or methods are introduced into a socialist factory in a planned town, no reduction in the work force should follow. Rather, the plant should be reconstructed so that all the old workers can continue to work and produce a larger output. This may require more space and equipment for handling a larger flow of raw materials and goods in process, as well as the installation of new production equipment. Additional space should usually be secured by vertical expansion.

The output of a socialist factory in a planned socialist factory town should be almost entirely determined by the size of the town, once it has been built, not by the demand for its product. When demand falls enough to reduce price below marginal cost for a long period, the product should be changed or replaced but the factory work force should remain stable.

If it is ever necessary to close down a factory in a planned town in order to remodel it, the old work force should be retained, perhaps retrained, given long vacations, and/or provided with other temporary jobs, such as rebuilding the plant or improving local gardens and playgrounds. No worker should suffer loss of income when a plant is renovated or replaced, and no factory in a planned town should ever be closed or torn down without being replaced by a plant which provides new jobs for all the old employees.

Of course, if the only factory in a planned socialist new town manufactures two or more similar products with the same kinds of skilled workers and the same machines, it should shift workers and machines from one product to the other whenever relevant selling prices and marginal costs change and remain changed for a long time. But a decline in the combined demand for both or all non-perishable products manufactured in such a factory should rarely if ever result in non-seasonal cuts in its total output and therefore in the town or factory work-force.

As noted earlier, the population and total work-force of each planned town should decline gradually as real wages rise, but this work-force decline should occur whether the demand for local factory products rises or falls.

It may be objected that the principle of continuous factory operation at near-capacity levels is unsound because output should be cut sharply whenever raw material costs rise greatly. However, we have explained that output should normally be at a level where marginal cost is two to ten times as high as average marginal cost. Therefore, even a 100% increase in raw material costs would rarely raise the marginal-cost curve enough to justify a substantial output cut. In any case, the elimination of extreme fluctuations in total factory output would itself greatly reduce the width of short-run changes in raw material costs.

More Inventory Changes — Another reason why socialist factory outputs should fluctuate far less than capitalist factory outputs is that inventory changes should replace or minimize output changes much more often and/or more fully than they do under capitalism. A socialist monopoly could borrow money to build up inventories much more easily and cheaply than most competing capitalist firms can do so. Moreover, if the managers of a socialist factory had to pay the rent for all vacant local housing formerly occupied by its employees, they would usually find it more economic to build up inventories and/or reduce prices rather than reduce their work-force when demand for their products declines.

Of course, inventory expansion should be only a temporary response to a fall in demand. If the fall lasts for more than a few months, it should be followed by a price cut and an inventory reduction.

Plants which process fresh seasonal food products must operate seasonally, but plants which experience seasonal changes in the demand for storable goods should operate at capacity throughout the year, building up stocks in the off season and reducing them in the season. It is much cheaper to store goods than to pay unemployment benefits to seasonally idle workers. And both the creation of monopolies and the elimination of style cycles and uneconomic model changes would greatly reduce the risk involved in storing seasonal manufactured goods.

More Price Changes — Capitalist factory managers often reduce the output of an existing plant in order to avoid a price cut when sales decline. Under socialism, price cuts and inventory expansions should nearly always make such output cuts unnecessary. Prices should equal marginal costs whenever possible, and should always balance supply and demand. But they should achieve this balance largely by changing sales and investment, not by changing the output from an existing factory. It is much easier and cheaper to change the price of a manufactured good than to change the output and work force of the plant which manufactures it.

The chief social functions of a socialist factory are to provide a desired amount of products and a desired number of stable jobs, not to earn a profit or to avoid a loss. If the sales of its products decline, it should first increase its inventories. If sales do not soon recover, it should reduce its prices enough to restore sales to the plant capacity level. The work force and wage rates should remain unchanged. The price cuts would reduce the total plant surplus (quasi-rent), which would discourage the construction of new plants producing similar manufactured goods. The resulting construction cut would usually cause prices to rise until old plants again yield large quasi-rents.

Proper determination of the prices of socialist factory output would help to keep factories operating continuously at near capacity levels by influencing exports as well as by influencing domestic sales. It would make it profitable and economic to increase exports whenever domestic demand falls, and vice versa, thus stabilizing total sales. Since marginal costs are normally far below all estimates of so-called average costs, very great export price reductions might be desirable in order to keep domestic plants operating at capacity when domestic sales decline.

Continuous Plant Operation — The above statement of the case for operating socialist factories at or near capacity not only justifies continuous capacity production during one or two shifts five days a week but also usually justifies continuous capacity production 20 to 24 hours a day 365 days a year. Higher wages should be paid night-shift and holiday workers, but the increase in wage costs would rarely raise marginal-cost curves enough to make night and holiday operation uneconomic.

As explained in Liberal Socialism (pp. 140-41), every rise in the amount of capital funds invested per worker increases the benefit from more complete utilization of capital facilities. And technological progress will continue to increase investment ratios indefinitely.

In 1970 the average wage of American factory workers was about $8,000 per year and the average investment in facilities and inventories about $16,000 per worker. The average pre-income-tax return on this investment was about 20%, or 40% of wages. The typical plant operated only forty hours a week or 2000 hours a year. If it had operated a second shift, it could therefore have afforded to raise wages for all extra workers about 40%, and still obtain the same return on its total investment. Such potential wage increases will rise steadily as investment per worker continues to rise faster than wages.

To help achieve continuous operation of their plants throughout the year, socialist factory managers should induce more workers to take part or all of their vacations in the off-vacation-peak months, especially in the winter. Managers should offer substantial financial inducements and/or longer vacations to those workers who take part or all of their vacations in less popular months. Wage rates should be significantly higher in summer months for the same reasons that they should be markedly higher for night-shift workers. They should vary from month to month just enough to achieve an equal work force during all months of the year.

Stable Wage Rates — If the output of an existing socialist factory is never reduced temporarily, it will never be necessary to reduce its wage rates in order to reduce its work force temporarily. Wage rates should normally rise slowly and steadily as the overall national real product of labor rises, but they should not be raised or lowered as a means or result of short-run factory output changes. However, wage rate changes needed to achieve and maintain capacity operation in an existing factory would nearly always be economic.

The wage rates of workers in unprofitable factories should be as high as those in profitable factories, other factors being equal, because wage rates should measure the marginal real costs of labor, which are unaffected by factory profit or loss. Moreover, a cut in factory wage rates caused by an operating loss would cause a decline in the factory work force, a decline which would reduce factory output below the optimum, near-capacity level, would leave some local housing vacant, and would reduce the use of local retail and other facilities. Finally, it would be difficult and uneconomic to cut the wage rates of factory workers, half the work-force in a planned one-factory town, without cutting equally the wage rates of other local workers, which would further change all local costs, prices, and rentals.

It may be objected that wage rates should measure marginal value products (vmp's), as well as the marginal real cost (pain) of labor, and that therefore socialist factory wages should fall whenever the price of the product falls. But workers' vmp's are rarely determinable (LS, 379-80). Moreover, marginal cost rises so sharply at or near capacity output that a very small, often insignificant, reduction in output can raise any determinable vmp of labor enough to keep it equal to the wage rate whenever the price of the product falls. And this very slight output cut is normally preferable to a cut in wage rates.

If a new planned town is built to house and service the workers in a new factory, and demand for its products later becomes insufficient to justify the original investment, the responsible trust, not the workers who settle in the new town and work in the factory, should be penalized. Therefore, the size of the work-force and the level of wage rates should not fall when demand falls. Of course, in a growing economy socialist monopolies should rarely overinvest in new factories, and, when they do, demand should soon grow enough to justify higher prices and wage rates. And any unexpected temporary loss in one factory town would usually be offset by unexpectedly high returns in other towns. Underinvestment should be as common as overinvestment.

No Output Planning — The principle that every socialist factory should be run at near-capacity levels throughout its existence implies that it would be unnecessary and uneconomic to plan the outputs of such factories in advance. Outputs would be determined at the time plants are originally constructed, not when current operating decisions are made. Or, more accurately, these decisions should always result in capacity operation, and capacity levels are determined when plants are built or rebuilt.

It may be argued that even if current output is not planned, investment in plant capacity should be planned, but this argument is unsound. Total investment each year must be economically allocated to individual industries and factory towns, but mere allocation is not economic planning. Such planning determines outputs and allocations in advance, before relevant costs and benefits can be known and before final decisions need be made. Future investments should be estimated or budgeted in advance, in order to prepare for and help coordinate final investment decisions, but such decisions should never be planned in advance (LS, 236-38).

Repair Parts Prices and Outputs — Most capitalist factories charge excessive prices for spare parts. For instance, the parts in an American automobile may sell individually for ten times their cost to the manufacturer. American car manufacturers earn more profit on parts than on new cars. In order to maximize these profits, each firm designs its parts to be different from those of competitors, and changes them frequently so that independent parts manufacturers must redesign and catch up after new models come out. Socialist monopoly and standardization should drastically cut such waste.

In a socialist society spare parts should be sold to repair shops and consumers at a price which just covers wholesale price (the price paid by the manufacturer) plus any distribution costs. Distribution costs of standardized parts should rarely exceed 50% of the producer's price to assembly plants.

It is extremely important that socialist factories produce enough of each spare part and distribute them so that repairs need never be delayed by the lack of needed parts. It is very uneconomic to have an expensive machine idle because one repair part is unobtainable. Hence, inventories of each spare part in each region should be more than adequate, and arrangements for fast delivery of each spare part to each repair shop should be made.

Many reports of the serious shortage of spare parts in the USSR have been published. The major reason for these shortages seems to be that central planners cannot respond properly to the needs of local consumers and repair shops. The adoption of liberal socialism would solve this problem because it would reform and decentralize output control.

E. Incentives for Managers

The use of suitable pecuniary and non-pecuniary incentives would induce factory designers and managers to be more efficient than they would otherwise be. Under capitalism the chief incentive for owner-managers is additional profit. This incentive often induces factory owners to adopt uneconomic policies — such as the creation of style cycles and the use of advertising. And the profits of factory owners are often increased by events beyond their control — such as reductions in raw material costs. Moreover, continuing marginal profits are always evidence of poor management (LS, 185-89). Sound socialist management of plants in decreasing-cost industries, notably manufacturing, would minimize marginal profits and losses, and would result in substantial continuing overall or total losses. Hence, a share in either marginal or total profits is a very poor incentive for socialist factory managers.

Of course, many capitalist factories are managed by salaried executives who receive no share of profits. For them the chief incentives to good work are the hope of promotion and of salary increases. Both of these incentives should be preserved under socialism. However, the reasons for promotion and salary increases should be quite different.

Under capitalism salaried factory managers are rewarded by promotion and salary raises whenever they help to increase profits, but many management policies which increase profits are uneconomic. Under socialism factory managers should be rewarded only for policies which increase economic welfare.

Those who decide when and where to build new factories should be rewarded for avoiding uneconomic overcapacity and undercapacity, and for minimizing the sum of freight-in and freight-out costs. Those who design new factories should be rewarded according to how well they maximize the rate of quasi-rent return from the new factory facilities. Those who operate the new factories should be rewarded according to how far they lower marginal-cost curves without reducing wage rates, and how well they minimize variable intra-marginal expenses without reducing outputs and wage rates. Every factory planner, designer, and manager would of course have a superior in a position to apply these incentive policies because all socialist factories would be operated by national monopolies.

It is usually impossible to measure the marginal value products (vmp's) of executive (LS, 379-80), and, even if they were determinable, executive salaries ought not to equal them (LS, 400-01). When executives improve their performance, they should receive small salary increases or bonuses, but no effort should be made to make these pecuniary rewards equal the increases in the relevant vmp's.

Praise and promotion should be the chief rewards used to induce socialist manufacturing executives to perform their functions effectively and efficiently. The higher the executive, the more emphasis should be place on these incentives because the highest executives are most influenced by them.

The president of General Motors, the largest American manufacturing firm, now receives about one million dollars a year in salary and bonuses. Such high incomes are a result of competition among employers for scarce, able executives, and also of the power of some top capitalist executives to fix their own salaries. The President of the United States is paid far less than the president of General Motors, but there is never any shortage of candidates for the office. If the salaries of all such executives were reduced by 90%, there would be no shortage of able applicants for the jobs. In a socialist America no senior executive should be paid more than two or three times the average wage of all workers. But such executives should have the use of impressive offices and be rewarded with medals, honors, and public praise whenever they achieve some important new product improvement or cost reduction.

Factory managers, like other executives, are much more interested in their relative salary ranking than in the absolute level of their salary. If top salaries were reduced by 90%, salary raises could be reduced equally without reducing their incentive effects. And any reduction in incentive would be more than offset by the benefits from the resulting reduction of income differentials.

F. Job Satisfaction

Every economic system performs two chief functions. It produces a large quantity of economic goods whose consumption gives pleasure to all consumers, and it also provides nearly all members of the workforce with jobs, the performance of which is usually pleasant, i.e., yields net job satisfaction. If all work were made as interesting and pleasant as it could and should be in an affluent society, the net economic welfare obtained from work might be larger for most workers than the economic benefit they obtain from consuming all non-essential economic goods. Thus a measure of economic income which includes only estimates of the value of the output of economic goods is a very imperfect measure of total economic welfare. However, it is very difficult to measure changes in the total national satisfaction from labor.

Up to the present time, economists have given nearly all of their attention to the problems involved in performing the first of these functions, the production of economic goods. They have largely ignored the problem of how to maximize and equalize net job satisfaction. They have given some slight attention to the problem of how to increase output by making work less painful and tiring, but they have rarely treated job satisfaction as a major and independent economic goal, one whose fuller achievement may require and justify a reduction in the output of economic goods and/or a very large investment in R and D and new capital goods.

Nearly all capitalist employers have grossly neglected the problem of optimizing job satisfaction because they have found it easy to secure new workers without trying to increase job satisfaction. As long as mass unemployment continues, most idle workers will be eager to accept offered jobs whether or not they have been designed to optimize job satisfaction.

Most of mankind has lived in dire poverty since the beginning of civilization. In a very poor country it is far more important to produce more food, clothing, and shelter than to make work safe and pleasant. But every increase in average real wages reduces the need for a further rise, and increases the relative demand for safe and pleasant work. In the most advanced countries there is already a rising chorus of demands for policies which will make work more interesting, more wholesome, and more satisfying. For instance, well-paid workers on automobile assembly lines are complaining more and more loudly about the dull monotony and creative frustration of their work. To emphasize their complaints, they have often failed to show up for work on Monday morning, have engaged in numerous wild-cat strikes, and have revealed their discontent in other ways.

In most advanced countries real wages will more than double again during the next fifty years and the number of dependents per worker will decline further. This will very greatly increase the demand for measures to make most jobs more interesting and satisfying. It will soon become justifiable to sacrifice substantial potential output in order to increase job satisfaction. Moreover, there are many ways to increase job satisfaction without sacrificing output. Indeed, some measures will increase output as well as job satisfaction.

Some things are being done to make jobs more satisfying under capitalism. The growth of vocational guidance, of free vocational and professional education, and of automation has helped. And every reduction in the hours of labor increase net job satisfaction. But a socialist government could and should carry these trends much further than any capitalist government can. Moreover, it could and should adopt certain policies which are not feasible under capitalism. The mere fact that a socialist government owns and operates all industries enables it to adopt policies which are not practical under capitalism.

It is highly desirable to make the distribution of work satisfaction among workers more equal, as well as to increase the total sum of work satisfaction. In the past, those who inherited unearned wealth have been able to secure an undue proportion of work satisfaction, as well as an undue proportion of money income.

Socialists have long agreed that the distribution of income is far too unequal under capitalism. Indeed, one of the major goals of the socialist movement is to make personal incomes less unequal. However, very few socialists have explained that the case for making labor satisfaction less unequal is similar to and as strong as the case for making personal income less unequal. For instance, the chief argument for minimizing income differentials is that this maximizes the pleasure of consumption. But it is equally true that by minimizing differences in work satisfaction we can maximize the amount of such satisfaction. Both rules rest upon the principle of diminishing pleasure. The addition of one hour of interesting work to the workday of a bored worker gives him far more pleasure than is lost by taking it from a worker all of whose work is or was interesting. And the latter worker will suffer much less pain from one marginal hour of boring work than the former.

If a socialist government made personal income relatively equal but left work satisfaction very unequal, men would still be very unequal economically. One man might earn $10,000 a year and a greal deal of work satisfaction, while another might earn the same income but receive far less satisfaction from his work.

It is of course impossible to assure all men equal satisfaction from their work, and it is not desirable to do everything that is possible toward this goal. But very great progress in this direction is possible and desirable.

While a socialist government should strive vigorously and continuously to maximize job satisfaction in all industries and occupations, it should make greater efforts in manufacturing than in most other industries, both because this is the largest industry and because most factory jobs now rank relatively low in job satisfaction. That is why job satisfaction is discussed more fully in this chapter than in any other chapter of this book. Most of the principles discussed here should also be applied in most or all other industries.

A wide variety of methods should be used to maximize the satisfaction secured from work, and nearly all of these methods would also help to equalize the distribution of job satisfaction among different jobs and workers. We have space to discuss only a few of the most promising methods here. They fall into three classes: (1) methods of helping each worker to choose the job which will give him the most satisfaction, (2) methods of altering jobs to make them more satisfying to workers, and (3) the introduction of daily job changes for most workers.

Improving Job Choices — One very good way to increase the job satisfaction of most workers is to give them much more and much superior vocational guidance, both before they choose a vocation and whenever they consider a job. A socialist America should train and employ several times as many vocational guidance experts as are now available. Every secondary school and college should employ enough such experts to test all students thoroughly and to give each student many hours of personal advice.

To further improve vocational choices, these schools should encourage or require most students to try out successively three or more kinds of work during vacations or as part-time work during the school year before they choose their vocations. And all such trial jobs for students should be designed so as to help students make wise vocational choices. The planning and provision of such student jobs would be far easier in a socialist economy because the government would own all industries.

Any policy which increases equality of opportunity for education enables students to make wiser vocational choices because it increases their freedom of choice. In Chapter VIII of Liberal Socialism, we recommended a number of such policies, including full government financial support of all university students by scholarship funds or personal loans.

Any policy which reduces unemployment, gives workers more freedom of job choice, enables more people to enjoy work, and thereby both increases the total amount of job satisfaction and results in a more equal distribution of it. The best method of achieving full employment, granting every worker the legal right to demand and secure suitable work, was discussed in detail in <u>Liberal Socialism</u> (pp. 143-45).

Any policy which gives job applicants a wider freedom of choice among suitable jobs enables workers to choose jobs which are better fitted to their personal qualities and needs. It reduces the number of square pegs in round holes. As explained previously, a socialist government could and should notably increase freedom of job choice by equalizing educational opportunities and by granting the right to demand and secure suitable jobs.

If workers were properly informed and free to choose among all suitable jobs, they would not choose dull or dangerous jobs unless the wage rates for such jobs were raised well above the levels paid for alternative interesting or safe jobs. For instance, assembly-line workers would have to be paid much more than salesmen. Such increases in wage rates for boring and/or unpleasant work would reduce the demand for such labor and encourage the substitution of machines for workers, both of which would reduce the amount of dull work and increase the total satisfaction from labor.

It may be claimed that individual workers have long been free to choose more pleasant jobs, even at the cost of lower output and wages, and that therefore the government need do nothing to make jobs more pleasant. However, most capitalist governments have adopted many measures to make jobs safer in spite of the claim that workers are free to choose the safest jobs and to refuse to accept dangerous jobs. The truth is, of course, that capitalist workers are rarely free to choose the safest or the most pleasant jobs, and that when they are free to do so, they nearly always lack the knowledge needed to make the best choice.

Producers have found it profitable to spend billions of dollars to alter consumers' goods, often annually, and to inform consumers of these changes. But it is just as economic to improve jobs and inform workers of such improvements as it is to improve consumers' goods and inform consumers of such improvements.

Improving Jobs — The managers of every socialist factory should make a continuous and serious effort to redesign and improve old jobs and to invent and design new jobs which are more interesting and healthful than old jobs, especially for the handicapped and the fastidious. It is far more important to design jobs which meet the widely varying needs of job-seekers than to design manufactured goods which meet the widely differing demands of retail customers. Capitalist firms spend ten times as much money on designing popular products as on designing pleasant and popular jobs. Socialist trusts ought to spend more on the latter than on the former. In an advanced economy it is more important for men to be satisfied workers than for them to be satisfied customers, because they spend more hours at work than shopping and because the potential extra pleasure from a well-designed and well-chosen job is much greater than any potential extra pleasure from consumption.

One possible method of improving jobs is to redesign them so that they are less monotonous. This method has often been suggested for application to jobs on assembly lines where workers perform the same operation over and over again all day. But the only practical redesign suggestion is to let each worker perform two, three, or more operations instead of one only. Such a change would usually require a worker to change tools one or more times every fifteen minutes, which would greatly increase the number of tools needed, would create difficult problems of coordinating assembly-line jobs, and/or would slow down the assembly line. And the increase in job satisfaction achieved by having each worker perform one or more additional simple operations on a long assembly line would probably be very small.

Some writers have suggested that workers would enjoy work more if they made an entire product. But it is not practical for one worker or work crew to make or assemble an entire automobile or airplane. He might assemble complete radio or TV receivers, but this would require more tools, equipment, inventory, and space per worker, and would also require more training per worker. Nevertheless, all such proposals should be carefully tested before being rejected.

Individual artists and craftsmen have long produced custom- or hand-made shoes, clothing, jewelry, ceramics, and other goods but their production costs are very high. The industrial revolution raised real wages to their current levels in advanced countries largely by replacing handicraft production with mechanized factory production. Any substantial return to handicraft methods would tend to reduce real wages greatly. The market for luxury hand-made goods may grow as real incomes continue to rise, in spite of income equalization, but arts and crafts will never provide employment for more than a very minor part of the industrial labor force of an advanced economy.

It is nearly always possible to make a production-line factory job less tiring and more pleasant without reducing output by redesigning the tools, equipment, and workplace. In his brilliant work on scientific management, Frederick W. Taylor suggested and emphasized several ways to improve these instruments of production, but he and his followers were primarily interested in increasing output, not satisfaction, per worker. Socialist factory managers could use their suggestions in order to increase job satisfaction.

Such simple measures as providing workers with comfortable chairs, foot rests, and arm rests often have a marked effect upon worker satisfaction. And many hand tools can be redesigned to fit the physical size and strength of the individual worker. It is as important to vary the size and strength requirement of machines and tools used by different workers as to vary the size of the clothing they wear.

Great progress has already been made in replacing manual tools with power tools, which make work much less tiring, but further progress is possible. And power tools must be made safer and quieter.

There is a marked trend towards the mechanization and automation of work which is especially tiring or boring, and this trend will long continue. For instance, more and more assembly lines will be completely automated, thus reducing the number of dull, boring assembly-line jobs.

It is often possible to increase job satisfaction by improving the conditions of labor. Smoke, dust, fumes, and noise may be reduced. Work spaces may be better heated in winter and better cooled in summer. Soft background music may be supplied. Workers should certainly be provided with all such conditions which they are collectively willing to pay for, and expert-advised managers should provide some the workers are not willing to pay for.

The redesign of tools, equipment, workplaces, and factory buildings and improvement of the conditions of labor have been so fully discussed by capitalist engineers that they deserve little elaboration here.

Slowing the speed of work, either uniformly throughout the day or by granting short rest periods during the day, usually increases job satisfaction. It reduces daily fatigue and gives workers more chances to talk with other workers. Social life on the job is a significant element in total job satisfaction. Every worker should have at least two brief rest periods a day — mid-morning and mid-afternoon — in addition to a lunch period. Perhaps there should be a rest period every hour.

The length and frequency of such rest periods should be determined by the workers, democratically when a group of workers must work and rest together, and individually when workers work alone. In all cases the workers should bear the full net cost of any resulting output reduction.

Every cut in the normal hours of labor increases average job satisfaction because the last hours of work each day are the most painful. Of course, the pain of marginal work may be more than compensated by the pleasure from the marginal consumption it permits. But every increase in average real wages justifies a reduction in the hours of labor if they were previously ideal, and real wage rates will double again in all advanced countries during the next fifty years. Moreover, the hours of labor are now probably excessive, due to cultural lag and lack of wise social control. Fear of unemployment causes most workers to welcome over-time work when they have jobs.

On the other hand, every policy which increases average job satisfaction reduces the need to shorten the normal hours of labor because it reduces the pain from the daily marginal hour of labor. Workers who have interesting jobs find the last hour of daily work much less painful than those who have dull or unpleasant jobs.

<u>Daily Job Changes</u> — We come now to the last, the least discussed, and perhaps the most promising new method of increasing job satisfaction for most factory workers, namely the practice of allowing or requiring workers to shift from one job to another at regular intervals — daily, weekly, or monthly. For instance, a man who works on an auto assembly-line during the first half of his daily work shift might work as a janitor, guard, stock clerk, or inspector during the second half of his shift. If such complete job changes are not possible for all assembly-line workers, a mere shift from one place on the line to another place on the line, one where different muscles are used, would yield some increase in job satisfaction. Moreover, many workers in nearby shops and offices might enjoy shifting to an assembly-line job in the second half of their shift if their white-collar job is monotonous and if they could earn more per hour on the assembly line.

Such daily job changes would be most beneficial for those workers who now have the most boring and least-satisfying jobs — assembly-line workers, truck drivers, trash collectors, office-machine operators, typists, etc. — and such jobs are the easiest to learn. However, such job changes would probably benefit the great majority of non-professional, non-executive, non-handicraft workers.

Daily job changes enable workers to use different muscles and organs, which reduces fatigue and mental strain. They enable workers to work in different environments — for instance, outdoors instead of indoors — and the change is normally pleasant. They allow sedentary or stationary workers to perform physical labor which improves their health, and they enable men engaged in hard physical labor to shift to sedentary work, which has a similar effect on health. Furthermore, they can distribute more evenly both the pain of dull work and the pleasure of interesting work.

Well-known economic principles tell us that the marginal pleasure of consuming any good diminishes as we consume more of it in a short period and that the marginal pain of enduring any bad increases as we experience more of it. These principles apply to the pleasure and pain of work, as well as to the pleasure and pain of consumption. It follows that a shift from one kind of work to another each day has the same effect as the shift from one kind of food to another during each meal. It increases the marginal amount of pleasure from work in each job. The cure for monotonous work, like the cure for a monotonous diet, is greater variety.

There are three major obstacles to daily job changes under capitalism which would no longer exist in a liberal socialist economy. First, capitalist trade unions try to restrict all jobs in each trade to their own members, and also restrict union entrance, because they fear unemployment. Secondly, different kinds of jobs are often controlled by independent firms which find it difficult to cooperate in any daily exchange of workers. And, thirdly, capitalist wage rates differ widely, and often unreasonably, from one kind of job to another. Few workers want to change daily from a higher-paying to a lower-paying job.

All of these obstacles would be ended or drastically weakened under liberal socialism. Unemployment would disappear and unions would cease to restrict entry. All firms in each town would have a common top management able to order desirable daily job changes. And the differences between average wage rates in different trades would be very greatly reduced.

There are several general principles which should be used to plan and arrange for daily job changes.

First, a daily job change from one kind of physical work to another is most beneficial when each kind of work uses and tires a largely different set of muscles. For instance, a daily job change from truck driving to freight loading or truck maintenance, or vice versa, would be very beneficial because it would enable workers to use more muscles and tire some of them much less.

Secondly, a daily change from mental or desk work to physical work (or vice versa) is usually much more beneficial than a change from one desk job to another, or from one form of physical labor to another, because it is a more radical change, i.e., because it involves a greater change in muscle and brain use. It produces notable health benefits for both mental and manual workers.

Thirdly, a daily change from monotonous repetitive work to creative work is especially beneficial. But an opposite job change may be beneficial for some of those previously engaged full-time in creative work. Many independent creative and professional workers have taken up monotonous, uncreative physical exercises — walking, wood-chopping, brick-laying, etc. — as a welcome change after hours at their desks.

Fourth, a more equal sharing of work which is inherently unpleasant throughout most or all of a working day — cleaning sewers, cleaning toilets, mopping floors, washing dishes, etc. — increases total job satisfaction. The workers who do less such work gain much more than the workers who do more such work lose. And wage rates can be raised enough to induce more workers to share in such unpleasant work.

Fifth, a daily change from handling things to handling people, or vice versa, would be pleasant for many workers. For instance, many bookkeepers would enjoy a change from bookkeeping to teaching once a day, and many teachers would enjoy a change from teaching to bookkeeping once a day.

Sixth, a daily change from working alone to working in a group, or vice versa, can increase job satisfaction. For instance, a maid or housekeeper who works alone in a house in the morning may enjoy a change to some kind of group work, perhaps in a restaurant, in the afternoon. And some restaurant help might enjoy working alone in a private home part of the day.

Finally, those who work in unpleasantly cold or hot work areas benefit markedly from a midshift transfer to a work area with a normal temperature. And those who take their place suffer less than the workers they replace would have suffered because they, the replacements, have been working in an area with a pleasant temperature. More equal sharing of a bad reduces its total harmful effect.

Daily job changes involve costs as well as benefits, most notably, increased costs of vocational education, plant management, and movement between workplaces.

If a worker shifts from one job to another each day, he must be trained to do two different kinds of work. However, the cost of training most unskilled and semi-skilled workers is small and the benefits of daily job changes for them are relatively large because their jobs are usually the most monotonous. By contrast, the high costs of professional education are an additional reason why few if any professional workers should be shifted from work in one profession to work in another each day. But professional workers could shift from one kind of job to another within their profession — for instance, from teaching to research — without requiring too much additional training.

Daily job changes would slightly raise personnel and plant management costs because they would greatly increase the number of men working in affected sections and offices during each day. Each such unit would have to keep time and payroll records for up to twice as many workers. Moreover, management would have to devote some time to planning job changes, and to coordinating the work done by different short shifts in each plant or office. Each additional shift change would involve some interruption or disruption of work processes and require additional managerial supervision.

Finally, job changes would require workers to waste some time in moving from one workplace to another. The amount of this waste would depend upon the distance between workplace and the means of transport, and could be minimized by ideal city planning. Moreover, those who plan such job changes should try to minimize the average distance.

All such costs of daily job changes should be carefully considered before each class of such changes is approved, but we believe that in a very large number of cases, probably for most workers, the benefits of suitable daily job changes would more than offset the costs. More research on the effects of such job changes is badly needed.

CHAPTER VII

MARKETING

Marketing has long been treated by bourgeois theorists as a division of the science of business administration rather than as a division of either pure or applied political economy. As a division of business administration, capitalist marketing theory suffers from the defects characteristic of that science. It is concerned exclusively with the problem of increasing the profits of private business. Since social gain conflicts with private profit at innumerable points, especially in marketing, the marketing theory developed by bourgeois theorists needs thorough revision before it can be accepted in a socialist economy.

In its most general sense, marketing includes all transport of goods from producers to consumers. However, transportation has been discussed separately, and this chapter is therefore restricted to other marketing activities of producers, wholesalers, and retailers. Only the marketing of consumers' goods is treated.

In 1970, 20% of all U.S. workers were engaged in wholesaling (5%) and retailing (15%). Competitive capitalist marketing also incurs heavy costs for transportation, advertising, and other outside services. As a result, almost half of every dollar spent on retail goods goes to pay for the cost of marketing. In a socialist economy the costs of marketing will be greatly reduced. One gas station on a corner will sell as much as the two, three, and four now there or in the immediate neighborhood. Vertical integration of industry will eliminate many marketing costs by transforming intercompany sales into intracompany transfers. Retail and wholesale distribution are relatively wasteful industries under capitalism because they are relatively competitive. Hence, socialism will accomplish greater immediate savings in these fields than in most others.

The following discussion of marketing theory is divided into three parts: (1) marketing by producers, (2) wholesale distribution, and (3) retail distribution.

A. Marketing by Producers

The establishment of a single state trust in every industry would automatically result in a virtual marketing monopoly in each industry. Monopoly in the field of distribution is desirable for a number of reasons. It eliminates all duplication of capital equipment and effort. It greatly increases the scale of clerical operations in marketing offices, thus reducing the cost of these operations. And it also simplifies the buying activities of wholesale and retail organizations because under monopoly they can get full information and service on each class of goods from a single agency.

In order to achieve a complete monopoly in every field of distribution, it will be necessary to sell all imported commodities through the marketing organization of the domestic producer of similar articles.

Standardization and Grading — The standardization and grading of commodities is ordinarily treated as a function of marketing. The principles to be followed in the simplification of manufactured goods have already been discussed (LS, 229-34). Proper simplification and the consolidation of each industry into a single unit will make grading and sorting of manufactured goods by wholesalers unnecessary. In the case of agricultural and other non-manufactured products, all grading and sorting should be done by the original producing trust in order to permit economy and uniformity in grading.

The number of grades should be greatly reduced and so named that the final purchaser will know their meaning. All grade names should be numbers — grade 1, grade 2, etc. — because this would make their rank clearer. The basic principle to be followed in deciding whether to increase the number of grades is to balance the benefit to consumers of an additional grade against the additional cost of grading and of carrying the higher inventories involved. Consumers should do this balancing and report their conclusions to the government in periodic opinion polls.

Direct Sales to Retail Stores and Consumers — The great bulk of tangible consumers' goods should be distributed through wholesale warehouses under socialism as under capitalism. But some goods should move directly from producers to retail stores or consumers. The entire output of some bulky, costly goods — pianos, autos, boats, etc. — should probably continue to be sold and delivered directly to retailers rather than to wholesalers in order to reduce shipping and warehousing costs. Moreover, direct distribution to retail stores may be necessary in order to speed up distribution and thus maintain the freshness of some food products.

Certain commodities, such as automobiles and gasoline, require separate and specially adapted facilities for both wholesale and retail distribution. Producers of such commodities should carry on their own wholesale and retail distribution. Thus garages, gas stations, and automobile sales agencies should be controlled by the trusts which produce the commodities sold in these retail outlets. The same principle applies to moving-picture theatres, although they produce services instead of commodities.

Such vertical integration of distribution would give better coordination between production and distribution. It would cause producers to give more consideration to the technical problems of distribution. It would centralize responsibility for proper supply and maintenance of such commodities, and would reduce bookkeeping and clerical costs by eliminating inter-trust transactions.

<u>Informative Advertising</u> — The aggressive salesmanship and deceptive advertising characteristic of capitalism should not be tolerated in a socialist economy. It will nevertheless be beneficial to give the consumer accurate information concerning the quality, durability, and uses of the article he purchases. The preparation of such information should be a function of the original producer, since he knows more about his products than anyone else. This information should be printed in annual catalogs and should also be summarized on printed tags attached to each article on sale, or on signs placed near such articles.

To illustrate the type of information referred to, we use men's shirts as an example. A typical question about men's shirts is whether one type of material, such as airplane cloth, will stand more laundering than another type, such as broadcloth. Another question is how much the collar and sleeves will shrink. The purchaser is the best judge of the aesthetic value to him of each type of material, but he knows very little about their relative durability, and the degree to which they will shrink or fade. Accurate information concerning the qualities of all products would notably increase the benefits received by consumers. Under competitive capitalism, it is not even possibly to rely on the customary information concerning collar size and sleeve length of men's shirts.

B. Wholesale Marketing

The proper functions of socialist wholesale warehouses are: (1) to reduce transport costs by pooling orders of many retail stores and thus making possible large-scale shipments by producers, (2) to speed up and cheapen transport by providing terminal facilities, warehouses, and delivery equipment which no individual retail store could afford to maintain, but which may be economically used by an organization supplying many

retail stores, (3) to carry local stocks in large
warehouses in low-rent areas, thus reducing the size
of stocks which must be carried in retail stores, and
cutting storage costs, and (4) to permit the return
and redistribution of surplus retail stocks without
their return to the factory. Of these four functions,
the carrying of local reserve stocks is the most
significant.

Under capitalism wholesalers perform additional
functions, such as extending credit, training and
financing retailers, facilitating aggressive sales
efforts of manufacturers, etc., but these functions
should not be performed under socialism. Extension of
credit should be concentrated in the hands of the
State Bank. Retail executives should be the best authorities on retail methods. Aggressive selling is
uneconomic.

All wholesale marketing should be carried on by
a single branch of the Marketing Trust. Centralization
of control over all wholesale warehouses would make
possible ideal design of warehouses, proper standardization of methods and equipment, accurate measurement and comparison of the results obtained by different local managers, and all the other economies of
large-scale management.

Every large socialist city should have one, and
only one, wholesale warehouse, which should serve all
local retail stores.

Wholesale Mark-Ups — Each wholesale price should
be the sum of a producer's price, freight-in cost,
and a wholesale mark-up. Socialist wholesale managers
determine only the latter, a very small part of the
total wholesale price.

Wholesale mark-ups should equal marginal costs
whenever these costs are determinable and such pricing does not increase the demand for wholesale services above capacity. The marginal-cost curve is
horizontal until capacity output is closely approached
or exceeded. Thereafter, marginal costs rise sharply
and are much harder to determine before they change.
Moreover, it then becomes much more important to
restrict demand quickly by raising mark-ups than to
fix mark-ups which measure marginal costs. Hence, the
chief effort should then be to balance current supply
and demand.

Since wholesale mark-ups should average less than
10% of retail prices, variations in these mark-ups
could have little effect upon the demand for retail
goods and, hence, for wholesale warehouses. Therefore
the demand for and supply of wholesale services should
be balanced mainly by properly regulating investment
in wholesale inventories and warehouses, not by raising

and lowering wholesale mark-ups. Fortunately, the growth of demand for monopolistic wholesale and retail services would be easy to predict under socialism.

It is more economic to store goods in producers' or wholesalers' warehouses than in retail stores. Moreover, fluctuations in orders from different retail stores may partly offset each other. Finally, each wholesale warehouse should give quick delivery, preferably overnight, to nearly all the stores it services, so that they can maintain minimum inventories without running out of any item. For these reasons, wholesale warehouses should assume the function of holding all reserve inventories. They should use inventory fluctuations to reduce the number of wholesale and retail price changes. A small unexpected rise in the wholesale sale of any item should normally result in an inventory reduction, not in a price rise. Only when increased demand has seriously depleted both producers' and wholesalers' stocks and required an expansion of output at higher marginal costs should the wholesale, and therefore the retail, price be raised. Price changes should be far less frequent than major wholesale inventory changes.

Quantity discounts based upon real variations in the unit cost of handling orders of different size should be granted all purchasers. Cash discounts would not be needed, since every retail store would be able to obtain ample funds, and credit sales should be prohibited.

Wholesale prices should be fixed f.o.b. the wholesale warehouse, and delivery costs should be added to them, in order to allocate delivery costs to those responsible for them.

<u>Methods of Operation</u> — Every wholesale warehouse should have railway connections and its own terminal facilities. Most goods should be shipped in containers designed so that they can be easily attached to or removed from flat cars by traveling cranes. These containers should also be used for storage purposes in wholesale warehouses.

Under capitalism nearly all wholesale warehouses and produce markets are located in highly congested business districts. The primary reason for this seems to be competitive salesmanship and the desire to be near possibly buyers. Under socialism this reason will disappear and it will become economic to locate wholesale warehouses on the outskirts of large cities rather than in their centers.

In order to speed up service to retail stores and thus permit a reduction in their inventories, a quick yet economical method of transmitting orders from retailers to wholesale warehouses should be used. Mail is far too slow for this purpose. Telephone is the quickest and most convenient means of all. However, a teletype system might prove more practical, since it would give an accurate written order to the warehouse.

As an additional aid to quick replenishment of retail stocks, all wholesale warehouses should operate day and night. Indeed, the major portion of the work should probably be done at night so as to enable each store to restock overnight.

Naturally, the Wholesale Division of the Retail Trust should make no effort to sell its merchandise to retailers. It should do no advertising and hire no traveling salesmen. It should merely fill orders sent to it by retail agencies. To facilitate ordering, however, it should prepare annually a complete catalog of all consumers' goods which it sells. This catalog should contain a description of each article, prepared by the producer of that article.

Mail-Order and Telephone Sales — In 1957 only 1% of U.S. retail sales were mail-order sales, and telephone-order sales may have been much smaller. In a socialist America such remote-order sales should probably account for well over half of all sales. And most of them should be handled by local wholesale warehouses.

There are several reasons why such an increase in remote-order sales would be economic. First, it would save a great deal of time now devoted to personal shopping, probably over two hours a week for the average adult. This time saving will become more and more important as more married women go to work outside the home. Idle women find shopping a pleasure, but busy women find it a burdensome chore. And all women would be able to work and earn men's wages in a socialist America.

Secondly, such an increase in remote-order sales would sharply reduce the volume of street traffic, which would reduce fuel consumption, air pollution, and street accidents.

Thirdly, such an increase would probably also reduce marketing costs. Handling remote-order sales in local wholesale warehouses would eliminate the retail stage in marketing. Wholesale warehouses would have to take on some retail functions, but they could perform them on a much larger scale, and therefore more economically. And the average distance goods must be transported would be sharply cut, for many buyers would live closer to the warehouse than to the nearest store.

The achievement of full socialism will make it far easier and more advantageous to order goods by mail or telephone. It will reduce by over 90% the number of varieties of goods offered for sale, which will permit listing and picturing all goods in a few mail-order catalogs. It will eliminate all shoddy goods, and provide accurate, honest descriptions of all catalog items. Personal inspection of goods before purchase will become far less useful. By creating marketing monopolies, socialism will make it easy for consumers to learn where to order goods by phone or mail, and what goods are available. By creating a delivery-service monopoly, it will markedly reduce delivery costs and/or speed up home delivery.

In an advanced socialist society every home should have a set of catalogs listing, describing, picturing, evaluating, pricing, and numbering all retail goods. Such catalogs would enable consumers to decide what to buy in the comfort of their homes, both before visiting retail stores and before ordering goods by phone or mail.

Each home should also eventually have a teletype ordering device connected with the nearest wholesale warehouse. This device, resembling a small adding machine, should enable any customer to order any good by punching a short catalog number on its face. It should show up to 100 different symbols, and should produce a tape order both at the customer's home and at the warehouse. The latter would be used to fill and bill the order, the former would enable the customer to check deliveries and charges.

If 100 different symbols (including letters as well as numbers) were used in each digit place of a catalog number, 100 million retail items could be given distinct numbers without using any number containing more than four symbols.

In America today, mail-order selling is done by national firms from a single warehouse or from regional warehouses, and by local firms from local stores. Some local stores also accept phone orders. In a socialist economy there should be no remote-order selling from national or regional warehouses. Local city warehouses should handle most mail, phone, or teletype orders. But some local stores, notably grocery and drug stores, might handle phone or teletype orders, especially orders for perishable foods. Only prolonged scientific research in a socialist society can determine which marketing agencies can handle which remote-order sales most efficiently in such a society.

The prices charged by wholesale warehouses to remote-order customers should be the same as those charged retail stores for like quantities. In both cases the delivery costs should be added to these prices. Of course, remote-order individual consumers

164

would normally buy in smaller quantities than retail stores, so they would normally pay higher prices, but these prices should be below retail prices.

<u>Delivery Service</u> — In a socialist economy all home delivery should be provided by a single home-delivery agency in each town. This agency should deliver milk, groceries, clothing, furniture and all other retail purchases not carried home by customers.

Nearly all deliveries should be made by large electric trucks, each staffed with four to eight workers, which move slowly and stop several times in each block. When they stop, all the delivery workers on the truck should remove packages from the truck for simultaneous delivery to the four or more nearest addresses. The delivery trucks should be designed to carry all kinds of deliveries and four or more delivery men.

Delivery men now waste much time waiting for people to answer the doorbell and open the door. This waste should be eliminated by requiring that all houses and apartment buildings be fitted with special delivery receiving facilities which enable a delivery to be placed inside the house or building, in a refrigerator if necessary, without aid from any resident.

C. Retail Marketing

Retail marketing is the last stage in the distribution of commodities. It may be defined as the sale and delivery of consumable commodities to consumers. It includes mail-order, telephone, and door-to-door selling, in addition to the work of retail stores.

The Retail Branch of the Marketing Trust should have charge of all retail stores in the nation. Garages and service stations, as has been noted, should be placed under the control of the trusts which produce the products sold in them, but they are not ordinarily considered to be retail stores.

The internal organization of the Retail Branch should be determined by the types of retail stores set up. The most fundamental division of authority would probably separate control over the distribution of convenience goods from control over the distribution of shopping and specialty goods. Convenience goods are those which are purchased frequently and in small amounts at the most convenient store. Groceries, drugs, tabacco, candy, soft drinks, etc., belong in this class. Shopping and specialty goods are relatively expensive and infrequently purchased, and are usually bought after some shopping. They include most clothing, furniture, household and garden equipment, hardware, musical instruments, toys, etc.

These two types of goods should be sold in different types of stores. Most convenience goods should be sold in local neighborhood stores scattered throughout the residential area of a community, by mail or phone from a warehouse, and by automatic vending equipment. Most shopping and specialty goods should be sold in department stores located at the center of each town and city, or by remote order.

The Structure of Retailing — In an advanced socialist society almost everyone should live in a well-planned town or city. The theory of how to organize retail marketing and how to locate retail stores is a part of the theory of socialist city planning, and was therefore treated in detail in Chapters III and IV. We shall not repeat much of that discussion here.

Each city and town center should include one large department store; each village center should include a large supermarket; and each community center should have a small shop selling a few convenience goods. The function, location, and size of these stores should be determined primarily by city planners, not by retail-marketing executives. For instance, it is far more important to locate stores so as to minimize street traffic and encourage walking than to locate them so as to minimize rent and other retail operating costs.

There should be a clear division of labor between city-center and town-center department stores. Metropolitan department stores should sell only the most expensive and/or least often purchased shopping goods — furniture, fur coats, musical instruments, silverware, TV sets, etc. The inconvenience of having to go into the center of a city to make a purchase is relatively unimportant when the cost of the purchase is large. And a metropolitan department store can offer a far larger variety of such goods and can achieve more economies of scale in handling them. Moreover, concentration in city-center stores of goods with low stock-turnover rates would greatly increase these rates, and thus reduce retailing costs.

Sound city planning and the elimination of competition should reduce the number of retail stores in a socialist economy to less than 10% of the number existing in the previous capitalist economy.

Retail Mark-Ups — A retail price includes a wholesale price, an in-freight cost, and a retail mark-up. Retail stores should determine only retail mark-ups, the prices of retail services.

In America retail mark-ups now average about 30% of retail prices, but this percentage should be much lower under socialism, due to standardization and simplification of retail goods, creation of retail monopolies, and other rationalization measures. Retail prices would be largely determined by producers when they determine their prices. Wholesalers and retailers should merely add small, independently-determined mark-ups to the prices and costs they pay.

Like all other prices of reproducible goods, retail mark-ups should balance supply and demand, and should also equal marginal costs when achievement of the latter result is consistent with achievement of the former. In the case of retail mark-ups, these results are often incompatible because the marginal costs of retailing may not rise when store sales exceed store capacity. The resulting store congestion creates external diseconomies in the form of various inconveniences to customers — crowded store aisles and queues inside and outside the store — but the marginal costs to the store may rise little if any. Therefore, the higher retail mark-ups needed both to prevent such congestion and to yield an adequate return on the investment in store facilities will usually be well above marginal costs.

While actual retail mark-ups should usually be well above relevant marginal-cost, any mark-ups above marginal cost may be thought of as including a basic mark-up equal to marginal cost and an extra mark-up or surcharge fixed so as to control total sales. Basic mark-ups should equal marginal costs and be relatively stable. Extra mark-ups should be unrelated to marginal costs, should be uniform for all goods in a store, and should change often.

Actual, effective retail mark-ups should never be less than basic mark-ups because the resulting marginal losses would measure net welfare losses. They should often be well above basic mark-ups in order to limit total store sales so as to prevent store congestion, and queues outside stores. Those who control investment in retail facilities should limit their investment in each store so as to make necessary extra mark-ups high enough to justify the investment.

It may seem that retail mark-ups should not be increased in order to prevent congestion because the costs of congestion fall on consumers who are free to prevent such congestion by shopping during other, off-peak hours. But when one consumer ceases shopping during hours of store congestion, most of the benefit accrues to other shoppers, not to him, so he never has adequate inducement to shop during off-peak hours. The use of extra mark-ups can give him an adequate inducement.

Most socialist stores sell hundreds of different goods, and for large numbers of similar goods marginal costs per unit of sale are the same, or almost the same. Hence, store managers should not try to determine the individual marginal cost of retailing each good. Instead, they should group all goods into a small number of classes and estimate average marginal cost per sales unit for each of these classes of goods. Classification should be based largely on the bulk and weight of the sales unit, not upon the value of the good sold.

Retail distribution costs are virtually independent of the cost of the article. The costs of buying, receiving, storing, and selling a $50 watch are very little more than the costs of buying, receiving, storing, and selling a $5 watch. The basic retail mark-ups on two different watches selling at these widely varying wholesale prices should measure the real cost of handling them. This cost will not be the same, but it would be far less of an error to mark up the price of each by the same absolute amount, $5 for instance, than to use the same percentage mark-up for both watches, as private retailers do. A uniform 100% basic mark-up would give a $50 mark-up on one watch and only a $5 mark-up on the other. Obviously, such a variation in absolute mark-ups is only justified to a very minor degree by the real differences in the costs of distribution. Moreover, under socialism these differences in costs of distribution would be much less than they are now. Both watches would be sold in the same store, the turnover of each would be rapid, credit losses would be eliminated, and there would be few losses due to mark-downs.

The marginal cost of selling one more unit of any good in a self-service retail store includes only the cost of receiving it, pricing it, displaying it, and handling it at the check-out counter. This marginal cost does not include rent, quasi-rent, heat, light, informative advertising, executive pay, property insurance, or any other cost which does not vary continuously with sales.

In a store which has clerks who wait on customers, the time a clerk spends on each sale is a marginal cost. If this cost varies widely from customer to customer and exceeds a minimum, perhaps five minutes a sale, it should probably be charged for separately, at so much per minute, the way most medical and legal fees are now determined. Under socialism, store clerks should be well trained and should earn almost as much per hour as doctors and lawyers. They should give very useful objective advice to customers, and should often advise against purchase of their merchandise.

In a socialist economy there should be a large number of very similar stores — like size, like volume of sales, like store layout, like selection of merchandise, etc. — in each major category of stores. If the marginal costs of selling each class of goods were carefully determined in a few of these stores and found to be very similar, such cost data could be used to determine retail mark-ups in all other like stores. This would reduce by 90 to 99% the total cost of determing such marginal costs.

Socialist self-service stores should charge separately for check-out counter service because the cost of such services per customer does not vary at all closely with the value of the goods purchased by individual customers. Every time a customer has his purchases added up, paid for, and bagged, he causes certain costs which he ought to pay for separately. A fixed sum (10 cents?) plus one cent per item might be charged. Of course, only careful research can determine how high these charges should be.

The task of balancing the supply of and demand for each retail good must be distinguished from the task of balancing the supply of and demand for the service rendered by a retail store. The former task should be performed by producers when they price their products and by wholesalers and retailers when they determine their inventories. The latter task should be performed by retailers. Retail mark-ups should rarely be changed in order to balance supply and demand for individual goods. Those who fix such mark-ups should devote their efforts primarily to fixing basic individual mark-ups which equal marginal costs and to fixing uniform store-wide extra mark-ups or mark-up surcharges designed to stabilize total store sales at capacity levels, i.e., to achieve optimum use of each retail store.

<u>Stabilization of Retail Sales</u> — One of the principal wastes of retailing under capitalism is the incomplete utilization of retail facilities due to marked and regular variations in the volume of sales. In capitalist retail stores, sales vary regularly from hour to hour throughout the day, from day to day throughout the week, from month to month throughout the year, and irregularly from year to year throughout the so-called business cycle. Socialism will eliminate business fluctuations, but special retail pricing methods ought to be used to reduce regular variations in sales volume due to other causes.

Few people realize the extent of these regular variations in retail sales. Between 11:00 and 12:00 a.m. retail sales are double or treble those between 8:00 and 9:00 a.m. Sales on Saturday far exceed those on other week days, and in many stores December sales are double those of any other month. This variation in sales means that every store is built and equipped to do between two and four times its average hourly volume of business.

The most practical method of securing a more even flow of retail business is that of regular uniform mark-up variation. If the preference of some consumers for shopping between 11 and 12 a.m., or on Saturday, makes it necessary to have a retail capacity much greater than actual retail sales, the consumers who make this necessary should pay the entire costs of the additional retail capacity by paying higher prices for the goods they buy. Here, as in many other cases, consumers should be allowed to buy, or do, whatever they please, but only if they are willing to pay the cost. It seems highly probable, however, that an appropriate increase in the retail mark-up of goods sold during peak hours would cause consumers to reduce sharply their peak-hour purchases. Similar pricing would distribute sales much more evenly between different days of the week, and different months of the year.

The principle that retail mark-ups should vary from hour to hour and day to day raises the problem of what price should be shown on price tags or signs. It would be costly and uneconomic to change quoted prices several times a day or week, or to list all different prices on each price tag or sign. The best solution would probably be to show both basic price and basic mark-up on all price tags and signs. Then the appropriate extra mark-up could be calculated and collected when the customer pays for his goods. Catalogs and store signs could advise customers of surcharge rates during different time periods.

Extra retail mark-ups used to limit store sales and to stabilize sales should be based upon and uniformly proportional to basic retail mark-ups, not to basic retail prices. The function of extra mark-ups is to control total store use, i.e., traffic in the store, not to control total dollar sales. If extra mark-ups were based on basic prices, they would raise the prices of costly goods far more than the prices of cheap goods, which would be uneconomic.

Since extra mark-ups should be based on basic mark-ups, the cashiers who calculate total mark-ups and prices must know both the basic mark-up and the basic price of each good in order to determine actual, final prices. Therefore, each price tag should show both items.

It may be claimed that customers could not buy wisely if they did not know the total retail price of each good they consider buying. However, if surcharge rates were announced on nearby signs, customers could add a surcharge to each posted mark-up. Moreover, they could usually compare different goods quite well on the basis of their basic prices, because surcharges would be fairly uniform, especially on like goods, and would usually amount to less than 10% of basic retail prices. When goods are sold by a sales clerk, he could figure the total retail price before the customer finally decides to buy.

While total retail mark-ups should vary during each day, wholesale mark-ups should remain stable during each day, and probably also during most weeks and months. A wholesale warehouse would not need to rely on markup variations to spread its sales evenly over the hours of the day. It could usually postpone action on individual orders for an hour or two. And sound retail mark-up variation would minimize daily fluctuations in both retail and wholesale sales. Moreover, sound seasonal variation in producers' prices would greatly reduce the need for seasonal fluctuations in retail mark-ups.

Store Hours — The kind of retail price cycles proposed above to reduce sales fluctuations during customary hours of store operation could also be used to achieve adequate sales during additional hours of store operation. Socialist stores should operate more hours per week, and should achieve optimum sales during these additional hours by reducing retail mark-ups, to the level of marginal costs if necessary.

Since non-marginal costs make up a large part, perhaps a half, of retail store costs, retail markups can be cut drastically without reducing them below marginal costs. And such price cuts would attract considerable patronage during added hours of store operation, especially for department stores, because of their higher mark-ups.

Only experience and research can determine how much the operating hours of retail stores should be increased in a socialist economy, but we believe that average hours should be increased by over 50% in a town built around a factory operating 24 hours a day 365 days a year.

The combined effect of daily, weekly, and other sales-stabilizing price cycles and increased hours of store operation should be at least a 50% cut in the per person cost of retail-store facilities.

Ideal Investments and Deficits — Wholesaling and retailing are industries of indefinitely declining marginal costs. Every well-planned increase in the size and output of a new wholesale warehouse or retail store lowers both average marginal cost and so-called average cost (however calculated). Therefore, investment in such facilities should be planned so as to result in both temporary deficits due to initial or occasional excess capacity and long-run overall or total deficits over the life of each facility.

A new store should be so large that it will have abnormally large deficits during the first decade or two of its operation if mark-ups are properly determined. However, as demand for its services grows, initial operating deficits should decline steadily due to rising mark-ups. But, before the mark-up rise has made possible an overall profit, it should be reversed by additional investment which would expand store capacity and require mark-up reductions.

No initial or additional investment in a retail store should be made unless the new store or addition to it could, with sound pricing and no new investment, earn a total rental and/or quasi-rent income over its life, equal to the total cost of the investment (chiefly interest and depreciation). But, in nearly all cases, the store should be expanded before mark-ups have risen enough to permit recovery of the total cost to date of the initial investment. Under socialism, added investments in decreasing-cost industries should be made as soon as they become independently economic, i.e., regardless of the effect on the income from old investments. Continuous total deficits are economic in all such industries.

Encouraging Multi-Unit Sales — The costs of retailing can be reduced by inducing customers to buy more than one unit of a good at the same time. The marginal cost of selling one more unit of the same good at the same time is always less, and often substantially less, than the cost of selling the first unit. For instance, when a customer aided by a sales clerk has found the shirt he wishes to buy — right style, fabric, color, and size — his decision to buy a second or third like article does not require more display of merchandise by the sales clerk or a separate sales slip. And when a gas station customer decides to buy an additional gallon of gasoline, no significant added retailing cost is created. It follows that in such cases the retail mark-up on the first unit sold should be much higher than the mark-up on any additional unit of the same good sold at the same time. In the case of gasoline, the mark-up on the first gallon should be 6 to 12 times as high as that on each subsequent gallon.

Even when a customer is not served by a sales clerk, i.e., buys in a self-service store, the sale of the first unit costs far less than that of the second unit. Both units can be handled almost simultaneously by the cashier, who can treat them as a single sales transaction and can often put them in the same bag or a little larger bag. Moreover, sales capacity per square foot of store space increases sharply when most customers buy two instead of one unit of each good.

It is noteworthy that nearly all the benefits of multi-unit sales result from buying more units of the same kind, not from buying more unlike goods. Only the former reduces the amount of time the customer must spend in the store selecting merchandise.

The ideal way to persuade retail customers to buy more units of a good at the same time is to reduce the mark-ups on all units after the first unit. The mark-ups on the second and later units should be equal to the lower marginal costs of selling these units in a single sale. These costs would be virtually uniform for all subsequent units, so only two total mark-ups need be set for such sales.

In many, perhaps most cases, the benefit to the customer of buying more units of a good at a time is substantial and independent of the effect on the costs of retailing. By buying more at a time, customers reduce the number of hours they must devote to shopping and to travel to and from stores. Socialist simplification and standardization of goods would make it much more economic for customers to buy more units of shopping goods at a time.

Special Charge for Special Service — In a socialist economy, retail stores should provide no special or extra customer services free of charge. They should collect extra charges for all such optional services in order to prevent overconsumption and to allocate costs to those responsible for them.

For instance, a special charge should be made for any clothing alteration, for marking or engraving any product, for gift-wrapping, for home delivery, and for approval sale. But no special charge for credit would be needed since all retail sales should be cash sales (LS, p. 125).

There should be no restriction of special retail services, other than the elimination of credit. However, these services should be sold for a price so that people will consume only what they are willing to pay for, and no customer will have to pay for services he does not use.

Sales Methods — The sales methods of retail stores in a socialist society should be entirely different from those used under capitalism. The average customer is the best judge of the benefit to him of price goods, and sales effort by clerks eager to earn commissions or a raise rarely improves his subjective discrimination in this regard. Therefore, retail stores should do no advertising, have no special sales, sell no "leaders" at a loss, and should instruct all sales clerks to refrain from persuading the consumer to buy more goods or to buy one good in place of another. The application of this principle would sharply reduce the cost of retail distribution.

This does not mean that the customer should be unaware of the quality and various uses of the articles he buys. Full and accurate information on these points should be contained in the catalogs published periodically by the Wholesale Branch and distributed free of charge to every retail store and consumer. The information in these catalogs, being supplied by the original producer in each case, would be far more complete and accurate than the knowledge of any individual sales clerk. Producers should carry on continuous research to determine the proper use of each article, the life of every article under several different types of usage, and so forth, and this information should be included in the sales catalogs, printed on tags attached to each article, or stated on nearby signs.

Vending Machines — A socialist marketing trust should use automatic vending machines far more extensively and intensively than any capitalist country. It should use them both to free retail stores of the costly handling of small-scale sales and to offer some goods for sale in areas where, or at times when, there are no stores open.

Vending machines are especially suitable for the sale of packaged snack foods, beverages, candy, tobacco products, newspapers, and other goods which have a low value per unit and are often purchased by people who buy nothing else at the same time. They should be placed outside all retail stores in order to reduce the number of store patrons, speed up service for customers, and provide service when the store itself is closed.

Under capitalism most retailers compete with vending machines, and therefore try to limit their use. They want customers who might use outside vending machines to come into their stores, hoping that these customers will see and buy something else. In sharp contrast, a socialist retail store manager should try to keep such customers out of his store in order to reduce his total costs. He should also try to discourage impulse buying, which is usually uneconomic for the customer.

The mere creation of a socialist retail monopoly would permit a far more intensive use of each vending machine because it would end competitive duplication of facilities in every suitable site. It would also facilitate the movement of such machines from one seasonal site to another. And it would sharply reduce the cost of manufacturing and selling these machines by standardizing them and guaranteeing a stable demand for them.

Automobile Dealers — New-car sales account for almost 25% of all U.S. retail sales, and the value of used-car sales may be even larger. Competition in auto marketing is unusually wasteful.

Most American cities are seriously congested and disfigured by a large number of competing new- and used-car lots and dealers. A socialist city should have only one retail automobile agency, and it should sell all used, as well as all new, cars. It should be located on the edge of the city, not in or near its center, because it would require acres of display area.

One agency per city would be sufficient and ideal because it would enable customers to look over all locally available cars, new and used, in a single place. The average customer now spends many hours and days visiting dozens of dealers scattered over a wide area. He is willing to travel long distances and visit many dealers because cars are expensive and price differences are large.

Concentration of all car dealing in each city on a single large lot would radically reduce selling costs. Each car salesman would be able to make many more sales a day with less effort. All useful information about each car, including detailed estimates of operating costs, should be presented to customers in printed form to reduce their questioning of salesmen. And, of course, socialist salesmen should waste no time trying to persuade customers to buy, or to buy one car rather than another.

All used cars should be repaired, reconditioned, and guaranteed, which would enable buyers to make their choice more quickly and confidently, and would also prevent many highway accidents.

Ideal simplification of new cars would reduce the variety of new and used cars by over 90%. This would reduce equally both the amount of space required to display all new cars and the time required by customers to make a decision, which would further reduce selling and buying costs.

The function of servicing and repairing automobiles should be almost completely separated from the function of selling new and used cars. These functions should be performed by different agencies, located in different places. The sale of new and used cars should be concentrated in one place in each city in order to enable customers to see and compare all offerings at minimum cost. Service stations and repair garages should be scattered through or around each city so as to enable motorists to reach them at minimum cost.

Automobile Service Stations and Garages — The combined sales of U.S. service stations amounted to about $50 billion in 1976.

Competition in the sale of gasoline and auto repair services has proven to be grossly inefficient. In most American cities there are now from two to five times as many gas stations as are needed. Some busy street corners have two to four gas stations, and some highways have over ten stations on a single mile of road. As a result, gas stations are much smaller and less efficient than they should be, and the amount of capital funds invested in them is over twice as large as it should be.

In a socialist economy urban service stations should be at least a mile apart. In an ideal planned new socialist city nearly all service stations should be located outside of town, on the margin of a greenbelt, because in-town private-car use should be prohibited.

Every urban service station should provide fairly complete repair service by a staff of skilled and specialized mechanics. There should be no separate repair garages competing with service stations. Socialist service stations should be few enough, and therefore large enough, to hire staffs of specialized mechanics and keep them busy. Moreover, it is much more convenient for auto owners to be able to secure gasoline, oil, and repairs at one place, the service station nearest to their personal garage.

All gas stations in a city should sell the same kinds of gasoline and oil. This would greatly reduce the number of separate pumps and tanks required. All like cars should be built to use the same tires, parts, and accessories. This would greatly reduce the cost of stocking and selling such goods, and would make it possible for service stations to carry much more complete stocks.

In a socialist economy lubricating oil should be sold and poured in only by gas station attendants, who should save all drained dirty oil for collection and recycling. In America today only 20% of drained oil is recycled, and the other 80% is disposed of in ways which pollute land and water. Socialist service stations should help customers to choose wisely between new and recycled oil, and the price of the latter should be low enough to assure sale of the entire supply.

Every socialist gasoline station and repair garage should function as an automobile inspection station. Every car which stops for gas should be given a superficial inspection for easily observable defects, and every car which has not received a more thorough inspection in its last 4000 miles should be required to submit to a longer examination.

Since socialist cars would be relatively standardized, and designed to facilitate such quick inspection, this inspection would be much easier and much more productive than it can be under competitive capitalism, and service station employees would have no incentive to damage cars and/or recommend unneeded repairs, as they often do today, because they could not profit from extra repair work. Nearly all automobile defects can endanger the lives and health of the drivers or of other highway users. Therefore, the repair of nearly all defective cars should be compulsory either immediately or within a very brief time.

Socialist service-station staff should also help to enforce laws against excessive automobile air pollution and noise, laws requiring the use of seat belts, and other safety laws. If a driver is not wearing a seat belt when he enters a service station, he should be fined then and there. If his muffler is missing or defective, he should be required to have it repaired within a few days. If his brakes are defective or worn out, he should be required to leave his car for repairs and given use of a rental car.

Most of the time of the staff of the enlarged service station prescribed above would be devoted to auto inspection and repair. Therefore, all service stations should be subordinate to the national automobile manufacturing trust. This would enable the executives of this trust to control the repair of their products and to learn as soon as possible of all defect in their products. It would help to induce auto-plant executives to design and produce cars which can be repaired more cheaply. It would enable the national government to grade such executives on the basis of auto repair costs, as well as on the basis of auto production costs.

The national oil trust should control the marketing of oil products up to the moment they arrive at the service station, but should not operate service stations. However, the wholesale and retail marketing of oil products used by automobiles should be closely coordinated.

CHAPTER VIII

FOREIGN TRADE

The economic theory of foreign trade has always received undue attention from bourgeois economists and statesmen. The exaggerated importance attributed to foreign trade and its regulation by the Mercantilists is well known. Mercantilistic economic theory is still dominant among businessmen and among the politicians, newspaper editors, and school teachers whom they control in all capitalist nations.

While classical and neoclassical political economists have placed less emphasis upon the need for foreign trade than the Mercantilists, they naturally criticized the errors of Mercantilism, and this in turn has tended to perpetuate the Mercantilistic overemphasis upon the importance of the theory of foreign trade.

Moreover, the nature of capitalism makes the question of free trade versus protective tariffs a perennial issue since it vitally affects the profits of many capitalists and the jobs of many workers. By eliminating the private-profit seekers who now benefit from limitations on imports, by uniting the interests of all groups of voters, and by abolishing unemployment, socialism will make the solution of the tariff question far easier and will thus greatly reduce the attention devoted to it and to foreign trade.

A. The Advantages of Foreign Trade

The advantages of foreign trade are the same as those of domestic trade. In the first place, all commerce makes possible an increase in the scale of production. The advantages of large-scale production, one of which is an increased division of labor, were described in Liberal Socialism. Both the scale of production and the degree of the division of labor are limited by demand. Every extension of trade, domestic or foreign, enlarges the market area and, hence, makes possible an increased scale of production and a further division of labor. The advantages of foreign trade, therefore, include all the advantages of large-scale production and the division of labor.

The importance of an increased division of labor depends upon the degree of the division of labor already achieved. The first steps in the division of labor yield the greatest returns, and subsequent steps, while always profitable if demand is large enough, yield a steadily diminishing return. Thus, a large or rich country which has already achieved a high degree of division of labor in all industries benefits much less from foreign trade than a small or poor nation which has not yet achieved an intensive division of labor.

A second significant advantage of foreign trade is that it makes possible the concentration of each industry in those nations where natural conditions are most favorable to it. Every nation has natural physical advantages — climate, accessibility, peculiar combinations of raw resources, etc. — which favor the production of certain goods, and these advantages should be exploited to the full for the benefit of the world as a whole.

Protective tariffs which discourage the importation of the products of irreplaceable natural resources are particularly unwise from the purely national viewpoint. The supplies of lumber, petroleum, copper, lead, iron ore, coal, etc., in the U.S., for example, will probably fall steadily while the demand for them continues to rise. To curtail imports of these raw materials is extremely undesirable, merely from the standpoint of conservation of our natural resources.

The theory that export trade is desirable or necessary under capitalism in order to dispose of surplus domestic products is widely held by both bourgeois and Marxian theorists. It is based upon a misunderstanding of the nature of foreign trade.

In the first place, exports of any given commodity do not eliminate a surplus, but rather tend to create a surplus available for export. In the absence of an export market, producers would cease to produce the alleged surplus now sold abroad or would find a profitable domestic market for it.

In the second place, exports result in visible or invisible imports of an equal value. They never decrease the total value of goods, services, and securities sold on the domestic market. Thus, low wages and the consequent low purchasing power of the workers cannot cause a net export of the products of their labor. Low wages always imply either inefficiency on the part of the workers, or high profits for the capitalists, or both. In the former case, there is no net surplus of goods to export, at least none due to the low level of wages. In the latter case, the high profits of the capitalists enable them to buy all the surplus products not purchased by the workers.

Although the advantages of foreign trade far outweigh the disadvantages, private businessmen who profit from restrictions on imports have popularized many unsound arguments against free trade.

Perhaps the most universally used and believed charge against free trade is that it causes unemployment. Almost every worker believes that the importation of foreign goods, particularly of the same kind of goods he is producing, results in increased unemployment in his own country. This belief is mistaken.

Under capitalism, foreign trade is divided into two distinct activities, either of which may be carried on independently of the other. These two activities are importing and exporting. The artificial division of foreign trade into these two functions makes it easy for uncritical observers to treat the effects of either one or the other as the sole effects of foreign trade. Those capitalists whose financial interests lead them to oppose certain imports speak as if the effects of importing foreign goods are the sole effects of foreign trade.

Actually, of course, foreign trade is merely a process of barter by which less valuable domestic goods are exchanged for foreign goods of a higher domestic value. Since imports cause equal exports, they cannot cause net unemployment, even under capitalism. The importation of coal reduces the demand for the labor of coal miners, but, at the same time, it increases by an equal amount the demand for labor to produce whatever articles are exchanged for the coal.

While foreign imports thus cause no net increase in unemployment, they may depress certain industries and put workers in those industries out of work. It is natural that under capitalism, which offers to displaced workers no guarantee of immediate employment elsewhere, the workers in these threatened industries should combine with their masters to demand tariff protection. Although potential imports ordinarily involve potential exports, and hence potential new jobs, no individual worker is sure of getting one of these new jobs and, consequently, no workers have an obvious personal interest in demanding free trade. Under capitalism, therefore, legislators receive many demands for protective tariffs from those voters who fear the loss of their jobs, while they seldom receive letters from those who expect free trade to give them jobs. Certain capitalists, of course, believe their industries will benefit from free trade, but the additional export sales made possible by free trade are less certain than the increased domestic sales made possible by protective tariffs.

Another common argument against free trade is the charge that it would reduce the high American wage level and standard of living by forcing American workers to compete with cheap foreign labor. Like the charge that free trade causes unemployment, this plea is based upon a partial and incomplete view of foreign trade. It is perfectly true that imports may reduce real wages in certain industries, but it is equally true that the compensating exports must increase real wages in other industries by an even greater amount. Foreign trade always increases the general average of real wages by reducing the cost of living.

No matter how great the difference in wages, it is impossible for cheap foreign labor to lower American wages so long as that labor is outside the U.S. The only way such labor can reduce American wages is by coming to live and work in the U.S. Even then the undesirable effect is not due to the cheapness, but solely to the quantity of the foreign labor. In other words, the immigration of an equal number of previously highly paid like workers would have the same unfortunate effect upon the wage level.

If all uneconomic restrictions on international trade were eliminated, advanced nations would specialize in the production of capital-intensive, high-technology goods like computers and airplanes, and backward nations would specialize much more heavily in the production of labor-intensive, low-technology goods like textiles and clothing. This international division of labor would especially benefit undeveloped countries, who now find it difficult to market their growing industrial output in advanced countries, but it would also benefit developed countries.

B. Methods of Increasing Foreign Trade

The mere eradication of unsound limitations on foreign trade would cause a great increase in the volume of foreign trade and the benefits from it. A number of other methods for increasing the volume of foreign trade deserve comment.

First, it is always possible to stimulate both exports and imports by granting a bounty upon either or both. Capitalist states have frequently granted bounties on exports. Due to their Mercantilistic prejudices, however, they have seldom granted bounties on imports. Both practices, nevertheless, serve to increase imports and exports in the same degree.

Bounties on exports and imports may develop new foreign markets, or extend old ones, and thus increase the scale of production. This lowers production costs in industries of increasing returns. But a bounty on exports of the products of extractive industries, such as wheat, cotton, and coal, obviously increases the cost to all domestic consumers.

Even in the case of industries of increasing returns, however, export bounties are undesirable. If exports were properly controlled, any saving from an increased volume of production would serve to the proper degree as an export incentive by increasing the marginal profit on exports.

Secondly, it is always possible to increase the volume of foreign trade by dumping domestic products in foreign markets or by permitting or encouraging foreign nations to dump goods in domestic markets. Dumping may be defined as sale to foreign buyers at a net price lower than that prevailing in the domestic market. It has something in common with the use of export bounties to encourage foreign sales, since both methods result in sales to foreigners at prices below domestic levels. However, bounties are government outlays, while capitalist dumping is practiced by private firms and does not increase taxes.

Dumping may be profitable to individual trusts under capitalism because most of them charge domestic prices far above their marginal costs. It is usually possible to dump goods abroad at a price below that secured in the domestic market, and yet above marginal costs, so that an additional profit results from the production and sale of the goods dumped abroad. This type of dumping will seem to disappear under socialism if domestic prices are reduced to the level of marginal costs, since the essence of dumping is the difference between foreign and domestic prices. Its disappearance will be only apparent, however. Dumping abroad will appear to disappear only because it will be accompanied by dumping in domestic markets at the same price, and this will eliminate the different between domestic and export prices.

Dumping is also occasionally practiced in order to retain existing markets until prices again return to normal profitable levels; in order to introduce new products in markets which are expected to be profitable when once opened up; or in order to drive competitors out of business and establish a monopoly. In such cases, the dumped goods may be sold at a price below the marginal cost of production.

As a method of international competition, dumping at prices below marginal costs would be far more practical and effective when used by the export agency of a socialist economy than when used by individual capitalist firms with relatively small resources. Nevertheless, it ought not to be used for this purpose. It would arouse international resentment and would lead to restrictions upon the trade of the socialist state using it and/or to bitter price-cutting wars with foreign trusts.

Thirdly, it is possible to increase the volume of foreign trade by using advertising, either for purely competitive or for educational purposes. Advertising may be used both to stimulate the sale of foreign commodities in domestic markets and to stimulate the sale of domestic commodities in foreign markets.

A socialist economy should not use competitive advertising to increase the sales of its own products in the domestic market, for reasons already made clear. Hence it ought not to permit the use of competitive advertising to stimulate the sale of foreign products in this market.

In the case of export trade, however, the interests of a socialist state conflict with the interests of the remainder of the world in regard to competitive advertising. The burden of such competitive advertising can and should fall entirely upon the consumer in the form of a higher price. It is clear, then, that the use of competitive advertising to increase export trade will benefit a socialist economy while at the same time it will harm the countries where such advertising is done.

C. The Disadvantages of Foreign Trade

Although foreign trade which enables consumers to get more for their money is ordinarily advantageous, unrestricted importation of certain classes of goods may be harmful.

In the first place, unrestricted foreign trade may result in dependence on foreign nations for commodities essential to the waging of war. If such goods are imported from abroad rather than produced at home, the military power of the importing nation may be considerably weakened, and the military power of other nations increased.

This argument against foreign trade applies only to industries essential to military power, and these industries are already more highly developed in America than in any other country. The great wealth, the large population, and the strategic isolation of the U.S. are also relevant. Under these circumstances, few if any protective tariffs are required to increase American military power.

The second real advantage of foreign trade is that under certain circumstances it may serve to check or prevent altogether the development of certain industries well suited to domestic conditions and which, once properly developed, could supply certain commodities more economically than foreign nations. The development of new industries can certainly be stimulated by restriction of imports. This is often desirable both for the nation in question and for the world as a whole. Experience has repeatedly demonstrated that the industrialization of backward nations increases both their imports and their exports. It also stimulates the progress of science, checks infectious disease, promotes democracy, and yields other benefits.

During most of the nineteenth century, the high American tariff was largely justified by the need for protection of infant industries. In Soviet Russia a high degree of protection for new and vital basic industries was long similarly justified. The case is quite different in modern Germany, England, and America, however, In these nations the great majority of industries are already highly developed and deserve no protection.

Another disadvantage of free foreign trade is that it may make a country unduly dependent upon imports or exports which foreign countries can radically curtail or stop, or whose prices they can change suddenly and greatly. Since 1900, exporters of several major U.S. imports — tin, coffee, oil, etc. — have formed cartels to force up the world prices of such commodities. The 1973 agreement among the major petroleum exporting nations was the most effective of such cartel agreements. It quadrupled the price of oil almost overnight, and was followed by an embargo of the shipment of oil to some nations. Other essential fuels and raw materials — coal, copper, iron ore, phosphate, etc. — may be similarly monopolized and/or withheld in the future. Hence, a socialist country should, when possible, avoid becoming highly dependent on imports of such scarce fuels and raw materials.

D. Methods of Restricting Foreign Trade

As explained above, it is sometimes justifiable to restrict both imports and exports (any restriction of one necessarily involves an equal restriction of the other) in order to protect or develop industries producing essential war materials and in order to encourage the establishment and development of promising new industries.

Under capitalism the most common method of restricting foreign trade is the imposition of a tariff or duty upon imports or exports. This method has a number of apparent advantages. It not only results in no burden upon the public treasury, but actually serves to bring in a very considerable revenue. Moreover, the additional revenue is not a direct or obvious burden upon domestic taxpayers. It comes in large part out of the pockets of foreigners. These are very persuasive considerations to the average politician.

Actually tariffs are undesirable because they hide the cost of protecting domestic industries and because they place this cost upon the wrong people. If national welfare justifies the protection of a certain domestic industry, this protection ought to cause an obvious cost to the state rather than an increase in its income, and this cost ought to be borne by the nation as a whole rather than by those who consume the products of the protected industry. Only under such conditions is it possible for voters and legislators to measure and give due weight to the costs of protection.

Duties on exports are undesirable for much the same reason. They appear to be profitable, since they bring in a large revenue, but actually they decrease the volume of foreign trade below the optimum level. If special considerations justify an effort to restrict certain exports, this should be done in such a way as to impose a financial burden upon the government so obvious that everyone will be aware that restriction of foreign trade is costly rather than remunerative.

A nation which has a monopoly in the production of a good, or is part of an international cartel, may profit temporarily by charging all foreign buyers a monopoly price, the domestic price plus a suitable export duty. However, such monopoly gains stimulate foreign research on substitutes and on better methods of production which, once discovered, may put an end not only to the monopoly profits but even to the trade itself. Duties on exports also create ill feeling abroad and increase the danger of war. Hence, a socialist state should never use them.

It is possible to reduce the volume of foreign trade by laying an embargo upon the import or export of any commodity, or by establishing either import or export quotas for individual commodities. An embargo or complete prohibition is the most drastic method of limiting foreign trade, and involves a greater social cost than any other method. This cost may be justified in certain rare cases, but an embargo normally is an unsound method of limiting foreign trade because it occasions no monetary cost to the government to call attention to the real economic cost. This same criticism holds for quotas, although the latter are less undesirable, as they place less of a bar upon commerce. Both embargoes and quotas also have the defect of being relatively inflexible and unresponsive to changes in market conditions. Quotas have the further disadvantages of giving rise to large profits upon the commodities imported. These profits, like the revenue from duties, tend to obscure the real economic costs involved.

One other method of restricting foreign trade, the granting of subsidies to domestic producers that are threatened by serious foreign competition, remains to be discussed. This is the method which should be used in a socialist economy. A subsidy granted to producers of war materials or to infant industries places an obvious monetary burden upon the state and, hence, upon taxpayers. This visible financial burden is highly desirable because it indicates a very real economic burden.

Another advantage of bounties over tariffs is that the former involve much less administrative expense. One government office in Washington could handle all bounties at a minimum cost, while the customs service now includes offices in all ports and border towns. Moreover, bounties do not result in smuggling and the resulting expense to the government of checking it. Smuggling is only profitable when prices are lower abroad than at home. Bounties can lower domestic prices to those prevailing abroad, plus costs of importation, and put an end to smuggling.

E. The Conduct of Foreign Trade

In a socialist economy all exports and imports should be handled by a single national Foreign Trade Trust. This organization should have branches in every foreign nation. At home the Foreign Trade Trust should have branch offices in every port and frontier point through which any appreciable volume of international trade passes. Wherever necessary, abroad or at home, this trust should have warehouse and storage facilities to care for its trade.

The basic economic problem involved in the management of foreign trade in a socialist economy is the problem of how to determine the nature and volume of imports and exports. We have already discussed certain methods both of increasing and of restricting the total volume of foreign trade, but these methods do not permit immediate and flexible control of individual or total imports and exports. Tariffs and bounties should not be changed from day to day. They ought to be used, if at all, merely to protect certain domestic industries, not to control the volume of foreign trade.

The problem of the control of foreign trade in a socialist economy may be divided into two parts; first, the problem of control over the volume of trade in individual commodities; and secondly, the problem of control over the total volume of imports and exports.

Controlling Individual Imports and Exports — Every individual commodity which moves in foreign trade should be placed under the control of specialists in that commodity or in a group of commodities including it. These specialists should have absolute control over the volume of exports and imports of the commodities placed in their charge. As explained later, control over the total volume of all imports and exports should be exercised in a manner which leaves complete freedom to these commodity specialists.

Two slightly different tasks will confront these commodity specialists; first, the task of determining what commodities ought to be imported or exported, and secondly, the task of determining the volume of imports and exports of each commodity.

The first question, that of determining what individual commodities should be imported or exported, ought to be settled by application of the following principle: any individual commodity which can be imported or exported at a profit should be imported or exported.

The justification for carrying on foreign trade wherever and whenever it yields a profit is precisely the same as that for producing whatever good or service yields a profit. With a relatively equal distribution of income and with a properly controlled monetary system, a profit is the best possible indication of a net margin of benefit over real cost.

The second question is that of determining how large a volume of each commodity should be imported or exported. Here again the proper method of control is similar to that used in controlling the production of domestic commodities. The volume of imports or exports of each good should be increased until marginal profits disappear, but no further. Of course, no exact equilibrium is possible, but the goal of all control over foreign trade should be to eliminate both marginal profits and losses by varying the volume of trade alone. Any effort to decrease such profits or losses merely by altering prices or business expenses would be unsound. Those who evaluate the success of executives of the Foreign Trade Trust should take two entirely different factors into consideration: first, the unit cost of doing business, and secondly, the volume of marginal profits and losses earned. This would tend to prevent the alteration of unit costs in order to reduce profits and losses.

All that was said in Chapter XIII of <u>Liberal Socialism</u> concerning the proper calculation of profits and losses resulting from the domestic production of commodities applies with equal force to profits and losses earned in foreign trade. It is marginal profit or loss that should be discovered and used for control purposes. Individual production-control statements for each commodity carried over each route should be prepared and used. Estimates of future or potential profits and losses should be the determining factors, rather than past profits and losses. This means, among other things, that profits and losses due to price changes, natural catastrophes, obsolescence, and other unpredictable factors should be ignored in controlling imports and exports.

The use of profits and losses to determine the volume of imports and exports of specific commodities is inconsistent with planning of such imports and exports. It will, of course, be good business practice to estimate in advance the volume of future imports and exports in order to prepare to handle them, but unpredictable fluctuations in domestic prices should alter profits and losses and, hence, the volume of imports and exports. In the last analysis, it is current profits and losses, rather than national plans, which should determine the volume of individual imports and exports.

In <u>Liberal Socialism</u> we argued (pp. 75, 208) that long-term buying and selling contracts are as uneconomic as coercive economic plans. However, this theory does not apply to foreign trade. The use of long-term contracts may secure better terms from foreign dealers. Hence, a socialist foreign trade agency should be allowed to use such contracts to obtain better prices or to stabilize the volume of trade in certain goods.

The foreign trade commodity specialists who control the import and/or export of individual goods should closely coordinate their plans and activities with those of the domestic producers of the goods involved. They should be well-informed concerning the relevant domestic cost schedules and investment pro‐ jects, as well as concerning domestic demand schedules and demand growth trends. And domestic producers should be well-informed concerning export demand schedules and import supply schedules for their products. Before any new domestic capital investment is made, full consideration should be given to an increase in imports as an alternative. The uneconomic competition between mutually uninformed importers and domestic producers typical of capitalism should cease.

<u>Balancing Total Imports and Exports</u> — As we have explained, the volume of imports and exports of each individual commodity should be independently determined by specialists in that commodity, regardless of the volume of trade in other goods. Since the total volume of imports or exports is merely the total of imports and exports of all individual commodities,

the former may appear to be determined by those who control the latter. However, since the commodity specialists are to be governed in all their decisions by marginal profits and losses, it is possible to give one agency complete control over the relationship between total imports and total exports by giving it power to influence sufficiently these profits and losses. This can be done by giving it complete control over the exchange rates between the domestic currency and foreign currencies. Such is the method of balancing total imports and total exports which ought to be used in a socialist economy. Absolute control over all foreign-exchange rates should be vested in a Foreign Exchange Branch of the Foreign Trade Trust and used by this division to secure the desired balance of trade.

Incidentally, the desired balance of trade will never be an exactly equal balance. There will always be other items, the so-called "invisible items," which involve international financial payments. It is the total payments of all kinds in each direction which must be balanced. The manipulation of foreign exchange rates will affect the volume of each of these invisible items in the same way that it will affect visible items. Thus, depreciation of the dollar will decrease American imports of all kinds.

Under capitalism control of foreign-exchange rates requires large financial reserves. Arbitrary authority over the conduct of private citizens also is ordinarily used to supplement financial measures. It will be far easier to secure the same ends in a socialist economy. Whenever the Foreign Exchange Branch desires a change in total visible and invisible imports or exports, it will merely alter foreign exchange rates so as to gain the desired result. All commodity specialists will immediately react to the new profits and losses created thereby in the trade under their control. The desired end will be quickly achieved without any large purchase or sale of foreign exchange because of the immediate effect upon the volume of imports and exports.

Many difficulties encountered in the control of foreign exchange under capitalism are due to the unsound purposes of such control. Under capitalism it is customary to use control over foreign exchange in order to stabilize the exchange, that is, in order to prevent natural reaction to economic forces generated by excessive imports or exports. Under socialism, however, control should be used to secure an immediate and proper reaction to such forces. When the nation is faced with an undesired surplus of imports, no costly effort to maintain the foreign exchange value of the domestic currency by deflating domestic prices ought to be made. Instead, the exchange rate should be lowered so as to eliminate all financial strain by stimulating exports and reducing imports. This method of balancing imports and exports would have a minimum effect upon domestic prices and business conditions. However, exchange rates should not be changed more often than once every three months.

To control all foreign exchange rates it is usually necessary to control the rate with one other foreign currency only. Thus, if Russia were to exercise control only over the exchange rate between the ruble and the dollar, it would automatically achieve all necessary control over other ruble exchange rates.

The method used by Russia to control the relationship between total exports and total imports is apparently an entirely arbitrary method. There is no difficulty, of course, in securing any desired balance between the total imports and exports of a socialist economy, just as there is no difficulty in determining an arbitrary plan of production for the domestic economy. The real difficulty, and one which the USSR has not solved, is that of securing the most economic volume of individual and total imports and exports. The great advantage of the method of balancing imports and exports suggested in this chapter is that it permits restriction of total imports or exports by curtailing all individual imports or exports in precisely the degree by which they ought to be curtailed, and vice versa in the case of an increase in total imports or exports.

It may be objected that a socialist state could not determine its foreign exchange rates because foreign nations might desire and strive to achieve different exchange rates. However, the method of rate determination we have prescribed would benefit all nations equally, and therefore should arouse little opposition from foreign socialist states. Of course, most capitalist governments still want to achieve what they call a "favorable" balance of trade. Since such trade balances are really unfavorable to other states, a socialist state should do nothing to oppose their achievement by capitalist nations. Rather, it should help capitalist states to achieve them whenever such states desire them. However, if socialist states acted thus, capitalist governments would eventually recognize that a favorable balance of trade financed by unbacked foreign paper money is in fact unfavorable, and would then welcome foreign exchange rates which prevent such a trade balance.

F. Foreign Finance

A socialist government should borrow all the capital funds (foreign exchange) it can obtain from capitalist countries and should use these funds to import capital goods and the components and materials needed to increase domestic production of capital goods (including housing). It should rarely if ever use borrowed funds to increase the importation of consumers' goods, because this would dissipate its national wealth.

A socialist state should borrow all it can abroad because capital is more productive in a socialist country — due to elimination of the wastes of competition and business fluctuations — and because interest rates in capitalist countries are normally far below the marginal product of capital investment. All capitalist governments impose heavy taxes on the income from marginal investment. As a result, capitalist firms cannot offer interest rates which measure anywhere near the full marginal product of investment.

Two good ways to increase domestic capital funds are to sell exports for cash and try to buy all imports for credit, the longer the better. A socialist state should use both methods, particularly when dealing with competing capitalist firms.

It is especially desirable for a socialist state to borrow large additional sums from capitalist countries when they are suffering from an economic depression which has lowered their export selling prices, reduced their interest rates, and made them more eager to maintain or increase their exports. At such times a socialist state should make special efforts to increase its imports and loans from depressed capitalist countries. This would help to restore prosperity in capitalist countries, as well as enrich the socialist borrower and importer.

The same reasons which justify maximum borrowing from capitalist countries also justify minimum lending to and investment in them. A socialist government should never lend to foreign firms or governments, except for compelling political reasons. It should invest in capitalist countries only for similar reasons, or to safeguard essential sources of scarce raw materials, or to open up very profitable markets.

CHAPTER IX

PUBLIC UTILITIES

As used in this chapter, the term public utilities or utilities includes gas, water, electricity, steam, sewer, telephone, telegraph, and cable television systems. It does not include transportation systems, which are dealt with in a separate chapter, or warehouses, dairies, ice companies, and various other industries sometimes called public utilities.
The public utilities covered in this chapter have much in common. All of them require a heavy investment in pipe or cable networks along public streets, usually underground, and these networks largely parallel each other. Most of them employ similar systems of measuring service and collecting charges from customers. For these and other reasons the problems of public utilities are similar, and differ from those of other industries.
The value of the output of American public utilities has been growing faster than American GNP for over a century and now is about 6% of GNP. This share will continue to rise indefinitely because: (1) water and fuel costs will rise faster than the price level, (2) the centralized provision of heat and hot water will expand and become the largest of all public utilities, (3) cable TV will also expand greatly and become a major public utility, and (4) telephone use will grow much faster than the consumption of other goods.
Capitalism has already developed an extensive literature on the theory of public utility operation. Most of this theory will be applicable in a collectivist economy. This chapter is therefore limited to a discussion of the major changes in the methods of operating utilities which will result from the introduction of socialism.
Most public utilities are already operated as monopolies under capitalism. Bourgeois economists commonly hold that utilities require government ownership more than other industries. Actually, however, it is the most competitive industries, such as retail stores, which require government operation most urgently, since only in such industries will government ownership achieve the economies of monopoly. Natural monopolies are much more suited to private ownership than are highly competitive industries since private

192

ownership of utilities does not result in the usual wastes of competition. However, government control over private monopoly is needed.

A. Utility Construction in New Cities

In our chapters on new-city planning we explained that all additional population and a small share of old population should be housed in planned new cities each year. Few if any additions to old cities should be built. This implies that the construction of new public utility facilities should be almost entirely restricted to new cities.

We also argued that each new city should be built all at once, as a single construction project, and, once populated, should decline gradually in population. If these principles were applied, the need to expand old utility facilities would probably be reduced by over 80%. The decline in the population of each old and new city would permit a steady increase in the consumption of each utility service without any expansion of facilities. It would rarely be necessary to dig up paved streets in order to replace old cables or pipes with new larger ones to provide more service.

The theory of where and when to build new utility plants and distribution facilities in new cities is a minor part of the theory of socialist new-city planning, and was therefore discussed in Chapters IV and V.

We also deal separately (in Chapter XIII) with the bright future of cable TV, which will become a major public utility. Cable-TV facilities should be installed with other utilities, perhaps in the same ditch, whenever new cities and towns are built.

All investment in utility plants and distribution facilities should be based upon the kind of total cost-benefit analysis prescribed in Chapter X of <u>Liberal Socialism</u>. The application of such analysis to utilities involves no major new or unique problems, and therefore needs no discussion here.

B. Consolidation of Utilities

In a socialist country all public utilities should be under a single national Public Utility Trust. In each metropolitan area and surrounding region all utilities should be operated by a single local or regional unit of this trust. Such a regional consolidation of operations would permit achievement of the maximum economies of common management and large-scale operation. These economies may be classified under three heads: (1) those due to unified construction and maintenance, (2) those due to consolidation of office work, and (3) those due to consolidation of facilities and operations. We have just noted our earlier treatment of the consolidation of original construction.

Consolidation of Maintenance — The maintenance work of different public utilities is very similar. Large economies are possible if all utility maintenance work in each area is done by the same organization. The same kind of skill and equipment is needed to dig up a street in order to repair a water main as is needed to dig up a street in order to repair a sewer, steam, or gas main. Moreover, an event such as a flood which injures one main is apt to injure the other mains.

The men and tools used to maintain telephone poles and lines are almost equally qualified to repair telegraph and power poles and lines. If a storm blows the wires down, there is no reason why the telephone company, the telegraph company, and the power and light company should all send repair crews to the same spot. And maintenance inspectors and trouble-shooters should inspect all overhead lines or underground cables on each street at the same time.

The merger of all utility maintenance work in the hands of a single agency would so increase the size and personnel of the average maintenance unit that marked improvement in organization and equipment would be possible. Thus, if all ditch digging for utility maintenance in each community were done by a single agency, it would pay to use more and/or bigger ditch-digging machines, and they would be more steadily employed. It would also become economic to increase the division of labor among both foremen and ditch-diggers. There are thousands of small towns and rural areas where the volume of maintenance work on independent utility systems is much too small to justify the use of labor-saving methods and equipment, but where the total volume for all utilities is large enough to justify it. Unification of all utilities would also permit the location of maintenance units closer to the utility customers in thinly settled areas, and this would speed up repair work.

Consolidation of Office Work — The accounting, clerical, and other business-office activities now carried on independently by up to five distinct private or municipal public utilities in each community should be combined and rationalized. Only one "accounts receivable" account for all utility services should be kept for each customer, and only one "accounts payable" account for each creditor. This alone would reduce by up to 80% the number of such accounts and would save an equal proportion of the paper, filing cabinets, and space required for accounts payable and receivable.

Each meter-reader should read all meters — gas, water, electricity, steam, etc. — in each building on his route, and should enter the reading for all meters at each address on a single page of his record book so that they could be simultaneously transcribed to the single accounts-receivable account and the single consolidated bill for each customer, without referring to more than one sheet of paper. Each customer should receive only one bill for all utility services, and should pay this bill by mailing a single check. This would reduce the number of separate bills required in the U.S. by over one billion per year. Each bill now costs the utility over 30¢ to prepare and mail, and receiving, entering and depositing the payment costs as much more. It also costs the average customer at least 40¢ to pay each bill, all of which adds up to over $1.00 per utility bill.

In order to reduce still further the costs of preparing, mailing, collecting, and paying utility bills, a socialist Public Utility Trust should prepare monthly lists of customers and amounts due and send these lists to local branches of the State Bank, where all customers would have checking accounts to which the amounts due should be directly debited without any effort by the customer. This would reduce the postage costs of bill collection by over 99%, and would also save customers the time now required to write and mail individual checks. Like many other socialist reforms, this policy would simplify life and free people from time-consuming repetitive chores.

All local operating units of the Public Utilities Trust should use the same standardized accounting system in order to facilitate comparison of the accounts of different operating units. The books and forms, the titles and definitions of accounts, the treatment of depreciation, the method of valuing inventories, the types of accounting machines, and all other significant features of the accounting system should be uniform throughout the country, except when new equipment is gradually introduced.

Consolidation of Facilities — The creation of a national Public Utility Trust which operates all utilities would permit, and should be followed by, the consolidation of nearly all utility offices and plants into much larger, more efficient and better-located units. For instance, all the small and middle-size sewage treatment plants in each metropolitan area could be replaced by one or a few much larger, more efficient, and better located plants. And similar plant consolidation and relocation should be carried out in other utility industries.

Electricity can be generated much more cheaply in large power plants than in small ones. Every increase in the size of a power plant reduces costs per unit of output. Therefore, a socialist public utility trust should replace most regional power plants with much larger plants. Small urban plants would be justified only as sources of steam and hot water to meet local needs.

The above remarks propose plant consolidation within single utility industries. There should also be considerable facility consolidation between utility industries. For instance, a single office in each city should house the office work for all local utilities, and a single maintenance yard or network of yards should contain the maintenance equipment, materials, and tools used in maintenance work on all local utility facilities.

Moreover, urban electrical generating plants should provide steam or hot water to heat all buildings in the city, and hot water for other uses, as well as generating electricity. No manufacturing plant, office building, hospital, or other building in a planned city should have its own equipment for producing steam, hot water, heat, or electricity. If emergency stand-by electrical capacity is needed in any building, it should be provided by stand-by facilities which have been planned and maintained by the Public Utilities Trust and which provide stand-by capacity for all local priority users, not for one user only.

Under capitalism many firms find it profitable to build and use their own power plants because public utilities are monopolies and charge a price above the cost of producing power in less efficient independent plants. Proper utility rates would make this unprofitable.

C. The Development of Central Heating

In America today nearly all electrical generating plants produce a large volume of spent steam which is condensed and cooled at great expense. In a well-planned socialist city the spent steam and its by-product, hot water, produced in urban power plants should be used for heating buildings and water throughout the city. In a new planned city the local urban power plant or plants should be just large enough to supply local demand for steam and hot water.

Only small areas in a very few American cities are now provided steam heating and hot water by central power plants. Over 90% of all American buildings have their own small and inefficient heating and hot water sources. We explained in Chapter III why this decentralized production of heat and hot water is inefficient and costly, and why all new and rebuilt socialist cities should have centralized heating and hot water systems. It is, of course, far cheaper to provide such systems in new cities than in old ones. That is one reason why socialist governments should rehouse most of their population in new or entirely reconstructed cities.

Steam or hot-water radiator heating is superior to warm-air heating, and is widely used in spite of the high cost of producing steam and hot water in small domestic boilers. Moreover, both steam and hot water can be used in heating systems which use pipes in floors, walls, and ceilings instead of radiators.

Central generation and town- or city-wide distribution of steam and/or hot water would not only reduce their cost but would also free the domestic consumer of many inconveniences of domestic production of steam and hot water. He would no longer have to buy and store coal or oil, or buy and maintain his furnace-boiler unit. And he would not have to get up early in the morning to fire his furnace with coal.

Most Americans now heat their homes and warm their water with oil or natural gas. Both of these fuels will soon be too scarce and costly to use for these purposes. They will be replaced by coal, which is far less suitable for distribution to and use in private homes. Thus the case for centralized production of steam and hot water will become far stronger as the domestic use of oil and natural gas declines.

Public utilities which provide steam and/or hot water should provide at least two kinds of service, firm and interruptible. And standby capacity should be used to provide firm service only when breakdowns in regular equipment occur.

D. Water Utilities

In the U.S., total water consumption now doubles every 20 to 30 years, and the real marginal costs are rising. By the time socialism is achieved, it will be an essential scarce mineral.

There are hundreds of independent firms and public agencies collecting, processing, and distributing fresh water in the U.S. Most of them are local monopolies, so the wastes of competitive distribution have been minimized, but they compete for both distant and underground water sources. A single metropolitan area may be served by a score of separate water suppliers, each competing with all the others for local and regional water sources. As a result, one part of a metropolitan area may suffer from a severe water shortage while nearby communities may have a water surplus. And the underground water level may fall steadily.

In a socialist country all water production, extraction, long-distance movement, and non-urban distribution systems should be managed by a single national agency, the Water Service Branch (WSB) of the Public Utilities Trust. However, in each city the maintenance of the water distribution system should be performed by the same joint agency which does this for other local underground utility networks.

The WSB should have complete control over the withdrawal of water from underground sources. No private person, firm, or government agency should be allowed to draw water from such sources unless it has received a permit from the WSB. And the WSB should control the use of each underground source so as to maintain an optimum underground water level, one which rises in wet years, falls in dry years, and minimizes pumping costs over the long run. Under competitive capitalism the water levels in underground reservoirs often fall far below optimum levels. This greatly increases well-drilling and water-pumping costs, and also causes land subsidence.

It is more economic to store surplus water underground than to store it behind high dams because dams are expensive to build and create flood risks. Moreover, underground water does not evaporate. Therefore, storage in underground reservoirs should be greatly increased.

In a socialist America no region or area should be allowed to retain for its own present or future use water needed more urgently in other regions of the country. All water should be sold to the highest bidder, regardless of his location, providing he pays the cost of transportation.

During the 21st century, if not before, it will probably become economic to transport by canal very large quantities of water from Alaska and Canada to arid areas of the American west. It will also become economic to supply most or all of the urban water used in some coastal cities by desalinizing sea water. Los Angeles, San Diego, and other neaby southern California cities will probably become the first American heavy users of desalted sea water. This will free large quantities of imported fresh water for use in inland areas. As fresh water becomes more and more valuable, it will become economic to divert more and more river water at points farther and farther inland, and meet the needs of more and more low-lying cities with desalted sea water and recycled fresh water.

As fresh water becomes more valuable, it will become economic to limit pollution of lakes and rivers ever more strictly, and to purify and reuse sewage and drainage water in all areas where fresh water is scarce Before America goes socialist, the purification and reuse of all irrigation run-off water in arid regions will probably become economic.

The ideal way to limit water pollution is to measure pollution and charge a uniform price per pollution unit high enough to reduce pollution to the optimum level, the level at which a further reduction would cost more than it is worth. To determine this level, the WSB will have to estimate carefully all the major disbenefits of water pollution, which will differ from place to place.

The use of pollution charges will permit a radical decentralization of decision-making concerning the methods and degrees of pollution control. This is desirable because local plant managers are more familiar with their local pollution-control problems than are central executives.

E. Controlling Investment in Public Utilities

All utility services are, or will soon become, necessities for urban residents in advanced countries. By raising average personal incomes and making them much less unequal, socialism will enable all families to consume all utility services. Hence, socialist new-city planners should provide all such services for all families.

When a planned new socialist city is built, the public utilities should be large enough to provide all tenants with the amount of utility services consumed by like tenants in older similar cities, plus a small margin for growth in demand. Since such cities should decline in population for many decades after they have been first fully occupied and since any later needed additional supplies of electricity should be supplied by regional superpower networks, there would rarely be any need to expand the capacity of the old utility plants in planned socialist cities.

Proper planning of the size of new utility plants requires total, not marginal, analysis. This total analysis should be applied to each proposed lumpy increment in the capacity of any utility plant. No such capacity increment should be added unless the expected consumers' surplus on the additional output is large enough to offset the expected deficit on the additional output. Changes in the suplus or deficit on basic output should be ignored. Thus the ideal deficit on the final increment in capacity should usually be small, even when the ideal deficit for the plant as a whole is large.

Moreover, investment in each utility plant should always be limited enough to justify relatively high peak-hour use rates, far above average marginal costs. This would compel peak-period consumers to pay a substantial part of non-marginal utility costs. Such limitation of investment would limit ideal deficits.

F. The Pricing of Utility Services

The welfare theory of utility rate determination has received little attention from capitalist economists, and has been virtually ignored by those who fix and review utility rates. Public utilities are natural monopolies with indefinitely decreasing marginal costs. Capitalist welfare economics is based largely upon the theory of perfect competition in industries with increasing costs, and is therefore not applicable to utilities.

Moreover, the managers of private public utilities have little if any interest in welfare economics. They fix their rates so as to achieve maximum permitted profits, not so as to maximize economic welfare.

In the U.S. the public officials who review nearly all utility rates are required by law and judicial decision to permit utilities to earn a fair return on a fair valuation of their assets. This is a legal, not an economic criterion, and it is a guide to profit control, not to price determination. There are usually many different possible cost and price structures, each of which would yield a desired fair return on investment. When public officials alter proposed utility rates, they do so in order to affect profits, not in order to achieve optimum rates. Indeed, they have no accepted theory of how individual rates should be fixed so as to maximize economic welfare.

As explained in Liberal Socialism, p. 70, those who fix socialist prices should ignore the effect of their pricing decisions on total profits. Only those who control investment should consider total profits, and they should only consider profits on proposed increments in investment, not on the net worth of a firm. Striving for a fair return on investment not only fails to yield ideal utility rates but is incompatible with the achievement of both sound investment and sound rates.

Most American public utilities now charge up to five different kinds of prices: (1) use rates, those which are stated per unit of service consumed, (2) connection rates, special charges for each connection and disconnection, (3) special equipment rates, additional fixed charges for special equipment, (4) special service rates, extra variable monthly charges for continuing special services, and (5) uniform monthly service charges. In Liberal Socialism, p. 199, we introduced the term multi-marginal pricing to denote the simultaneous use of two or more prices like those listed above.

Use rates are and should continue to be the largest sources of utility income, and therefore deserve the most attention here.

Use Rates — The most basic principle of socialist utility use-rate determination is that use rates should equal marginal costs, defined as necessary variable cost at the margin, whenever such rates do not cause demand to exceed supply. Rates should of course be raised above marginal cost whenever this is necessary to balance supply and demand.

In Chapter IV of Liberal Socialism, we explained that in industries producing tangible goods the best way to achieve prices equal to marginal costs is to separate the function of pricing from the function of output control. With such a separation of functions, those who fix prices need only apply the simple rule of setting prices which will just move the entire supply of each good. These prices would result in marginal profits or losses which should cause those in charge of output control to increase or decrease the supply of each good until marginal cost is just equal to price.

Such a separation of function is not possible in the case of utilities because their products are services which cannot be produced for inventory and stored. It is impossible to fix prices in such a way as to move an independently determined supply because the price itself directly determines the supply, which is equal to the amount consumed.

It may appear at first glance that this is unimportant since capacity to serve is available as a substitute for supply in the process of price-output control. However, capacity cannot usually be increased as rapidly as supply from existing plants, and it ought never to be reduced merely because it is temporarily unneeded.

Since a separation of functions is not practical, the use rate for and the output from existing capacity must be simultaneously controlled and, since consumers control output, this control must take the form of price control.

Utility use rates equal to marginal costs would be far below capitalist utility rates, except when peak demand would exceed capacity. Marginal cost is only a minor fraction of any estimate of the average cost of utility service because construction and interest costs are very high and account for most of any estimate of average cost. Once a utility system has been built, the costs of operation are relatively small. Hence, the cost of producing and selling one more unit of below-capacity service is relatively small. In the case of an electrical utility using steam power, for instance, the only significant cost of producing and selling additional electricity is the cost of the additional fuel. Even repair and maintenance costs on the system as a whole are largely independent of the quantity of electricity produced and consumed. The marginal cost of providing one more unit of any utility service to a domestic consumer is identical with the cost of providing one more unit of service to a commercial or industrial consumer. Therefore, the rate charged should be the same for all consumers.

Marginal costs of utility services are very stable from hour to hour through the day and from day to day through the year as long as the peak load each day is less than the capacity of the system. Hence, little if any variation in use rates during periods when demand is less than capacity is justified. On the other hand, as soon as the demand for service at the existing rate approaches closely the capacity of existing fixed plant, rates should be raised enough to keep demand below capacity.

The use of any utility service varies from hour to hour throughout each 24 hours, and from day to day throughout the year. It would be fairly easy to establish different rates for off-peak months, and this should be done. It would be more expensive to install meters which record the time of day as well as the amount of service consumed. However, technological progress may soon make it economic to vary the use rates charged most customers of water, gas, and electricity according to the time of day. Capitalist telephone rates for long-distance calls already vary in this way, and should continue to do so whenever peak demand exceeds capacity.

Capitalist economists have long taught that utility rates should yield "a fair return on a fair value." To apply this principle, utility managers have often raised their use rates to compensate for a decline in demand. Under socialism such use rates should never be raised because demand has fallen. They should be raised only when demand has increased and/or marginal cost has risen.

A socialist utility should never grant quantity discounts. Such discounts may at times be desirable under capitalism because they lower use rates and bring them closer to marginal costs. But socialist use rates should always be as low as marginal costs, for both small and large consumers, except when higher rates are needed to balance supply and demand.

Some reformers have recently begun to argue that utility use rates should increase as individual consumption increases in order to induce individuals to reduce their consumption. This proposal is unsound. It ignores the well-known principle that the total benefit from consumption of any good can be maximized only by permitting all consumers to increase their consumption until their marginal benefit, measured by the price paid, is equal for all consumers.

<u>Free Provision of Utility Services and Goods</u> — The question of whether a specific utility service or good should be treated as a price good or a free good requires welfare, not profit, calculation. Most of the benefits of free distribution accrue to the public, not to utilities, and therefore do not affect their profit calculation. And some of the costs of price distribution, for instance, the costs of paying bills, are paid by customers, and therefore do not affect profit calculation. In this case, as in so many others, rational economic calculation is impossible or impractical under capitalism but possible and practical under socialism.

In the case of utilities which provide a physical commodity — gas, water, steam, electricity — it is impossible to charge a use rate unless a meter is installed to measure consumption. The use of meters creates not only meter investment and maintenance costs but also the costs of meter reading. Moreover, collecting use-rate charges from customers involves substantial costs, both to the utility and to consumers. Free provision of a utility service avoids all these continuing costs. It increases use, but in many cases the real cost of the increased use is less than the real cost of preventing excessive use by means of installing meters and collecting use rates.

Under capitalism many private building owners provide one or more utility services free of charge to their tenants. They do so because they believe that the cost of installing meters and collecting use rates is greater than the resulting gain to the landlord, and their belief is usually correct.

The smaller and less elastic the consumption of a utility service by a consumer, the stronger is the case for free provision of that service. Thus water should usually be provided as a free good to tenants of apartments and other small houses who do not have gardens to water or swimming pools to fill. Electricity also should usually be a free good to such tenants, unless it is used for heating, cooling, charging automobile batteries, or some other elastic use.

Another, less general but more conclusive, reason for treating some utility services as free goods is that their marginal cost is zero or insignificant. For instance, when the marginal cost of water is zero and the water distribution system is large enough, water should be a free good to all customers. And when the marginal cost of telephone service is zero and the automatic phone system has the capacity to handle all free calls, telephone service should be free. Even when service should not be free during hours of peak use, telephone service and domestic water should be free during off-peak hours under the above conditions.

If all electricity in a city is generated by hydropower stations or other stations with negligible marginal costs, electricity should be a free good, at least to typical domestic users in off-peak hours. The marginal cost of electricity generated in nuclear plants may be negligible.

The service of cable-TV systems should be free because marginal use creates no marginal cost, and any use rate or service charge would reduce consumption below the optimum level.

The use of sewer systems is now, and should remain, a free good to domestic consumers because it is far too costly to measure use by such consumers. However, it would be economic to measure the volume of sewage created in plants which produce large amounts of industrial sewage. They should be charged use rates which allocate to them the costs of treating sewage, so as to optimize pollution and improve cost calculation.

In many areas of the world natural gas produced in the process of oil extraction is still being locally "flared" or burned unproductively to dispose of it safely. When pipelines and distribution systems are first installed to send such costless gas to consumers, no use rate should be charged until demand exceeds supply.

Charges for Optional Equipment and Services — In a planned socialist new city the cost of the original investment in utility plants and distribution systems should be allocated to individual buildings in the same way as the costs of streets and sidewalks are allocated. The interest and non-use-caused maintenance costs of utility facilities should be treated like the similar costs of buildings. They should be covered by rentals paid by tenants. Only optional costs incurred after a new city is built, due to the decisions of individual tenants, should be allocated to these tenants by means of use rates, connection charges, special equipment charges, and other such prices.

It may be objected that some tenant rentals should not cover the original investment in all utilities because some tenants would not use all utility services. But socialist income-equalizing policies should permit all domestic consumers to use all local utility services.

Socialist utilities ought to collect special extra charges for all optional services — temporary disconnection, information calls, telephone answering service, etc. — and for all optional extra equipment — fancy telephones, computer connections, water purifiers, etc. Such charges would allocate the extra costs to those responsible for them. Free provision of such goods would result in gross overconsumption of them.

The extra charges for optional service should equal the marginal costs of providing these services. The extra one-time charges for optional equipment should equal the lumpy costs of producing and installing the equipment.

It is noteworthy that such extra charges are economic even if the relevant basic utility service is a free good. Even when there is no use charge or periodic charge for the basic service, those who demand special services and equipment should pay for them.

Charges for Non-Optional Services — Some non-optional one-time or periodic utility services should also often be charged for separately in order to help cover total costs and reduce deficits without raising use rates above marginal costs. Such services include original connection, final disconnection, and periodic billing service.

The preparation, submission, and handling of periodic bills for utility services create significant costs which do not vary with the amount of services consumed. These costs should be recovered by adding a fixed sum, a billing charge, to each bill submitted. This charge should equal the average marginal cost of bill preparation, submission, and handling when bills are paid promptly. The extra costs of special collection efforts for delinquent accounts should be covered by other special collection charges.

Ideal Deficits and Periodic Service Charges — All public utilities have indefinitely declining marginal-cost curves. Every well-planned increase in the capacity of a utility plant reduces investment and operating costs per unit of output at planned capacity. Since utility investment costs per dollar of output are relatively high, any reduction in these costs achieved by an increase in scale is unusually significant. Therefore, optimum investment in any socialist utility, with optimum pricing, should result in relatively large ideal deficits, even without any free distribution.

In most industries ideal deficits should be fully covered by subsidies from the national treasury because there is no practical method of allocating such deficits to the industries and consumers responsible for them without raising prices above marginal costs and/or restricting consumption unduly in other ways. In the case of utilities, however, otherwise uncovered non-marginal costs can be allocated to consumers by means of periodic service charges. Such charges are widely used by private utilities to permit the lowering or non-use of use rates. Under socialism, much higher periodic service charges could be collected. This could make each utility profitable and self-supporting without raising use rates above marginal costs, or even without charging use rates.

Such periodic charges are uneconomic whenever they prevent some potential consumers from consuming a utility service they ought to consume, a common effect of such charges under capitalism. But in a mature socialist economy, one with high average real wages and no unemployment or poverty, periodic utility charges would have far less effect on consumer use of utility services, especially in planned new cities. Nevertheless, there would be some harmful effect, and the costs of collecting periodic uniform utility charges would be significant. Therefore, it would be better to finance all utility ideal deficits out of the general revenues of the government.

CHAPTER X

INSURANCE

The private insurance industry employed about 1.5 million Americans in 1976. It is one of the least efficient capitalist industries. A socialist reorganization should radically change the structure and operating methods of the industry, markedly increase insurance coverage and protection, and also drastically reduce operating costs.

Private insurance has long been provided by private firms which hire salesmen to sell individual insurance policies to individual customers, collect insurance premiums, and keep accurate records of all premiums paid by, and all benefits paid to, each insured person. As a result, their operating costs have been very high, often larger than the total benefits paid to beneficiaries. In 1974 the operating costs, profits, and taxes of American life insurance companies amounted to about $16 billion, $30% of the total premium income and 43% of total benefit payments. These data include a large volume of group insurance, which has relatively low operating costs. For the typical individual life insurance contract the proportion of costs to benefit payments is much higher.

Private auto accident insurance companies are even less efficient. Their total operating costs and profits now amount to about 40% of their premium income, and often exceed benefit payments.

It is noteworthy that some of the largest American insurance firms are mutual non-profit or cooperative firms, but they have the same high costs as the capitalist, profit-seeking firms. It is not capitalism but competition which is responsible for most of the waste under competitive capitalism.

So far as I am aware, no economist has ever tried to state the theory of an ideal insurance system, either for a capitalist or a socialist society. The major reason for this neglect is that private insurance firms cannot apply, and therefore do not need, a theory of ideal insurance. Moreover, in capitalist countries social insurance has been created and used primarily to supplement private insurance, not to provide an ideal system of insurance.

Public insurance, broadly defined, has been growing much faster than private insurance since 1900 in all advanced countries. In other words, the insurance industry has been increasingly socialized. In most advanced countries, benefit payments by public insurance systems now exceed benefit payments by private insurance and pension systems. They will continue to grow faster.

Social insurance is less comprehensive in the U.S. than in most other advanced countries, but by 1973 public insurance benefit payments equaled total private insurance payments to policyholders. If public welfare payments — $27 billion in 1973 — are treated as insurance benefits, as seems proper, the total of public insurance benefits in 1973 exceeded total private insurance benefit payments by about 40% and amounted to 9% of total American disposable personal income.

A. The Functions of Insurance

Insurance is usually defined by capitalist economists as a system of pooling risks which converts large irregular private costs or losses into small regular costs. For a socialist economist, the most important fact about personal insurance is that it redistributes income from the less needy to the more needy. It collects a part of the income of many persons and distributes most of the proceeds to those who have become more needy because of a sudden large, individually unpredictable loss of property or income. Thus all of our arguments for equalization of personal income (LS, Ch. XV) can be used to strengthen the case for universal insurance of personal incomes and property.

Although insurance benefits flow from the less needy to the more needy, they tend to restore the income structure which would have existed if there had been no insurable losses. They need not, and ordinarily do not, redistribute original or pre-loss incomes.

Even when insurance does not redistribute income or property between income classes, it benefits low-income classes more than high-income classes. A poor man suffers much more from the loss of part or all of his income than a rich man does. Therefore, it is much more beneficial to provide adequate personal insurance to the poor than to provide it to the rich. Yet private insurance firms concentrate their expensive sales effort on the well-to-do, and fail to sell adequate insurance to most poor men. Only a socialist state, or a capitalist state which socializes all insurance, can provide adequate insurance to the poor, those who need it the most.

We have mentioned two major functions of insurance (1) risk reduction or regularization, and (2) redistribution (usually restoration) of personal incomes and wealth. Insurance systems may also be used to: (1) turn unpaid costs of production or consumption, so-called external diseconomies, into paid costs, (2) minimize general business depressions, (3) aid or compel individuals to save more, and (4) turn price goods into free goods.

Compulsory workmen's industrial accident and illness insurance converts many production costs previously paid by workers into costs paid by insured producers. Compulsory auto accident liability insurance converts costs previously met by innocent injured parties into costs met by insured car owners.

Unemployment insurance reduces the decline in total personal income when a business recession occurs. Insurance of bank deposits also helps to maintain spending at such times.

Endowment life insurance policies are designed to persuade or compel insured persons to save more than they would otherwise save. Term life insurance, which involves no saving, is ignored or played down by most life insurance salesmen because it yields lower commissions.

In a capitalist society where health care and legal services are not free goods, health insurance and legal insurance may turn health and legal services into free goods for insurance beneficiaries. Such insurance should be unnecessary under socialism because both health care and legal services should become free goods. But the taxes which finance such free goods closely resemble the taxes which finance social insurance.

Most capitalist economists have asserted that risks which are unpredictable in total cannot be insured against. But the burden of any unpredictable loss can be shared more equally by dividing it among many persons. And insurance is essentially a system of dividing up losses and equalizing net income after losses. Private insurance companies cannot safely insure individuals against losses unpredictable in total, but any government can do so. And the definition of insurance should not depend upon the nature of the economic system or the insuring agency.

Most capitalist insurance theorists distinguish sharply between welfare payments and insurance benefits, presumably in part because welfare needs are unpredictable in total as well as individually. Another possible reason is that welfare payments are based upon need, not upon previous insurance premium payments. But the essence of insurance is the social sharing of sudden individual losses, and poverty is usually the result of such losses. If all persons were ideally insured against all possible losses — unemployment, accident, sickness, etc. — there would be little if any poverty in an advanced country. Thus a public welfare system is a supplementary catch-all social insurance system. It collects and redistributes income so as to reduce the risk of becoming very poor. However, welfare systems segregate, mark, and stigmatize the very poor, who naturally resent such treatment.

Many old-age pension systems are a combination of saving for old age and insurance against poverty in old age. If some of the insured who survive and are pensioned receive total pension benefits larger than their contributions, there is an element of insurance.

It is important to distinguish between saving and insurance. Many so-called insurance systems, like most pension systems, combine saving and insurance. If an insurance system creates reserves and/or creates cash values for policyholders, it is a combination of saving and insurance. Such a combination may be beneficial and/or profitable under capitalism, but it would be unnecessary and undesirable under socialism, for reasons to be given later.

Some large corporations do not buy insurance from outside firms but instead carry their own insurance, i.e., practice self-insurance against some or all insurable risks. They find this profitable when they have many stores, plants, and/or offices because large numbers reduce their risks, as they reduce the risks of insurance firms, and self-insurance saves some of the costs of external insurance.

Self-insurance requires no formal organization or special cost. The mere pooling of all costs, including those due to insurable losses, in a single consolidated profit and loss statement achieves the benefits of insurance, without buying insurance, if the self-insured firm is large enough and its plants are sufficiently separated.

Such self-insurance is so different from the purchase of insurance from outside agencies that it will be treated as a substitute for insurance, not as insurance itself, in this chapter.

The Need for Insurance under Socialism — In a liberal socialist society the need for insurance would be far less intense than in a competitive capitalist society. First, every socialist trust or department would be so big that it could largely carry its own insurance, i.e., dispense with insurance, against most risks. The mere increase in scale of organization would make most previously unpredictable risks far more predictable, and thus reduce the need for insurance against them.

Secondly, a socialist society would suffer far less unemployment, especially prolonged unemployment, which would radically reduce or end the need for unemployment insurance.

Thirdly, personal incomes would be far less unequal in a socialist society. This would reduce the need for personal income insurance because very poor people need such insurance much more than other people.

Fourthly, socialism would sharply raise the average level of real income, which would further reduce the need for personal income insurance for the same reason.

Fifth, a socialist society should radically increase the level of compulsory personal saving, which would enable uninsured individuals to suffer income and property losses with much less suffering.

Finally, every increase in the provision of non-collective free goods — education, child care, school lunches, health care, etc. — reduces the need for insurance. Thus in Great Britain, where most health care is free, the need for health insurance is far smaller than in the U.S., where most health care is still sold for a price. In a mature, advanced liberal socialist economy, the share of free goods in national income should probably exceed 50%, i.e., should be about twice the level among most advanced capitalist nations today.

Although the need for insurance is far less extensive and intense under socialism than it is under capitalism, the basic case for insuring all individuals against all remaining risks remains sound, and the cost is much lower. Therefore, a socialist state should insure all persons against all substantial remaining risks, including those against which insurance is not now available.

B. Organization

In capitalist America there are many thousands of competing firms issuing hundreds of different varieties of each kind of insurance policy. In a liberal socialist country there should be only one firm whose principal business is insurance, the Department of Social Insurance, and it should provide only one variety of each kind of insurance.

As explained later, some other agencies should provide certain forms of insurance closely related to or involved in their main economic function, but none of them would be primarily insurance carriers or brokers. And each should be a monopoly.

The elimination of competition and of duplication of local facilities and services would notably reduce the operating costs required to provide insurance. It would also facilitate standardization of equipment, forms, and procedures throughout the insurance industry.

This, in turn, would further justify substantial continuing research and development to improve the standardized objects and procedures. The more widely a given machine or method is used, the more beneficial is an improvement in it.

The geographic boundaries of the operating divisions and subdivisions of a socialist department of social insurance should usually differ from those of other national trusts and departments because its operating methods would differ from theirs. As explained in Liberal Socialism, there should be no regional or local units of government performing two or more social functions.

National insurance monopolies should not be subordinate to agencies which control tax rates or compulsory national saving since the executives of such agencies would be tempted to raise insurance taxes in order to finance government spending or investments for non-insurance purposes.

C. General Operating Policies

Let us now consider the major operating policies which should be applied to two or more kinds of insurance. Policies which should or could be applied to one kind of insurance only will be discussed in the next section of this chapter.

The enforcement of these general operating policies should probably be assigned to the Department of Social Insurance. Some central supervision of all insurance systems would be necessary to coordinate their activities and enforce general operating policies.

Social Insurance Only — In a socialist country there should be no voluntary individual insurance policies. All insurance should be compulsory group or social insurance. No individual should be allowed to refuse to pay for insurance because such refusals may compel other persons to support him when he is in need. Of course, public support of the needy is socially beneficial, but no individual who can support himself and pay for insurance should be allowed to become a burden on the community through refusal to buy insurance.

Moreover, the costs per person of social insurance are far less than the costs of voluntary individual insurance. Social insurance saves the cost of writing and selling individual insurance policies. It increases the amount of insurance in force and facilitates standardization of operating methods, both of which reduce costs per person insured.

Social insurance is financed by taxation, not by voluntary premium payments. The cost per dollar of collecting taxes is much less than the cost per dollar of collecting voluntary premium payments. In many cases, social insurance taxes can be mere additions to existing taxes, and an increase in an existing tax has relatively little effect on tax-collection costs, especially in socialist states.

No Combination of Saving and Insurance — In capitalist countries both life insurance and social insurance often combine saving with insurance. The premiums or taxes are large enough to build up surpluses which are invested in various ways. In a socialist country, insurance premiums and taxes should be just sufficient to cover current insurance benefit payments. Annual deficits should be as frequent and as large as annual surpluses.

The volume of annual saving should be determined by an agency responsible for that function only. Any combination of insurance and saving would divide authority over total saving. It would also confuse consumers and voters, who would find it more difficult to learn how much they were paying for insurance alone, and how much for forced saving.

Universal Coverage — A socialist insurance system should protect all citizens against all substantial risks. In capitalist countries private insurance companies write policies which specify and limit insurance coverage. And social security laws also specify and limit insurance coverage. A socialist legislature should not specify or limit insurance coverage, except to rule out insurance against losses too small to justify verification and compensation. The legislature should merely order the national insurance agency to insure all persons against all losses large enough to justify the costs of insurance.

The law establishing such an insurance system should state only major general operating policies and should be less than a thousand words in length. All of the more specific operating policies of each national insurance agency should be determined by the agency itself, not by the legislature, because the agency officials and experts would be much better qualified to determine these policies.

Under socialism no individual should be able to determine what risks he is insured against or how much coverage he has against any individual risk. Insurance benefits everyone, and therefore everyone should be insured against all significant risks. Furthermore, the costs of providing different kinds and amounts of insurance for different individuals are very high. Finally, socialist insurance agencies would be much better judges of how much insurance the average citizen should have than the citizen himself. In capitalist countries it is impossible to obtain insurance against some kinds of risks — such as the risk of having a defective child or the risk of becoming blind or insane — and insurance against other risks — floods, earthquakes, riots, etc. — is so costly that few people buy it. Moreover, those who are most in need of insurance — the poor, the sick, and the handicapped — are the least likely to buy voluntarily the available insurance they need, and are often denied it because of high risks. Hence, a socialist policy of uniformly insuring all citizens against all risks would greatly increase the number of persons insured and the number of risks covered.

Furthermore, such a policy would save the very large sums now spent to write and interpret non-uniform insurance policies and laws which specify and limit differently the insurance coverage of each class of insured person. It would also relieve all citizens of the often difficult task of deciding how much of each kind of insurance to buy.

<u>Incomplete</u> <u>Loss</u> <u>Coverage</u> — While socialist insurance should cover all persons and risks, it should not cover losses of less than some prescribed minimum amount, and it should pay benefits less than the full amount of most verified large losses.

Socialist insurance should not cover small losses because the cost of handling a small insurance claim is relatively high, often more than the amount of the claim. Moreover, almost everyone suffers a small loss occasionally, so failure to compensate for them would fall fairly equally on all persons. And the labor required to investigate small claims by almost everyone could be used more productively in many other ways. By refusing to investigate and pay losses of less than some minimum amount, society can achieve savings which benefit all citizens and are larger than the real costs to all those who suffer from this policy.

Only careful research can determine how high this standard insurance-benefit deduction should be, but it should probably be at least $200 in America today. Every increase in real wages will justify a rise in this minimum, both because it will increase claim handling costs, and because it will reduce the pain of a given insured loss.

Furthermore, socialist insurance should not pay the entire amount of verified property losses because those who suffer such losses are usually partly responsible for them, and it is difficult and costly to determine how responsible they are. Therefore, such losses should be largely but not entirely covered by insurance. Extensive research is needed to determine the ideal percentages of coverage.

A <u>Single</u> <u>Benefit</u> <u>Payment</u> <u>Office</u> — In capitalist countries each city has many offices which make insurance benefit payments. In a socialst country each community should have but one such office. No person should have to visit more than one office to apply for and receive any kind of insurance benefit.

We shall recommend below that different agencies should determine and pay different kinds of insurance benefits, but all of these agencies should receive applications and make benefit payments through a single office in each community.

<u>Death</u> <u>Benefits</u> <u>and</u> <u>Penalties</u> — In a socialist society no lump-sum death benefits should be paid because this practice would preserve a form of inheritance. If the deceased person had no dependents, his death does not even justify a pension. If he had dependents, they deserve pensions until they grow up and/or become self-supporting. But such pensions should be provided by an income-assurance system, not by any other insurance system, and should be unrelated to the past earnings of the deceased.

While no death benefits should be paid in a socialist society, the agency responsible for an avoidable death should be required to pay a large penalty to the national Treasury. This penalty should be based on estimates of the average value of human life, and should serve to induce each local plant manager to spend the optimum amount of money to prevent deaths of employees, customers, and others due to any cause over which he has control.

<u>No</u> <u>Court</u> <u>Review</u> — In capitalist countries the insurance awards of private insurance firms are subject to court review. This is reasonable because such firms are profit-motivated, and often deceive or defraud their beneficiaries.

It is profitable for a private person suing for denied insurance benefits to spend money on legal services if he can thereby increase his award by a larger amount. The difference between his legal costs and his award is a net benefit to him, but not to society. All legal costs of both parties to the suit are a real social cost.

The awards of a socialist national insurance system should not be subject to court review. A socialist non-profit agency would have far less incentive to deceive and defraud the public. Moreover, court trials are now very costly, and it may take a long time for a socialist government to simplify and rationalize them. Finally, administrative review tribunals within

the national insurance system would cost much less
and would become far more expert than regular courts
in handling appeals concerning insurance awards. Hence,
all such appeals should be heard and decided by such
tribunals only. These tribunals should sometimes
reduce awards, and should charge fees for unjustified
appeals, so that only well-justified appeals will be
made.

It should not be necessary for benefit claimants
to receive professional advice and aid in presenting
their insurance claims, but, if it is necessary, such
advice and aid should be provided by salaried experts
employed by the relevant insurance agency, or by a
separate national legal service agency. No such advisor or lawyer should be able to profit from encouraging individuals to make insurance claims or to
appeal insurance benefit decisions.

No Taxation of Insurance — Capitalist insurance
firms pay a wide variety of taxes. A socialist insurance system should not pay any taxes designed primarily to raise revenue. It should pay some special-purpose taxes, but few special-purpose taxes would
apply to an insurance system. Among these few might be
sales taxes on some or all of the equipment, materials,
and fuels which it purchases.

The chief activity of a socialist insurance system should be redistribution (restoration) of income
and wealth. There is no good reason why such redistribution should be taxed. Operating costs should amount
to less than 4% of the redistributed funds, and only
this small part of the expenditure of a socialist
insurance system should be subject to special-purpose
taxation.

Insurance benefit payments should be tax-free to
the beneficiary because they do not increase his
wealth or income; they merely restore lost wealth or
income.

Nearly all the numerous taxes now paid by private
insurance firms — license taxes, sales taxes, corporate
income taxes, etc. — are uneconomic, for reasons
detailed in Chapter XV of Liberal Socialism.

Allocation of Insurance Costs — Whenever it is
possible and economic, insurance should be financed
by taxes or charges which allocate insured losses to
those directly or indirectly responsible for them,
and which therefore induce these responsible persons
to alter their behavior so as to reduce insurance
losses. It is not always possible and economic to
determine who is responsible, and, when it is possible
and economic to determine who is responsible for an
insured loss, it may be impossible or too costly to
make them pay for such losses — for instance, large
losses due to crime.

The ideal is allocation of losses to individual persons or firms, but this is usually impossible or too expensive. However, allocation of certain classes of insured losses to classes of people collectively responsible for them — young automobile owners, boat owners, smokers, etc. — is usually possible and desirable.

Some insurance losses should be allocated to consumers of the goods whose consumption creates or permits these losses. For instance, the costs of fires caused by cigarette smokers should be allocated to these smokers by means of sales taxes on cigarettes. Such taxes would reduce the number of such fires by reducing the number of cigarettes smoked.

Some insurance losses can and should be allocated by producers who use equipment, processes, and/or raw materials whose use causes insured losses. For instance, the full costs of commercial airline accidents should be allocated directly to airlines, and indirectly to those who ship and/or travel by air.

No Premium Payment Records — It is still customary to keep records of each person's payments to a social insurance system in order to determine the benefits due him. Under socialism there should be no direct relationship between the amount of insurance payments collected from an individual and the amount of insurance benefits paid to him. Benefits should be based on losses or needs, not on the amount of insurance premiums previously collected. Hence, no records of insurance tax payments by individuals should be kept. This policy would greatly reduce the cost of operating a social insurance system.

We have provided for a relatively high rate of compulsory personal saving which would be credited to individual interest-earning savings accounts spendable only after retirement from work (LS, pp. 123-5). The creation of such savings accounts would make unnecessary the provision of old-age pensions based on previous social-security tax payments. And there should also be some voluntary saving for retirement.

Finally, the great reduction in personal income differentials recommended in Liberal Socialism (Part Five) would greatly weaken the argument for differentials in social insurance benefits based on insurance premium or tax payments.

No Income Redistribution — In capitalist states some social insurance systems are used both to provide needed insurance and to redistribute income from the rich to the poor. The rich pay higher social-security taxes and/or receive lower benefits in proportion to their taxes. This may now be desirable because capitalist personal incomes are too unequal, but it would be very uneconomic in a socialist state which has provided for proper initial determination of personal incomes.

Furthermore, it is always unsound for an agency to try to perform two or more possibly conflicting functions such as insurance and income redistribution. Taxes designed to finance insurance properly cannot also serve to redistribute income properly. And insurance benefits which measure insurance losses cannot also help to redistribute income properly from one social class to another.

All insurance systems redistribute income among individuals in order to restore lost income or wealth. But they need not and should not redistribute income in order to make original ideal incomes less unequal. This function should be performed by a separate agency which has no other function.

D. Kinds of Socialist Insurance

Having stated the basic operating policies of a socialist insurance system, we turn now to a discussion of the application of these and other policies to individual kinds of insurance. To minimize repetition, we shall not explain the application of each general policy to each kind of insurance. Rather, we will discuss only the most novel and/or important applications.

<u>Income Insurance</u> — Under socialism the most important form of insurance would be income insurance, which should insure every family and single adult against any continued substantial lack of or reduction in real income due to death, accident, illness, unemployment, or any other cause largely or entirely beyond the control of the insured person. Such income insurance would include or largely replace unemployment insurance, disability insurance, welfare payments, and old-age pension systems. It would also replace the income-maintenance provisions of some health insurance, accident insurance, and life insurance systems.

We shall provide below for separate financing of income insurance benefits made necessary by fires, auto accidents, crime, and industrial accidents and diseases. But all such benefits should be determined by one agency, the income insurance branch of the Department of Social Insurance.

Wage-rate reductions would often be necessary to control the distribution of labor among plants and occupations, but all such wage cuts would be relatively small and/or temporary, usually both, as well as economically desirable. Hence, income insurance should never offset or diminish the effects of such wage cuts.

Income insurance benefits paid to the sick or unemployed should not be related to length of employment or amount of insurance taxes paid. They should be based entirely on recent or possible earnings and/or current needs. They should not fully restore lost income because this would encourage fraud and because unemployed workers do not need as much income as employed workers, but they should restore over 60% of lost income.

Moreover, income insurance should assure adequate incomes for all persons who have never been able to work because of physical or mental handicaps, and it should liberally supplement the incomes of handicapped workers unable to earn an average wage income. For instance, blind or crippled workers who earn wages well below average wages should receive income supplements which raise their wage earnings to or above the average level. These income supplements should be paid by the insurance system, not by employers because such supplements do not measure real costs of production.

It is just as desirable to insure people against the income effects of a birth defect as to insure them against the income effects of blindness or any other disability incurred later in life. And men should be insured against unemployment before they secure their first job as well as afterwards.

Socialist income insurance would make it unnecessary and undesirable for any socialist trust or department to grant sick leave or pensions to its employees. The costs of sick leave and pensions not due to industrial accidents or illness are social costs, not production costs, and should not be included among the operating costs of any organization.

When sick leave is granted by an employer, it is more apt to be abused than when granted by an independent outside agency. In America today most employees regard sick leave as a form of vacation leave, and use of their full sick leave whether or not they are sick. A socialist income insurance monopoly could use the state health system to verify sick leave claims. And sick-leave benefit payments should be well below lost wage payments.

The elimination of pensions paid by individual employers would remove a serious obstacle to the employment of older workers. The burden of pension payments would fall on the income-insurance system, not on individual employers.

Income insurance should be financed in part by funds transferred to the insurance agency by other government agencies responsible for insurance claims, including the national police force, the national fire prevention and control service, the national auto accident insurance agency, the national industrial accident insurance agency, and the agencies responsible for unemployment. We will explain the reasons for such contributions in discussing the individual agencies. The most general reason is that this allocation of certain income insurance costs will help to make them optimum.

The uncovered remainder of income insurance costs should be financed out of general government revenues because such costs should not fall more heavily on one person or organization than on any other.

Automobile Accident Insurance — In America automobile accident insurance has become one of the two most important forms of insurance. In 1974 about $19 billion of insurance premiums were collected. And this private insurance system did not cover all autos or all accident risks for those covered. A socialist insurance system should cover all cars and all risks. The heavy costs of competition, advertising, and salesmanship should be eliminated by creating an insurance monopoly and making insurance coverage compulsory.

Since a socialist country should provide free medical care for all accident victims, the need for automobile accident insurance would be much less intense then it now is in the U.S. And the creation of a comprehensive income insurance system would also greatly reduce the need for automobile accident insurance. However, such insurance would still be needed to cover property losses, to help finance income and health insurance, and to limit auto use.

Automobile accident insurance can and should be financed by taxes which allocate the costs of auto accidents to those classes of persons and consumers directly or indirectly responsible for them, according to the degree of their responsibility, because such allocation would help to reduce the number and cost of auto accidents. Those who drive private cars for pleasure or convenience should pay the full costs of such benefits, and consumers of goods moved by truck should pay the full costs of truck use.

Any auto accident insurance system which collects premiums from car owners does allocate accident costs to those who cause and/or benefit from them, but the allocation is now very crude. Private insurance firms achieve such allocation by classifying car users and basing their annual insurance premiums upon rough estimates of the risk involved. However, they have been unable or unwilling to determine the mileage and speed at which each insured car is driven, and these are among the chief factors determining accident risks.

A socialist country should finance all auto accident insurance benefits by sales taxes on gasoline and tires. Every additional mile a car is driven increases both gasoline and tire consumption and accident risk. Likewise, every increase in the speed at which a pleasure car is driven (above 30 miles an hour) increases more than proportionally gasoline and tire consumption and accident risks. Other risk-increasing driving practices — jackrabbit starts, fast turns, sudden stops, etc. — also increase gasoline and tire consumption. Hence, financing auto accident insurance by suitable sales taxes on gasoline and tires would markedly improve the allocation of auto accident costs to those who ought to pay them. And it would also minimize the costs of collecting the revenue needed to finance auto accident insurance. Sales taxes, especially increments in sales taxes, cost little to collect, and cause minimum inconvenience to the taxpayer. He pays them in small amounts, at his convenience, when he must pay something anyway.

Moreover, the proposed sales taxes would turn auto insurance costs into marginal costs which would be considered by drivers whenever they consider marginal use of their cars. Periodic fixed insurance premiums do not equally limit car use.

If certain kinds of motor vehicles have much higher accident rates than other kinds, the extra insurance costs above the lowest level should be financed by special sales taxes on the more accident-prone cars and/or by extra sales taxes on the gasoline used by such cars.

If certain classes of drivers — juveniles, alcoholics, etc. — are proven to have abnormally high accident rates, they should be denied driving licenses or required to pay higher gasoline and tire sales taxes than other drivers, or their benefit payments could be reduced. Their cars could be clearly marked so that every gas station attendant would know that they should pay higher sales taxes.

The gasoline and tire sales taxes used to finance automobile accident insurance should be high enough to cover all the social costs of auto accidents. Under socialism these would include the costs of free medical care and the income insurance benefits made necessary by automobile accidents. Thus the auto insurance system should finance part of the costs of health care and of income insurance. The allocation of these costs to auto users is necessary to enable users to control properly their use of cars and trucks, i.e., to balance marginal social real costs against marginal social real benefits.

There should, of course, be no duplication of benefits to individuals. That part of insurance benefit payments which covers health-care costs and lost earnings made good by income insurance should be paid directly to the agencies which provide free health care and income insurance. Only that portion of the accident insurance benefit payment which covers pain and personal property loss should go directly to the accident victim.

In America today the owner of an insured car damaged in an auto accident must obtain repair cost estimates from three or more garages, a time-consuming task, before he can apply for insurance benefits to cover such costs. This would be unnecessary under socialism because there would be only one auto repair system. Moreover, this system would have no inducement to conspire with car owners to defraud the insurance system, a common practice under capitalism

Air and Water Transport Insurance — Much of the above discussion of auto-accident insurance clearly applies also to air and water transport insurance, and will not be repeated here.

Insurance of privately owned planes and boats should be provided without issuing individual policies. It should be largely financed by extra sales taxes on the fuel used by private planes and boats. Such taxes should raise enough revenue to cover all accident costs, including health care and income maintenance.

The national airline agency and the national water transport agency should each carry its own accident insurance financed by additions to passenger and freight charges. Each should investigate its own accidents, and determine and finance insurance awards to employees and customers for pain and loss of property. Each should also reimburse other agencies for health care costs and income maintenance payments due to its accidents.

Fire Insurance — Fire insurance should be handled by fire departments; and should continue under socialism, but should be radically reformed. Fire insurance for residential and commercial tenants should become universal, uniform and compulsory; should be largely or entirely financed by special fire-prevention taxes. These taxes should be designed by the national fire protection service to reduce the use of the most combustible building materials and furnishing, to discourage customs and practices responsible for many fires, and to allocate the costs of fires to those who create fire risks.

If there were no combustible buildings and furnishings, there could be few destructive fires in buildings. Men use combustible building materials and furnishings in order to save money or create superior products. They cannot balance costs against benefits when deciding to use such materials and furnishing unless they are required to pay and consider the social costs of fires resulting from their decisions.

Hence, these social costs should be determined and should be measured by direct money costs paid by builders and tenants.

Private fire insurance companies have tried to measure fire risks and base their premiums on such risks, and a socialist fire insurance monopoly should use all the knowledge they have gained to allocate fire costs to those responsible for them. In addition, it could use methods of cost allocation not available to private firms. For instance, it could and should impose sales taxes on combustible roofing materials, cigarettes, matches, and alcoholic beverages. A great many destructive fires are started by cigarette smokers and drunks.

It will require considerable scientific research to determine the relative fire-causing effect of each fire-causing factor and the ideal level of the sales taxes on such factors. If these taxes are properly determined, they will bring in a total revenue just sufficient to cover all the costs of destructive fires, including lost wages, free health care, death charges, and fire protection costs.

Every sound increase in government spending on fire departments reduces both fire losses and fire insurance benefit payments. It is the sum total of such spending and payments which should be determined and properly limited. Whenever an increase in fire department spending cuts fire losses by a larger amount, it is economic. Whenever a decrease in such spending raises fire losses by a smaller amount, it is economic. Taxes on combustible materials and furnishings should be designed to reduce fire fighting costs, property losses, and insurance benefits. And fire fighting methods should be planned and controlled so that they do not increase fire insurance benefit payments unduly.

Finally, every residential and commercial fire should be investigated by fire department experts, both to determine the cause and the cost of the fire and to help fire departments improve their performance. It would be uneconomic to require a separate insurance agency to duplicate most of this investigation in order to determine the amount of the fire insurance benefit payment. For all these reasons, such benefit payments should be determined and paid out by local fire departments, not by a separate insurance agency. A single local agency in each area should provide both fire protection and fire insurance.

Such a combination of fire protection and fire insurance is best suited to the handling of fire insurance against fires in residential and commercial buildings. It is not well suited to fire insurance for transport facilities, petroleum wells and refineries, large factory buildings, mines, and other major producing plants. The managers of such plants should be chiefly responsible for reducing, determining, and allocating their fire losses. They should pay the fire protection service in full for all services rendered, and should carry their own fire insurance.

Crime Insurance — All citizens of a socialist state should be automatically and uniformly insured against losses and expenses due to any kind of crime.

Most criminals convicted of non-violent crimes for the first time should be paroled and required to begin paying for the insured losses they have caused. Their installment payments should go to the crime-insurance system, not to their victims, who would already have received their insurance benefits.

All insurance benefits to individual victims of crime should be determined and paid by local police departments. This would help local police determine the total costs of local crime, the optimum expenditure on each form of crime prevention, and the effects of each change in methods of crime prevention.

The goal of each local police department should be to minimize the total local cost of crime, and it cannot determine this total cost unless monetary murder penalties are determined, all victims of crime are fully compensated, and the total cost of such payments is determined. The quickest way to learn this total cost is to determine and pay the compensation payments. Moreover, the police must investigate each crime in any case, so it would be inefficient to have an outside insurance agency duplicate this investigation in order to determine the insurance benefits. Finally, if police departments handled compensation payments by paroled criminals, they would learn something useful for police purposes about the behavior of these parolees.

Local police departments should reimburse the Department of Health and the Income Insurance Branch for costs incurred in providing health care and interim income to the victims of crimes in their area.

Crime insurance benefit payments to victims of violent crimes should include an allowance for any pain and suffering caused by personal violence or threat of violence. Police officials cannot decide how much to spend on crime prevention unless they have money estimates of the total real cost of crime. Moreover, crime victims deserve compensation for such pain and suffering, and criminals ought to pay for the pain and suffering they cause.

The system of crime insurance prescribed above should be applied to all crimes against individuals and to crimes committed by outsiders against the property of socialist trusts and departments, but it should not be applied to non-violent crimes — theft, embezzlement, bribery, etc. — committed by employees against their employers, because the victimized employers could prevent such crimes. Each socialist agency should carry its own insurance against such internal crimes and make an optimum effort to prevent them. Repayments for such crimes should be paid directly to the employers.

<u>Industrial Accident Insurance</u> — All workers in a socialist state should be fully and uniformly insured against the costs of industrial accidents and illness. The provision of free medical care and adequate income insurance would radically reduce (by 60-90%) the worker's need for industrial accident insurance benefit payments, but it would still be desirable to use insurance taxes to allocate the full costs of industrial accidents and sickness (including health-care costs) to those plants and processes responsible for them. Such allocation would help plant managers choose their raw materials and production methods so as to minimize social costs. It would also improve the final selling prices of all goods and induce consumers to reduce their relative consumption of those goods whose production causes the most industrial accidents and sickness.

All socialist trusts and departments would be large enough to carry their own insurance against industrial accidents and illness, and self-insurance would help to allocate the costs of such accidents and illness to those responsible for them. Each agency should investigate industrial accidents and illnesses in its plants and determine the costs and benefit payments. It should reimburse the national Department of Health for the latter's costs in treating its victims of industrial accidents and illness. It should also allocate its total accident and illness costs to those local plants and plant units responsible for them.

Trusts and departments which carry their own insurance should pay a separate death penalty or charge for each death in their plant due to their activities. The revenue from such charges should be used to cover the costs of pensions for dependents. No death benefits should be paid to heirs, for the same reason that inheritance should be largely abolished.

In order to determine the charges for insured deaths, it will be necessary to place monetary values on human lives. This is a difficult task, but the use of any reasonable rough estimate is better than either ignoring the value of human life or treating it as of infinite value

The problem of how to value human lives will be discussed more fully in our chapter on health care because such valuation would be most needed in the control of spending on health care. We shall there suggest that this valuation be based primarily on age and prospective earnings.

A doctor could easily determine the age and earnings of each of his patients and base his health care upon such data, but a socialist plant manager who has workers of many different ages and skills working together in his plant could not economically devise a different safety program for each worker based upon his age and wage rate. Therefore, the death charge against his self-insurance system should probably be uniform for all workers' deaths in his plant. Such charges should be determined by independent insurance experts, not by the agencies which pay them.

Uniform charges for the deaths of insured workers at work should vary with average real wages and interest rates. If real wages rise 100% during a given period, these charges should also rise 100%. Thus it is impossible to say now how high such charges should be at some future time. But we can suggest what death charges might be in terms of average annual real income.

If the interest rate is about 10%, a death charge of ten times average annual wages at the time of the accident would seem reasonable because it would yield an interest income about equal to average wage earnings. The fact that this decision would ignore probable future increases in wage earnings by the victims is about offset by the fact that such a death benefit would purchase an annuity higher than 10% interest on the death benefit. Of course, it would be easy to make nicer calculations, but this seems unnecessary here.

The typical American worker now earns about $10,000 a year, and the interest rate on savings accounts is 5%, so the above reasoning implies that U.S. death benefits should now average about $200,000. This is far more than U.S. workmen's compensation laws now provide, but far less than some generous juries have provided for the heirs of accident victims.

Customer Insurance — The customers, clients, and visitors of all socialist trusts and departments should be insured against all negligence-caused accidents which they incur on the premises of these agencies, and against accidents due to product defects. This would help to induce all such agencies to spend optimum amounts to prevent such accidents.

Every socialist trust or department would be large enough to carry its own customer accident insurance. It should investigate all such accidents and determine accident costs and awards. Most of the awards should go to the Department of Health to pay for the heath care received by accident victims and to the Department of Social Insurance to cover income benefits paid to victims. Only compensation for suffering and property loss should go directly to victims.

Insurance against medical malpractice is a form of customer insurance. The national Department of Health should carry its own malpractice insurance, investigate all malpractice claims, and determine and finance all malpractice insurance benefits.

Insurance against accidents incurred by passengers on planes, buses, ships, and other means of transport is also a form of customer insurance. The highway transport branch of the Transport Trust should carry its own passenger and freight accident insurance, which should be largely financed by gas tax refunds. It should investigate all accidents involving its vehicles, evaluate the resulting property damage claims, and determine all benefit payments for pain and for property losses. It should also reimburse health care and income insurance agencies for their costs due to injuries to its passengers. This system would minimize the costs of investigating accidents, and would help highway transport managers learn how to prevent accidents and how much to spend on accident prevention.

Insurance of school and college students against accidents on school premises is a form of customer insurance. The Department of Education should carry its own insurance against school accidents due to its negligence.

Other Accident Insurance — Private accident or casualty insurance firms sell insurance against many kinds of accidents not discussed above. A socialist insurance system should insure all citizens against an even wider range of accidents, but it should do so in a radically different way. Instead of selling private insurance policies, it should provide compulsory social insurance. Instead of charging one private premium to cover many different kinds of risks, it should use separate taxes to finance each kind of accident insurance, so far as this is possible and economic.

For instance, a socialist insurance system should determine the probable total annual costs of accidents due to the use of power lawn mowers and should impose on such machines special sales taxes just sufficient to cover all resulting benefits, including health care and income insurance benefits. If risks differ, it should have different taxes for each class of power lawn mower. And all other consumers' machines and products whose use causes insured losses should be similarly treated. The use of such taxes to finance accident insurance would reduce the use of the most dangerous consumers' products by raising their post-tax prices, and would help to allocate accident costs to those responsible for them.

<u>Life Insurance</u> — Life insurance is one of the two most important forms of insurance in advanced capitalist countries, but there should be no life insurance in a socialist country. Life insurance creates substantial estates for heirs, and all inheritance, except that of personal family property, should be prohibited in a socialist country. The income insurance prescribed earlier would protect all unemployable dependents of deceased worker.

CHAPTER XI

HEALTH CARE

Health care has become one of the largest industries in advanced countries. Americans now (1977) spend about 9% of their GNP on health care.
We use the term health care to include the services of physicians, surgeons, dentists, psychiatrists, nurses, therapists, laboratory technicians, pharmacists, and all other persons engaged in providing health care services.

A. Organization and Personnel

Monopoly and Centralization — In a socialist country all free or subsidized health services should be provided by salaried personnel of a single national agency, here called the Division of Health. The term health is more inclusive than the term medical service used in Liberal Socialism.
This Division should include a Health Care Department, which should operate all clinics, hospitals, nursing homes, pharmacies, ambulance services, and other health care delivery facilities. In each regional and local division of the department there should be a similar monopolistic concentration of control over all health delivery services, in order to permit coordination of these services. The national and regional offices of the department should employ consultant specialists who visit and advise local clinics and hospitals, but the latter should have complete operating control over their services.
In addition to a Health Care Department, the Division of Health should also include: (1) an Education and Research Department which operates all medical, dental, nursing, and other health care schools and classes, and all health research programs, (2) a Food and Water Control Department which regulates the production and distribution of all food and water so as to improve public health, (3) a Drug and Appliance Department which produces and distributes all drugs, vaccines, blood elements, appliances and other items used only or chiefly to heal the sick and aid the disabled, and (4) an Industrial Health Department which tries both to limit pollution and to improve working conditions responsible for industrial accidents and sickness. These department should be

organized on a functional, not a geographic basis, and should not be controlled by regional or local units of the Health Care Department.

Administration and Supervision — A socialist national health care system should be managed by a new class of professional managers, men who have been professionally trained in health care administration. Clinics and hospitals should not be managed by doctors. Training and experience in a medical specialty does not prepare one to manage a clinic, hospital, or group of such facilities. Of course, students of health care administration should be taught a great deal about various forms of health care, but they should not be taught how to treat patients.

Health care managers should perform all business functions, including the hiring of all personnel, but they should not evaluate or supervise the work of professional personnel. These functions should be performed only by professional colleagues. For instance, the medical head of the department of surgery in a hospital should be chosen by his local fellow surgeons or by a regional chief of surgery, and should be professionally supervised by the latter, not by the manager of his hospital.

In a socialist country all health care personnel, including physicians and surgeons should be supervised. Their professional work should be reviewed by supervisors competent to detect and penalize malpractice and to detect and reward superior practice. The economic incentive to malpractice would end under socialism but all men make occasional mistakes, and in health care such mistakes can have tragic results. Moreover, men in every profession differ widely in their knowledge and skill. Proper supervision of health care personnel would assure better selection of personnel for each kind of work, and retraining or elimination of the least competent.

Regional and national health care managers should require the periodic preparation and submission of statistical and cost data which will help them both to allocate funds rationally and to evalute the performance of local and regional managers. These data should reveal the average and marginal cost of each health service.

Group Medical Practice — Nearly all health care should be provided by clinics, hospitals, and other group-care facilities. The practice of medicine by individual doctors or partnerships in isolated individual offices should cease, except perhaps in very small, remote villages.

Group medical practice is superior to individual medical practice for several reasons. It facilitates specialization and division of labor among doctors and nurses. It permits fuller use of all specialized medical equipment. An individual doctor practicing alone must have a wide variety of equipment, much of which is little used. A clinic specialist needs only the equipment designed for his work, and uses this equipment far more intensively. Moreover, in a clinic, each doctor's office can be located near those of fellow specialists, laboratory technicians, X-ray experts, physical therapists, and other health care workers, which makes it much easier for doctors to consult with other specialists, and also much easier for patients to go from one office to another. Finally, group medical practice facilitates proper supervision of the work of all health workers.

Clinics and Hospitals — In a planned socialist city each village (population 5 to 10 thousand) should have its own small clinic, specializing in maternity, child care, and minor health problems. It should be located in the village shopping center. In old unplanned cities there should be such a clinic for every 5 to 10 thousand persons, located next to a school or a shopping center. Each clinic should serve all residents of its area, and should provide dental as well as medical services.

The location of clinics next to intermediate schools would enable many young children to visit clinics for regular examinations and treatments without being taken by their parents and without risking traffic accidents. Moreover, their parents could visit clinics as quickly and easily as their children could go to school. No home should be more than a mile from the nearest clinic.

Schools which do not have clinics adjacent to them should be visited periodically by mobile pediatric clinics so that school children can receive basic medical care during the school day with a minimum of interruption of their school work and a minimum of inconvenience to their parents.

In a planned new socialist city each town center should have a large polyclinic. This would permit most workers to visit the clinic before, during, or after working hours with a minimum of effort, cost, or loss of working time.

Next door to each polyclinic there should be a hospital, a nursing home, and one or more apartment buildings planned to meet the special needs of partially disabled and/or chronically ill persons who need health care far more frequently than other people.

Specialized hospital facilities and services which cannot be provided efficiently and economically in general hospitals should be provided in specialized hospitals located in the center of each large city. For instance, all cobalt-bomb and heart-lung machines should be installed in such hospitals, and all organ transplants and open-heart surgery should be done there. Town hospitals should contain no costly equipment which is idle most of the time, and should serve only local residents. Moreover, local hospital surgeons should perform no operations which are so infrequent that local surgeons cannot become and remain highly proficient in performing them.

All clinics and hospital data on the care of individual patients should be kept on standardized forms and filed in standardized filing cases used throughout the nation, at least until computers can store this data more economically. Whenever a patient moves from one clinic area to another, his medical records should automatically follow him immediately.

Hours of Clinic Operation — Clinics should operate two or three full shifts a day — for instance, two six-hour shifts (8 a.m. to 8 p.m.) or three five-hour shifts (7 a.m. to 10 p.m.). Such multi-shift operation would radically reduce the necessary investment in clinic buildings and equipment, and would give the public a much wider range of visiting hours. The savings on interest costs would permit the payment of higher wages per hour, which in turn would permit and induce a reduction in the hours of labor.

Clinics should also have small night shifts to handle accidents, heart attacks, and other sudden night-time emergencies. Anyone who becomes ill during the night should be able to secure immediate advice by phone, or ambulance service and personal attention from a nearby medical clinic.

Clinic workers should be allowed to choose their own normal hours of labor either collectively or individually. Those who are members of work teams should decide their hours of labor collectively. Those who work individually should choose their hours of labor individually, but should pay the full costs of any resulting decline in output. No individual or team worker should be allowed to benefit himself at the expense of other workers or of the public.

Every clinic should operate 365 days a year, both because people get sick and need health care every day of the year and because continuous operation would sharply reduce the necessary investment in clinic buildings and equipment. This rule does not imply that clinic workers should have no weekly or annual holidays, but only that they should not all have simultaneous holidays.

If some shifts or work schedules are more desired by workers than others, clinic and hospital managers should attract the needed number of workers to each shift or work schedule by varying wage rates. For instance, night-shift workers might be paid 20% to 50% more per hour than day-shift workers. Weekend day workers might also be paid 20% to 50% more than other day workers.

Ambulance Service — In America today ambulance service is one of the weakest links in the chain of health services. Most ambulances are ill-equipped and ill-manned, and usually take much too long to arrive where they are needed.

In a socialist society every hospital should have its own fully equipped ambulance manned by a professionally trained crew, including a doctor, prepared to render specialized medical care before the patient is moved and during transit to the clinic or hospital. The crew should be connected with its base by two-way radio so that it can obtain specialized advice and also warn base personnel of the emergency care which will be needed as soon as the ambulance returns to its base.

Ambulance doctors and assistants should be specially trained to give emergency care to accident victims, heart-attack victims, and other emergency cases. When not on the road, they should always be within 200 feet of their ambulance and free to leave immediately.

Since police are often the first to arrive at the scene of an accident or other health emergency, they too should all be trained in preliminary emergency health care — stopping the flow of blood, reviving a person who has stopped breathing, and so forth. And all police vehicles should have two-way communication with the nearest hospital.

Increased Specialization Among Doctors — Socialist medical schools should train nearly all doctors and dentists as specialists. Group practice of medicine in clinics and hospitals would virtually eliminate the need for general practitioners. When a patient first enters a clinic or hospital he should be initially interviewed by a diagnostician or his assistant. Diagnostics should become a new specialty. Diagnosticians should merely diagnose patients roughly, i.e., by specialty, and then send them to the appropriate specialist for more specific diagnosis. Diagnosticians should never treat patients or operate on them.

When working in their field, specialists are much more competent than general practitioners. Moreover, the training of specialists can and should be made much less costly than that of general practitioners.

In America all medical specialists must now be trained as general practitioners before they can begin their training as specialists. The chief reason for this seems to be that, when medical school training of doctors began, all doctors practiced individually as general practitioners after graduation. As a result of cultural lag, medical specialists must still be trained as general practitioners, even though few of them ever engage in general practice.

Most current medical specialties should and will be divided up into two or more less general specialties. For instance, pediatrics and geriatrics are too broad, and should be divided up into several new and/or old specialties. A pediatrician is really a general practitioner for children, and would be as out of place as a general practitioner in a socialist clinic or hospital.

The number of specialties is probably already too large to permit socialist clinics to have a specialist of each kind on its staff full time. And the number of specialties will grow. Therefore, these clinics should employ many specialists part time. And some specialists — surgeons, anaesthesiologist, etc. — should work only in hospitals.

In socialist hospitals all operations should be performed by surgeons who are specialists. Eye operations should be performed only by eye surgeons, heart operations only by heart surgeons, ear operations only by ear surgeons, and so forth. And each specialized surgeon should have his own specialized operating room and staff. Moreover, within each surgical specialty, surgeons and teams should specialize in individual operations, and repeat them at least 200 times a year. Only such extreme specialization can result in the finest surgical performance and reduce surgical complications and death rates to the optimum degree.

Female Doctors — In a socialist country over 60% of all doctors should be females. Modest women prefer to be examined and treated by female doctors. And most small children are more at ease with female than with male doctors because they have been cared for by women all their lives.

Moreover, health care occupations are occupations for which women are especially suited. They do not demand great physical strength or frequent travel away from home. Rather, they demand such peculiarly feminine qualities as sympathy, gentleness, and tact. That is why the great majority of nurses have always been women.

Then too, many women want shorter working hours than men so they can spend more time with their children or at home, and it is relatively easy to provide part-time work in clinics and hospitals. Also, most female doctors will live closer to their local clinic than to most other places of employment, which would shorten the time they spend away from their children.

Finally, every city needs a wide variety of health services. As a result, female doctors can follow their husbands wherever they move and be confident of finding suitable employment in their new home town.

It has been claimed that the long and costly period of medical training required of doctors makes the medical profession unsuitable for women. But the radical increase in specialization in medical education and practice advocated earlier would cut this period of training in half.

B. Health Care Policies

Having considered the basic principles for organizing the provision of health care facilities and services in a fully socialist economy, let us turn now to the operating policies. It is possible to discuss here only the most novel and significant of these policies.

Free and Compulsory Health Care — All essential health care services which are both effective and economic should be free goods. Many cosmetic operations and treatments are non-essential and/or uneconomic. Many, perhaps most, psychiatric treatments have never been proven to be effective. And some effective health treatments are uneconomic, i.e., cost more than they are worth to society. These last three classes of health treatments should be available for a price which covers all costs, unless they have been proven to be harmful. But, if unproven treatments, like Freudian psychoanalysis, are offered for a price, patients should be fully and repeatedly advised that they are unproven.

Health care which is essential, effective, and economic should be provided free of charge, rather than sold for a price, primarily because this would notably increase the consumption of such health care. When health care is sold for a price, many people fail to visit their doctor or dentist because they cannot afford to pay for needed health care, or because they wish to save money. And, under capitalism, the people most likely to need health care — the aged, the very young, the poor, and the handicapped — are the least likely to be able to pay for it.

Free health care for all children and pregnant women is especially desirable in order to make opportunities for success in adult life less unequal. Competition for success in life will continue to be less efficient and productive than it should be as long as some children receive much better health care than other children.

Moreover, many health services benefit the public by reducing the risk of infection and the need for public support of the sick and needy. Taxpayers can both reduce their taxes and protect their health by paying for such free health services.

Many doctors who sell their services for fees prescribe unnecessary or harmful treatments, operations, or drugs in order to increase their incomes. Free provision of most health care would largley end this evil, and thus improve health care. For this reason, free provision of most health services would be much preferable to adequate, universal health insurance. Such insurance merely guarantees payment of medical fees, which induces doctors to perform more unnecessary and/or harmful services and operations.

The provision of free health care makes health insurance unnecessary. Most systems of health insurance have administrative systems which absorb 10 to 30% of the premium income. This large expense can be saved by providing health care free of charge.

Finally, free provision of essential, basic health care is desirable because it redistributes real income (1) from families with one or two children to those with three or more children, and (2) from families with little illness to those who suffer much illness. It performs the same income redistribution function as health insurance. (See LS, 367-75, 419-20.)

It may be claimed that free provision of all essential health services would lead to gross overconsumption and waste of them. However, health services are provided by professional workers who can easily limit consumption. Overconsumption and waste of free tangible goods — for instance, free food and clothing — is very difficult if not impossible to prevent, even with rationing, itself undesirable, but overconsumption of free professional services can be prevented by the salaried professionals who render these services. And such professionals are precisely the persons best qualified to limit the consumption of their services. Furthermore, the public is unlikely to overconsume free medical services, even when permitted to do so, because most medical treatments and operations are painful, frightening, and/or demeaning.

The social benefits of an increased consumption of many kinds of health care are so great that some consumption should be compulsory. All persons should be required to have annual or semi-annual medical and dental examinations, timely vaccination against certain diseases, and treatment for some diseases. Such coercion would protect the public against infection and higher taxes, as well as protect coerced persons against sickness and disability. It would, for instance, permit the elimination of venereal disease within a decade, which would notably increase the pleasure from sexual relations.

We have argued that all basic or essential health care should be free. In addition, many non-essential or luxury health services should be sold for a price. For instance, nearly all cosmetic or beauty treatments and operations — massage, face lifts, bust lifts, treatments for baldness and dandruff, etc. — should be sold for a price. Also, circumcision should be a price good. And luxury accommodations in hospitals, nursing homes, and other health care facilities should be sold for prices sufficient to cover added costs. Extra nursing care desired by patients but not prescribed by doctors should be similarly treated. In gneral, patients should be allowed to secure for a price any kind of beneficial health care not provided free of charge. Socialist near-equalization of income would prevent any serious overconsumption of such health care.

Computer Diagnosis and Treatment — It is already possible to secure complete case histories by computer. When laboratory and case history data have been fed into a diagnostic computer, it can diagnose both physical and mental illness better than most physicians and psychiatrists. And medical computers are being steadily improved. They will soon be able to both diagnose and prescribe treatment for most illnesses.

The creation, operation, maintenance, and constant improvement of medical computers would cost more than any individual clinic or hospital could afford. Hence, centralization of these functions is essential.

The use of such computers in the offices of doctors practicing medicine alone or with one partner is uneconomic, but it would be economic in a socialist clinic. In such a clinic nearly all case histories should be obtained and preserved by computers, nearly all diagnoses should be made or confirmed by computers, and nearly all health care programs (including drug prescriptions) should be prepared or confirmed by computers.

Such use of medical computers will radically reduce the amount of training required by most diagnosticians and specialists as soon as computers become more competent than the average diagnostician or specialist. Of course, some very highly trained diagnosticians and specialists will always be needed to plan R and D projects, to supervise the work of ordinary dianosticians and specialists, and to program computers.

Drugs — In capitalist countries the great majority of drugs in use are ineffective, superfluous, or harmful.

They are sold to poorly informed doctors and laymen, chiefly by means of false or deceptive advertising. For instance, in the U.S. over $100 million was spent in 1975 on advertising to persuade people that one kind of pain killer — aspirin, Anacin, Bufferin, Excedrin, etc. — is superior to the others. As a result, few people in pain know what pain killer to buy. And those who consult more than one doctor often find that their doctors disagree.

In a socialist state all drugs should be carefully tested to determine how safe and effective they are, and the results should be clearly stated in all advertisements, labels, brochures, drug manuals, and other sources of information. Such tests would almost certainly justify prohibiting the manufacture and use of the great majority of both patent medicines and prescription drugs now in use in America. Oligopoly among capitalist drug manufacturers has resulted in a vast overdiversification of drugs.

In a socialist society all drugs should be sold in pharmacies located in clinics and hospitals. There should be no outside drug stores. The names of all drug buyers should be recorded, and later reviewed by local clinic staffs, to control use.

Patent medicines are those sold without a prescription. In capitalist states people often buy patent medicines in order to save the cost of medical advice. In a socialist state such advice would be free, so people would be far more willing to seek it. But many would still rely on patent medicines if they were available. This would be undesirable because nearly all people in pain need medical advice. Pain is a symptom of illness, and it is usually a mistake to treat the symptom rather than the illness. Hence, no drugs should be sold without a prescription in a socialist country. Of course, some prescriptions should permit repeated purchase of relatively safe drugs like aspirin, but no one in pain should be allowed to buy any pain killer until he has been examined at his local free health clinic. This rule would assure earlier detection and treatment of millions of illnesses each year.

In a competitive capitalist state it is very difficult and costly to enforce laws against the sale and use of harmful drugs because private businessmen are eager to make a profit, many men are unemployed, and many policemen are corrupt. In a socialist society it would be easy to enforce such laws, partly for reasons explained in the next chapter.

Controlling Air and Water Pollution — The function of ideally limiting air and water pollution should be largely or entirely assigned to the Division of Health because it would be best qualified to determine the health effects of such pollution. This function should not be assigned to polluting agencies because they would often be biased against adequate pollution control.

Pollution control should be largely achieved by means of sales taxes on polluting products and use taxes on polluting machines and processes. For instance, those who smoke cigarettes should pay special extra sales taxes, and those who burn trash should pay use taxes designed to measure the marginal health damage caused by such conduct. These taxes should be determined by and eventually transferred to the national Division of Health. It should also have the authority to prohibit certain health-damaging polluting practices.

Food and Water Control — The function of determining and inspecting methods of purifying and modifying water, beverages, and foods for health reasons should be assigned to the Food and Water Control Department (FWCD) of the Division of Health. It should prescribe water purification and medication standards (including fluoridation) for all domestic water systems. It should prescribe pasteurization and health standards for all dairy products. It should also prescribe enrichment of bread and some other food products with vitamins and minerals. It should prohibit the production of very harmful foods and drinks. And it should adopt many other rules to make foods and drinks more wholesome.

The FWCD should limit the amounts of salt, sugar, animal fat, and other unwholesome constituents in a large variety of processed foods in order to reduce morbidity and death rates. For instance, it should limit the amount of sugar in canned fruits. Both salt and sugar are harmful to many, probably most, people. Moreover, they can easily be added to any food by those who want more salt or sugar.

The amount of sugar, salt, fat, or other constituent in foods should rarely be reduced sharply and suddenly. Any desired new limit should normally be introduced so gradually that consumers will not sense any single step in this process.

Food Taxes and Subsidies — In every advanced society a great variety of foods and beverages is produced, some of which are harmful and some of which are much more wholesome than the average food or drink. Production of some of the most harmful should cease under socialism but other methods of influencing the consumption of food and beverages should be used, including both consumer education and a tax-subsidy system.

All foods and beverages should be classified into three groups: (1) those whose consumption is harmful for most consumers, (2) those whose consumption is neither harmful nor especially beneficial, and (3) those whose consumption ought to be increased because they are close substitutes for harmful or more costly products, or for other reasons. The FWCD should impose special excise or sales taxes on class one goods, and should use the proceeds to subsidize the production of class three goods.

It is impossible to say now which foods should be taxed or subsidized at some future time, or how high such taxes and subsidies should be. Our knowledge concerning the health effects of different foods and drink is growing rapidly. However, if such a tax-subsidy program were being considered today, we would recommend a sales tax of 10 to 20% on most beef and pork, and a subsidy of 10 to 20% on most fish and fowl. Even higher sales taxes would be desirable for candy, cake, and sweet beverages. The proceeds could be used to subsidize fresh fruit and green vegetables.

<u>Health Education for Consumers</u> — In capitalist countries an enormous number of newspaper and magazine ads and radio and TV commercials misinform and mislead the public concerning drugs, health care equipment, and medical treatments. Often they flatly contradict each other an/or recommend drugs, equipment, and treatments which are harmful or ineffective.

In a socialist country the Department of Health Care Education should use advertisements and commercials to educate the public on health care. For instance, it should use them to teach people how to recognize early symptoms of disease, how to diet wisely, how to stop smoking, how to avoid alcoholism, and so forth.

Moreover, every school and college student should be required to devote one hour a week each school year to a course in personal hygiene, emergency health care, child health care, or some other health subject. These courses should teach all students the serious evils of smoking tobacco, drinking alcoholic beverages, overeating, overdoing, failing to seek prompt medical attention when ill or injured, relying on quack medicines and doctors, and using narcotics.

All health advertising designed to increase the profits or incomes of private health care providers should be prohibited under socialism. But doctors in private practice should be allowed to advertise their place of business, professional training, medical school grades, and professional experience.

<u>Eugenics</u> — Scientific research has revealed that an ever-increasing number of human defects which require medical treatment are inherited, i.e., are carried in the genes. Future research will reveal many more such defects. In most cases the early detection of hereditary defects and illnesses requires the use

of medical procedures. Moreover, the most effective methods of eugenic control, sterilization and artificial insemination, are medical procedures. Hence, the functions of detecting hereditary defects and illnesses and carrying out eugenic programs should be entrusted to the national Department of Health Care.

There should be two major kinds of eugenic programs, one which helps individuals to marry eugenically and to decide whether to bear children, and one which strives to raise the average national level of hereditary health and intelligence in other ways. The former programs are already politically feasible, and some doctors are now giving valuable advice to individuals on choice of mate and on decisions to bear children. The latter programs are not yet politically feasible, but will probably become so during the 21st century. Once adopted and developed, such programs will produce far more beneficial and striking results than any program of advice to individuals.

The first major eugenic program beyond giving advice to individuals should probably be compulsory sterilization of the least fit — the insane, the feeble-minded, chronic criminals, known carriers of specific harmful genes, and so forth. The percentage of persons sterilized for eugenic reasons should begin at a very low figure, less than 1%, and should then gradually rise to at least 10% as eugenic knowledge grows and public support rises.

The ideal method of raising the general level of inherited health and intelligence is to examine and grade all individuals and then use sterilization and artificial insemination to restrict male insemination to an ever smaller group of very superior males. Under this program, only the most seriously defective females would need to be sterilized. The vast majority of women should bear two or three children conceived by means of artificial insemination. This system would preserve the natural family, yet would permit rapid eugenic progress. Sterilization of males does not decrease the pleasures of sex; indeed, it probably increases them. And artificial insemination does not involve adultery in the usual sense of the term. Moreover, most parents will increasingly take pride in having superior children. This pride alone will result in a growing voluntary use of artificial insemination for eugenic reasons before it becomes compulsory. It will, or course, soon become possible for parents desiring superior children to choose among a wide variety of classes of semen donors — males classified by race, size, temperament, artistic gifts, etc.

In a democratic country, we must emphasize, no coercive system of eugenic reform affecting most citizens should ever be adopted until after it has gained the support of a large majority of the voters. But minor eugenic measures affecting less than 10% of the population do not require such overwhelming support.

Birth Control — For at least ten thousand years overpopulation has been the chief cause of poverty. And every country in the world is still seriously overpopulated today. In other words, a large reduction in its population would raise real income substantially. And the degree of overpopulation is rising steadily.

While overpopulation is not an obvious health problem, every reduction in poverty and every increase in average real income improves public health. Moreover, nearly all efective means of birth control require medical advice and/or surgery.

The free basic health care provided by a socialist health system should include professional advice on birth-control pills and devices, abortion, sterilization, and other approved means of birth control. Free provision of these services is highly desirable because it will increase the use of them and help to lower the birth rate. They should me made readily and confidentially available to all unmarried adults and teenagers, as well as to married persons. This would reduce sharply the number of illegitimate births and unwanted children.

Unfortunately, the chief method of birth control in all advanced countries is still abortion, the most expensive and the most harmful method. A socialist government should use the schools, the press, the radio, and television to persuade more people to use less costly and dangerous methods of birth control. At present, the cheapest, the most effective, and probably the least harmful methods of birth control is male sterilization. And the cost and danger of female sterilization has recently been radically reduced. While it is impossible to predict accurately future advances in birth-control technology, we believe that male sterilization will long continue to be the best method of birth control.

To achieve a stable or declining population, socialist governments should limit the average number of children per family to two or less. Moreover, the pleasure of bearing and raising children should be almost equally distributed among parents. The argument for near equalization of this pleasure resembles closel the argument for making money incomes far less unequal. The pleasure of raising children, like the pleasure of spending money on consumers' goods, is subject to the principle of decreasing pleasure. The pleasure per child decreases as the number of children increases. Moreover, it is unnecessary to grant parents higher child-raising quotas in order to induce them to produce more economic goods. Hence, these quotas need not be nearly as unequal as money incomes. Indeed, they should be almost equal. Eugenic goals should be achieved largely by wide use of artificial insemination, not by inducing superior families to have more than two children.

Infanticide — For thousands of years infanticide was a common method of restricting the number of children. It was widely practiced in Europe as late as the Nineteenth Century, and in China until 1950.

In advanced countries infanticide is no longer needed as a means of population control but it is needed as a means of reducing the number of dependent and/or unhappy persons. No infant who is likely to be bedridden should be allowed to live. The money required to care for him could be much better spent to provide proper care for normal children, many of whom now starve to death each year.

Moreover, most of the children for whom infanticide is appropriate are doomed to lead unhappy lives because of their defects. And their presence in the world causes sadness and unhappiness to those who associate with them or care for them. Infanticide is the kindest of all possible treatments for such children.

Suicide and Euthanasia — All men must die, but there is no good reason why anyone under medical care must die slowly and painfully. Any aged and/or fatally ill person who wants to hasten his death in order to avoid the cost, degradation, and pain of a lingering death should be permitted, perhaps encouraged to do so. His doctor should provide him with a drug which will permit him to die painlessly and peacefully whenever he wishes to do so. The mere knowledge that such a drug is readily available would itself greatly reduce the common fear of death, especially among aged persons. Moreover, suicide by the dying injures no one, so no law or rule against it can be justified. Mere moral dogmas cannot justify state control of personal conduct.

Some men who want to avoid the degradation and pain of slow death or of long dependency and pain may be paralyzed, or fall into a prolonged coma, and thus become unable to end their terminal suffering and dependency. It is natural for most dying persons to postpone suicide until they are very sick and have lost hope of recovering. By then they are usually bedridden and unable to secure the means of suicide. Their relatives, doctors, and nurses, are now unwilling to help them for religious or legal reasons. Thus the dying may become unable to end their suffering and may die in agony. It is very important, therefore, that socialist hospital doctors practice euthanasia on terminally ill patients who cannot commit suicide and have previously requested euthanasia.

Under capitalism some heirs are tempted to speed their parents' death in order to inherit their property. This risk is far less in a socialist society where inheritance and unearned income have been largely abolished. Moreover, the functions of facilitating terminal suicide and practicing euthanasia should be entrusted to doctors, not to relatives.

A large number of hospital and nursing-home beds are occupied by terminal patients who require more care than other patients. By facilitating suicide and practicing euthanasia, socialist doctors could free these beds and nurses for more productive uses.

When terminal patients commit suicide, they are benefiting other men as well as themselves, and both benefits deserve careful consideration. As men become more socially minded, they will give more and more consideration to the social benefits.

Alcohol and Drug Addiction — Alcoholism and drug addiction are major causes of accidents, illness, violent crimes, and death in all capitalist states. It is estimated that half of all U.S. auto-accident deaths involve one or more persons under the influence of alcohol. And a large share of all burglaries and robberies are committed by drug addicts desperate to secure money to pay for another fix.

In a capitalist country it is impossible to enforce laws prohibiting the production, sale, and use of narcotic drugs and alcoholic beverages because many men are unemployed, because the police are corrupt, and because there are millions of unsupervised profit-seeking private firms. Capitalist efforts to enforce such laws cause more harm than good. They increase police corruption, popularize law-breaking and contempt for the law, result in many deaths from drug overdoses and bad liquor, greatly increase the number of violent crimes, enrich the underworld, and in other ways injure society. Under socialism, however, it would soon become possible to enforce such laws. We predict that most socialist states will enact and enforce strict laws against the sale and use of hard liquor and hard drugs before 2100 A.D.

In the meanwhile, the treatment of alcoholics and drug addicts should be a function of any socialist Department of Health Care. It should treat chronic alcoholics by segregating them in work camps or isolated towns, where no hard liquor is available, for at least one year at a time. It should treat drug addicts by providing them with maintenance doses sufficient to avoid the pains of withdrawal. Addicts on maintenance doses can live normal lives, unlike alcoholics, and therefore do not need to be segregated and confined. But addicts who continue illegally to increase their consumption of drugs and become unable or unwilling to work should be segregated in isolated work camps like unreformed alcoholics.

The frightful consequences of smoking tobacco have only recently become known. It now seems certain that smoking cigarettes shortens the average life span of smokers by about seven years, or 10%. Moreover, smokers cause innumerable fires and many deaths due to fires each year. They also pollute the air breathed by non-smokers, scatter trash in public places, cause auto accidents, and stink of tobacco.

It is not possible to enforce laws against smoking in capitalist economies, but it is possible in a socialist economy. Therefore, a socialist Division of Health should recommend complete prohibition of the smoking of tobacco as soon as public opinion polls reveal that most voters support such a prohibition. In the meantime, it should impose ever-increasing sales taxes on all tobacco products, and should use most of the proceeds to finance a powerful educational campaign against smoking. For instance, nearly all the space on the outside of each cigarette package should be devoted to warnings of the dire effects of smoking cigarettes.

In addition, before prohibition, a socialist government should decrease each year the percent of harmful ingredients in tobacco products it sells. This should be done so gradually that smokers cannot detect the results of any individual reduction, but as fast as possible within this limitation. By this means, cigarette addiction could be ended in a decade without any noticeable withdrawal pains.

Autopsies — Diagnosis is one of the most important and difficult health-care services. The percentage of patients who receive a mistaken or incomplete diagnosis is still very high, and results in a great deal of ineffective or harmful treatment.

One of the best ways to improve success in diagnosis and to determine which doctors are the best diagnosticians would be to increase greatly the number of autopsies. In a socialist society at least 20% of all corpses should undergo autopsy to determine not only the precise cause of death but also the causes of any other chronic ailments. The findings should be used to correct misdiagnoses, to test and improve diagnostic and medical procedures, to grade doctors, and to improve eugenic records. Doctors who receive grades below some minimum level, should be denied the right to practice diagnosis, at least until they have been successfully retrained. And all diagnosticians should receive salaries which vary with their grades.

Use of Cadaver Parts — The use of cadaver parts — corneas, kidneys, hearts, bones, etc. — has been increasing steadily in recent decades. It is likely that surgeons will learn to use an ever-greater variety of such parts and will make more frequent use of the kinds of parts they now use.

Already some cadaver parts are in very short supply, and many persons die or remain blind or ill because their doctors cannot obtain the needed parts. These parts are scarce chiefly because our laws prohibit their removal and reuse unless the deceased had given written approval before his death and/or unless his relatives consent after his death. These laws should be reversed. All cadaver parts should be available for medical use unless the deceased had rejected such use in writing before his death. If this legal reform alone does not result in an adequate supply of all cadaver parts, the government should start paying for each scarce part used by surgeons, and should raise the prices high enough to secure adequate supplies. Both of these policies would increase the supplies of cadaver parts without compelling any person to violate his religious principles.

C. Medical Education and Research

A socialist government should radically reorganize the education of health care personnel. It should sharply increase the total enrollment in medical and nursing schools in order to train the staff needed to provide adequate free health care to all citizens. It should eliminate all economic bars to entry into and graduation from such schools by making such education free or by providing liberal scholarship loans to be repaid out of the additional earnings assured by this education. This policy would increase the number of doctors enough to eliminate nearly all the difference between doctors' wages and the average wage for all workers.

In addition to training doctors and nurses, socialist universities should train assistant doctors, persons with qualifications about halfway between those of a registered nurse and an M.D. Group or clinic practice of medicine would greatly facilitate an increased division of labor, including a division of labor between assistant doctors and doctors. Assistant doctors could perform many functions now performed by doctors, and would cost much less to train.

Nearly all doctors, assistant doctors, and nurses should be educated as specialists. Most of the medical training now given to American doctors and nurses is useless to specialists. An oculist does not need to know the names and functions of all the bones, nerves, arteries, and other parts of the human leg, arm, abdomen, or chest. Nor does he need to know how to treat any disease of or injury to these organs. And a nurse who assists an oculist does not need to know most of the subjects now taught to registered nurses. No doctor should be trained as a general practitioner before beginning his training as a specialist. From the beginning of his medical training, he should be taught only what will be useful to him in his specialty.

Elimination of general medical training now given to doctors and nurses would not only radically shorten the period of training, probably by more than half, but would also permit a more thorough training in the specialty to be practiced. It would radically reduce the cost of medical education, and permit doctors to begin practicing medicine two or three years younger than they now do.

It is uneconomic to teach many or all health care specialties in a single school. This practice limits specialization among teachers and training facilities, or results in too small classes and underutilization of facilities. Hence, each socialist medical school should specialize in the training of one or two related specialties, and should teach only those courses required for these specialties.

The Department of Health Care Education should determine each year the number of students who begin their professional training in each department of each medical or other health care school. It should not permit the training of unneeded specialists of any kind, but should assure full quotas of each class of students in each school. In order to help attract the desired number of qualified students to each entering class of each medical, dental, or nursing school, the department should offer financial inducements sufficient to achieve this goal. These inducements should vary from school to school and from year to year, when necessary. If health care training is free, the living allowances to students should vary. If such training is financed by loans, the terms of the loans should vary.

Of course, the salaries paid health personnel should also be controlled so as to help balance the supply of and demand for each class of health workers, but fluctuations in student financial aid would have a more direct and immediate effect on young people planning their occupational and school choices. Vocational advisors of all secondary-school students should be promptly and fully informed of all prospective changes in such student financial aids.

All professional health workers should be required to continue their formal professional education throughout their working lives. Technological advance is rapid in most health care fields. Moreover, most professional workers need periodic review of basic health care principles and practices.

Continuing professional health care training could take several forms — supervision and tutoring by senior local specialists, weekend classes, TV demonstrations and lectures by specialists, return to medical school for regular classes, etc. Each class of specialists might need a different combination of such continuing education programs. But all health care professionals should be required to devote 5 to 10% of their working hours to continuing formal professional education.

As explained in <u>Liberal Socialism</u>, all pure research should be conducted by a national Department of Pure Research because the results of pure research are nearly always useful to two or more industries. But all applied research on health care drugs, equipment, and procedures should be conducted by the Division of Health.

At least 10% of the division budget should be assigned to this function. In advanced capitalist countries funds invested in health research have been highly productive, and the prospects of further notable scientific advances are very bright. Moreover, all citizens in advanced countries are eager for further improvement in their health care.

Applied health research should be conducted both by full-time researchers and by part-time health care practitioners. Many doctors should be encouraged to spend half their time treating patients and the other half working on research projects, especially projects designed to improve the kind of medical care they provide. This combination of work and related research would both enrich research and make life more interesting and satisfying for many doctors.

The Research Branch should receive or have access to copies of all personal medical records, and should be able to require the collection of any research-useful personal data on the standardized case-history forms used by all doctors. It should conduct statistical studies to determine the correlation between each kind of illness and each of many personal traits and habits. The terrible effect of cigarette smoking on health, the most important health discovery of the last generation, was discovered primarily by such statistical research.

The Branch should also determine the correlation between each type of medical treatment and patient cures. The results should be used to train medical practitioners and to program the computers they use in determining which treatment to use.

D. Financing Health Care

The Source of Health Division Funds — If most health services are provided nearly free of charge, as we have recommended, they will have to be financed by taxation. In Liberal Socialism and in earlier chapters of the present work we prescribed certain special-purpose taxes and compulsory insurance premiums designed to allocate some health care costs to those consumers responsible for them. Such taxes include sales taxes levied, solely for health reasons, on cigarettes, alcoholic drinks, narcotics, etc. These taxes should be fixed by the Division of Health, and the proceeds should accrue to it. Moreover, a large share of the taxes fixed by police and fire-protection agencies to allocate the health care costs due to crime and fire should also accrue to this division and be used to cover such costs. And any other special taxes or insurance premiums designed to allocate health care costs should be so treated.

It may also prove economic to charge all clinic patients a small fee, perhaps one dollar per visit, in order to discourage unjustifiable visits to clinics. However, no fee should ever be charged for a visit which results in a needed health examination or treatment.

While customary well-justified health care services should all be largely or entirely free, some less necessary or optional services like cosmetic surgery for adults, should be sold for a price. And some doctors should be allowed to engage in private individual or group practice in order to enable demanding patients to obtain more personal attention than they would receive in public clinics. However, no doctor employed full-time by a public agency should be allowed to engage in private practice since this would induce him to overwork and/or neglect his public patients.

The total revenue from special-purpose taxes, insurance premiums, and fees described above would probably finance less than half of the budget of a socialist Division of Health. The remainder of its budget should be financed out of the proceeds of the general revenue tax prescribed in Liberal Socialism.

The Total Appropriation for Health Care — The national legislature of a socialist state should appropriate each year a total sum to finance the Division of Health. This sum would normally be less than that requested by the division because specialists always overrate the relative importance of their fields, and because executives usually wish to expand their personal empires. Only a legislature can impartially evaluate competing demands for scarce revenue by separate national agencies.

The size of the annual appropriation for health care in a democratic socialist country would depend upon the desires of voters and their representatives. But these desires would be greatly influenced by information as to the marginal cost and benefit of each proposed health care expenditure, especially as to the cost and benefit of saving one more life, for each class of persons.

Health care provides a great variety of widely differing benefits: prevention of many kinds of pain, prevention of many kinds of both temporary and permanent disablement, preservation of sight and hearing, prevention of apathy and depression, etc. To spend health funds wisely, socialist health care managers must try to allocate available funds among a great variety of uses and persons in such a way that the marginal dollar devoted to each use yields the same amount of benefit. But such marginal benefits can be measured and compared with each other and with marginal costs only if they are measured in a common unit of measurement, namely the monetary unit.

We need a new science of medical care cost-benefit analysis to help doctors decide how much to spend on treating each kind of illness for each class of patients. When most health care was sold for a price, each patient decided, with the advice of his doctor, how much should be spent on his care. But already over half of all health care is a free good in advanced capitalist countries, and nearly all such care is free in communist countries. Yet we have developed no substitutes for price allocation except arbitrary decisions by legislators and doctors. We need large-scale continuous research to determine the personal and economic benefits of each kind of health care on each class of patients, and how to measure all of these benefits in money, so they can be compared with the costs of each kind of health care. The resulting pecuniary cost-benefit estimates could be used both to control total national spending on health care and to allocate health care services among individual patients. These estimates should be prepared by the Research Department.

Whenever the Division of Health requests funds to perform new functions or to expand old ones, it should submit to the national legislature copies of cost-benefit studies which justify the initiation or expansion of these functions. Such studies should be prepared for all new programs and program expansions considered or proposed by any unit of the division as well as for those which are finally recommended by the division.

To aid in the preparation of such studies, the division should conduct periodic public opinion polls to determine how much the public desires major new or expanded health services. All persons polled should be informed of both the probable individual tax costs and the probable personal benefits of each proposed increment in health services.

The Allocation of Health Funds and Services — Having considered the determination of the total budget of the Division of Health, we turn now to the problem of allocating the funds to specific uses. This problem includes three major parts: (1) how should the available funds be divided among the departments of the Division of Health, (2) how should the Health Care Department allocate its funds to regional and local units, and (3) how should these local units allocate funds to the care of individual patients.

The allocation of total health funds among the departments of the Division of Health should be done by senior national executives of this division, not by the national legislature, because these executives would be more familiar with and expert in the problems involved in this allocation. Moreover, they would have no constituents demanding favors for their local areas, they could devote more time to these problems, and could act more quickly to change such an allocation whenever conditions change. They too should try to allocate funds so as to maximize the total national benefit, which would require achieving an equal benefit from the last million dollars spent by each unit, a very difficult task.

Most of the total Health budget would probably be allocated to the Health Care Department, so its internal allocation problems deserve special attention. It should distribute its funds among regional districts, and they among local districts, very largely on the basis of population because there is rarely a good reason why the inhabitants of one area should receive more health care per person than the residents of other areas. However, local epidemics and catastrophes would justify minor temporary differences in local per-person spending on health care. And differences in average age might also justify minor but more lasting differences, for reasons given below.

We come now to the fourth major health allocation problem, namely that of how each clinic and hospital should distribute its service among individual patients. The easiest and most obvious answer to this problem is to prescribe that all patients with like symptoms should be treated alike, regardless of their age, earnings, and other personal features. This rule is likely to be more popular politically than any alternative rule, but its application would not yield optimum economic benefits.

To achieve such optimum benefits, local health care delivery agencies should discriminate among patients on the basis of age and, perhaps, on the basis of earnings. They should discriminate on the basis of age because it is far more economically productive to save the life or health of a twenty-year-old worker than to save the life of a day-old infant or a ninety-year-old person. The twenty-year-old is the product of a large investment in child care and education which has just begun to yield a return to society and the individual. No such investment has been made in the infant, and the investment in the old man has already been fully amortized and can yield little if any further return. Indeed, the old man is probably a burden on society, and may also be suffering many chronic aches and pains. Therefore, much more should be spent to preserve the life and health of a young worker than to preserve the life of an infant or the life or health of an aged person. How much more is very difficult to say, but socialist doctors should spend at least two or three times as much to heal a young worker or housewife as to heal any aged person.

From birth to age 20, the economic value of an individual normally increases steadily, and from age 30 on it normally decreases, slowly at first and then ever more rapidly. Careful studies are needed to determine more precisely how age affects the value of an average human life.

The discrimination on the basis of age suggested above should be applied only in deciding on expensive treatments and operations. There is no good reason why a patient of any age should be denied relatively inexpensive drugs, treatments, and minor operations which are known to be effective.

A great deal of research is needed to determine how much discrimination in health care on the basis of age is economic. All we wish to assert here is that such discrimination would be economic.

Some discrimination in health care based on earnings would also be economic under socialism. However, differences in personal earnings would be far smaller under socialism than they now are under capitalism. We have recommended (LS, Ch. XVI) that average wages should be almost equal in nearly all occupations.

One easy, acceptable way to achieve some such discrimination would be to allow certain health care services to be sold for a price. For instance, special or extra nursing care, treatments, and the use of private hospital rooms could be sold for a price which only the better-paid workers could afford to pay.

It would be very difficult to discriminate in the provisions of free health care on the basis of earnings, and would probably also be politically unpopular. Hence, we shall not discuss such discrimination further.

On the other hand, political opposition to discrimination on the basis of age should be relatively weak, and should decline steadily as its economic benefits are more widely grasped, because it would affect all social classes and most persons equally. The members of every social class pass through childhood, maturity, and old age. And nearly all of us would benefit from discrimination in health care based upon age. Unfortunately, half of us would suffer from discrimination based on earnings.

CHAPTER XII

PUBLISHING

In terms of number of employees or value of output the publishing industry is relatively small. It employs less than 1% of the national work force. But publishers of newspapers, magazines, and books have a great influence upon public opinion, and therefore upon the rate of social and economic progress. Publications multiply the benefits of all scientific research and development, to which over 10% of GNP should be devoted. They also facilitate all education, another 10% of GNP under socialism. In these and other ways, they yield large external economies.

Critics of socialism have often warned that socialism will end or reduce freedom of the press, and government control and censorship of the press in communist countries have made this warning very plausible. Therefore, we have decided to devote a separate chapter to the publishing industry, in spite of the fact that the market value of its output is now, and will remain, relatively very small.

A. Organization

The very tentative Organization Chart for a Socialist Economy on p. 114 of Liberal Socialism lists an "Amusement Trust" in the Division of Vendible Services. We would now like to rename this "The Information and Entertainment Trust." Both major forms of public information, namely publishing and broadcasting, should be included in this trust. Entertainment also should be included because nearly all forms of public entertainment should be published and/or broadcast. And libraries are a major means of information.

The publishing industry should constitute a branch of this trust. This branch should include separate national agencies for periodical publication, book publication, and printing plant operation.

There are three basic principles of organization which should be applied to all socialist systems of public-opinion formation, including publishing: (1) operational centralization, (2) editorial decentralization, and (3) professionalization.

Operational Centralization — In a socialist country all physical means of commercial publishing should be planned, designed, maintained, and operated by a single national agency in order to achieve all the benefits of large-scale production and management. This agency should perform all functions except collecting news and manuscripts and determining what is published.

The principle of operational centralization includes more than the principle of monopolistic organization. Organization of a newspaper monopoly with a single printing press in each city centralizes operational control over newspaper operations in each city. But it does not centralize control over newspaper operations in the nation as a whole. Hence, we have stated the more general principle of national operational centralization.

Editorial Decentralization — The general principle of complete national centralization of control applies to all economic activities except the creation and spread of ideas by scientific research, education, publication, broadcasting, entertainment, and other means. In these activities it is far more important to achieve and preserve a free and varied expression of opinion than to minimize the costs of production by eliminating the wastes of competition.

Freedom of expression promotes scientific, technological, and social progress because it permits and favors the development and spread of useful new ideas. Many new scientific ideas and nearly all important new social reforms originate as unpopular minority views which rulers and censors would like to ignore or suppress for religious, moral, economic, or political reasons. Those nations which have advanced most rapidly during the last 500 years are precisely those nations in which scientists, writers, journalists, and reformers have been most free to express new and dissenting views. Hence, for purely practical reasons, it is vital that a socialist government should permit and encourage free expression of opinion and facts in all media of public communication. Moreover, every articulate and creative individual is happier when he is free to express his own personal opinions on all subjects.

While freedom of expression on social, political, scientific, religious, and other general issues promotes social progress, the same cannot be said for freedom of expression in communication media about private personal conduct. For instance, critical newspaper comment on individual divorces, sexual acts, crimes, illegitimate births, drunkenness, etc., rarely promotes social reform and nearly always injures the individual criticized. Hence, socialist writers, editors, and broadcasters should not be allowed to criticize or publicize any individual acts of non-political persons, and their criticism of political leaders should apply only to political qualifications and acts. The courts alone should be allowed to criticize or punish men for individual non-political acts, and their proceedings and verdicts should be unpublicized.

To help assure a free and varied expression of published opinion on public issues, a socialist state should radically decentralize editorial decision-making in each publishing industry, and should strive to make editors independent of economic and political pressure. Every publishing unit should have a staff of journalists largely independent of outside control. And no such staff should control more than one publication. Each staff should be self-perpetuating, selecting new members by co-option, or should be chosen directly or indirectly by some independent local or regional organization of readers, journalists, and/or other professional men. Perhaps some chief editors should serve a fixed term, or for life, and be assured an ample pension on retirement or dismissal. Every journalist, as well as every editor, should be as free as possible of opinion control by the central government. Moreover, freedom of entry should be carefully maintained.

Professionalization — The third basic general rule for socialist publishing is that nearly all non-fiction editors, authors, and reporters should have professional education both in writing and in the subjects about which they write. Editors and reporters who handle political news should have a degree in political science or political economy. Those who report on developments in scientific research should have a degree in the relevant natural science, and so on. A university degree in English or Journalism, desirable as it is, should not be treated as sufficient qualification for writing news stories or editorials on income-tax reforms, education, eugenics, or any other subject.

Few if any laymen are qualified to express informed opinions on social and scientific problems, or to summarize well the speeches and publications of those who are experts. Most such problems are already complex, and are steadily becoming ever more complex. Even professional men are usually unqualified to write well on subjects outside of their specialty in their professional field.

One good way to insure that all publishing units are controlled and manned by competent professional editors is to require that the senior editor of each unit be chosen by a national, regional, or local committee of his professional organization. This method of selecting editors, however, should not be imposed on the publishing staffs of self-supporting voluntary political, educational, and religious organizations, who naturally care more about the ideology or prejudices of their editors than about their professional competence. But the publications and broadcasts of such organizations should receive no state financial aid.

B. Newspapers

In capitalist countries, newspapers are major means of news dissemination and political indoctrination. In 1972, U.S. newspapers had gross revenues of $8 billion, and their private owners had great political influence. In a socialist society, both functions of newspapers should be far less important.

The Need for Newspapers under Socialism — Capitalist newspapers are supported largely by advertising, which should be reduced by over 80% under socialism. This would increase the price of unsubsidized newspapers by over 200%, which would radically reduce their sale.

Moreover, all local and national news can be broadcast by radio or TV much faster and much more cheaply than it can be printed and distributed in newspapers. And most news now published in newspapers should not be published at all, for reasons given later. Also, an ample quantity of thoughtful commentary on the news can be published in magazines and books. Finally, newspapers consume a vast amount of timber, and produce a great amount of street litter and household refuse. For all these reasons, the case for continued publication of large daily newspapers under socialism is rather weak.

Newspapers still have some advantages over news broadcasts. One can read a newspaper when and where he pleases, can skip stories in which he is not interested, can find desired stories more easily, and can clip and preserve them. Also, most newspaper news stories are now much longer and more detailed than broadcast news stories. But the latter could easily be made more detailed, and weekly news magazines could provide detailed news stories to supplement brief broadcast news stories.

The case for continuing to publish suburban and small-town newspapers is stronger than the case for continuing to publish metropolitan newspapers. When metropolitan newspapers publish local community or suburban news, most of their readers (who live in other communities) are uninterested and skip it. And news of city-wide interest can be broadcast by stations which serve the entire city. But no broadcasting station can serve a single community or suburb as a suburban newspaper can. Suburban newspapers can concentrate on local news and deliver it only to local residents.

To determine whether a city or suburb should have its own newspaper, the government should conduct a public opinion poll or local election. The voters should be informed of all the prospective costs and benefits of publishing such a paper. If a paper is published, local residents should pay all costs, partly by local taxes and partly by paying prices equal to marginal costs.

In the following discussion we assume that national, metropolitan, and/or suburban newspapers will be published under socialism. They could be published daily, twice a week, or weekly, as local voters decide.

Newspaper Contents — Most American city newspapers now contain 40 to 100 large pages on weekdays and 200 to 600 on Sundays. Most of their space is devoted to advertising and to publicity stories supplied by advertisers. A socialist city paper should probably have no more than eight pages, and should devote less than one quarter of its space to advertisements. No commercial publicity stories should be printed.

Socialist city and suburban papers should print only advertisements of purely local interest — local theater, radio, and TV programs; notices of local sporting events and lectures, etc. Advertisements for nationally distributed goods should appear only in national periodicals and catalogs. This policy would help to minimize the cost of printing and distribution.

The size of newspapers should be further reduced by eliminating most editorials, nearly all feature stories, and several important classes of news stories.

Socialist newspapers should contain no editorials by local editors, or commentaries by columnists, except on purely local or regional policies. Editorials and comment on national policies and international events should be published only in national magazines and books. Such comment is of interest to some people throughout the nation, but not to all readers in any city, and is worth preserving longer than daily newspapers are kept. Editorials printed in national magazines need not be set in type in many or all cities. Moreover, it is desirable to keep daily newspapers small in order to conserve paper and labor.

It may seem that this policy would reduce unduly the variety of opinion on national issues to which citizens are exposed, but if each national magazine is required to publish a variety of different opinions, readers would be exposed to a much wider range of opinion than they now find in the typical capitalist or communist newspaper. Also, there could be many national magazines and books.

Capitalist newspapers print many feature items — book reviews, fiction, comic strips, humorous stories, kitchen recipes, gardening advice, crossword puzzles, etc. — in addition to news stories, publicity, and advertising. Nearly all such features are of more than temporary local interest, and do not require prompt publication. Hence, they should be published in magazines and books, which can be preserved and reread much more easily than newspapers. They should not also be published in local newspapers because this would require duplicate or multiple typesetting, printing, and distribution of the same items.

Most newspaper readers ignore some or all of the special features listed above. They must pay for features they do not want. If these features were published only in specialized magazines and books, this waste would be drastically reduced.

Capitalist newspapers feature news stories of sensational local and national crimes, criminal trials, divorce proceedings, and other scandals. In the process they ruin the reputations of innocent as well as guilty men, cause witnesses to hide or give dishonest testimony, bias many jurors and judges, give criminals and criminal methods undue publicity, and prompt some persons to commit crimes.

Socialist newspapers should print no news which would injure any individual, except complaints about poor performance by elected officials and their subordinates. Divorce proceedings and testimony should be ignored. Most local crimes should also be ignored, and, if any major crimes are reported, no names of arrested suspects should be printed until they have been finally convicted. Criminal trials should rarely be reported, and then only in very summary form.

To publish the crimes and trials of criminal suspects is as indelicate and vulgar as to publish the ill health and medical diagnosis of patients who do not want such personal facts publicized. It is socially desirable to publish frequent detailed crime and health statistics, but not to name the individuals involved.

Local newspapers should publish no book reviews, play reviews, musical criticism, and other criticism of national interest, but they should publish reviews of purely local dramatic, artistic, and sport events because such reviews would be of interest only or chiefly to local residents.

Socialist newspapers should print no sport news, except announcements of local sporting events, because radio and television broadcasts can provide much more vivid and much more prompt news about such events. It is far more pleasant to see a football game on television than to read about it afterwards.

Socialist newspapers should print little if any news of private social events. There would be no millionaires to give elaborate parties. Moreover, public reporting of such social affairs is vulgar and arouses envy and resentment. However, papers should print advance notices and news of local civic, reform, learned, and other association activities which are open to the public.

Most or all of the space devoted to financial and business news in capitalist newspapers could be saved. There would be no daily security and commodity price changes to report because there would be no security and commodity markets. And there would be no news about private profits or losses, or about the sale of real estate.

A socialist government should of course publish many reports on economic progress in each major industry, but most such reports should be published in weekly or monthly periodicals, not in newspapers, because the former are more apt to be preserved for much longer periods of time and because many readers are uninterested in most such reports.

Few if any letters to the editor should be published in socialist newspapers. Such letters usually report familiar ideas, or contain false statements, or make charges which should be carefully investigated before they are published. Moreover, they often give a false impression of public opinion. Public opinion should be measured by scientific public opinion polls, not be counting or reading letters to the editor or to legislators. Finally, the few constructive letters by qualified, lucid authors should be published in a magazine or book which will not be discarded the day it is received.

Reducing Duplication of News Stories — Nearly all large U.S. cities still have two or more daily newspapers distributed throughout the metropolitan area, and a number of daily or weekly suburban newspapers distributed in individual suburbs. There is very extensive duplication of news content between these papers, even when they are monopolies. A socialist city should have no more than one metropolitan paper, and no news or feature story printed in it should be published in any suburban paper. Moreover, a metropolitan paper should not print any items of interest only to the residents of a single suburb.

A similar division of labor should be established between national and metropolitan papers. All news of nationwide interest (and no other news) should be published in a single national newspaper. Such a division of labor between national, metropolitan, and suburban papers would reduce by over 80% the cost of collecting, printing, and distributing any given amount of printed news.

In a large country the national newspaper should be printed in and distributed from local printing plants, but all of the stories and comment should be collected, edited, and sent out by a national office, which should have equipment to set type in all local printing plants by wire. Many of the news stories distributed by the national office should be written by local metropolitan reporters and editors, but many others should be prepared by foreign and national reporters and editors employed by the national office of the national newspaper.

We have been speaking of a national newspaper, a metropolitan newspaper, and a local suburban paper as if they were separate physical entities. If they are separate entities they should be folded together and delivered as a single paper. But it would be more economic to print them locally as separate sections of a single paper.

The creation of a newspaper monopoly in each city would make it unnecessary to send more than one newspaper reporter to any local news event. Furthermore, metropolitan coordination of all local news-gathering agencies would make it unnecessary for radio news departments to send their own reporters to news events.

Centralization of control over all news-gathering agencies in the nation would permit a radical reduction in the number of reporters who attend national newsmaking events. For instance, the number of reporters who attend White House press conferences could be reduced from over 400 to 10, or less. Better yet, such press conferences could be ended and replaced by printed news releases. The questions reporters now ask in person, often as a form of exhibitionism, could be asked and answered more thoughtfully and correctly in writing.

Only one issue of a daily newspaper should be published each day. Earlier and later news should be provided by radio and television broadcasts.

The single edition of each paper should be published for afternoon delivery. People have much more time to read papers in the evening than in the morning, and evening papers are less expensive to publish and deliver because they require less night work.

Pricing and **Financing** — The relatively small and inexpensive newspapers we have proposed for a socialist country should be free goods, delivered to all homes in each city. They should be free for the first copy because charging a price for all copies would cost something and would yield little benefit. Price distribution would reduce consumption below the optimum level without reducing total costs significantly. The marginal costs of consumption are small. Only extra copies should be sold for a price, equal to the marginal cost of production.

If most newspapers are delivered to all homes gratis, and the rest are sold for a price far below any estimate of average cost, every newspaper plant will incur a large deficit. This deficit should be covered by the national treasury in such a way as to minimize national and local political control over the preparation of news stories. The national legislature should allocate a lump sum to the Information and Entertainment Trust, without specifying how it is to be allocated to individual media. This Trust should then divide this sum among its major branches without specifying how it is to be allocated among subordinate units. The publishing branch should use some objective index or measure of social benefit — number of subscribers, number of readers, opinions polls, expert evaluations, etc. — to allocate its funds among individual publishing firms, including newspapers.

C. Periodicals

In capitalist countries the costs of publishing most periodicals are met largely by advertisers. As a result, magazines are much cheaper than books, and magazine sales have risen above the ideal economic limit. Socialism will cut periodical advertising by over 90%, and this alone will sharply reduce the proportion of printed matter published in magazine form and increase that published in book form. Moreover, for other reasons, much, perhaps most, of the material now published in popular capitalist magazines ought to be published in books, not in magazines.

Contents — Socialist periodicals should publish only material which is unsuitable for publication in newspapers and books. They should not reprint news items published in newspapers because this would require unnecessary duplication of services. However, a single weekly news magazine which condenses and summarizes the national and international news might be justifiable.

Magazines should publish no fiction, poetry, drama, history, health advice, recipes, chess games, bridge lessons, how-to-do-it instructions, and other material of continuing interest because quick publication is unneeded and because all such material can be more easily preserved and consulted in book form. Magazines should print only news stories and other items which are too specialized and/or detailed for publication in newspapers and which should be published as soon as possible. All stories and reports which do not need to be available before they can be published in book form should be published in books.

Newspapers should print news items of general interest because papers should go to all homes and should be much more widely read than any magazine. Periodicals should print news items of interest only to limited groups because the circulation of each magazine or learned journal would be restricted to the relevant group of specialized readers. Most news is not of general interest.

Magazines should also print comment on the news which ought to appear soon after the news event has occurred. They should print book reviews, drama criticism, and comment on current national radio and TV programs because such criticism is needed to help book buyers, playgoers, and broadcast viewers as soon as possible. Moreover, most such criticism dates fast and is not worthy of permanent preservation in book form. However, the best criticism of the more significant current artist events should be reprinted later in book form.

Specialization — Hundreds of periodicals should be published in a socialist economy, but each should specialize and appeal to a limited group of readers. No general magazines including fiction, popular science, political comment, travel stories, etc., should be published. Each periodical should appeal to a national but special group, a group interested in a single profession, trade, hobby, sport, science, art, or other limited subject.

The more a periodical specializes, the more likely its readers are to be interested in all of its contents. When specialists read general magazines, most of them ignore many of the articles because they fall outside their special interest. And laymen too have widely varying special interests — hobbies, sports, politics, and so forth. Hence, magazines which fail to specialize publish a great deal of material which remains unread by most subscribers. Every increase in specialization decreases the number of such unread pages, and such pages are evidence of economic waste.

This reasoning applies also to learned journals. For instance, the <u>American Economic Review</u>, which now publishes articles on all branches of economic theory and policy, should cease publication, and all articles on economic theory and policy should be published in more specialized journals on price theory, rent theory, interest theory, wage theory, monetary theory, and so forth. The circulation of each specialized journal would be smaller, but subscribers would be far more likely to read all articles and to preserve the magazine for future reference. Moreover, it would become far easier to assemble and review the literature on any subject.

There ought to be a single general magazine covering all fields of economic theory, policy, and practice, but it should contain no original reports on research or theory. Its function should be to review in simple language, i.e., for laymen and experts in other fields, the most important recent developments reported in specialized economic journals. It should present a general survey like that now provided by Society or Psychology Today.

No two periodicals should ever print the same, or very similar, articles because this would require duplicate writing, typesetting, printing, and distribution costs. Nor should any magazine reprint news stories or comments already published in the national newspaper. However, each specialized national periodical should list articles in other periodicals most likely to be of interest to its readers.

Editorial Decentralization — All periodical publishing activities except writing and editing should be carried on by a single national agency. All printing not done on newspaper presses should be done in one or a few printing plants located so as to minimize printing and delivery costs.

On the other hand, the government should exercise no control over the content of the vast majority of periodicals, those not published by state agencies. The editors of art, literary, hobby, sport, reform, religious, political, scientific, and other non-government periodicals should be chosen by political parties, by professional associations, and/or by other relevant groups. The selection of these magazine editors should be highly decentralized in order to help achieve maximum independence and freedom of the press. Any private person or association which wishes to publish a magazine and is able to finance it should be allowed to do so and to choose its editorial staff.

In capitalist magazines, editorials are written by members of the staff and usually state the views of the owner. In communist countries, editorials are written by editors selected or approved by the communist party and state the party line only. In a liberal socialist society nearly all newspaper and magazine editorials should be written by outside propagandists hired by numerous private non-profit political parties and reform associations, and should be clearly labeled as political propaganda. Equal space should usually be given to both or all sides of controversial issues. During political campaigns free editorial and advertising space should be allocated to political parties on the basis of their total vote in the last election. These policies would help to decentralize control over opinion formation. They would help readers to distinguish more clearly between news and propaganda and to identify the source of each item of propaganda.

<u>Pricing and Financing</u> — While socialist newspapers should be free goods, all popular magazines should be price goods. Such magazines would be much larger and more costly than newspapers. Also, they would be more specialized, and most would serve only a very small proportion of the total population. Moreover, some persons would want to receive several magazines, and others none.

Magazine prices should equal marginal cost, i.e., current cost at the margin, which includes no writing, editing, composition, interest, rent, or overhead costs, only the cost of printing and selling one more copy. Since most capitalist magazines are now heavily financed by advertisers, they sell at prices much nearer marginal costs than do learned journals and books which carry little or no advertising. Thus the adoption of marginal-cost price-output control would reduce magazine prices much less than it would reduce the prices of books and learned journals.

Learned journals, unlike popular magazines, should be free goods, in order to increase their readerships. They would publish all the results of a very costly national research program, whose benefits would be reduced by charging prices for the final published results. An advanced socialist society should spend over 10% of its national income on R and D, and the annual results should be worth many billions of dollars. It would be grossly uneconomic to restrict these benefits by charging prices in order to finance part of the small costs of publishing research reports.

Most learned journals are now purchased by university libraries and professors, by other researchers, and by doctors and lawyers. We explained in <u>Liberal Socialism</u> why most education, health care, legal services, and research findings should be free goods. These arguments support our conclusion that learned journals should be free goods.

Periodicals which are published to entertain, to report on sport or art, to further political or social reform, and to comment on current events should be sold for a price equal to marginal cost. To enable the publishers of these journals to cover most or all of the resulting deficits, the government should provide suitable subsidies. These subsidies should be large because all publishing creates heavy intra-marginal costs which would not be covered by prices equal to cost at the margin.

If some non-learned journals of opinion are subsidized and others are not, there will be discrimination against certain journals and their opinions. Therefore, all journals of opinion should be equally subsidized. The subsidies should probably be based upon the number of words printed and the number of subscribers when prices equal marginal costs.

Production Policies — Eventually, most periodicals will be produced only on microfilm, but in the meantime, those printed on paper should be bound like paperback books — as most learned journals are now — and should be of standard book format, so that they can be more easily stored on standard book shelves. Most non-professional magazines are now discarded within a week or two because they consist largely of advertising, contain many articles of little interest to the reader, and do not fit well in standard bookcases. If advertising were largely eliminated, if magazines were more specialized, and if they were printed in book form, far more of them would be preserved in public and private libraries. And increased preservation and use of old magazine issues would decrease the demand for new magazines and books.

All magazines of each class should be printed on the same kind of paper, one proven by careful scientific research to be the most suitable for use in such magazines. The use of tested standardized papers should reduce publishing costs, make reading easier, and make library copies last longer.

All magazines of each class should be printed with the same size and kind of type, that proven by careful scientific research to be the most suitable for use in such magazines and books. This type should be designed primarily, perhaps solely, to facilitate rapid reading. However, private persons and groups should be allowed to use any paper and type they wish in unsubsidized publications.

The cost of printing and storing all publication could easily be reduced 10 to 20% by the universal use of simplified spelling (tho for though, etc.) and a few score standard abbreviations (Am. for American). This would save hundreds of millions of dollars a year and, much more important, would increase reading speeds. A socialist state should gradually and continually reform its written language so as to increase these benefits every year.

D. Books

In the coming socialist society, book publishing should expand sharply both in relative and absolute importance. As explained earlier, a great deal of material now published in capitalist magazines and newspapers should be published in books because it is of continuing interest. Moreover, most periodicals are now heavily subsidized by advertisers, and such subsidies would be drastically reduced. Finally, book prices would be reduced much more than periodical prices by the marginal-cost price-output control appropriate for all publications sold for a price under socialism.

In 1972 the cost of publishing America's newspapers and periodicals came to about $11 billion while the cost of all books and pamphlets was only about $3 billion. The elimination of nearly all advertising and the adoption of other policies recommended in this chapter would probably raise the annual value of book output well above the combined total for newspapers and periodicals.

<u>Contents</u> — As explained earlier, newspapers and magazines should not publish any material more suitable for publication in books. Books are more durable and can be more carefully written and edited than periodicals. Therefore, all manuscripts which are of continuing interest and do not require rapid publication should be published in books. Such manuscripts provide most of the non-advertising matter now published in newspapers and popular magazines, which are normally discarded soon after their receipt. Publishing such material in book form would not only make it easier to preserve, but would also make it far easier for librarians to classify and catalog it. Moreover, readers can find desired matter in specialized and cataloged books much more easily than they can find it in old newspapers or magazines.

If a short story or a novel is worth publishing in a newspaper or magazine, it is worth publishing in a book. To publish a novel in both magazine and book form is wasteful because it doubles the publication costs. Moreover, when a short story is published in a newspaper or magazine, many, perhaps most, of the subscribers do not read it. They have not specifically chosen to buy or receive it. On the other hand, when people buy books, they choose each book individually, and are therefore far more likely to read it. The publication of pages which are never read is obviously wasteful.

All fiction, all verse, all artistic pictures, all biography, all how-to-do-it articles, all travel reports, all kitchen recipes, all histories of doctrine, all surveys of current thought, and so forth should be published in book form only.

Nearly all non-fiction books should contain an index and a detailed table of contents designed to help the reader find what he is looking for as quickly as possible. Most users of such books are looking for information on specific points, usually found on a few pages, and do not want to have to read an entire book, or even an entire chapter to find it.

Each non-fiction book should also contain a one-page summary review of the author's education and experience. These summaries should be written so as to help the reader determine how well-qualified the author is to write on the subject of the book.

In addition, each such book should contain one or two very brief critical reviews by impartial experts. These book reviews should call the reader's attention to the chief merits and demerits of the book. Book reviews published in newspapers and magazines are seldom easily available to readers when they consider whether or not to read a particular book. Reviews published in non-fiction books would help book readers to buy more wisely and to understand better what they read.

Professionalization and Decentralization — For book publishing, as for newspaper and magazine publishing, the two chief principles of editorial organization are decentralization and professionalization. All senior editors should be professionally trained men chosen by their professional colleagues, by the appropriate learned association, or by some university. And ultimate editorial decisions should be decentralized in order to minimize dogmatic, political, religious, and clannish control over the expression of opinion and over literary trends and styles.

There are various ways in which editorial responsibility for the publication of books could be decentralized. First, a socialist state could establish many competing independent editorial staffs, each free to publish any book it likes. If this policy is adopted, each staff should probably be located in a different region in order to subject it to a different intellectual environment. And an author whose manuscript has been rejected by one staff could send it to another until it has been accepted, or has been rejected by all. The chief editor of each regional staff could be chosen by a different regional professional group. This method of editorial decentralization would continue much of the waste of competitive capitalist selection of book manuscripts, but it would help greatly to assure the expression of a wide variety of intellectual and literary opinion.

Another way to decentralize book editing would be to establish a single central editorial staff with several senior editors in each field and make each senior editor independent of his administrative and editorial colleagues and superiors. Then, each manuscript rejected by one senior editor could be passed on to other editors in the same office, any one of whom would be empowered to authorize its publication. This policy would make manuscript submission much easier. It would assure considerable freedom of expression in books if editors were properly selected. Such freedom is most needed for artists, reformers, and social scientists.

A third way to decentralize the choice of books to be published is to allow each university to have its own publishing committee to approve books for publication by a single national book publishing agency. And, of course, any author whose book manuscript has been rejected by all editors should be allowed to publish it at his own expense.

Other methods of editorial decentralization could be suggested. It is the principle of editorial decentralization, not any specific method of application, which is vital.

When there are many independent publishers handling similar books, literary agents can perform a useful social function. They can save the time of writers and publishers by seeing that manuscripts go first to those firms or editors most likely to accept them, and by speeding up re-submission. In a capitalist society literary agents refuse to serve those writers who most need their services, new or unknown authors, and compete vigorously to serve those who least need their services, namely successful authors. In a socialist society, they should devote nearly all their time to new and/or unsuccessful authors. They should be paid by the hour not by commissions or royalties. They should not be allowed to try to switch authors from one publisher to another, or to bargain for higher royalties. And one monopolistic literary agency, including many independent agents, should serve all authors.

<u>Authorship</u> — Even in the richest and largest capitalist states very few men, probably less than 200 in the U.S., are able to earn a living by writing books. The vast majority of books are written by individuals employed as teachers, lawyers, doctors, civil servants, and so forth, who must write in their very limited spare time. As a result, nearly all books, including most textbooks, are poorly written. For this

and other reasons, over 99% of all book manuscripts are rejected by publishers and never published. Moreover, of those published, the great majority lose money for the publisher and yield the author less than $1000 in royalties. And, as noted in Liberal Socialism, royalties measure no real marginal cost and always raise book prices further above the ideal level.

In a liberal socialist economy these conditions of authorship should be radically changed. Most non-fiction books and all textbooks should be written by teams of authors, not by individuals. In almost every field of knowledge the mass of written material is far too great to be mastered by a single man. Moreover, even when this is possible, the composite opinion of several authors is more reliable and significant than the opinion of a single author. And mastery of a subject is rarely combined with skill in lucid exposition. Hence, every non-fiction book written by authorities in a given field should be revised and edited by men skilled in exposition, including specialists in graphic presentation, in literary style, in bibliography, and in the preparation of indexes.

The average textbook should be the product of at least ten man-years work by three to five authors and editors. If a book is the product of a single author, it should be criticized in detail by both subject and style editors and returned to him for further revision at least once, and usually several times. The greater the expected sales, the larger should be the investment in writing and editing a non-fiction book. The most widely read non-fiction books should be revised every few years, both to keep them up to date and to make them more and more readable and stimulating.

The method of financing authors should also be radically changed. A socialist America should put thousands of book authors on an annual salary so that they can devote full time to their research and writing. No gifted author should be required to teach or hold some other job to supplement his income from writing. Of course, many authors enjoy a combination of authorship with some other part-time work, especially teaching, which should be facilitated, but most very gifted authors prefer to devote their full time to writing.

The selection of persons to become salaried writers should be highly decentralized, so as to prevent central control of public opinion. Most salaried authors should be selected by regional professional associations, and/or by independent universities.

Every university should be allowed to appoint each year a quota of new probational salaried writers, and these should be supported by the publishing branch for a trial period of perhaps three to five years. At the end of this period, the most promising probationers should be given permanent appointments. They should receive annual salaries largely independent of the volume of their output. Furthermore, all university professors should be allowed time off with pay whenever they desire to write a book in their field of study. And any unsalaried author who writes a valuable or successful book should be offered a position as a salaried author.

The salaries of non-fiction authors should depend upon unbiased evaluations of their work by professional colleagues chosen by professional associations. The salaries of other authors should vary with the total sale of their books. But the best-paid author should earn no more than three times that of the worst-paid full-time authors should not significantly exceed the average salary of any other profession.

Translated Books — The number and proportion of foreign books translated and published in English should be very greatly increased. Indeed, translation should soon provide the majority of books published in English. Nine out of ten people in the world are non-English-speaking. It is therefore very likely that their authors and publishers now produce, or will soon produce, more books which deserve publication in English than do all English-speaking authors.

In 1970 only 5% of the new book titles published in the U.S. were translations. The primary reason why so few foreign books are translated into English and published in America is the cost of translation. Although this cost is usually less than the cost of writing an original book in English, translation costs must be paid by the publisher before the manuscript is finally approved for publication. If he pays the cost of writing a book in English, he normally pays it after publication, and then usually in part only.

Another major reason for the small number of translated books published in America is the fact that publishers make no systematic effort to discover foreign books which should be translated and published here. American book publishing is carried on by many small firms, no one of which has the personnel and resources needed to review most or all foreign-language books, and competition results in costly duplication of the limited review of such books. These limited efforts are concentrated on France and Germany, which provided about half of the books translated and published here in 1970. There are almost as many Spanish-speaking people as English-speaking, but only 39 books were translated from Spanish and published here in 1970. The USSR published about as many books as the U. S. in

1970, but only 139 were translated and published in the U.S.

Under socialism some American publishing agency should be assigned the function of reviewing all new books published abroad in foreign languages and deciding which of them should be translated and published in English in America.

Imported Books — In 1970 over one billion books were sold in the U.S., but less than 5% of them were imported. Yet publishers in other English-speaking countries published about half as many new book titles as were published in the U.S. Clearly there are high tariffs and/or other uneconomic restrictions on the number of books imported.

Instead of importing books published in English abroad, American publishers have such books reprinted here. This duplication of printing costs is costly and uneconomic. It is required in order to give more work to American printers and publishers. Under socialism full employment could easily be achieved without the use of protective tariffs, which should be largely abolished. Certainly there should be no tariffs on books.

No book published in English in a foreign country should be reprinted or republished in the U.S., and each such book should be announced, reviewed, and distributed in the U.S. in the same way as any similar American book. The application of this policy would vastly increase the importation of English-language books published abroad, and would result in a division of labor between foreign and American publishers which would sharply reduce total book publishing costs. Moreover, foreign authors of English language books would make far greater efforts to please and inform American readers.

The publication of all domestic books should be heavily subsidized in order to permit their sale at prices equal to cost at the margin, or their free distribution. The amount of and need for these subsidies could be sharply reduced by encouraging foreign publishers to print books in English and sell them ("dump" them) in the U.S. at prices close to marginal cost. In many cases, an American socialist government should subsidize foreign publishers in order to induce them to dump their English-language books in the U.S. because such foreign subsidies would make unnecessary larger subsidies to domestic publishers.

Moreover, books written by American authors and published by American publishers should be printed abroad whenever this reduces printing costs enough to reduce total publishing costs significantly.

Book Design — The chief problem of a capitalist publisher is to induce readers to buy his books. Therefore, he concentrates his efforts on securing favorable book reviews, writing misleading advertisements, and designing books and jackets which will attract attention. In a socialist society, book publishers should spend far less on advertising and publicity, and advertisements should be purely informative. Most books should be designed primarily to minimize production costs, to make reading easier, and to facilitate library use and preservation.

Capitalist publishers often print books on thick paper, and/or in large type and/or with abnormally wide margins in order to deceive customers as to the amount of reading material contained. They also design books in odd sizes, or striking colors, or with elaborate jackets in order to attract the attention of customers. Standardization of books could save many millions of dollars.

For instance, printing nearly all books on thinner pages with narrower margins could reduce the library shelf space used to store books in private and public libraries by over 40%. Private publishers ignore all such external economies, but socialist publishers should give them full consideration.

Colorful book jackets are expensive and easily damaged. They serve primarily to catch the eye of the browsing book-store customer and to display misleading advertising. The useful information now printed on book jackets should be printed within the book, and customers who desire artistic book jackets should be required to pay extra for them.

So far as we are aware, no capitalist publisher or research organization has ever bothered to find out what kinds of printed pages are the easiest to read. This is an extremely important problem since most knowledge is acquired by reading. A socialist state should spend large sums in research on this problem. It should study the effects of page grain, color, and size; the effect of print color, shape, and size; and the effects of all other factors affecting readability. It should design and experiment with new type faces, inks, and papers. And all subsidized publishers and printers should be required to use the type, ink, and paper which permits the most rapid reading.

The rapid growth of higher education and scientific research will continue to make libraries more popular and more essential. But the rapid growth of knowledge and of library use will make library problems ever more complex. Hence, when designing books and magazines, socialist publishers should pay far more attention to these problems than private publishers do. They should drastically reduce the variety of book sizes in order to enable librarians to store more books in the same space. They should adopt simplified spelling, use thinner book paper and covers, and leave narrower margins on book pages for the same reason. They should print national library catalog numbers on all hard-cover books and jackets because it is much cheaper to do this when books are printed than when they are being prepared for library use. Moreover, book stores, book buyers, and readers with private libraries will find such catalog numbers useful. All books should be ordered and inventoried by these national catalog numbers, not by name or by publishers' catalog numbers.

Book Grading and Marking — Book buyers need far more helpful advice than they now receive from publishers and book-store clerks. Book buyers cannot trust the advertisements and jacket blurbs printed by profit-seeking publishers, and the reviews of competent critics are rarely if ever available at the point of purchase, or when the book buyer is planning his purchase.

In a socialist economy all books should be read and evaluated by competent critics, usually a committee of three or more, before they are offered for sale. These critics should rate all books on a scale of perhaps one to five, and their rating should be clearly printed on each book and jacket, perhaps in the form of one to five gold stars, with five stars indicating the highest rating.

The grading and marking of books should probably be a function of the national library because this agency would be much less biased than any publisher, and would also have to assign catalog numbers to all books. It would of course be free to use independent outside critics, such as university professors and book reviewers who write for popular magazines. It should decentralize the work of book rating.

To specify in detail an ideal system of book review and evaluation would require a separate book, and this task does not belong to political economy. But the principle of product grading belongs here.

To those who deny that a useful evaluation of books is possible, we reply that many commercial products which are difficult to grade — fruit, meats, vegetables, dairy products, etc. — are already being usefully evaluated and graded. We are certain a very helpful system of grading books can be developed.

Book Prices — Books which are not used in any school and which are not primarily educational — novels, poetry, short stories, religious books, game books, comics, and so forth — should be sold for a price equal to marginal cost. They should not be free goods because there is no valid reason in increase consumption of them beyond the level which would result when their prices equal marginal costs.

Textbooks and other books which are primarily educational — popular histories, biographies, healthcare books, how-to-do-it books, etc. — should be free goods for the same reasons that most education should be a free good. But no individual should be given more than one free copy of any such book. Additional copies should be sold at marginal cost.

E. Output and Price Control

All publishing involves problems of output and price determination. All publications are produced in batches, i.e., in separate, often large, printings. Output cannot be currently controlled at the margin. Rather, every decision to publish is a lumpy investment decision. This truth becomes even more evident and significant if we include in publishing costs the large lumpy one-time investment in researching and writing the manuscript.

Since the decision to publish any manuscript is a lumpy investment decision, it should be based upon total cost-benefit analysis, which considers intra-marginal non-monetary costs and benefits as well as total monetary costs and income. Consumers' surplus is the largest non-monetary benefit. The consumption of publications yields relatively large consumers' surpluses because most publications are unique.

There is a second important class of social benefits ignored by capitalist publishers which deserves consideration in such total analysis, namely, external economies of consumption. These are benefits to third parties and are therefore ignored by buyers when making price offers. They include such social benefits as more intelligent voting, better care of children, better treatment of other persons, the reduction of anti-social behavior, the reduction of welfare costs, the prevention or cure of contagious diseases, and the stimulation of scientific research and invention. Since most non-fiction publications are educational, they yield all the external economies produced by education.

When all intra-marginal and external real costs and benefits are properly considered, total analysis reveals whether a proposed book or periodical should be published. If publication can yield a net benefit at some batch size, publication is justified. If it cannot, publication is not justified, i.e., is uneconomic.

A socialist publisher must decide not only whether to publish any given manuscript but also how many copies of it to publish at one time. The latter decision requires a marginal cost-benefit analysis. The size of each printing should be increased until the resulting predicted marginal benefit (price, plus the estimated value of any external economies of consumption) equals marginal cost. Thus these economies must be considered both in total and marginal analysis. The external economies of intra-marginal consumption should be considered in total analysis, and the external economies of marginal consumption in marginal analysis.

Of course, external economies may be estimated by a government agency and measured by subsidies to producers. In this case, publishers need not estimate these economies, and should increase the size of each edition until the sum of the resulting predicted price and subsidy per book equals marginal cost.

In the publishing industry marginal cost is always much less than any estimate of so-called average cost. Therefore, the sale of all the copies of any printing at a price equal to marginal cost would yield a big deficit. The smaller the printing, the larger the deficit would be as a share of total costs.

Pricing publications at prices equal to marginal costs would yield large deficits for two reasons: (1) publishing is an industry with decreasing marginal costs — the larger the edition, the lower the cost at the margin, and (2) fixed costs are very high relative to marginal costs. The latter reason is usually more important than the former, especially for small printings.

Fixed publishing costs include the costs of researching and writing. For scholarly non-fiction articles and books these costs alone are usually several times as high as total printing and selling costs because such items are usually published in very small editions. Moreover, editing, typesetting, and advertising costs are fixed costs which together may also be several times as high as marginal costs.

In sum, the application of ideal marginal-cost price-output control to publications would result in large ideal deficits. And these deficits would be greatly increased if prices were reduced below marginal costs in order to allow for relevant external economies of consumption, which are substantial in the case of most non-fictional publications.

F. The Microprint Revolution

A major technological revolution, the most important since the invention of printing, has already begun in the publishing industry. This is the substitution of microprint film slides and tapes for printed paper pages. Less than 1% of American publications are now on microprint film, but the revolution will continue until most magazines and non-fiction books are published only on such film, and many more publications are produced on film as well as on paper.

It is already possible to publish an entire million-word book on a single small slide, called a microfiche, and such a slide occupies less than 1% of the shelf space required for a book of equal length. Moreover, the marginal cost of producing one more copy of any microprint publication is already, or eventually will be, far less than the marginal cost of producing one more standard printed copy of the same material.

Some newspapers — for instance, the New York <u>Times</u> — are already being published on microprint film tapes, as well as on paper, primarily to help libraries store and handle old issues. This practice will grow steadily, and libraries or reprint publishers will gradually microfilm more and more copies of the old newspapers now congesting library shelves. But most newspaper copies may continue to be published on paper because most subscribers prefer paper copies and/or because printing is a faster method of publishing.

The most important use of microfilm reproduction will be in the publication of non-fiction books and magazines, especially in the original publication of scholarly books and learned journals. Such books and journals are now published in small editions and read almost solely by professors and research scientists, all of whom will eventually have microfilm projectors and large libraries of microfilm books and journals. Within less than 100 years the great majority of learned books and journals will be published only on microfilm. This will radically reduce both the total and marginal cost of publication.

G. Public Libraries and Bookstores

Libraries are not commonly considered a part of the publishing industry. But they are already engaged in extensive duplication (xeroxing and microfilming) of the publications on their shelves, an activity which will grow rapidly and indefinitely. Moreover, a socialist national library should establish uniform editorial, printing, and bookbinding standards for all publishers. Hence, it is appropriate to include a section on public libraries in this chapter. We shall also have something to say about bookstores because we believe they should be merged or closely affiliated with public libraries.

An advanced socialist country should have a comprehensive integrated public library system which performs nearly all functions now performed by the best American public libraries and also many functions not performed by such libraries. Every citizen should be served by one or more public libraries.

All public library operations except book selection should be managed by a single national library agency because this would sharply reduce the cost of buying, cataloging, and storing library books.

The U.S. national library should have at least one copy, usually two, of every publication in English, and many millions of publications in other languages. No local library should have any publications not found in the national library. No reader or scholar should ever need to visit or write more than one library to complete his search for any publication in his country.

The national library should buy and preserve not only all the publications referred to above but also all unpublished letters, manuscripts, typescripts, diaries, theses, statistical data, government and business records, architectural plans, musical compositions, TV and cinema scripts, and other similar matter worthy of temporary or permanent preservation. To protect its vast holdings, the national library should deny admission to the public, including government officials, but it should quickly supply local libraries with microfilm or microfilm copies of any item in its collection. Every central city library, every university library, and every new-town library should have a complete microfilm catalog of the national library, which should supply copies of any item by air mail direct to the individual borrower within 48 hours. The national library should operate 24 hours a day, 365 days of the year, to assure prompt response to all loan or purchase requests.

The national library should operate a computerized information-retrieval and bibliographic system serving the entire country by wire or overnight mail service. To improve such service, it should require all writers of non-fiction books and articles to use standardized scientific terms approved by their respective professional associations whenever this does not prevent them from saying what they wish to say. The library should also require that each such book should include both a summary and an index stated in such standard terms, as well as in the author's new or preferred terms, to aid bibliographers and information-retrieval programers. In the summary and the index the standard terms used by these experts should be printed in bold-faced type or otherwise distinguished. Book titles and tables of contents should also be stated in these standardized terms.

Many old and modern manuscripts and publications are deteriorating. The national library should microfilm all scarce items before they fall apart. It should also require that the new domestic paper publications it acquires be printed on long-lasting paper and bound in a durable manner.

As noted earlier, the coming microfilm revolution in publishing will reduce the cost of most publications and will permit each library to increase its stock of publications a hundredfold without expanding the shelf space. Indeed, for publications on microfilm, the catalogs of most large libraries should include a copy of each publication immediately after each catalog card. When a library user finds a microfilm book behind its catalog card, he would take it to a nearby copying machine and return it to its place in the catalog after he has produced a copy, a copy which he could then add to his own home or office library.

Of course, every local socialist library should eventually include rows of projectors for use in reading microfilm tapes and/or cards in the library.

The main public library in every socialist town and city should contain a bookstore for new and used books, as well as a library, and no city or town should have any other bookstore. Such a combination of library and bookstore services would permit most book-buyers to inspect in the library the books they may consider purchasing in the bookstore. This would protect new unsold books from damage, would reduce duplication of stocks, and would vastly increase the number of books available for inspection by bookstore visitors. Moreover, it would make it easier for would-be book borrowers to buy copies of new library books which have waiting lists. And it would greatly reduce the size of the inventory which bookstores must carry. Finally, it would induce some potential book-buyers to borrow rather than buy the book they want, and this would conserve the agents of production used to manufacture and distribute new books.

It is noteworthy that under capitalism any proposed combination of public library and bookstore facilities and services is certain to be opposed by capitalist book publishers and retailers precisely because it would reduce the sale of new books, and thus conserve economic resources. Profit-seeking here, as so often elsewhere, is antisocial.

A bookstore in a public library should stock chiefly publications published during the last year or two. The library should be able to meet the current demand for any older book on its shelves. When bookstore customers want to buy paper books not in stock, the bookstore should order them from a national or regional book warehouse, which, under monopolistic socialism, should be able to fill each order the day it is received.

All rare used paper books should be sold through a single national mail-order bookstore managed by and adjacent to the national library. This affiliation would make it easier for the national library to locate and buy rare books for its own shelves. The centralization of all rare-book sales would also make it easier for all local book-buyers to locate desired rare books.

Libraries are a means of public-opinion control. A head librarian who buys only or mostly liberal or conservation publications can gradually change public opinion in his town. As explained earlier, no socialist central government should be able to control public opinion. One good way to minimize the control of such a government over public opinion would be to decentralize radically the choice of publications for inclusion in public libraries. Those librarians who make such choices should be appointed by and responsible to local committees of professional men — social scientists, writers, librarians, etc. — not to higher executives in the national library system. However, librarians who perform other operating functions in local libraries should be appointed and supervised by higher library executives.

As explained in <u>Liberal Socialism</u> (p. 324), nearly all public library services should be free goods because they are educational and have very low marginal costs, but some or all non-educational services should probably be sold for a price because free provision of them is not justified by these reasons. For instance, if there is a waiting list for a popular new paper novel or jazz record, it would be economic to charge a rental for its use. This would reduce the number of copies the library needs to buy, and would help to allocate a scarce good to those who most desire it.

The case for providing other non-educational books and records free of charge is very weak. Hence, a small rental should be charged for all paper novels and non-educational records. And a small charge should be made for all copies of microprint films and slides of such books.

CHAPTER XIII

BROADCASTING

Radio and television broadcasting are much newer industries than printing and publishing, but they are growing faster and will soon have more influence on public opinion. Moreover, a socialist government should drastically curtail publishing — by eliminating over 80% of all advertising and non-news items, creating newspaper monopolies, and so forth — while it should greatly expand both radio and television broadcasting. Finally, broadcasting can be used to create and control public opinion. Therefore, a separate chapter on broadcasting is appropriate.

On the average, Americans now (1977) spend over 1000 hours a year listening to radio and TV broadcasts which cost less than $5 billion per year. Thus the cost per listener is less than $.03 per hour. The average value of the personal benefit received is far higher. In other words, there is an enormous consumers' surplus. Moreover, this consumers' surplus could be very greatly increased by eliminating commercials, which now occupy 10% to 30% of broadcast time in the U.S., by increasing the number and variety of programs, and by coordinating programs.

Public demand for entertaining, informative, and educational television programs will continue to grow indefinitely as real incomes rise and the hours of leisure increase. When men earn more, they can afford to spend more on non-essentials like TV programs, and when their hours of labor decline, they have more time to spend watching television. Therefore, the industry which creates and broadcasts radio and TV programs is likely to grow much faster than most other major industries during the next century or two.

A. Organization

Since both publishing and broadcasting are means of information, education, and entertainment and should often present the same facts or ideas in the same words, they should be major branches of the same national agency, the Information and Entertainment Trust.

While publishing and broadcasting should be managed by a single national trust, each should have its own separate national organization. There should be no regional and local offices which handle both publishing and broadcasting. But the top executives of the I and E Trust should assure a sound division of labor and full local coordination of services between publishing, broadcasting, and entertainment.

Since the production of moving-picture films for television will soon be more important than film production for theaters, and since all theater films should also be shown on television, all film-making should be managed by a section of the Broadcasting Branch.

The same reasoning applies, to a lesser degree, to all musical, dramatic, dance, and other performances in theaters. Under socialism, all the better stage performances should be shown on television as well as in the theater. Such theatrical performances should be managed by a section of the Broadcasting Branch, or by a separate branch of the I and E Trust.

The Broadcasting Branch should also include a film and tape preservation section which stores, preserves, and periodically duplicates all broadcast films and tapes which might be suitable for rebroadcasting at some future time. Copies of all of these films and tapes should be stored in two or more widely separated bomb-proof, air-conditioned underground storage rooms, so that they cannot be lost by fire, earthquake, riot, or war. Capitalist firms have already allowed many costly films to be destroyed or to deteriorate.

Within a few more decades, the backlog of fine old films and tapes will become so large that they can fill most broadcast hours. In time, fine old films and tapes will become far more valuable than the most valuable old manuscripts and paintings because they will give a much more vivid and informative picture of the past.

<u>Centralization of Control over Operations</u> — Control over all broadcasting operations except the preparation and choice of programs should be highly centralized in order to permit a proper division of labor between radio and TV broadcasting and in order to achieve the many economies of large-scale management. All equipment and facilities used by local broadcasting stations should be developed, designed, and purchased by a single national agency. All office equipment and supplies used by local broadcasting stations should be purchased by a single national purchasing office. All operations managers of local stations should be appointed by national executives or their regional subordinates. And in many other ways national control over the daily operations of local broadcasting stations should be fully achieved.

Moreover, in each local area all local TV and radio stations should be managed by a single area manager, and all the offices of these different stations should be housed in the same building, partly in order to facilitate control over them by a single local chief operating executive. Also, all broadcasting stations in a city should use the same broadcasting facilities whenever this reduces costs.

<u>Decentralization</u> <u>of</u> <u>Control</u> <u>over</u> <u>Programs</u> — While control over all broadcasting facilities and operations in a socialist state should be highly centralized, control over both program selection by local program directors and program creation by film studios and other producers should be highly decentralized.

The program director of each local TV or radio station should be entirely free of central control. He should be a professional chosen by and responsible only to a local unit of his own professional association, by a local independent consumers' co-op, by a local university, or by some other independent local group. Here as elsewhere, the principle of decentralization is vital, the method of applying it less important.

One good way to decentralize the selection of programs to be broadcast by TV or radio is to abolish or radically curtail the operations of national networks because they centralize program control.

National radio and television broadcasting networks were organized in the U.S. primarily in order to sell advertising time and programs to large national advertisers and to create or buy programs suitable for sale to national advertisers. It is far more convenient and efficient for a national advertiser, like General Motors, to deal with one or two national networks than to deal with hundreds of local broadcasting stations and program producers. And national advertisers spend 60% of all money spent on broadcast advertising.

If a socialist government reduces advertising by over 80%, as we have recommended, and decentralizes control over program creation and selection, there would be little if any need for national TV and radio broadcasting networks, except for broadcasting news and events of immediate nationwide interest. Most such news should be broadcast by radio, so a single national news-broadcasting radio network would be justified, but the need for a national news TV network under mature liberal socialism seems doubtful. Most TV programs would be films or tapes which could be distributed by mail and broadcast on different days by different stations.

Television programs already consist largely of films prepared by more or less independent producers. The chief function of a local socialist TV program director should be to choose among such available films. If these films were all produced by a single state film-making trust with centralized decision-making concerning the kind of films to be produced, the range of choice of TV program directors would be sharply restricted, and government control over public opinion would be greatly facilitated. To minimize these evils, a socialist state should carefully decentralize all decision-making concerning the kind of moving-picture films produced for theaters and television stations. At least 50 different independent film-producing agencies, each controlled by a different group of people — universities, cooperatives, dramatic societies, etc. — should be created in the U.S. All should be heavily subsidized so that they can cover costs and rent films to users at marginal film-reproduction costs. Within each film category — western, science fiction, drama, etc. — subsidies should vary with theater attendance and TV-program popularity ratings, and should cease when a film producer proves unable to produce popular or well-rated films.

A single monopolistic agency should provide all of the facilities, equipment, and auxilliary services used by these independent producers, but the latter should hire and supervise their own directors, writers, actors, and other creative assistants.

Moreover, a liberal socialist Broadcasting Division should encourage amateurs to produce TV films as a hobby. It should assure a fair test and evaluation of all promising films produced by amateur groups. It could give such films and performances a trial run on a single broadcasting station and determine audience response by sampling methods. It should strive to create free and effective popular use of the broadcasting system.

Professionalization — All TV and radio broadcasting program directors should be professionally trained and should have advanced university degrees in broadcast programing. They should begin their careers as assistants to program directors on small stations. No actor, accountant, engineer, or operating executive should ever become a program director unless he has returned to school and received professional training in programing. Then he should begin work as an assistant to the program director of a local station. Perhaps all local program directors should be appointed by their local professional associations. As explained later, there should be over 50 local TV and radio stations in each urban broadcasting area, so there would usually be many local professional programers.

All film producers and directors should also be professionally trained and experienced before they are allowed to control the production and direction of TV films.

Cable TV — The broadcasting industry is going through a technological revolution, namely the shift from wireless to cable program transmission. This revolution has just begun. In the U.S. less than 10% of viewers were served by cable connections in 1970, but this percentage will rise steadily until nearly all viewers are so served. Cable connections markedly improve TV reception and permit a great increase in the number of TV channels and programs. It will eventually be possible for each metropolitan area to have as many different cable-TV channels as it wishes.

It would be far less costly to install a cable-TV system in a planned new socialist city than in any old city. The builders of a new socialist city should install a cable-TV connection in every residence, office, and store. The costs of installing such connections should be added to other construction costs and covered by housing rentals, not by special installation charges or monthly payments.

The costs of installing TV cables in individual homes could also be sharply reduced by combining telephone lines and TV cables in a single cable. It would cost little if any more to install this dual cable than to install either single line individually. And in socialist cities every residence and office should eventually be equipped with both telephone and cable-TV connections.

B. Program Creation and Selection

In a socialist society the volume of commercials broadcast by radio and TV should be reduced by over 90%, and those which are broadcast should never interrupt a program. They should be bunched together and broadcast on only one radio station and one TV station in each broadcasting area. They should never urge people to buy, but should merely announce price and product changes, local entertainment and sport events, local lectures and exhibitions, and other local public meetings.

Program Coordination — Certain kinds of programs are more suitable for broadcasting by television than by radio. If all TV and radio stations were controlled by a single public agency, it would be possible to require that both TV and radio stations broadcast only those classes of programs best suited to their facilities. For instance, nearly all lectures, readings, book reviews, non-political news, and purely musical programs should be broadcast by radio. It costs much more to broadcast such programs by TV, and the audience benefits little from observing the movements and facial expressions of speakers and musicians. However, candidates for political office should be allowed to talk on TV programs to help listeners evalute them as persons.

On the other hand, nearly all dramas, dances, operas, musical comedies, travelogues, wild-life films, and other programs which require or benefit from pictorial representation should be shown on television. But most news reports do not have relevant pictures, and therefore should be broadcast by radio.

The broadcasting of news by radio and TV has already partly replaced the publication of news in daily newspapers. This trend will probably continue indefinitely. Broadcasting news is faster and cheaper than printing it. Newspapers consume a vast amount of paper, and are discarded, often in public places, soon after being partly read. As the relative real cost of newspaper production continues to rise, and that of news broadcasting continues to fall, more and more news should be broadcast.

When broadcasting stations compete with each other, each tries to attract the largest audience. To do so, they may show similar or identical programs at the same time because part of a large audience may be larger than all of a small audience, and because sharing a large audience reduces greatly any competitor's share in this audience. This competitive policy sharply restricts program variety and the program choice of all consumers. Like many other capitalist business practices, it is uneconomic but profitable.

In a socialist country broadcast programs should be planned and coordinated so as to maximize the total audience for all justifiable programs. Therefore, the great majority of broadcasting stations in each local area should deliberately provide programs which are not the most popular but which will add to the total listening audience.

To help achieve optimum variety of choice and to aid listeners in locating desired programs, each radio and TV broadcasting station should specialize in one kind and one artistic level or program — sport, comedy, westerns, soap operas, heavy drama, light opera, ballet, etc., etc. And no program, no matter how popular, should ever be broadcast simultaneously by two TV stations, or by two radio stations, in the same city.

Political Programs — All socialist TV and radio broadcasting stations should be required to assign a nationally determined number of hours per year to political programs prepared by political parties and candidates and used both to discuss political policies and ideas in off-election months and years, and to support candidates in election years. Station program directors should have no control over these programs.

But it would be desirable to have an impartial national agency which reviews all political talks and calls attention to serious errors of fact and to grossly illogical and misleading arguments. This agency should have adequate radio time to publicize such errors and bad logic.

In a socialist society nearly all political campaigning by parties and candidates should be done in periodicals and in TV and radio broadcasts, and all such campaigning should be publicly financed. Moreover, the state should pay the living costs of major-party candidates during their active political campaigns. Few if any private campaign contributions should be permitted, certainly no large ones.

The allocation of broadcast time among political parties and candidates should be based upon popular support, as measured by public opinion polls and/or the number of ballots received in one or more previous elections.

Broadcasting stations should also be required to broadcast all propaganda prepared and fully paid for by non-profit, social, educational, religious, and other organizations.

Educational Programs — A large proportion of total radio and TV broadcasting time should be assigned to formal educational programs prepared by educational organizations. The amount of time and its allocation among both educational units and broadcasting stations should be determined by a national agency, perhaps a committee representing the Department of Education, the Broadcasting Branch of the I and E Trust, and the national legislature. No local broadcasting program director should have any control over this allocation, or over the content of any formal educational program. But he might help to coordinate individual educational programs with other broadcasting programs.

Many educational radio programs, as well as many entertainment programs, should be devoted to reading articles and books over the air. Reading a book is the cheapest form of radio program, and can be very educational. The books read should include non-fiction written for adults as well as texts written for students. At least 1000 complete books should be read over the radio each year in each broadcasting area.

Educational television programs should include complete laboratory courses in many sciences, maps and travel pictures designed to teach geography and social anthropology, historical films useful in teaching history, field trips useful in teaching botany and biology, trips through factories and other productive facilities, and many other films designed to assist teachers and/or promote self-education at home.

In a socialist society most secondary and higher education should take the form of radio broadcasts of lectures by the most gifted teachers in the nation, radio broadcasts of the reading of books and articles written by the best experts and authors in the country, TV broadcasts of educational travelogues, and other kinds of educational broadcasts. Such broadcasts should almost entirely replace lectures and demonstrations by local teachers and professors.

News Programs — In a mature advanced socialist state, radio and television broadcasting stations should greatly expand and improve their news programs. At least one TV station and two radio stations in each city should broadcast news 18 to 24 hours a day every day of the year. One or more radio station should broadcast news stories in considerable detail. But long full news stories such as those now published in the New York Times should be provided in weekly periodicals, not in daily newspapers or in news broadcasts.

All national news should be assembled and distributed by a single national non-partisan professional agency. There should be only one national TV news network and one national radio news network. But most of the domestic news stories they assemble should come from local journalists working for local independent broadcasting stations. This would help to minimize centralized control over bias in news stories.

To help listeners find the TV and radio news programs in which they are most interested, the stations which broadcast detailed news stories should announce and follow a suitable subject schedule. This would enable listeners interested in foreign news but not in sports to hear foreign news without having to be bored by sports news.

Television stations should broadcast only news stories for which they have revealing new film illustrations. They should not read news stories which can be broadcast equally well by radio. Radio broadcasting is much cheaper, radio sets are much more numerous and mobile than TV sets, and radio channels will probably always be more numerous than TV channels in each city.

Free Access to News Sources — The owners of private firms are legally entitled to keep confidential records and files, i.e., to prevent researchers and journalists from using their files. Moreover, they are eager to do so because they fear that publicity would aid their competitors, disclose illegal or unpopular behavior, help their workers to obtain higher wages, and otherwise reduce their profits.

In a socialist economy none of these reasons would justify the denial of free access to the meetings, correspondence, and other records of state trusts and departments. Since all these agencies would be monopolies, there would be no competitors who could benefit from such publicity. Since they would be publicly owned, the public ought to be fully informed about all major decisions and the reasons for them. And all illegal behavior ought to be revealed and publicized in any society

Therefore, in a socialist economy the meetings, files, and other records of every trust or department should be open for observation and study by all researchers and journalists at all times, upon payment of a reasonable fee covering any added expense to the agency. Radio journalists should be informed of and invited to attend all executive committee meetings, and/or should receive copies of the minutes of all such meetings.

Most large private firms and government agencies now have public relations departments which provide information and propaganda to the media and/or the public. In a socialist economy the propaganda should be eliminated, and all such departments should be staffed or replaced by journalists on the payroll of some national or regional news agency. These journalists should strive only to meet the needs of the public, not those of the agency whose activities they report.

There should of course be certain minor exceptions to the above general rule of full exposure to researchers and journalists. Military authorities should be allowed to prevent disclosure of certain military information. The executives in charge of foreign relations should be allowed to keep some of their decisions and records secret. Nearly all medical and psychiatric records should be confidential. And most police and judicial hearings and records should never be published. But 99% of all other business and government meetings and records now closed to the public should be opened to public scrutiny.

<u>Commercial Entertainment Programs</u> — In a capitalist country many costly live dramatic, operatic, ballet, and other stage and outdoor productions are never shown on TV because the producers fear that this would reduce their profits and/or because TV broadcasters cannot afford to pay the fees demanded. In a socialist state all live productions suitable for TV broadcasting should be filmed and shown repeatedly on television. Decisions as to the broadcasting of such live productions should always be based on economic calculation (felicific calculus), never on profit calculation.

The filming and/or live broadcasting of all such live commercial entertainment programs for use on television would sharply reduce the need to create live entertainment for TV broadcasting only. Since such live TV shows are both costly and/or inferior, their creation should decline sharply when better and cheaper substitutes become available.

In capitalist countries it is customary to show the best new moving picture films in theaters for months or years before they are broadcast because this enables film producers to maximize their profits. In a socialist society all new films should be shown on TV before they are first shown in any theater. This would sharply increase the total pleasure derived from seeing each new film by increasing the number of viewers, and would also sharply reduce theater attendance, which would equally reduce the need for investment in theater buildings and the cost of operating theaters.

All live entertainment — Plays, operas, sports events, etc. — should also be seen on TV at the same time they are first seen live locally, for similar reasons.

Nearly all radio and television programs should be written, designed, and produced for a national or international audience. The larger the audience, the lower the original production cost per hearer and/or the larger the possible economic investment per program. Most programs now produced locally for local audiences are very inferior because they must be cheaply produced.

However, programs produced for national audiences need not be broadcast simultaneously by local broadcasting stations in different cities. All live programs should be filmed or taped, and the films and tapes could then be broadcast at different times in different cities throughout the world. The transmission of tapes and films to local stations by mail is usually cheaper than transmission of live shows by wire. It follows that national radio and TV networks providing the same live or film program simultaneously in many cities should be far less important under socialism. Capitalist film producers like to have their new films shown simultaneously in many theaters so that all can benefit from national publicity and advertising, but there should be no such publicity and advertising under socialism.

<u>Foreign Films</u> — The desire to reduce domestic unemployment causes most capitalist governments to restrict both the importation of foreign moving-picture films and the use of foreign locales and workers

in producing domestic films. And communist governments have severely restricted the importation and exhibition of foreign films in order to limit the influence of foreign ideas and fashions.

A liberal socialist American government should radically increase the importation of foreign films. The Broadcasting Branch should employ a staff to review all foreign films and select those suitable for broadcasting in America. Every foreign film which appears to this staff to be better than the worst American film should be exhibited or broadcast in one American city to determine its popularity, and should be shown nationally if it rates higher than the worst American film so shown.

The adoption of this policy would sharply reduce the amount of money which needs to be spent to produce American films and would also improve the level of films broadcast in America.

It costs a great deal of money to produce a high-quality film. The vast majority of films now produced for television are low-quality because they are low-budget films. Importing more foreign films would permit, indeed compel, domestic film producers to spend much more per film.

To further increase domestic broadcasting of the better foreign films, a socialist American Broadcasting Branch should offer to share in the cost of producing those foreign films expected to be more suitable for broadcasting in the U.S. And it should try to induce more foreign film studios to make films with two sets of leading actors, one speaking American English, to improve acceptance of their films in America. Once a movie scene has been set up and filmed with one set of speaking actors, it costs little more to refilm it with a different set of speaking actors. It would be much cheaper for the U.S. to meet this extra cost than to produce another similar film in the U.S.

C. Output Control

The production of either radio or TV programs can be increased in three ways: (1) by building and operating a new broadcasting station, (2) by broadcasting an additional off-peak-hour program from an existing station, and (3) by spending more money on producing more or better programs. Since the production of any program involves a substantial investment in a durable product, a film or tape which may be rebroadcast many times over many years, and since the broadcast of any program yields lumpy units of pleasure (including consumers' surplus) to many people over many years, every decision concerning changes in the output of radio and TV programs requires total or lumpy cost-benefit analysis.

Private radio and TV broadcasters must limit the number of broadcasting stations and the cost of programs they broadcast enough to make a profit from advertising. The number and variety of programs broadcast is determined by the demand of advertisers for advertising time, not by public demand or need for such programs. In a socialist society the demands of advertisers should be ignored, and the cost, number, and variety of radio and TV programs should be controlled so as to maximize the net social benefit to viewers. The output of each class of program should be increased as long as it seems that the total benefit from an additional station or program — including consumers' surplus and any external economy of consumption — will exceed the total cost. We believe that the application of such analysis would now increase by over 100% the number of American TV broadcasting stations and programs. And, as incomes and the hours of leisure increase, the demand for radio and TV programs will steadily grow.

All national broadcasting executives and all independent program producers should be trained in the specialized kind of total and marginal analysis most suitable for the control of expenditures on program creation and/or on the construction of local broadcasting stations.

The major obstacle to the use of refined economic or felicific calculus in the decision to produce individual broadcast programs is that few listeners pay prices for the services they receive. As a result, money income from listeners and demand curves based on price offers cannot be used to measure welfare.

Technological progress has made it possible to build so-called "pay-TV" receivers which permit TV broadcasters to charge a price for each program received by each set. Since marginal program reception creates no marginal cost to the broadcaster, charging a price for TV reception is very uneconomic. But it might be desirable to use pay-TV temporarily in isolated TV-program-testing areas to help determine how much money should be spent on non-educational TV broadcasting and how this total should be allocated among TV programs. For instance, the San Francisco Bay area could be used as such a testing area, and many new programs could be tested there. The government could provide every family with one or more free pay-TV sets and prohibit the use of other sets. All reception should be by cable. Prices should be set so that if collected throughout the nation they would recover about half the total cost of each program, only half because there would be large consumers' surpluses. If subsidized test-area viewers voluntarily paid enough to suggest that a national pay-TV showing would cover over half the total costs of the program, the original decision to invest in the program would be justified. Unfortunately, such testing is possible only after a TV program has been produced.

The residents of any testing area should be liberally compensated for their added TV costs and other inconvenience by a general tax reduction or by fixed subsidies, neither of which should influence their TV program choice.

It would also be possible to invent pay radio sets and use them to determine the demand schedule for non-educational radio programs.

If pay-TV and radio sets are not so used, demand for TV and radio programs could be more crudely measured by the use of questionnaires, public opinion polls, and intensive study of radio and TV audience behavior. And the Broadcasting Branch could investigate how much people pay for an equal amount of entertainment in other forms.

In America public TV and radio stations which accept no advertising have been able to cover most or all of their costs by appealing to their listeners for gifts. Any station or program which can support itself in this way should be encouraged to do so under socialism. All religious broadcasts should be so supported in order to maintain separation of state and church.

Moreover, it might be desirable to measure public demand for each entertainment program by requesting donations from all satisfied viewers or hearers. Then more public funds could be spent to produce and broadcast the kind of programs which brought in the most money, and less on other kinds of programs. This method of measuring public demand would work even if the gifts received covered only a very small share of programming costs.

D. Financing Free Broadcasts

In a socialist economy all broadcast reception should be a free good, for several reasons. In the first place, such reception has from the beginning been a collective good, i.e., a good which is collectively consumed, like national defense. Broadcasters have been unable to measure individual consumption and charge a price per unit of compensation. This situation may continue for many years.

Secondly, even if it becomes possible to equip all listeners with pay-TV and radio sets and charge a price for each hour of listening to each individual program, the extra costs of building, installing, and operating these sets, and of paying and collecting the charges made, will to so high that they will make it uneconomic to treat broadcast programs as price goods.

Thirdly, prices should never be higher than marginal costs when supply is abundant. The supply of any broadcast program is unlimited, because, when one or more person tunes in to a program he does not reduce the supply available to other listeners. And the cost of tuning in is zero.

Finally, most radio and TV broadcasts yield significant educational benefits. Therefore, most or all of the arguments for free provision of education apply to broadcasting.

It would be possible, of course, to finance part or all of the costs of broadcasting by collecting annual license fees from the owners of receiving sets. This method of financing would be far less uneconomic than charging prices for individual program receptions because it would not limit marginal consumption by set owners. But it would substantially reduce the purchase and preservation of sets, and thereby reduce the total broadcast audience, and the pleasure from listening to broadcasts, without reducing by a penny the total cost of broadcasting. By contrast, free provision of broadcasts would substantially increase the number of listeners and their pleasure, without raising broadcasting costs, and would also save the costs of collecting and paying license fees.

In a socialist economy, therefore, all the costs of operating broadcasting stations, including the costs of producing and renting programs, should be met by the national government out of general revenues. The national legislature should appropriate annual lump sums to be allocated among individual broadcasting stations and program producers by the Department of Education and by a national broadcasting agency.

The problems of now non-educational funds should be allocated to individual stations, and by them to individual programs, are difficult, but would not be new. Advertisers and broadcasters have always found these problems difficult, and almost any reasonable socialist allocation would probably be much superior to the allocations made by capitalist firms.

E. Program Announcement and Rating

A printed television and radio program guide is very useful to TV and radio listeners. The coming increase in the number of broadcasting stations will make such guides more and more useful. If a newspaper is published in a socialist city, it should print a TV and radio program guide which lists all programs on all local TV and radio stations.

If no newspaper is published, a full TV and radio program should be published in a local weekly magazine. The elimination of all but one national TV network would make the publication of national guides in national periodicals uneconomic.

All radio and TV program guides published in a socialist state should enable viewers to learn in advance concerning each program at least: (1) its title, (2) its subject-matter classification — mystery, western, science-fiction, etc., (3) its intended or actual audience — children, highbrow adults, middlebrow adults, etc., and (4) its tested popularity rating with this audience.

Capitalist broadcasters have long hired independent rating experts to determine how popular their programs are, and these experts have developed efficient popularity-rating methods, but the results have rarely been made available in program guides, because private broadcasters do not want to help consumers find the programs that would most please them. Each broadcaster wishes to secure as large an audience as possible for his own programs, regardless of the effect on the consumers' pleasure. In sharp contrast, socialist broadcasters should help consumers find the programs which will please them the most during each hour, regardless of the effect on the number of people who hear their programs.

It is, of course, much more difficult to determine the level of the intended or actual audience than to determine the size of any program audience, but literary critics and professional reviewers of plays and films have long engaged in such evaluation. While their judgments are often conflicting and debatable, their majority or consensus opinion on any radio or TV broadcast would be very helpful to consumers trying to decide which broadcast to hear. Any such rating system devised by thoughtful critics would be better than none, and it would cost very little compared to the benefit it would yield. As long as the average person spends over two hours a day listening to broadcasts, any reform which increases the pleasure or satisfaction received from radio and TV programs yields enormous social benefits.

We suggested earlier that the allocation of non-educational funds to radio and TV program producers and broadcasters should be based in large part on the popularity of the programs they produce or broadcast. Therefore, all evaluation and rating of programs should be done by an independent rating agency within the Broadcasting Branch, one responsible directly to the head of this Branch.

Program classification and ratings should be announced together with the title of the program at the beginning of each radio or TV program, as well as being printed beside the program title in all program guides.

CHAPTER XIV

LAW ENFORCEMENT

As used here, the term law enforcement covers not only police protection, but also all legal, judicial, and penal services used to enforce the law. Such law enforcement now costs the U.S. about 1.5% of its GNP. In spite of these enforcement efforts, crime costs Americans another 1.5% of their GNP in the form of property loss or damage and personal injuries. And almost 1% of the American labor force is employed in criminal activities, or locked up in prison, rather than engaged in productive labor. But less than 1% of all crimes now result in the conviction of the perpetrator.

It is unusual, perhaps unique, for a book on the principles of political economy to include a chapter on law enforcement. But basic economic principles apply to law enforcement as fully as they do to agriculture or health care. The chief reason economists have rarely discussed law enforcement is that most law enforcement services have long been free goods. Most economists believe that price or value theory is the heart of economics. In fact, however, all free goods should be produced as economically as possible, and economic theory should tell us how this can be done. Moreover, the question of whether or not law enforcement services should be free is itself a vital economic question.

Science versus Ideology — When professors of law and jurisprudence discuss problems of law enforcement, they usually base their arguments on prescientific religious or philosophic moral principles and/or natural rights. As explained in Liberal Socialism, we believe that all statements of such principles and rights are literally senseless (pp. 27-30). Appeal to them merely enables men to dignify and exalt their own irrational personal prejudices or biases. For instance, a dogmatic opponent of euthanasia does not say that euthanasia is wrong because he dislikes it. Rather, he claims that it is immoral, or violates natural law. This elevates his opinion from a personal prejudice to a divine or natural law.

In this chapter we shall use only utilitarian or felicific calculation to support our conclusions. This method of reasoning is traditional in political economy.

Its use enables economists to view law enforcement in a novel and enlightening way. Thus, to an economist, justice is never an absolute or priceless value. Rather, its value is a welfare quantity which can and should be measured and compared with its cost. Expenditures on law enforcement should be increased only when the marginal or total benefit exceeds the marginal or total cost. In other words, the economist believes that additional crime is tolerable, i.e., a lesser evil, whenever it would cost too much to prevent it, and he can define and measure "too much."

Capitalism, Socialism, and Crime — In The Case for Liberal Socialism (1976) we explained that a competitive capitalist society is almost perfectly organized so as to cause and facilitate crime. It allows enormous private wealth and poverty to exist side by side; it tolerates large unearned incomes; it permits heavy unemployment among young people, those most likely to commit crimes; it allows competition to threaten small business men with bankruptcy and push them into arson and dealing in stolen goods; it facilitates the secret payment of bribes and ransom, and the concealment of illegal income; and it promotes crime in many other ways.

In Liberal Socialism, and in earlier chapters of this volume, we explained a variety of ways in which the mere adoption of socialism would reduce crime, for instance, by ending unemployment, by providing liberal pensions for those unable to work, by making earned incomes far less unequal, by providing free health care, and so forth. Such methods of indirect crime prevention need no further discussion in this chapter, which is devoted to the theory of how to directly prevent, detect, and penalize those crimes which would occur in spite of all these social reforms.

Socialists have been persecuted and oppressed in all countries, and have therefore usually opposed measures which would increase the powers of police, prosecutors, and judges. Hence, we fear that most socialists will reject off-hand some of the law enforcement measures advocated in this chapter. These policies are based upon the belief that the substitution of democratic socialism for semi-democratic capitalism will greatly reduce the danger of police and judicial oppression of political minorities. If this belief is sound, it should be far less necessary to hamper and restrict the police and the courts in order to protect political dissenters under democratic socialism.

B. The Organization of Law Enforcement

All law enforcement functions, except the internal law enforcement functions of other organizations, should be performed by a national Department of Law Enforcement. This new name is preferable to "Department of Police" (suggested in LS, p. 114) because police work is only one law enforcement activity.

This Department should be divided into four major branches: (1) the Police Branch, (2) the Court Branch, (3) the Detention and Rehabilitation Branch, and (4) the Research Branch.

Within each of these branches, operating control should be highly centralized, but this principle does not rule out decentralized selection of regional judges by local professional associations, which should be experimented with. Such decentralization might reduce the danger of political repression by the national government.

The chief national executive of the Department should be independent of both the chief executive and the national legislature because he might need to arrest and/or prosecute high administrative officials and national legislators. He might be selected by his own immediate subordinates, by a national professional association, or in some other way, but he should not owe his appointment to any political party or leader. Probably he should serve for a fixed term different from that of national chief executives and legislators.

The Case for Free Distribution — In capitalist countries many law enforcement services — private guard service, private detective service, the services of criminal lawyers, etc. — are sold for a price. In a socialist economy all law enforcement services should be free goods. All guards, detectives, and criminal lawyers should be employees of the state, which should not charge for their services.

Most of these services are individual, not collective goods, i.e., they can easily be sold for a price. They should remain or become free for five reasons. First, free provision increases consumption of such services. If they are sold for a price, many consumers will not buy as much of them as they should buy, in their own interest. The benefits of police protection, like the benefits of insurance, are uncertain future benefits for which many improvident consumers are unwilling to pay for voluntarily. Hence, all consumers should be required to pay taxes to finance such benefits.

Secondly, private buyers of law enforcement services ignore the substantial external economies produced by their consumption of these services. When one individual helps police to catch and/or convict a criminal, he protects the entire community from possible future harm by this and other criminals. The government could, of course, subsidize the private purchase of law enforcement services, but it would be very hard to determine how high such subsidies should be on each service. And, in any case, there are other reasons why these services should be entirely free.

Thirdly, if police or legal protection were sold for a price in a socialist community, some persons would be able to buy more of it than others, and this would give the former persons and their children an uneconomic advantage in competing for success in life. All competing persons should enjoy equal protection against criminal assault, fraud, and loss of property. Every social policy which makes competition between persons more equal benefits society because it stimulates such competition.

Fourth, free distribution of law enforcement services, including legal advice and judicial hearings, improves these services. Unequal or biased justice is inferior to equal and objective justice. When rich men accused of crime can buy superior legal advice, more competent representation in court, and more appeals to higher courts, law enforcement and justice are unequal and inferior to free and equal justice. They are less effective in preventing crime and resentment.

Finally, most consumers are incompetent to buy legal services intelligently. For instance, they do not know enough about the education and record of individual lawyers to select one wisely. On the other hand, a state agency which employs many lawyers can keep records of their education and performance, and can therefore assign them to cases much more wisely than can individual consumers of purchased legal services.

The Control of Spending on Law Enforcement — Total spending on law enforcement should be determined by the national legislature, which should try to make marginal spending yield equal marginal benefits in all departments providing free goods. The legislature should employ a staff of advisors who specialize in estimating such marginal benefits.

The Department of Law Enforcement also should have a staff of such experts, who should help the Department prepare and justify its annual requests for funds.

To determine the marginal benefits of spending on law enforcement, it will of course be necessary to value in money all significant non-monetary benefits, including the decrease in fear of crime, more use of streets at night, the reduction in the pain caused by violent crime, and the cut in home protection costs. This will be difficult, but the use of any estimates made by an expert will be better than complete neglect of such benefits.

While the national legislature should determine the total annual appropriations of the Department, it should have no control over the allocation of such totals among individual departmental functions and units. The Department executives should be much more competent to perform this allocation because they would be experts in law enforcement.

B. Reform of the Criminal Law

We explained in <u>Liberal Socialism</u> (pp. 105-7) why all local and regional self-government should cease in an advanced socialist economy. If this policy were adopted, criminal law would become uniform throughout the nation. In America this reform alone would reduce by over 90% the number of criminal laws and the time devoted to enacting and interpreting them. Court precedents also would become uniform in all parts of the country. As a result, it would become far easier for judges, lawyers, and laymen to learn what the law and court precedents say. Furthermore, the consolidation and integration of local, state, and federal government would eliminate the often confusing problem of deciding which government unit has jurisdiction over certain crimes, would end or facilitate extradition, and would make it much more difficult for local law enforcement officials to evade or escape responsibility for certain law enforcement duties by claiming that these duties should be performed by some other unit of government.

It is as irrational to have different laws and court precedents in different parts of the country as to use different medical theories and drugs to treat the same kinds of patients in different parts of a country. The best law and court precedent, like the best medical treatment, should be used throughout the country.

There have been many proposals to repeal laws against so-called victimless or non-coercive crimes. Such laws fall into two quite different classes: (1) laws against acts (mostly sexual) which are deemed immoral by most conservatives, but which do little if any harm — adultery, prostitution, sodomy, etc. — or may even be beneficial in most cases — birth control, abortion, euthanasia, etc. — and (2) laws against acts which may or may not be considered immoral, but which are in fact very harmful to the performers — smoking, heavy drinking, regular use of narcotics, etc. A socialist government should repeal all laws in the first class, and should retain or enact and effectively enforce many laws in the second class. Repeal of all laws in the first class would sharply reduce the work-load of the police, and would also make all men more free.

In capitalist countries nearly all laws against victimless crimes should be abolished because it is very difficult and costly to try to enforce them. The history of prohibition in America in the 1920's illustrates this fact, and recent vain and harmful efforts to enforce laws against the sale and use of hard drugs emphasizes it.

In a socialist society, on the other hand, it should be possible to enforce laws against both classes of victimless crimes because the police would be far more honest and efficient. And victimless crimes of the second class are very harmful to society. Therefore, they should be prohibited.

American criminal laws should be reduced in length by over 90% under socialism. It is much better to allow judges to interpret brief general laws than to have Congress write long and detailed laws, both because judges are better trained in criminal law and because national legislators are far too busy with other important work to be able to spend the time required to write and/or evaluate details of long criminal laws. Moreover, judges can change their rulings more quickly than legislators can change laws.

C. The Organization of Police

The organization of police services in a mature socialist economy should differ radically from the organization of such services in Anglo-Saxon countries today. The most important change should be the complete nation-wide integration and centralization of police work.

<u>Centralization</u> — Nearly all American metropolitan areas have several independent police departments, and some have over twenty, each with its own criminal files, jail, communication system, budget, administrative staff, and so forth. In a socialist country there should be only one police organization in each metropolitan area, and it should be a subordinate unit in a national police force.

The consolidation of all police units in each metropolitan area would yield many benefits of large-scale operation and management. All local jails could be consolidated into a smaller, more efficient system with lower operating costs per prisoner, and each jail could be used for a different class of prisoners. All uniforms and equipment could be standardized and purchased by a single office at lower costs. All police officers could be continuously trained and upgraded in a larger, and therefore more efficient, local police academy. A single, more highly paid and more able police chief and staff could supervise all policemen in the metropolitan area. And a much greater division of labor could be practiced. Some detectives could specialize on burglaries, some on robberies, some on car thefts, and so forth. As a result, each would become more proficient in his work.

Supervision of local police forces by regular and/or national police executives would yield many benefits. It would assure the selection of more competent local police chiefs. Local officials without police experience are not competent to appoint local police chiefs. Only superior executives professionally trained and long experienced in police work are competent to appoint and supervise local police chiefs.

National supervision would facilitate the national standardization of all police uniforms, equipment, jails, training schools, statistics, methods, and so forth. And the national police experts who choose and standardize such items and methods would be much more highly educated and able than the local police chiefs who now choose them.

National supervision would also aid the collection and use of national police files which would best assist local police forces in identifying suspects and stolen property. These files should contain the fingerprints, photograph, voice-print, address, employer, etc., of every citizen or resident alien over age ten. And much more data should be filed on all convicted felons.

In a national police force every employee should be able to obtain easily a transfer to any other police unit in the country. He should pay all transfer costs, and should also suffer a temporary pay cut after his transfer, to offset the reduction in his productivity in a new environment. Knowledge of the community is a great aid in police work. But no local police chief should be able to prevent individual moves by policemen. If any local force is losing too many men, it should raise its wage rates. And, if it is gaining too many men, it should lower its wage rates. Such wage variations should be the chief means of control over such job transfers.

In a capitalist country many public agencies and private firms employ their own armed guards and detectives. In America private guards may outnumber police. In a socialist country all law-enforcement services by armed guards outside or inside individual plants and offices should be provided by the national police force.

When a guard or detective is hired by a single agency or firm, he restricts his activities to protecting that agency or firm. For instance, a bank guard may ignore crimes committed just outside a bank, and he may fail to look inside his bank for persons wanted by the police for non-bank crimes. If all such guards were members of the local police force, they could patrol more territory, perform more police functions, and prevent more crimes. They would also receive better training and more professional supervision. Finally, city police chiefs would learn of many crimes not now reported to them by private security forces.

<u>Crime Insurance</u> — In a socialist society every person should be almost fully insured against all injuries and property losses due to crime. This insurance should be financed by police funds, and all benefits should be paid by local police offices. This method of crime insurance would induce citizens to report all crimes to the local police, and would permit much better calculation of the local and national cost of each kind of crime. Such calculations, in turn, would help local and national police executives decide how much to spend in preventing each kind of crime in each local area. At present, less than half of all crimes are reported to police in the U.S.

The total national cost of crime includes both the costs of law enforcement and the losses to the victims of crime. An increase in spending on law enforcement is economic whenever it decreases the costs of crime by a greater amount. Police cannot determine whether any additional spending is economic unless they can measure its effect on crime costs. The best way to make police aware of all relevant crime costs is to require them to pay directly all personal and other crime costs, or at least a high uniform fixed percentage of them.

The medical and hospital bills of all persons injured by criminals should be paid by the local police department. The costs of pensions paid to persons partially or completely disabled by criminals and the unemployment or sick benefits paid to victims of crime should be similarly treated. All direct and indirect costs of crimes preventable by the local police should be paid by the local police. Of course, losses due to some business crimes, like embezzlement or theft by employees, cannot be prevented by the police, and therefore should not be allocated to local police forces.

Regional and national police supervisors cannot evaluate properly the work of local police chiefs unless all local costs of crime are fully and accurately reported. If the losses suffered by victims of crime are ignored, some local police chiefs will try to make a good impression on their supervisors by cost cutting which actually increases the total costs of crime.

Requiring local police units to compensate fully all local victims of crime would give them a major added inducement to prevent crime. Local police chiefs should be evaluated partly on the basis of their total spending per person for both police work and victim compensation. Finally, requiring such compensation ould make it unnecessary for individuals to buy special crime insurance.

Firemen as Policemen — In each socialist city the operations of the local police and fire units should be placed under a single manager, and should be coordinated in ways which will reduce their total costs, including crime and fire losses. Every policeman should be trained as a junior-grade fireman, and every fireman as a police patrolman. This would enable firemen to aid policemen better in emergencies, and vice versa. It would also permit many firemen to perform routine police patrolling near their fire stations between fires.

Firemen are now idle most of the time between fires. One or two firemen on each shift at each fire station should patrol nearby streets in a police car between fires. When a fire call is received at the station, firemen patrolling nearby should be notified by radio and should drive directly to the location of the fire, where they would rejoin their station mates and serve as firemen until the fire is out.

When a big fire occurs, the need for firemen is temporarily much greater than the need for policemen, and some policemen should work as firemen. When a major riot occurs, the need for policemen is temporarily greater than the need for firemen, and some firemen should work as policemen, often using fire department equipment for police functions.

Furthermore, whether or not the previous suggestion is adopted, all junior firemen should serve as policemen for half of each day. Sitting in a fire station waiting for a fire alarm is monotonous work. A daily change from work as a fireman to work as a policeman would make each day's work more interesting and satisfying for most firemen.

The firemen who serve as policemen for half of each day should be replaced in their fire stations by junior policemen serving as firemen for half of each day, for the same reason. In affluent countries it is much more important to make work interesting and satisfying than to make it more productive, but the suggested daily changes in work routine might make police and firemen more efficient because it would make their work less tiring and more interesting.

Mailmen as Policemen — Mailmen visit all homes and businesses on their route daily, and become well acquainted with the customers they serve. In a socialist society they should work as police aids, as well as mailmen, when they deliver mail. They should be trained to detect evidence of crime, and should report all suspicious persons and behavior to the police. Before starting on their rounds each day, they should study the pictures and descriptions of several of the most-wanted local crime suspects, and should look for these persons while delivering mail. Mailmen working as mailmen should rarely make arrests or pursue armed suspects, but instead should usually report their observations to police headquarters by telephone or two-way radio. This additional police work should interfere very little with the delivery of mail.

Most mailmen should work as mailmen only half of each day, or perhaps every other day. The rest of the day or week they should serve as regular police patrolmen in an area including the same neighborhood where they deliver mail and where they know nearly all the residents and their vehicles by sight. The knowledge gained as mailmen would make them superior patrolmen in this neighborhood.

The Training of Policemen — In Amerca today most policemen and firemen have only a high-school education or less, and few police executives have had professional training in police work. But police work has always been complex and demanding, and is becoming more and more technical each year. Police make innumerable critical decision about whom to arrest and how to treat suspects. In a socialist society all policemen should be college graduates with training in both police work and fire fighting. All police and firefighting executives should have one or more years of graduate university work in their profession. Moreover, every policeman and fireman should complete one university course in his profession each year.

All police and firemen should also be taught how to give emergency medical care of the kind they most frequently have the chance to give. Police and firemen often reach accident and crime victims before any doctor arrives, and they ought to know how to give temporary emergency care.

D. The Reform of Police Methods

We turn now to consider a variety of ways in which a socialist government should rationalize and improve the work of its police force. We shall not try to cover all needed reforms, but shall feature those which would yield the greatest benefits, and/or which would be easier to adopt under socialism. The application of these reforms would notably reduce the cost of police work and/or markedly improve the results of such work.

Payment by Check — There is one major economic reform which would do far more to prevent crime and aid the detection of criminals than any other, namely the substitution of payment by check and/or bank credit for all significant payments by cash, and the efficient police use of the resulting personal bank records. And it would be far easier to introduce, enforce, and exploit this reform under socialism because a socialist government would own all banks and business firms.

As explained in Liberal Socialism (p. 196), no town or city should have more than one bank, and every resident should be required to receive all significant income (over $5?) and make all significant payments by checks which pass through his local bank and are reported in his monthly bank statement. Each person should have only one checking account, so that nearly all of his income and expenditures would be recorded in his one monthly bank statement. The possession of large sums of cash (over #50?) should be illegal, and all paper money should be dated, and valid for one year only, to discourage accumulation of hidden stocks of cash and to make such money difficult to spend. At the end of each year, no one should be allowed to exchange more than $50 of old paper money for new paper money, and no individual should ever be allowed to deposit paper money or specie in any personal bank account. All deposits in personal accounts should be made by check, so that bank records can reveal all sources of personal incomes. No unit of paper money should be worth more than $1. And every check should reveal the chief purpose of the expenditure it covers.

All personal bank statements should be standardized, showing total spending for each major purpose in the same place on each statement. And all bank statements should be routinely available to the police. Bank computers should be programmed so that they automatically select for police inspection all statements showing a suspicious change in personal income or expenditure. And police personnel should work in the accounting office of each bank. Such regular reviews of personal bank records would make it far more difficult to receive, conceal, and spend illegal income.

If no person could obtain large amounts of cash from his bank, no one could pay kidnappers, blackmailers, extortionists, and corrupt officials without leaving obvious traces of such criminal transactions. Moreover, large sums of stolen cash could not be spent if all landlords and stores refused to accept significant cash payments. Finally, if all income payments were made by check, income-tax collectors would find it far easier to audit income-tax returns. Indeed, this might be added to the functions of bank computers.

It may be objected that such a use of bank checks and records would be an unjustified invasion of personal privacy. In fact, there is no such thing as personal privacy. There are only persons who wish to conceal some of their acts. A major reason for this desire is that many personal acts which are common and harmless are illegal — abortion, sodomy, prostitution, adultery, etc. — and some legal acts would result in social, economic, or political discrimination if revealed — for instance, infection with a venereal disease or a gift to an unpopular political party or to an atheist organization. But many laws against victimless crimes should be abolished. And socialist police should be discrete.

Another major reason why many persons wish to conceal certain personal acts is that these acts are illegal and socially harmful. Most capitalist business men and politicians have performed illegal acts which ought to remain illegal — bribing buyers, defrauding customers, paying or receiving political bribes, paying or receiving kickbacks, splitting professional fees, selling stolen goods, etc. But any invasion of privacy which prevents or penalizes such illegal acts is socially beneficial.

Nearly all of the routine review of standardized bank statements advocated above could be done by computers in such a way as to prevent or minimize clerical or police knowledge of the legal acts of individuals. Only suspicious bank statements selected by computers would require police study. The chief effect of such inspection of personal bank statements would therefore be to prevent and detect crime.

Moreover, even this minimum degree of police knowledge of private personal behavior could be drastically reduced by substituting identification numbers for names on bank records submitted to police study. Names could be revealed only to senior police officers, and only after police have decided that they wish to talk to the suspect and/or to his relatives and associates.

Incidentally, the virtual elimination of money and the use of bank checks and records to detect most crime was proposed, perhaps for the first time, by the Austrian economist, Theodore Hertzka, in his widely read utopian novel, Freeland, published in 1890. Unfortunately, such brilliant social engineers receive little credit for their great social inventions.

Identity Cards — Every teenager and adult should be required to carry an identity card which contains at least his picture, description, fingerprints, address, employer, and signature. This card should also serve as a social security card, a driver's license, a universal credit card, a pass to his place of work, and perhaps for other purposes. The identity number on this card should be tattooed on each person's body so that police can easily relate cards to persons and identify corpses. The universal use of such identity cards would enable police to catch wanted persons more quickly and to question suspects more effectively. It would also help banks and stores identify customers, and therefore would radically reduce the number of bad checks.

The identity card should be designed so that when one end of it is inserted in an identification machine — every police car and station should have one — an immediate response from a central computer will tell whether the bearer is wanted by the police anywhere in the country, and whether the card is a counterfeit or false card.

The identity card should also be designed so that when it is inserted in an electronic fund transfer machine — every store should have one — the funds specified will be credited to the retailer's account, or the retailer will be informed that the customer's account is insufficient to permit this. And this machine could serve as a police identification machine while performing its fund-transfer function.

Whenever a person buys a valuable durable article in a retail store, the store should stamp the buyer's identity number on it. This would help police discover stolen goods and return them to their legal owners.

No Jail or Bail for Suspects — If all the methods of catching and identifying suspects proposed above were adopted, it should be relatively easy to catch any fugitive from justice in an advanced socialist country. The very nature of a socialist economy would itself make successful flight, relocation, and reemployment in a new community very difficult, and also very costly. Every adult in a socialist society should have a large savings account and/or pension which he could not take with him or use when a fugitive. And large sums of cash should be unavailable and almost useless. Moreover, we shall urge later that nearly all persons convicted of a first offense, and many convicted of a later offense, should be fined rather than imprisoned. For these and other reasons, it would be unnecessary to jail or bail any sane first-time criminal suspect. To jail a man not yet convicted of a crime is a gross and often undeserved indignity.

Most suspected repeaters should also remain free without bail until they are again convicted. Their offenses would usually be minor, and the penalty a fine. Only repeaters previously convicted of a serious offense should be jailed until their trial.

Wiretapping — Wiretapping is a very useful and inexpensive method of crime detection and prevention, but it is generally illegal and little used in the U.S. today. Perhaps the main reason it is unpopular is that we have so many laws against victimless crimes. The repeal of these laws should greatly reduce opposition to wiretapping because it would make the average citizen much less eager to conceal his personal behavior from the police.

Most serious crimes are committed by a very small proportion of the populace, a proportion consisting largely of ex-convicts. If the police are not permitted to wiretap everyone, as they should be, they should at least be permitted to listen in on all phone calls by or to ex-convicts.

It should, of course, be illegal for police to make public outside of court any information obtained by wiretapping, or to use it for any purpose except the prevention and detection of crime and the conviction of suspects. No wiretapped information about innocent persons should ever be published.

Lie Detectors — Lie detectors are extremely useful in police interrogation of criminal suspects. They would be much more useful if suspects were denied the right to remain silent. Opponents of the use of lie detectors have claimed that they often fail to function properly, and/or that the men who operate them are often insufficiently trained or incompetent. The same argument may be used against many medical instruments and methods, like the use of X-ray machines. The relevant question is not whether such instruments and methods function perfectly but whether they function well enough to improve and/or cheapen law enforcement and medical care. There is ample scientific evidence that the use of lie detectors can substantially improve and/or cheapen law enforcement. For instance, it often helps detectives to locate missing pieces of physical evidence, like guns and corpses. And the efficiency of lie detectors and their operators will improve as time passes.

If narcoanalysis, the use of truth serums and drugs, or hypnosis proves to be more effective than lie detectors, or a valuable supplement to them, they too should be used in socialist criminal investigations.

It may be objected that the use of these methods of investigation is an invasion of personal privacy, or that it degrades the person investigated, but if an innocent man is indicted for a crime, he will much prefer a quick acquittal achieved by such means to a long trial and possible conviction which preserves his privacy and/or his dignity. And it is more desirable to preserve the privacy and protect the dignity of possible victims of crime than to give such protection to those who, if mistakenly acquitted, may injure and degrade more victims.

No Right to Silence — In America all suspects questioned by the police are legally entitled to remain silent. Until recently, only the well-educated and well-advised were aware of and/or accorded this privilege, but knowledge and use of the right is growing steadily. The law providing this right ought to be repealed because it seriously handicaps the police and the courts. This right originated in an age when police and prosecutors used torture and threats to compel accused persons to testify as the authorities desired. It would not be needed in a socialist state which had eliminated such coercion of suspects.

A clever lawyer can advise a guilty client how to limit or control his testimony in such a way as to reduce his risk of conviction. Such advice benefits the client, but impedes the administration of justice, and therefore harms society as a whole. Under socialism no criminal suspect should be advised by his lawyer when interrogated by the police.

While no suspect or witness should have the right to remain silent, none should ever be questioned for more than a reasonable period of time, perhaps four hours a day. And, of course, no suspect or witness should ever be threatened, bribed, or physically coerced.

Rewards for Aiding Police — Every person who aids the police should be liberally rewarded. A single tip to the police may save hundreds of man-hours of police work and prevent one or more serious crimes. In such cases the reward to the informant should equal at least half of the cost saving.

If any person comes to the aid of a policeman trying to catch or arrest a suspect, he should be well rewarded. If he is injured in a chase or struggle, he should not only receive full compensation for any lost time or wages, but should also receive a large cash reward for risking his life and/or his property. To protect him against possible revenge, the police should keep his name and address secret.

The payment of suitable rewards to all persons who aid police in the performance of police functions would greatly increase the number of persons who voluntarily aid the police, which, in turn, would lower the costs and/or improve the results of police work.

Handgun Control — About two thirds of some 20,000 U.S. homicides per year are committed with guns, nearly all handguns. Over 100 American policemen are now killed each year by gunfire. And the number of persons seriously injured by guns in the hands of criminals is about ten times as high as the number killed. Guns are also involved in over 10,000 U.S. suicides and 2500 accidental deaths each year. From 1900 to 1974 over 800,000 Americans were killed by civilian guns, one third more than in all American wars during this period.

In a socialist society, the manufacture, sale, and possession of all kinds of handguns and handgun ammunition should be prohibited. The sale of police and military handguns to civilians, and their possession by civilians, should be illegal. All sport and target rifles owned and used by city dwellers should be kept in the lockers of gun clubs when not in use. Only isolated rural residents should be allowed to keep rifles in their homes.

All police and military handguns should be designed to use distinctive ammunition sold only to authorized buyers, and the distinctive barrel markings and numbers of all such handguns should be recorded and filed with the national police office before such guns are sold. This would enable the police to identify the licensed owner of the gun from which any recovered intact handgun bullet has been fired.

It would be far easier to enact and enforce such gun control measures under socialism because all guns would be produced, imported, and sold by state agencies. No private person could profit by the manufacture, importation, or sale of guns.

E. Court Trials

After a suspect has been arrested, he must be tried in court. We shall now consider some of the major reforms which should be adopted in order to reduce the excessive costs of American criminal trials and/or in order to make these trials more efficient, i.e., to obtain more correct court decisions.

The Adversary System — All Anglo-Saxon criminal courts use the so-called adversary system of obtaining and presenting evidence and stating cases. The state hires prosecutors whose function is to convict those accused of crime. Most of the accused hire, or are provided with, defense lawyers, whose function is to secure the acquittal of their clients. The court room is the arena of an often dramatic verbal duel between the prosecutor and the defense lawyer.

The adversary system of securing and presenting evidence in criminal trials is obsolete. It was a step forward when it superceded trial by combat or trial by biased state prosecutors and judges, but it is inferior to non-adversary trial by impartial state investigators and judges, which is quite feasible in advanced capitalist states today, and would be much more feasible in an advanced socialist state.

When lawyers function as adversaries, each tries to win his case, not to obtain a correct verdict. Each tries to hide or minimize evidence against his client, and to confuse and mislead witnesses and the jury whenever this will aid his client. Many books have been written on trial tactics telling lawyers how to confuse and entangle honest but hostile witnesses, and how to keep relevant evidence out of court. For instance, most trial experts advise lawyers to ask witnesses only those questions to which they already know the answers, because, if they ask other questions, the answers may reveal a fact or opinion which would benefit their adversary.

Whether or not trial lawyers use such methods, it is certain that the more able the lawyer, the more likely he is to win a favorable verdict for his client. And the ablest lawyers usually defend the richest suspects.

A socialist state could, of course, radically reduce income differences and hire more and better public defenders, but it could never assure equal justice to all, under the adversary system. Differences in the ability and performance of criminal lawyers will distort court decisions as long as the adversary system survives.

If criminal prosecutors, lawyers, and investigators worked for the state, as they should under socialism, and if they were trained and instructed to help courts arrive at sound decisions, not to win cases, the costs of investigation and presentation of evidence would fall sharply, due to the elimination of duplication of labor, and courts would arrive at sound verdicts more often and more quickly. Hence, a socialist state should end the adversary system of obtaining and presenting evidence in all trials.

If this system is, nevertheless, retained for a time under socialism, the government should pay all the costs of legal defense, as well as the costs of prosecution, and should assure that in every criminal trial the funds available to the defense are as large as those available to the prosecution. This policy would increase the already large duplication of investigation and legal research work by the prosecution and the defense, but it would yield much fairer trials and verdicts.

Another good way to make adversary trials more fair would be to require that lawyers be chosen by lot. This would assure that the lawyers defending poor men are as competent as those defending rich men.

No Plea Bargaining — American criminal trial costs are so obviously and grossly excessive that voters and legislators have refused to appropriate more than a very minor part of the funds required to pay for court trials for all indicted persons. If the government had to pay all legal expenses of accused persons, it would be even more reluctant to finance costly criminal trials.

Lacking funds and courts sufficient to try most indicted persons who initially plead innocent, American public prosecutors have developed an alternative method of securing convictions, namely plea bargaining. They keep the accused in jail, on bail, and/or in fear or prosecution until he is eager to secure release from jail or a final decision, and then they offer to reduce the charge against him, and the possible penalty, if he will plead guilty. Such a plea to a reduced charge saves the cost of an expensive trial, and reduces the burden of the prosecutor. Plea bargaining has grown so much that 9 out of 10 indicted Americans now eventually plead guilty to a reduced charge. This has saved the nation billions of dollars in trial costs, but it has distorted the entire system of justice. Nine out of ten convicts escape punishment for the crime they actually committed, and are punished for a lesser offense. This seriously weakens both public respect for the law and the deterrent effect of criminal penalties.

In a socialist state, trial costs should be reduced at least until the government is willing and able to try all indicted persons who plead innocent to the initial charges. Plea bargaining should almost cease. Ending it would not increase the number of trials by anywhere near 900% because many more suspects would plead guilty to the original charges in order to reduce their penalties. And the reduction in costs per trial would further limit the effect of the elimination of plea bargaining on the total cost of all trials.

Plea bargaining also grossly distorts criminal statistics and the criminal records of individual criminals. Serious crimes are wrongly reported as less serious crimes. This makes scientific research on the causes and treatment of crime much more difficult, for all science is based on measurement, and the more accurate the measurement, the better the science.

While plea bargaining to avoid trial costs is uneconomic, plea bargaining to induce suspects to witness against their partners in crime, or to reveal evidence needed to convict the latter, may often be economic.

Prompt Trials — The drastic reduction in criminal investigation and trial costs previously recommended would make it far more feasible to create and maintain enough courts to provide prompt trials, without plea bargaining, for all accused persons. In a socialist society no one accused of crime should have to wait more than two months for his trial, and the vast majority of felony trials should begin within one month, and should last less than one week.

Justice delayed is often justice denied. Witnesses die, disappear, or forget. The accused lives under a cloud, and, if he is innocent, his pain is prolonged unnecessarily. The direct connection between crime and penalty is weakened. And the cost of investigation may increase.

Double Jeopardy — It is a basic principle of Anglo-Saxon law that no person should be tried again for the same offense. This principle was developed in an age when English kinds and their agents often persecuted their critics by trying them more than once on the same charge. It would be superfluous and harmful in a democratic socialist country.

Important new evidence is sometimes discovered after a criminal trial is over. The more prompt and economical such trials become, the more often will such belated discoveries occur. To disregard new evidence which might change a criminal verdict is as irrational and harmful as to disregard new medical data useful in the diagnosis and treatment of a sick man. It is much better to convict and punish criminals late than never. And under socialism the state would pay the full costs of all trials, so a second trial and acquittal would not penalize an innocent man financially.

Abolishing the rule against double jeopardy would remove a major bar to the holding of prompt trials. Prosecutors now often delay trials to secure more evidence because they know that new evidence found after the trial cannot be used against the suspect.

No Juries — One of the chief reasons why our criminal trials are far more costly than they should be is the common use of twelve jurors to decide questions of fact. The average jury trial lasts over twice as long as the average non-jury trial.

The employment of jurors has other disadvantages. Most jurors are inexperienced and therefore relatively incompetent. Jurors need professional training in judging the facts as much as judges need such training in judging the law, but such training would be expensive for temporary jurors. Moreover, it is illogical to require twelve men to judge the facts, but only one to judge the law. And jury selection often takes an entire day or more. Many members of the jury panel, as well as the jurors selected, must wait until the jury is chosen.

Jurors are now grossly underpaid, so part of the excessive real costs of American criminal trials is shifted to jurors. If jurors are used in a socialist society, they should be paid wages equal to their normal wages at work, and nearly all potential jurors would be employed. In a capitalist society there are millions of idle housewives, unemployed men, and able-bodied retired persons who can serve as jurors with slight loss of production. In a socialist society almost everyone should have a job, so the real social costs of employing twelve jurors would be much higher than they are now.

For these reasons socialist courts should abandon the jury system and allow judges to judge both the law and the facts. In major trials one judge of the law and two of the facts might be used, or all judges might be professionally trained to judge both the law and the facts. In minor cases one judge should suffice.

If the jury system is retained, the number of jurors should be radically reduced, perhaps from 12 to 5, and juror should be encouraged to ask questions and to take notes.

New Rules of Evidence — In American criminal trials, evidence concerning previous convictions of the accused is usually inadmissible because it is believed that such evidence would prejudice the jurors. But judges and jurors ought to be influenced or prejudiced by such evidence. A man who has committed one or more previous crimes is more likely to be guilty when accused again, especially when the latest crime closely resembles a previous crime. To refuse to consider such evidence in a criminal trial is as unreasonable as it would be for a physician to refuse to discover and consider a previous illness of a new patient he is beginning to care for. A previous criminal conviction is as significant as a previous medical diagnosis. At times neither is significant, but only a judge or doctor familiar with the relevant record can determine how significant it is.

Another old Anglo-Saxon rule of evidence is that hearsay evidence is inadmissible. One reason for this rule is that the original source of such evidence cannot be cross-examined in court. It is, of course, desirable that a source of hearsay evidence be cross-examined, when this is possible at a reasonable cost, but often this is impossible.

Hearsay evidence can be very helpful in arriving at sound verdicts in criminal trials. A competent and experienced judge can weigh such evidence and reject it when he believes it to be unreliable or false. Hence, there should be no general rule barring hearsay evidence from criminal trials.

In Anglo-Saxon criminal courts, one mate cannot be compelled to testify for or against his or her mate. This rule is based upon the legal fiction that both mates are legally one person, and upon the legal rule that a person cannot be required to testify against himself. The fiction should be abandoned, because it is fiction, and the rule should be repealed, for reasons noted below. It is far more socially desirable to convict the guilty and acquit the innocent than to avoid embarrassing the mates of accued persons. And mates often have very important and relevant knowledge about their mate's criminal behavior.

The rule that no accused person should be compelled to incriminate himself increases the length and cost of many criminal trials. It was developed in order to protect innocent persons in an age when torture, threats of torture, and prolonged pretrial imprisonment were often used to compel innocent men to incriminate themselves. This rule would perform no useful function in a socialist society which did not use such methods to compel self-incrimination. Indeed, it probably does more harm than good in the U.S. today. Its repeal would help to reduce trial costs and convict the guilty.

During an American criminal trial the defendant is allowed to remain silent unless his lawyer calls him to the stand; and his lawyer is seeking an acquittal, not justice. Under socialism this legal right should be abolished in order to help courts discover the truth at a minimum cost. Every defendant should be required to testify in his defense, and to answer all relevant questions. Judges and jurors can evaluate the claims of a witness or defendant better when he testifies in person and undergoes critical cross-examination.

<u>No Insanity Defense</u> — In socialist courts no one should be allowed to plead innocent by reason of insanity. The function of socialist criminal trials should be to determine who committed a given crime, not who is morally guilty.

All convicted criminals, sane or insane, should be required to make restitution or provide compensation to their victims if they are able to do so. No insane person should be allowed to benefit from crime.

And he must be found guilty before restitution or compensation can be required.

After a criminal has been convicted, he or his judge should be able to plead insanity as a reason for special treatment of the criminal. Insane criminals should be treated differently than sane criminals, but no one should be declared innocent of a crime on the ground of insanity. If insane criminals really are less likely than others to be deterred from future criminal acts by fines, they should be imprisoned much oftener, and for much longer periods, than other criminals, and should be treated by psychiatrists.

"Probably Guilty" Verdicts — The rule that an accused person must be proven guilty "beyond a reasonable doubt" was developed in an age when most felonies were punished by execution. It was then a beneficial protection against the execution of innocent persons, but today it serves chiefly to inflate trial costs and make conviction too difficult. If imprisonment were replaced largely by fines and probation, the need for this rule would be further diminished.

The rule should be abolished and replaced by a rule which permits judges an additional verdict, probably guilty. The penalty for being found probably guilty should be less than that for begin found guilty beyond a reasonable doubt, and should rarely be imprisonment, but no one found probably guilty should escape all penalties. Adoption of this new rule would increase the number of convictions, and would also reduce average trial costs.

The verdict, probably guilty, should be roughly defined in percentage terms. For instance, it might be defined to mean that the odds are at least three to one that the accused is guilty.

Many judges and jurors now declare some accused persons guilty beyond a reasonable doubt because they believe that they are probably guilty, and therefore should be convicted. The rule change proposed here would legalize such common behavior.

More Division of Labor — Political economists have long taught the advantages of the division of labor, but most courts and lawyers do not specialize enough. In a socialist society all judges and lawyers should specialize far more than they do today. No judge should try both civil and criminal cases, and no lawyer should work on both kinds of cases. But specialization should procede much farther than this. Each criminal court judge and lawyer should specialize in a certain kind of criminal case. This division of labor should proceed until no two judges or lawyers in a city handle the same kind of case.

As economists have often explained, the size of the market limits the degree of specialization, and the normal market for most lawyers and judges is a single city. A greater, interurban division of labor would further improve the product or lower its unit costs, but would increase transportation costs unduly, except perhaps when very unusual and difficult cases are being tried. Careful and long-continuing scientific research will be needed to determine the ideal degree of interurban and inter-regional division of labor among criminal court judges and lawyers.

Lawyers and judges who specialize should, of course, receive a very specialized legal education. No lawyer should be required to undergo an expensive general legal education before he begins his specialized legal training. A lawyer who specializes in trials for theft does not need to take courses in divorce law, contract law, constitutional law, and other subjects which would not help him to try theft cases. Thus, proper specialization in legal education would radically reduce the time and cost of educating lawyers and judges.

Trial-Cost Reduction — Most of the methods suggested earlier for improving the prevention and detection of crime would also help to shorten trials and reduce trial costs. For instance, if all large payments were made by check, it would be easier to prove that any criminal had received or paid illegal sums, or had failed to make tax payments. And, if lie detectors were used systematically, it would be easier to determine the truth in both civil and criminal trials, which would reduce their length and cost. Likewise, the elimination of juries and the adversary system would markedly reduce trial costs. However, some additional general comments on the problem of how to limit criminal trial costs are appropriate.

In the U.S., criminal trials now cost over $1,000 a day. A socialist state should use economic theory to control trial costs, which include all legal and investigation costs. Justice is not priceless. It is an economic good which should be produced only when and where its economic benefit exceeds its economic cost. The costs of a trial should always be less than the probable benefit from the resulting court decision.

It is uneconomic to spend $10,000 to determine whether an accused person has stolen an article worth less than $100, or to determine whether an official has accepted a $100 bribe. It is probably uneconomic to spend $1,000 to solve such questions. How much, then, is it economic to spend? This problem deserves a great deal of study. One plausible answer is that trial costs should rarely exceed the value of the alleged criminal gain. This limit may be too low or too high, but it is surely reasonable that trial costs should be closely related to the economic cost of the alleged crime, measured in money.

The mere private sale of legal services tends to increase average trial costs unduly. Lawyers earn higher fees when court trials last longer. They have no incentive to make trials less costly. And most men accused of crime place an inflated value on their acquittal, especially when the state pays their trial costs. However, the substitution of fines for most imprisonment, recommended later, would radically reduce this common overvaluation of acquittal. And socialization of legal services would radically reduce lawyers' incentives to prolong trials, but it would not solve the problem of how much should be spent on each kind of trial.

In capitalist states no public agency is responsible for the limitation of trial costs. As a result, many trials now cost over $200,000 apiece, and some cost over $1,000,000. A 90% reduction in the cost of most such trials would probably change few verdicts, and would free large sums for more productive use. When society spends $1,000,000 on a trial, it gives up an equal dollar value of new housing, education, health care, or some other economic goods. Therefore, it is uneconomic to spend an additional million on court trials unless the resulting economic benefit is greater than that which could be produced by spending this sum on other economic goods.

Spending on court trials should probably be controlled by the same senior law-enforcement executives and legislators who control spending on police forces. This system would enable them to compare and balance the social gain from spending any given sum upon additional police work with that from spending it to prolong and improve criminal court trials. The ability to shift funds from criminal courts to police work would alone induce higher officials to drastically reduce the average cost of criminal trials. One man-year of police work is now far more productive than the last man-year devoted to criminal trials.

The social gain from conducting a criminal trial does not vary proportionally with trial costs. A 100% increase in average trial cost would not double the benefits from such trials, and a 50% cut would not reduce such benefits by anywhere near half. Expenditures on criminal trials yield rapidly diminishing returns.

Moreover, the radical reduction in criminal penalties in the last century has greatly reduced the social cost of unjustified convictions. It costs society and the victim far less to serve an undeserved prison term of three years than to serve one of thirty years. And in a socialist society prison terms should be shorter and far less common than they are now. A socialist state should substitute fines for imprisonment in most cases, and an undeserved fine injures society and the victim much less than a prison term because the fined convict can continue to work and support his family. Hence, the need to prevent incorrect criminal convictions has long been shrinking, and will shrink much further when socialism is adopted.

It may be claimed that it is impossible for the government to decide rationally how much should be spent on each trial. But in fact the government now does decide how much is spent to prosecute each indicted person, and when the accused uses public defenders, it also decides how much is spent to defend him. Unfortunately, these decisions are not based on economic analysis or upon scientific experimentation.

The rules of evidence and court procedure developed over many generations by judges and legislators, most of whom previously worked as private lawyers, have grossly inflated criminal court costs. These men were not trained as economists or efficiency experts, and their previous trial experience made them adverse to economy in the operation of the court system. A socialist society must, therefore, train experts in judicial economy and efficiency, and must spend large sums on research in such economy and efficiency.

F. Criminal Penalties

In primitive societies it is not practical to use imprisonment as a punishment. Society cannot afford, and/or does not know how, to establish secure prisons with full-time prison guards. Therefore, such societies rely heavily on physical punishment — beatings, mutilation, execution, etc.

In societies which practice slavery, it is not practical to punish slaves by imprisonment because they are already deprived of personal freedom. Hence, physical punishment must be used.

Imprisonment is most practical and is most widely used as a method of punishing criminals in advanced capitalist societies. During the first half of the twentieth century, European countries probably had a larger proportion of their population in prison than ever before.

<u>Fines versus Imprisonment</u> — Further social advance will make it increasingly feasible and desirable to replace imprisonment with purely economic penalties for the great majority of crimes. The higher the standard of living and/or the lower the level of

unemployment, the easier it is to collect fines high enough to seriously deter crime. And the collection of fines is profitable, while the operation of prisons is very costly.

When a convict is working to pay a fine and support himself and family, he is a productive member of society. It costs as much to keep a convict in prison as to send a student to Harvard, and the educational benefits of life in prison are small, indeed often negative. Moreover, the state must not only pay the high cost of maintaining a convict in prison, but may also have to support his wife and children while he is in prison.

Religious thinkers assert that crime is a sin, and that criminals should be taught to become penitent in institutions they therefore called penitentiaries. Non-religious, philosophic moralists believe that criminals should be morally reformed in institutions therefore called reformatories. The scientific solution for most crime is to make it unprofitable by catching and fining criminals. But this is impossible under capitalism. Unemployed men cannot pay fines.

In a liberal socialist society monetary fines should replace imprisonment as the chief means of deterring crime. The great majority of convicted criminals should be required to pay fines rather than to spend time in jail or prison. Only criminals convicted of violent crimes and considered likely to repeat them should be imprisoned after conviction. And they also should pay fines.

The fines imposed for serious crimes should be heavy. They should usually be more than large enough to cover all the social costs of the crime — including full compensation for the victim, crime detection costs, and court costs. The police and the criminal courts of a socialist society should be largely or entirely financed by fines levied on convicts.

Most men convicted for the first time have committed other crimes for which they were never tried. Fines should be high enough to make crime unprofitable. Therefore, they should vary with police success in catching criminals. If only one half of all crimes are solved and followed by conviction, fines should be at least twice as high as the costs of their proven crimes. If only one quarter of all crimes are solved, fines should average more than four times the cost of proven crimes. In addition, fines should cover all relevant police and trial costs. Thus, if a criminal turns himself in promptly, confesses his crime, and requests no trial, his total fine should be much less than it would be if the police spent many hours on catching him and his trial lasted a week or more. This system of fine determination would induce many more suspects to confess and plead guilty before trial, which would reduce the costs of law enforcement.

In a capitalist society most convicts find it difficult to get work after their release from prison, and, when they do get work, it is often temporary and low-paid. Moreover, some criminals are so rich that heavy fines have little deterrent effect. And capitalist governments are so inefficient that they cannot keep track of paroled convicts and collect fines over a long period of time.

In sharp contrast, a socialist government could and should provide steady well-paid jobs for all paroled convicts, and could easily collect any fine by deducting it from wages, perhaps for 50 years. All the income of each convict should pass through his own personal bank account, where his fine could be deducted monthly. And no convict could avoid payment by fleeing because he would be unable to secure shelter or a job elsewhere under a different name. Indeed, he would be unable to rent or buy any good or service costing more than a very small sum in any other place in the U.S. if our banking rules were adopted.

A criminal who has killed or seriously crippled a victim should be required to pay a monthly fine equal to over half of his take-home pay for the rest of his life. A criminal who steals $100 in cash or merchandise, and then turns himself in and pleads guilty, should pay a fine of less than $200.

Monetary fines are the ideal deterrent to the commission of crimes committed for gain because they can take the profit out of crime. They ought to be high enough to make such crimes obviously unprofitable on the average, and they ought to be certain enough to make the chance of a profitable, i.e., unpunished, series of crimes very small indeed. But even if these goals are not achieved, the substitution of fines for periods of costly imprisonment would reduce radically the net social cost of crime.

<u>Sterilization</u> — Sterilization should be widely used as an extra penalty for major crimes and as a deterrent to crime. It is much superior to imprisonment of non-violent criminals because it costs far less than even a very brief imprisonment. It is superior to monetary fines because it does not reduce economic incentives, and because it prevents a criminal from having additional children. Most criminals are inferior parents. Their children are much more apt to become criminals than are the children of other parents. This is true even when criminals are not eugenically inferior, because children tend to admire and imitate their parents, and because criminals provide a less stable and secure home for their children.

Moreover, the burden of supporting pregnant wives and additional children may drive a convict to new crimes. And, the more children he has, the less his ability to pay a heavy fine and compensate his victims.

Finally, the kind of men who commit serious crimes are the kind who most object to being sterilized. Thus the threat of sterilization can be a real deterrent to serious crime.

All persons convicted of serious crimes should be sterilized after their first conviction. Also, all persons repeatedly convicted of minor crimes should be sterilized.

<u>Prisons and Work Camps</u> — Sterilization and/or suitable fines would be adequate penalties for the great majority of first-time offenders. But it would be necessary to segregate in prisons or penal work camps most first offenders guilty of heinous crimes — murder, arson, gross personal injury, etc. — and many chronic offenders guilty of three or more minor felonies. The chief purpose of such segregation should be to protect society from crime, not to reform the criminals. Most of them should be segregated for very long terms or for life, but they should be segregated in work camps, not in prison. Confinement in prison should be reserved for prisoners who must be segregated, but who refuse to abide by the rules in penal work camps.

Work camps should vary widely in the work they offer, in the class of convicts they take, and in living conditions. Some should operate mines; others, farms. And violent convicts should not be mixed with non-violent ones. The most pleasant camps should be reserved for the most cooperative and industrious prisoners.

Penal work camps are more economic than secure prisons because they are much cheaper to construct, and because the inmates can more easily engage in useful labor. Work camps should be located in remote, isolated areas, and should be largely constructed, maintained, and operated by the inmates. Wives should be allowed to live with their husbands in some work camps, but all inmates should be sterilized. The danger of successful escape would be slight because no escapee would be able to pay for food or get a job in our socialist economy.

All prisoners convicted of killing or crippling prison or work-camp guards should be executed painlessly, without any publicity. Public and/or publicized executions brutalize the public. It might also be desirable to execute all persons convicted of killing policemen.

Compensation for the Innocent Accused — Every suspect who is arrested, indicted, and/or tried and found not guilty should receive full compensation for time lost, wages lost, legal costs, and public humiliation. Compensation should come out of law-enforcement funds, and records of such compensation should be considered whenever a police chief is considered for promotion.

Under socialism all attorneys and investigators would work for the state, so the need for such compensation would be less than it is under capitalism, but there would still be ample reason for compensation, especially when the criminal charge is a serious one. The payment of such compensation would make police act more cautiously in making arrests and charges. It would place the costs of mistakes on the agencies responsible for them.

G. Scientific Research

Investment in scientific research and development (R and D) should be greatly increased in all fields of law enforcement. The social sciences are so new, and religious and philosophic prejudices against R and D in these fields have been so strong, that very little such R and D has been done. In the U.S., investment in such research is now running far below 1% of total spending on law enforcement. It should exceed 10%.

Every proposed investment in such R and D should be subjected to cost-benefit analysis, both before and after it is carried out. Those who make such an analysis before an investment is made should not make the audit analysis after the investment has been made and has yielded results, because they would be strongly tempted to justify their pre-investment analysis. Their pre-investment analysis should be evaluated and graded on the basis of the final post-investment analysis. This would enable executives to grade the analytical work of subordinates, and would help all cost-benefit analysts to improve their methods of analysis.

Each of the proposed new methods of law enforcement recommended in this chapter should be tested by local experimentation and careful scientific observation before it is applied nationally. If such experimentation significantly injures any local population, they should be compensated in some way.

Since few of the old or conventional law enforcement policies have ever been tested scientifically, most of them also should be subjected to scientific experimentation, usually by ceasing to apply one of them in a single city for some years and observing the effect upon local crime.

INDEX

Accidents, indus., 26, 130, 137
Advertising, 160, 163, 173, 183, 238, 240, 257-8, 262, 265, 267, 273, 281, 283, 285, 290
Air transport, 75-6, 116, 122
Agriculture, farm accounting, 13-4; machinery, 19-20; rentals, 10, 12-4, 16; farm size, 3-5, 19; farm towns, 5-7, 14; irrigation, 20; specialization in, 8-9; wages, 10, 12-8
Architecture, 77, 84, 88
Athletic facilities, 82, 84, 88, 101
Auto dealers, 76, 135, 159, 175
Auto repairs, 38, 135, 175-7
Automation, 136, 140, 153

Banking and crime, 307-8; bill collection, 195, 309; & farm accounting, 13-4
Bicycle use, 72, 86
Birth control, 242-3
Books, authors of, 270-1; contents of, 259, 263, 267; design of, 273; editors of, 268; grading of, 274-5; import of, 272; marketing of, 279-80; microprint, 277-80; pricing of, 274-5; royalties, 270; subsidies for, 272; translation of, 271-2
Broadcasting, cable TV, 55, 74, 285; facilities, 81, 84, 283, 291-5; financing, 292-4; foreign films, 290; networks, 283, 288-90; organiza. of, 281; output control, 291-3; pricing of, 262, 292; program rating, 294-5; programs, 260-1, 282-9
Building height, 67-9, 83, 88; size, 55, 84
Bus service, 72, 90

Central heating, 27, 39, 72

Centralization, 2-3, 109, 132, 161, 229, 254-6, 282-4, 299, 302-3
City growth, 44-6, 51, 59
City planning, agency for, 49, 53-4; & auto use, 47, 71-2, 86-7, 90-1; & city forms, 54-7; & city location, 49-51; city size, 43-4, 58-9; city centers, 80-4, 155; construction rate, 50, 60-2; export plants, 7, 69-71, 85; house size, 62; import-export balance, 70-1, 86; megastructures, 55-7, 88, 93, 97, 100; nat'l policies, 48-53; need for, 43-7; principles of, 57-79; & plant location, 80-4, 87-8, 134, 162; & reconstruction costs, 62-3; & warehouse location 76, 162
Community planning, 99-101
Competition, wastes of, 2, 12, 23, 25-7, 37-9, 43-7, 107-110, 116, 136, 176, 207, 211, 286, 295
Compulsory employment, 17
Compulsory retirement, 18
Conservation, of farm land, 20-1, 27-8; of minerals, 28-36, 48, 53, 72, 176, 204; pro & con, 28-31; & recycling, 36, 137; & standardization, 37, 136; & substitution, 35-6
Consumers' surplus, 14, 15, 21, 275, 281, 291
Containerization, 75, 112-115
Contracts, sales, 40, 188
Cost-benefit analysis, 15, 199, 250, 275-6, 292
Crime, & capitalism, 297; cost of, 297, 304; detection, 397-12; insurance, 219, 224-5, 304; lie

326

detectors, 310; news of, 259; prevention, 72, 298, 307-9, 323; punishment of, 309, 321-5; victimless, 301, 308, 310

Criminal law, double jeopardy, 315; handguns, 312; reform of, 301-2; standardization of, 301

Court trials, adversary system, 312-4; cost reduction, 319-20; evidence rules, 316-7; insanity defense, 317; juries, 315-6; plea bargaining, 314-5; probably guilty verdict, 318; prompt trials, 315; right to silence, 311; specialization 318-9

Cultural facilities, 6, 49, 58-9, 81, 84

Decentralization, of cities, 64-5, 84, 94; of opinion control, 254-9, 264-9; of judiciary, 299

Deficits, ideal, 128-9, 205, 262, 276

Division of labor, in agriculture, 4-9; in medical education, 246-7; in foreign trade, 178; in health care, 233-4; in legal work, 318-9

Drug addiction, 244-5

Economic calculation, 188, 201, 276, 289, 292, 297, 304, 319-20

Economic planning, 15-6, 32, 132, 145, 188

Education, 234, 246, 287

Educational facilities, 5-6, 49, 88, 94-6, 99

Editorial decentralization, 255, 264, 268-70, 274, 280, 282-4, 287

Entertainment, 254, 282, 289-90, 293

Eugenics, 240-1

Euthanasia, 243-4, 297

External diseconomies, 27, 44-9, 52, 60, 75-8, 85, 129-30, 137, 177, 209

External economies, 254, 273, 275-6, 292, 299

Extraction taxes, 53, 323

Fire protection, 222-4, 305
Foreign finance, 191
Foreign trade, advantage of, 178-83; balance of trade, 179, 190; in books, 272; & bounties, 181-2; & conservation, 25-6, 33; control of, 187-8; dumping, 182-3; 272; embargoes, 185; exchange control, 188-90; infant industries, 183-4; & military needs, 183; organization of, 186; & quotas, 185; & subsidies, 186; tariffs, 33, 179, 183-5, 272; & unemployment, 180; & wages, 179-81

Free goods, books, 275; broadcasts, 292-4; health care, 209-11, 236-6; law enforcement, 297-300; learned journals, 265; legal services, 209, 299; library services, 280; mass transit, 127; newspapers, 262, 265; utility services, 203

Freedom of the press, 254-6, 258, 264, 268

Freight rates, 117-26, 133

Furniture, home, 78-9

Gas pipelines, 27
Gas utilities, 73-4, 196
Gasoline stations, 26, 36, 88, 159
Gasoline taxes, 129-30, 220-1
Greenbelts, 52, 60, 63-4, 85, 88, 94, 96, 100

Handicrafts, 152-3
Health care, allocation, of funds, 251-3; ambulance service, 233; autopsies, 245-6; cadaver parts, 246; clinic location, 231; computer diagnosis, 237; drugs, 237-8; facilities, 80, 87, 95; female doctors, 234-5; financing of, 249-51, 304; food control, 239-40; free care, 220, 235-6, 249; group practice, 230-1;

327

insurance, 236; management of, 230, 232; organization of, 229; professional education, 229; & specialization, 233-4; 246-7
Highways, 6, 75-6, 83
Hours of labor, 18, 27, 83-4, 97-8, 234
Housing, 91-2, 96-102

Identity cards, 308
Incentives, 17, 146-7
Income equalization, 138, 149, 208, 211, 217, 242
Increasing returns, 3-5, 25, 108, 135, 140, 181
Infanticide, 243
Inheritance, 215, 228, 244
Insurance, accident, 227; airline, 222, 227; auto accident, 220-2; crime, 219, 224-5, 304-5; financing of, 216-7, 220, 224; fire, 217, 219, 222-4; functions of, 208-11; health, 236; income, 218-20; industrial accident, 28, 209, 215, 226-6; life, 209, 215, 228; need for, 210; organization of, 211-2; self-insurance, 210, 224-5; social, 207-8, 212-8; taxation of, 216; universal coverage, 213; & welfare, 209-10
Inventory control, 11, 26, 41, 142, 162
Investment, 19, 21, 34, 130, 140, 144, 171-2

Job changes, daily, 28, 154-7, 305-6
Job choices, 150, 303
Job improvement, 147-57

Large-scale production, advantages of, 44, 50, 61, 87, 178, 302
Law enforcement, 297-325
Legal services, 313, 318-9
Libraries, 80, 273, 277-8
Life, value of, 225, 252
Literary agents, 269

Magazines, 260, 262-7

Manufacturing, inventory control, 142; marginal-cost curve, 139-46; multi-shift operation, 143-4; organization of, 131-2; price-output control, 138-46; plant location, 132; product improvement, 136-7; specialization in, 134; wages, 143-4
Marketing, of books, 273; catalogs, 174; deliveries, 165; of imports, 159; mail-order, 163-4; multi-unit sales, 172; by producers, 158-60; quantity discounts, 202; retail, 76, 81, 84, 87, 95, 165-77; sales stabilization, 169-70; special retail charges, 173; store hours, 171; vending machines, 174; wholesale, 160-5
Mineral imports, 25-6
Mineral production, coal, 26-8; mine towns, 42; oil, 24-8; organization of, 23, pricing, 39-40; prospecting, 24
Mobile communities, 18, 19-20, 61
Monopolies, 3, 23, 27, 66-7, 86, 90-1, 106-9, 131, 158-9, 175, 192-3, 229, 284

Neighborhood plans, 101
Newspapers, contents of, 258-63, 286; financing of, 262; as monopolies, 260-1; need for, 257-8; prices of, 257, 258, 262

Parking lots, 82, 89
Parks, public, 60, 78, 88, 92, 97, 104
Plant location, 7, 27, 42, 82, 85, 132-3
Plant size, 3-5, 19, 134-5
Police, centralized control of, 302-3; & crime insurance, 224; firemen as, 305; mailmen as, 305-6; methods of, 306-12; rewards, 311; training of, 305

Pollution, 27, 44-9, 52-3, 60
    72, 75-8, 85, 129, 137,
    177, 238
Price change frequency, 121-2
Price discrimination, 118-21
Price theory, agricultural, 10-4;
    for broadcasts, 293-4; factory
    products, 138-9, 142-5; magazines, 265-6; minerals, 40;
    railroads, 117-26; retail,
    164-73; utility, 200-6; wholesale, 161-2
Privacy, personal, 259, 289,
    308, 310
Professionalization, 256, 268-9,
    284-5
Public utilities, cable TV, 24,
    192; central heating, 192,
    196-7; consolidation of, 193-6;
    construction of, 6, 44, 49, 52,
    193, 199; electrical, 27, 196,
    201-4; & free services, 203-4;
    investment in, 199, 204; maintenance of, 194; prices, 200-6;
    telephone services, 192, 204;
    water, 49, 197-9
Publishing, 254-80

Quasi-rent, 12-6, 140-6

Railroads, abandonment of, 107,
    114-5; car size, 116; location
    of, 75-6; rates of, 117-26;
    reorganization of, 106-8;
    unit trains, 115
Reconstruction of old cities,
    102-5
Recreational facilities,
    78, 82, 99-101
Repair costs, 37-8, 135, 145
Research & development, 4, 21-2,
    34, 212, 248-9, 273, 325
Rentals, 10, 12-4, 16

Saving, 209-10, 213, 217
Science vs. ideology,
    297-8, 322
Seasonal employment, 18, 27
Scale of production, 3-5, 26,
    135, 140
Segregation, residential, 97-102
Sewage treatment & use, 20-1,
    36, 74, 204

Simplification, 26, 135-7,
    175
Simplified spelling, 266, 274
Smoking, 223, 245, 301
Social life, 65, 93, 100-2
Socialism, advantages of,
    37, 39, 67, 74, 106, 136,
    176, 207, 286, 295
Specialization, 8-9, 134,
    181, 233-4, 246-7, 286,
    318-9
Standardization, 26, 37,
    136-7, 159, 211-2, 232,
    273, 302-3
Street names, 79-80
Streets, 44, 54, 83, 88-90,
    96
Subsidies, for publications,
    262, 265, 272; for films,
    284; for food, 239-40;
    for conservation, 33; for
    transport, 127
Suicide, 243-4

Taxes, discriminatory, 4, 92;
    extraction, 32-3, 53; as
    insurance premiums, 220-3,
    227-8; on insurance, 216;
    price, 130; revenue, 128;
    & subsidies, 32-3, 239
Town planning, 54, 84-93, 166
Transport, intercity, coordination of, 108-14; costs
    of, 51, 133; cross shipment, 25, 132; freight
    reallocation, 111-2; investment in, 128-9; organization
    of, 107-9; pick-up &
    delivery, 114; rates, 117-26;
    subsidies for, 128; taxation of, 129-30; terminal
    unification, 75-6, 113; by
    truck, 108, 111, 116

Unemployment, 17-8, 67, 141,
    151, 210-1
Unions, labor, 155
Universities, 81
Urban transport, 29, 47, 71-2,
    90-2, 105, 127
Urbanization, 43, 49-50

Village planning, 84-5, childless villages, 98; one-building villages, 97; one shift villages, 97-8; village centers, 95-6; village size, 94; village layout, 96-7

Wage determination, in agriculture, 10, 14-8; & foreign trade, 179, 181; in manufacturing, 133, 144; in mining, 28; & mobility of labor, 60; in old cities, 104; for police, 303
Wage trends, 148-9
Water treatment, 239
Work shifts, 83-4, 88-9, 97-8, 143-4

THE AUTHOR

Born in Carthage, Missouri, in 1904, and raised largely in Pasadena, California, Burnham Putnam Beckwith was graduated from Stanford University with a B.A. in philosophy in 1926. He spent the next two years at the Harvard Business School and, after three more years of full-time study, received a Ph.D. in economics from the University of Southern California in 1932. He held a postdoctoral research-training assistantship under Dr. Edward L. Thorndike at Teachers College, Columbia University, from 1935 to 1937.
After a brief university teaching career, Dr. Beckwith was employed by various federal war agencies from 1941 to 1949. At the peak of McCarthyism he was blacklisted in 1951, and has been unemployed since then. In addition to his books on liberal socialism, the cause of his blacklisting, he has published Free Goods, The Theory of Free or Communist Distribution (1976); Government by Experts, The Next Stage in Political Evolution (1972); The Next 500 Years, Scientific Predictions of Major Social Trends (1967); and Religion, Philosophy, and Science, An Introduction to Logical Positivism (1957).